D0414643

LITERATURE AND THEOLOGY AS A GRAMMAR OF ASSENT

For Zephyra Porat

Literature and Theology as a Grammar of Assent

DAVID JASPER

University of Glasgow, UK and Renmin University of China, Beijing

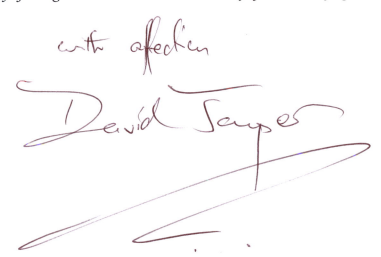

with affection

David Jasper

ASHGATE

© David Jasper 2016

All rights reserved. No part of this publication may be reproduced, stored in a retrieval system or transmitted in any form or by any means, electronic, mechanical, photocopying, recording or otherwise without the prior permission of the publisher.

David Jasper has asserted his right under the Copyright, Designs and Patents Act, 1988, to be identified as the author of this work.

Published by
Ashgate Publishing Limited
Wey Court East
Union Road
Farnham
Surrey, GU9 7PT
England

Ashgate Publishing Company
110 Cherry Street
Suite 3-1
Burlington, VT 05401-3818
USA

www.ashgate.com

British Library Cataloguing in Publication Data
A catalogue record for this book is available from the British Library

The Library of Congress has cataloged the printed edition as follows:
Jasper, David.
 Literature and theology as a grammar of assent / by David Jasper.
   pages cm
 Includes bibliographical references and index.
  ISBN 978-1-4724-7524-4 (hardcover : alk. paper) – ISBN 978-1-4724-7525-1 (ebook) –
 ISBN 978-1-4724-7526-8 (epub) 1. Religion and literature. I. Title.
 PN49.J387 2016
 809'.93382--dc23

                                                                 2015027686

ISBN: 9781472475244 (hbk)
ISBN: 9781472475251 (ebk – PDF)
ISBN: 9781472475268 (ebk – ePUB)

Printed in the United Kingdom by Henry Ling Limited, at the Dorset Press, Dorchester, DT1 1HD

Contents

Acknowledgements   *vii*

Introduction: The Study of Literature and Theology –
A History since 1982   1

PART I   THE DURHAM CONFERENCES

1   Humanism and Belief in Literature: Seeking a Grammar
     of Assent   13

2   A Habit of Mind: Religion and Imagination – John Coulson
     and John Henry Newman   27

3   Making the World Bearable: Ulrich Simon   43

4   Choosing Commitment: Martin Jarrett-Kerr CR   59

5   Finding the Otherness of God in Literature: Werner G. Jeanrond   73

PART II   THE LOSS OF AND THE RETURN TO THEOLOGY

6   'A Tone Born out of the World of Ruins': Robert Detweiler   87

7   Returning to Theology: Nijmegen, 2000   99

8   Seeking Forgiveness and Retrieving a Theological Sense of
     Being Human: Leuven, 2014   111

PART III   THEMES AND THE WIDER WORLD

9   Poetry: The Poetry of the Oxford Movement   127

10   Sacrament: The Eucharistic Body   143

11   The Bible: The Bible as Literature – *Parergon*   159

12   Europe and Australia: New Worlds   189

13   Europe and China: Old Worlds Meet   205

PART IV   CONCLUSIONS

14   Becoming Innocent Again: Looking Back on Theory in
      Literature and Theology   221

15   Conclusion: Prospero's Books   235

Brief Bibliography   *251*
Index   *255*

Acknowledgements

It is impossible to thank everyone who contributed directly and indirectly to the making of this book. There are many voices from the past, and some of them, no doubt, would be critical of my judgements. Old friends who can review, with me, this history in full, will have different readings and interpretations, and here I am thinking of Elisabeth Jay, Stephen Prickett, David Klemm and a few others. I thank generations of my students, some of whom, like Andrew Hass, have gone on to become colleagues. Andrew in particular has distinguished himself by his labours over many years in editing the journal *Literature and Theology* and his heroic work as Secretary of the International Society for Religion, Literature and Culture which continues to sustain the biennial conferences today. The next meeting is scheduled to be held in the University of Glasgow in 2016. Voices from around the world will be heard in the following pages, but particular thanks are due to my two anonymous readers who made many wise suggestions and saved me from a number of gross errors. Those that remain are entirely my own. If I may be permitted to reproduce the words of one who remarked on the writing of the book that 'it is a way of integrating two (traditional) ways of thinking that itself is no longer being practiced, or being practiced in *this particular manner*, and the reasons why it is not – which importantly is what this book is about – is the very reason it ought to remain'. I hope that this is the case.

Above all I thank my wife Alison and three daughters, who have endured my obsession with literature and theology these many long years, my many hours spent in my study when I might have been better employed more sociably, and the perhaps inevitable onset of a cast of mind that looks back to better times as increasing years battle with ever faster and more mysterious technology and seeks on shelves for dusty volumes that are ever more difficult to find – though I know that they are there somewhere.

October 2015

An earlier version of Chapter 1 was published in *Literature and Theology*, vol. 26, no. 3, September 2012, 252–64.

An earlier version of Chapter 5 was published in *Dynamics of Difference: Christianity and Alterity*, ed. Ulrich Schmiedel and James M. Mattarazzo, Jr (London: Bloomsbury T&T Clark, 2015).

An earlier version of Chapter 8 was given as the keynote lecture to the biennial conference on Literature and Theology in the University of Leuven in September 2014. This version was published in *Literature and Theology* vol. 29, no. 2, June 2015, 125–37.

An earlier version of Chapter 9 was published in the *International Journal for the Study of the Christian Church* (IJSCC), vol. 12, nos 3–4, 2012, 218–31.

An earlier version of Chapter 10 was published in Ramona Fotiade, David Jasper and Olivier Salazar-Ferrer (eds), *Embodiment: Phenomenological, Religious and Deconstructive Views on Living and Dying* (Farnham: Ashgate, 2014), pp. 131–42.

Chapter 12 was first given as the keynote lecture in the third conference of The Sacred in Literature and the Arts (SLA) at the Australian Catholic University, Sydney, July 2015.

Permission to reproduce Paul Celan's poem 'Psalm' from *Poems of Paul Celan*, 3rd edition, trans. and intro. M. Hamburger, 2007, is given by Anvil Press Poetry.

Introduction

The Study of Literature and Theology – A History since 1982

It is often remarked that all writing is to a degree autobiographical. I suspect that this becomes more the case as one grows older, though it takes different forms from that of preachiness, to nostalgia or reminiscence and so on. It would be true to say that the genre of autobiography must be, with some notable exceptions, one of the most self-indulgent, not to say boring, of literary forms. Airport book shops are full of hastily contrived volumes describing the lives of 'celebrities', many of whom are barely old enough to have absorbed much more than the tinsel of their celebrity status, and are liable to be forgotten within a short space of time. Nevertheless, at a certain point, perhaps before it is too late, there may be something to be gained in reflecting on many decades of experiments in thought, encounters with people and ideas, and the effects, both mental and spiritual, of experiences that are both the result and the cause of certain defining moments not only in one's life but in the life that is shared between a number of people. Such moments in a life may participate, in a minute way, in the larger cultural, intellectual and religious events that are ongoing and around us all of the time, whether we are aware of them at the time or not, and at the very least these defining moments may act as reflectors, however distorted, of such large scale events in the world and society.

On 23–25 September 1982, the first National Conference on Literature and Religion took place in Hatfield College in the University of Durham, England. Such conferences have been held every two years since then to the present time in various universities in Great Britain and Europe. They gave rise to a society, at first known as the National Conference on Literature and Religion, with its own modest newsletter that later became the journal *Literature and Theology*. By the time the conferences became international, meeting in Nijmegen, Holland, in 2000, the society had grown and been renamed as the International Society for Religion, Literature and Culture (ISRLC). My present concerns are primarily with the earlier meetings in the 1980s, though some attention will be given to the meeting in Nijmegen as it ushered in the new millennium, and finally to the most recent conference, at the time of writing, held in Leuven in 2014. I am seeking for the imperatives which drove us in the early meetings. The history of the later conferences will be for others to pursue if they think it worthwhile.

Why did such a conference on the subject of the relationship between theology and literature take place in Durham in 1982? Why has it persisted, with increasingly worldwide participation, in a field of study that has continued to fascinate but has never really commended itself to any university system, spawning no departments or career paths for the many younger scholars from Europe, North America, China and elsewhere who seek to gained doctorates in 'literature and religion'? Not long after the birth of the conferences, in 1987, the journal *Literature and Theology* began its life under the imposing academic protection of Oxford University Press, and it flourishes to this day, despite being suspended precariously between two academic disciplines. In 2012, the journal, under the editorship of Andrew Hass, published a 25th Anniversary Special Issue to which I contributed an essay that forms the basis for the early chapters in the present book. Other contributors to that issue include Elisabeth Jay, one of the few people who have also travelled the journey from the 1982 conference without a break. In his Introduction, Andrew Hass acknowledges the uncertain, changing and sometimes precarious enterprise in the ongoing study of literature and theology. In this respect, it may be said, little has changed.

> The questions, the tensions, the ambiguities continue to persist, no matter how many texts, how many voices, how many theories they have been filtered through. The enterprise remains still too formative to rest on definitive accomplishments or illustrious achievements. So the essays below continue the interrogations, the cross-examinations, the fierce exercise of doing and thinking interdisciplinarily in the context of religion, literature, theory, and culture.[1]

A recent volume of essays entitled *Poetry and the Religious Imagination* (2015), edited by Francesca Bugliani Knox and David Lonsdale, identifies the founding of the journal as a key moment in the establishment of 'an important movement in recent and contemporary scholarship in Europe, North America and elsewhere, in literary studies, philosophy and theology'.[2] In 1991, Stephen Prickett and I established the Centre for the Study of Literature, Theology and the Arts in the University of Glasgow, and its work continues to this day in spite of all bureaucratic attempts to stifle it.[3] These events, and the academic questions to which they give rise, are inextricably bound up in my own life – but their roots and branches spread far more widely, and in complex historical, spiritual and intellectual ways, into the history of thought and religion. Such events at the end of the twentieth century are the starting point of this book, but they are

---

[1]   Andrew Hass, Introduction, *Literature and Theology*, vol. 26, no. 3 (2012), 249.

[2]   Francesca Bugliani Know and David Lonsdale (eds), *Poetry and the Religious Imagination: The Power of the Word* (Farnham: Ashgate, 2015), p. xi.

[3]   There is little money to be made in such interdisciplinary work.

only that, for its concerns must entertain a theological complexity which only the perspective of some 40 years can even begin to acknowledge if they are to avoid the inevitable triviality of impetuous intellectual decisions and superficial cleverness. The actual nature of what one is engaged in academically can take a long time to begin to dawn, and patience, it seems, is rarely a virtue in the contemporary university.

I began my thinking about this book with a careful re-reading of the three volumes that contain the most significant papers from the first three conferences of 1982, 1984 and 1986, all held in the University of Durham. They are entitled *Images of Belief in Literature* (1984), *The Interpretation of Belief* (1986) and *The Critical Spirit and the Will to Believe* (1989), all of them edited by myself, though in the last case with a co-editor, T.R. Wright. What is immediately apparent is that all three titles have one word, or a variant of it, in common – 'belief'. They are concerned with what we believe in, with how we believe or, perhaps, how belief can begin to fail and come to an end. I am struck, as I read these books after their many years remaining unopened on my bookshelves, at how they represent a form of writing, and even scholarship, that has now fallen almost entirely out of fashion. And yet they are dense, full of often difficult and recondite learning, generally beautifully written (and style does matter), and, above all, devoted to close readings of the texts to which they give their attention. In them, reading and writing are arts which have strange and powerful beauties. In their various ways these books reminded me that these conferences held in the 1980s were characterized by a daily event that would probably be unthinkable at such academic conferences today: the participants (or many of them) gathered each morning to say their prayers together. Of course, that presupposes that most of them shared a common tradition of belief – indeed, these were, on the whole, very *Christian* gatherings. Still, the point is worth making as a reminder that, even in a world now much more conscious of the multiplicity of beliefs, or none, that the study of religion (or theology) and literature cannot simply be a merely intellectual or academic exercise, and that the literary participates in this excess beyond the academy as much as (and perhaps even more than) the theology and religion. Whether we like it or not, and however uncomfortable this may be to people driven by SMART objectives that are measureable, achievable and so on, the anxious matter of belief, and perhaps also faith, come into the picture, and to acknowledge such is to be committed to forms of language and processes of thought that are awkward within the largely secular context of a modern university. The study of theology or religious studies may be one thing – the study of literature and religion (or theology), though not unrelated, will always be another, often demanding more of us than we are willing to admit or able immediately to articulate.

This book, then, will trace the history of 10 years of meetings on the subject of literature and theology from 1982 to 1992. In those 10 years we can see happening a massive period of change in European self-consciousness. Addressing the question of what impelled that first meeting in 1982, we must go back to the dark days of the post-Holocaust generation and in the figure of Ulrich Simon visit again the unutterable trauma of the mid twentieth century in those who had suffered and endured the murder of 6 million Jews and other victims of the concentration camps. The figures who guided those first conferences are now largely forgotten – a fact which says more about us, and our capacity to forget, than about them. I did attempt to acknowledge them by name in my introductory essay to *The Oxford Handbook of English Literature and Theology* (2007)[4] and most of them will figure largely in the ensuing pages, but they are, perhaps, too old fashioned to be much remembered now. Nevertheless, they were all scholars who had lived through the dark middle years of the twentieth century and whose Christian theology, in so many ways conservative and untouched by the later 'turn to theory' had, in various degrees, been rendered problematic or even mute by war, suffering and conflict. The turn to literature was partly a seeking for an alternative voice – but for all of that it was deeply theological inasmuch as theology itself was so often rendered silent, or perhaps more precisely, helpless.

My feeling is that there was in those meetings a sense of seriousness, a rootedness in tradition and an atmosphere of radical urgency that was later lost as Christian theology somehow, and in various ways, recovered its voice and its claims. The sometimes strident and dismissive assertiveness of such theological enterprises as Radical Orthodoxy was beyond us, and recently Rowan Williams has accused me of 'indulging' in a form of negativity in my approach to word and image – an indulgence (if that is what it is) for which I make no apology. I prefer to call it something else.[5] The later study of religion and literature in both Europe and North America, with the founding and establishment of such journals as *Literature and Theology* in the wake of those early conferences somehow became more proper, less uncomfortable, more professionalized and more politically correct: and something was lost. To begin with we began to forget the deep historical roots of what we were doing which were both ancient within classicism and Christianity, and more immediately in Romanticism and its hermeneutical traditions in seminal figures such as S.T. Coleridge and

---

    4   Andrew Hass, David Jasper and Elisabeth Jay (eds), *The Oxford Handbook of English Literature and Theology* (Oxford: Oxford University Press, 2007), p. 21. The names noted here are Martin Jarrett-Kerr, F.W. Dillistone, John Coulson, John Tinsley, Ulrich Simon and Peter Walker.

    5   Rowan Williams, *The Edge of Words: God and the Habits of Language* (London: Bloomsbury, 2014), p. 169. 'Allowing for some discomfort at the way in which Jasper's rhetoric indulges the idea of a *cancelling* of word and image rather than their relocation or radical opening up in the way I have been suggesting ...'. Perhaps the discomfort is a good thing, in the end.

Friedrich Schleiermacher. There was also a profound pedagogical instinct present, and these two facts come together in the opening lecture and essay by John Coulson in the proceedings volume of the 1982 conference, entitled 'Religion and Imagination: (Relating Religion and Literature) – A Syllabus.' Coulson's opening words were these:

> In almost all the classics of English or European Literature written before the nineteenth century, their authors assume the truth of the Christian faith. It does not have to be justified. The onus of disproof rests with the unbeliever.[6]

We were rooted in the religion, the literature and the issues of belief and unbelief that began in the nineteenth century and not before. Coulson was primarily a Newman scholar, and that was no accident either. The figure of John Henry Newman is at the very heart of much in our concern with the relationship between theology and literature and will reappear time and again in the pages to follow. Our early conferences were not only theological, they were deeply, if problematically, religious. By this I mean, as I have said, that prayers and a daily Eucharist were part of our proceedings – which would be almost unthinkable, perhaps even politically incorrect, in an academic conference of this kind today. Among the university academics gathered in Durham there was also a large number of parish clergy who then still read (and often wrote) serious and scholarly books and were troubled by the questions that they posed. Part of this story is the rapid decline over the past 40 or 50 years within the Christian churches of a broad tradition of learning and genuine theological enquiry. At the heart of this tradition for us, I think, was the vision of the Church as proposed by Newman – and so at the heart of the conferences were profound theological issues that sought for guidance outside the realms of academic, doctrinal or systematic theology in exploring the question of the conscience and issues of right and wrong (in what Newman in the *Grammar of Assent* would have known as the Illative Sense) in the realms of literature and the art of poetry. If the study of literature and religion began in the shadow of the Holocaust and the problem of evil, it lay also in the shade of the Second Vatican Council and Newman's arguments for consulting the laity in the Church, the 'laity', in a sense, being represented by the poets and writers to whom we gave our attention. In two senses Newman's essay *On Consulting the Faithful in Matters of Doctrine* (1859) was similar to our early conferences. Newman begins his essay with an important if, at first sight, rather drily academic discussion on the precise meaning of the word 'consult'. In Latin and the theological sense, 'to consult' means to take counsel with or, more broadly, to have regard to, rather

---

6   John Coulson, 'Religion and Imagination: (Relating Religion and Literature) – A Syllabus', in David Jasper (ed.), *Images of Belief in Literature* (London: Macmillan, 1984), p. 8.

than seek advice from. That would reflect well our concern for literature in a context that, as with Newman's essay, was clearly and firmly theological. Like those of Newman, also, our discussions were at once deliberately 'old fashioned' (or perhaps, better, traditional) and at the same time profoundly radical, seeking to recover a cultural note in theological discussion that was, and now is, in danger of serious erosion. John Coulson, some years before the meeting in Durham, had expressed this well:

> Both he [Newman] and Coleridge conceived the contrast as one between two worlds – an older one which valued poets, philosophers and theologians, and sanctioned the generous unworldliness of the whole (or holy) man; and a new one of shrewd, knowing men of business and imperial rule, whose piety was dangerously unlearned and unenlarged.[7]

The language may be somewhat dated now, but such an observation points, perhaps, to the subsequent failure of the study of literature and theology in the contemporary university, a place of shrewd and knowing people of business, and the Church of which the piety is no longer grounded in the patient and habitual reading of both the classics of theology and the literary culture with which they coexist.

If the first two conferences in 1982 and 1984 established the theological sense of what we were trying to do, after the Holocaust and after Vatican II, as well as the hermeneutical roots in English and German Romanticism, the third conference in 1986 moved us inevitably into the nineteenth century. Once again it is Newman and the essay on aesthetics by John Coulson[8] which defined the tone of the meeting and the subsequent volume of essays. Returning to Newman's *Essay in Aid of a Grammar of Assent* (1870), the question is addressed as to how we may come to believe what cannot be precisely understood or proven. Although in Coulson it is the literary references that drive the argument – from G.M. Hopkins, Dostoevsky or T.S. Eliot – the tone is very much the same as that of Newman in its central concern with the role of education, of an 'educated laity' that goes back to Coleridge's idea of the *clerisy*, a secular and cultural intellectual élite within Church and state.[9] In such discussions the place of both theology and literature within the university was at the heart

---

[7]   John Coulson, *Newman and the Common Tradition: A Study in the Language of Church and Society* (Oxford: Clarendon Press, 1970), p. 143.

[8]   John Coulson, 'Hans Urs von Balthasar: Bringing Beauty Back to Faith', in David Jasper and T.R. Wright (eds), *The Critical Spirit and the Will to Believe* (London: Macmillan, 1989), pp. 218–32.

[9]   See Ben Knights, *The Idea of the Clerisy in the Nineteenth Century* (Cambridge: Cambridge University Press, 1978).

of our conversations as it was in Newman's writings.[10] And as in Newman in his *Discourses on the Scope and Nature of University Education* (1852), so the idea behind the study of literature and theology was the maintenance of an equilibrium and balance that is maintained within the complex interdependent web of the university's studies. Theology simply cannot be studied alone inasmuch as it participates in the complex unity of which it is a part and which is alone accessible through the broad exchanges made within culture. Once these become unravelled (as is arguably the case in the contemporary university with its high departmental walls, its advancing bureaucracy and limited aims) we are left, in Newman's words with 'a sort of bazaar, or pantechnicon, in which wares of all kinds are heaped together for sale in stalls independent of each other'.[11]

At the time, in 1986, we seemed to be focusing on the theme of the Victorian crisis of faith with its doubting clerics in literature, the rise of science and the will to believe as the sea of faith ebbed away from Dover Beach. In fact, I now think that the underlying theme we were addressing was, in the end rather different and even more important. It lay within the processes of education itself, the nature of language and the withering of theology when (as Newman feared for the Church when it forgot its organic nature by the emphasis on the magisterium as expressed most starkly in Vatican I) it forgets its place within the complex discourses of humane and creative activity. It was a lesson that we have once again forgotten, and it is why the study of literature and theology or religion has, once again, receded into the background as, at best, a rather undisciplined option in the curriculum, while theology is not unique in its increasingly traditional, isolated and fortress mentality. The lessons of the imagination have again been neglected.[12]

The essays after the fourth conference of 1988, which was almost the last to be held in Durham,[13] were published in a volume entitled *European Literature and Theology in the Twentieth Century: Ends of Time* (1990). It was to be the last volume which I myself edited, this time with Colin Crowder of Durham University. This conference marked a radical turn and in some ways it was

---

[10] Coulson had already edited a volume entitled *Theology and the University* (London: Darton, Longman & Todd, 1964) containing essays from such distinguished figures from theology, literature and philosophy as Alan Richardson, L.C. Knights and Anthony Kenny.

[11] J.H. Newman, *Discourses on the Scope and Nature of University Education* (Dublin: James Duffy, 1852. Facsimile reprinted by Cambridge University Press, 2010), V, p. 139.

[12] Knox and Lonsdale's volume on *Poetry and the Religious Imagination* would seem to contradict this statement, though I suggest that their work, though impressive, does little more than repeat old lessons rather than carry the conversation into the present.

[13] The last Durham conference, held in 1990, was entitled 'The Rebirth of Tragedy'. It was the first conference not to have a dedicated conference volume published after it. Instead there was, just before the conference, a special issue of the then new journal *Literature and Theology*, with contributions from, among others, George Steiner and Stewart Sutherland.

the beginning of the end, even though the conferences remain active until the present time. It will be discussed in some detail in Chapter 6, through the specific contribution of Robert Detweiler. The central question of that conference was posed by myself in the Preface to the published volume:

> This collection of essays is very much of and for its time. It traces the literature of the twentieth century in Europe through modernism and postmodernism to the point when the crucial question cannot be avoided: how does theology respond to the moment of the apparent collapse of coherence in language, meaning and reference, to the denial of logocentricity and the radical suspicion cast upon the whole Western metaphysical tradition?[14]

When I say that this was the beginning of the end, it has to be admitted that 'ends' were very much the theme of the conference. Moving from the *fin de siècle* of the nineteenth century to the sense of apocalyptic gloom at the end of the twentieth century was to find ourselves inhabiting a very different place. It was also the moment when our primary emphasis turned from theology to literature. I put the matter quite clearly: 'The essays are concerned with literature rather than with theological debate as such.'[15] I now think that this was a mistake. Clearly we were then still absorbing the largely literary expressions of the turn to the post-modern, and if some of the earlier and older voices remained (Martin Jarrett-Kerr, Peter Walker), the most significant new essay in this collection was by the younger American scholar Robert Detweiler. His essay, 'Apocalyptic Fiction and the End(s) of Realism', which I will study in more detail later, was both a continuance and a break. It was a continuance inasmuch as it begins with a reflection made by Paul Tillich in 1948, and recognizes the transformative effect of the Second World War (an effect now largely forgotten by theology). It was a break in that no theological works, apart from a brief reference to Tillich's *The Protestant Era*, are so much as mentioned by Detweiler. We had begun to move away from theology to religion and then further towards what Detweiler calls a new kind of realism that finally denies both.

And yet the conferences continued, though I think that in many ways the heart and soul had gone out of them. The study of literature and theology was by now well known enough for people to study it at doctoral level, and the Centre for the Study of Literature and Theology continues in Glasgow University to this day, though now in a very attenuated form. St Andrews University also continues to promote its rather different Institute for Theology, Imagination and the Arts, and books in the field continue to be published. (In the United

---

14   General Editor's Preface to David Jasper and Colin Crowder (eds), *European Literature and Theology in the Twentieth Century* (London: Macmillan, 1990), p. vii.
15   Ibid.

States programmes in literature and religion sprang up in major universities such as Chicago, Emory and Virginia, but died quickly from the lack of depth of soil and they failed to gain any institutional footholds. Universities were changing and unwilling and unable to accept the dark vision of the early conferences.) Robert Detweiler was the co-editor (with Gregory Salyer) of the volume of essays entitled *Literature and Theology at Century's End* (1995), papers drawn from the sixth conference now held in the University of Glasgow in 1992, a full decade from our beginnings in 1982. This book has a quite different sense to it – as much American as British and now with a proper sense of political correctness. This had never really bothered us, for better or for worse, in the early days! Issues in feminism and gender are here of central concern, and the wider world was beginning to press upon us in the form of an essay from Australia by John Strugnell. It was the eve of the millennium and Detweiler's Preface reflects a new sense of globalization, issues in ecology, the collapse of the Soviet Union and the end of apartheid in South Africa. The world had become more complex, more conscientious, more theoretical – and less theological. By the time the conferences became international in the University of Nijmegen in 2000 theology was beginning to return to our agenda, though in rather different ways. As we shall see in Chapter 7, it was through the themes of memory and forgiveness and through a renewed and close attention to the texts of literature, to reading as salvation, that we were struggling to find our way back. As we moved into the new century, and the older memories of war faded, we found ourselves in a wider world, as reflected in the themes discussed in the third part of this book. They are rooted in the old addresses to poetry and the Oxford Movement (John Keble in his Oxford *Lectures on Poetry* being linked to the contemporary Australian poet and writer David Malouf), the sacraments and the Bible read as literature, but these ancient traditions opening up into the new theological worlds of Australia, and even more startlingly, China.

My purpose in writing this book, however, has been first to return to an older world which is now less easily defensible and hardly known at first hand now by more than a very few. But my claim is that in the study of literature and theology we were, to a degree unconsciously, addressing profound theological questions that, in the end, were more radical and perhaps, dare I say it, more important, than the immediacies of the present age too frequently allow for. But I quite deliberately end in the meeting of two old worlds, the second being that of China (where I have been privileged to teach for part of my time in the past six years), wherein I perceive the roots of a growing and vital theological and literary energy that recognizes its own trauma in the Cultural Revolution, just as Ulrich Simon lived within the violence of the Holocaust. (See Chapter 13 on the writings of Yang Huilin).[16] I am perfectly well aware of the criticism from other theologians to which I am exposing myself. And I end on a note of hesitancy. In an age when, it might be said, people do not read as much in either literature or theology as in the past, and when the literature that could be taken for granted in 1982 is now generally unread and unknown, we need to recall the deep traditions within which we are formed and whose principles and ideas still govern much of what we say and think, although we are not aware of it. In them more profound and radical questions relating to the nature of theology and the place of humanity within the span of its history and *sub specie aeternitate* still dwell, and are forgotten at our peril. At a time when the formal institutions of higher education and religions are in dire peril to the point of collapse, such questions need to be asked again. There are signs of hope in our world, but the failure to ask such questions or even to find ways in which they might be asked with a creativity that acknowledges our continuity with the past, may well turn out to be a failure of our very humanity.

---

[16]   Yang Huilin, 'The Contemporary Significance of Theological Ethics: The True Problems Elicited by Auschwitz and the Cultural Revolution', in *China, Christianity and the Question of Culture* (Waco, TX: Baylor University Press, 2014), pp. 61–75.

PART I
The Durham Conferences

Chapter 1

Humanism and Belief in Literature: Seeking a Grammar of Assent

On 23–25 September, 1982, the first National Conference on Literature and Religion was held in the University of Durham. It was from this event and its successors in the biennial series of conferences that continue to the present day that the journal *Literature and Theology* was born, although even by then, only five years later, the literary and the theological climate in Britain was beginning to change. The papers that were later published from the 1982 conference might seem to us now, in many ways, to belong to another world both in their language and in their frames of reference. Their authors were largely, though not exclusively, Christian, clerical and male, speaking and writing in what one of them, John Coulson, quoting Cardinal Manning, who was speaking rather disparagingly of J.H. Newman, called 'the old Anglican, patristic, literary, Oxford tone'.[1] It was naturally assumed then that each day of the conference should begin with prayers or a Eucharist in the college chapel. This was a time before the advent of continental theoretical thinking in literary, cultural and later theological studies, and both literary and theological references in the essays are to an older generation of scholars, redolent of a Catholic and Christian humanistic spirit that has its roots in the nineteenth century in the prose works of Coleridge and Newman's *Grammar of Assent* (1870), and behind them to Pascal and, eventually, Erasmus. Contemporary English poetry then seemed to have reached its peak in *The Four Quartets*, and behind Eliot lay the seventeenth-century Metaphysical poets, Shakespeare, Virgil, the Greek tragedians, and, of course, the Bible, a book which still, for such scholars, 'found them' at the very root of their being.[2] Yet F.W. Dillistone, the chair of the conference, conveys some sense of the innovative nature of the proceedings when he writes in his Introduction to the published essays of the 'hesitation, even suspicion in academic circles in this country when attempts have been made to suggest that theology and English Literature have much to contribute to one another and

---

[1]   John Coulson, *Newman and the Common Tradition: A Study in the Language of Church and Society* (Oxford: Clarendon Press, 1970), p. 148.

[2]   S.T. Coleridge, *Confessions of an Inquiring Spirit* (London: William Pickering, 1840), p. 13: '... in the Bible there is more that *finds* me than I have experienced in all other books put together ... and [] whatever finds me brings with it an irresistible evidence of its having proceeded from the Holy Spirit'.

to learn from one another,'[3] though he admits that this was not entirely the case in the United States, where the powerful voice of Nathan A. Scott Jr, among others, could be heard in an interdisciplinary programme in the University of Chicago that was civic and Tillichian in its preoccupations and owed much to particular readings of Matthew Arnold. The Durham conference was only what Dillistone called 'a welcome and promising beginning' and a 'withdrawing of blinds',[4] yet from the start, in England, there were two differences from the Chicago programme. First, it was more precisely theological, indeed, liturgical in its nature, drawing on its nineteenth century Tractarian roots. Second, it was, in some respects, more strictly philosophical. Neither of these notes in the study of literature and theology sound so clearly and in the same way in current studies in the field. In 1982, it was the presence of the Wittgensteinian philosopher D.Z. Phillips that intellectually braced the conference, demanding what Phillips called strict 'grammatical requirements', and if we infringe them, 'we shall soon find ourselves engaged in trivialities or nonsense. The most common infringements come about by trying to sever a concept from the conditions of its application'.[5]

There was little here of abstraction but there was a deep learning in and respect for the texts of literature. What was particularly significant about this moment in England in the early 1980s? The study of the humanities was soon to change radically and adopt the new language ('jargon' it would then have been called by the older generation of scholars) of postmodernity and deconstruction, while theology and the Church were very much part of wider debates in society which, after Bishop John Robinson, still listened seriously to what it was to be honest to God.[6] But the Durham conference was a meeting of generations. The five senior figures to whom I shall return in more detail shortly – F.W. Dillistone, John Coulson, Martin Jarrett-Kerr, Ulrich Simon and Peter Walker – were men who, in different ways, had been deeply involved in the bloodbath that was mid-century Europe, in the armed forces, in the struggle in South Africa, in the horror of the Holocaust, or had been taught theology at first hand by

---

[3]   David Jasper (ed.), *Images of Belief in Literature* (London: Macmillan, 1984), p. 1.

[4]   Ibid., p. 6.

[5]   D.Z. Phillips, 'Mystery and Mediation: Reflections on Flannery O'Connor and Joan Didion', in David Jasper (ed.), *Images of Belief in Literature* (London: Macmillan, 1984), p. 25.

[6]   Robinson's *Honest to God* was published in 1963. Then the world of theological publishing remained largely clerical and church-orientated. The general editors of Dillistone's major book, *The Christian Understanding of Atonement*, published a little more than 10 years before the conference, in 1968, could still write that it was their hope that it 'might find a useful place on the shelves of the clergyman and minister, no less than on those of the intelligent layman. Perhaps we may have done something to bridge the gulf which too often separates the pulpit from the pew' (Welwyn: James Nisbett & Co., 1968), p. viii.

Karl Barth, Paul Tillich and the Niebuhrs. At the other end of the age spectrum were younger scholars, myself included, who had no such memories and looked forward to a different world which was less particular and perhaps less devout. It was a meeting point that found, in different ways and for various reasons, a common language for religion and theology in literature.

The ground for that common language was initially the nineteenth century, and above all the intellectual heritage of S.T. Coleridge. It was no accident that the second Durham conference in 1984 should focus on Coleridge and Schleiermacher, both of whom died in 1834. Behind the theological movements broadly represented in the United States by Tillich, and in England by Anglican clergymen like John Robinson, which regarded theology from 'the bottom upwards', lay an understanding of language which primarily regarded it not as analytic but as, in Coulson's word, 'fiduciary'.[7] For Coleridge words are energetic, living things and language a living organism which resists any tendency towards reductionism into what he calls 'a Chaos grinding itself into compatibility'.[8] Rather, by a process of 'de-synonymization', meanings should be kept distinct and from such careful diversity the life and vitality of metaphors have their being. In this way the language of poetry cannot be reduced or replaced by any 'literal' equivalence. At the same time for Coleridge, the poet, whose vision may be characterized as a 'unity in multeity', must be 'impelled by a mighty inward power under whose "obscure impulse" the poetry reveals "a bright, and clear, and living Idea"'.[9] It is to the imagination that this Idea alone can become apparent, closely related to what Coleridge describes in *The Statesman's Manual* (1816), speaking of the language of the Bible, and above all the writings of the prophets, as a symbol, that is as making possible the revelation of the universal in the particular which is a living part of the whole which it represents.[10] In the theology of the Tractarians and the work of J.H. Newman, such an understanding of symbol is taken up into a sacramental theology that, for Coulson, finds its deepest literary expression in Newman's *Grammar of Assent*, which he summarizes succinctly in describing the claims of his own book entitled *Religion and Imagination* (1981): 'The chief contention or grammatical principle of this book is that religious belief originates in that activity we call imagination, and that its verification thus depends now, as in the past, upon its first being made credible to imagination.

---

7   Coulson, *Newman and the Common Tradition*, p. 4.

8   A.D. Snyder, *Coleridge on Logic and Learning* (New Haven, CT: Yale University Press, 1929), p. 138.

9   S.T. Coleridge, *Treatise on Method: As Published in the Encyclopedia Metropolitana* [1818], ed. A.D. Snyder (London: Constable, 1934), p. 63.

10   S.T. Coleridge, *Lay Sermons*, ed. R.J. White, *The Collected Works*, vol. 6 (Princeton, NJ: Princeton University Press, 1972), p. 30.

The phrase (and claim) are Newman's ...'.[11] Throughout the careful distinctions made in Newman's book, of which the deepest concerns are theological in the defence of Catholicism, between assent, inference, certitude and the nature of the 'Illative Faculty', he continually employs literary methods and examples. Newman returns repeatedly to the plays of Shakespeare and particularly in a lengthy discussion of whether an early text of *Henry V* is corrupt (the question being how do we establish the 'real' Shakespeare?) – he concludes that 'if the text of Shakespeare is corrupt it should be published as corrupt'.[12] The truth, for Newman, lies in the 'concrete' and lively text as we have it before us and this is always to be preferred to that which is strictly 'correct'. This is not to say in the least that we should abandon the rigours of careful attention and scrutiny in the understanding of texts or in reasoning. Rather, in a sentence that well would characterize the critical spirit of the 1982 conference, Newman writes:

> Reasoning in concrete matters ... does not supersede the logical form of inference, but is one and the same with it; only it is no longer an abstraction but carried out into the realities of life, its premisses [*sic*] being instinct with the substance and the momentum of that mass of probabilities which carry it home definitely to the individual case ...[13]

The later Coleridge of *Aids to Reflection* (1825) is referred to in and permeates the *Grammar of Assent*, not least in the establishment of the nature of the Illative Sense whereby (Newman is drawing closely also on Bishop Joseph Butler) assent arises from the accumulation of probabilities. This is despite the Cardinal's declaration in extreme and forgetful old age that he 'never read a line of Coleridge'.[14]

Aids to Reflection also permeated at a deep unconscious level the spirit and thought of the Durham conference of 1982. If in many respects Coulson was the conference's intellectual guide, it was Ulrich Simon's lecture on Job and Sophocles that was its brilliantly dark and feeling centre. Simon was Professor of Christian Literature at King's College London. He was born in Berlin in 1913 into a cultivated Jewish family (his father was a noted concert pianist and composer) which gave him opportunities to meet Thomas Mann and

---

[11] John Coulson, *Religion and Imagination: 'In aid of a grammar of assent'* (Oxford: Clarendon Press, 1981), p. 46.

[12] J.H. Newman, *An Essay in Aid of a Grammar of Assent* [1870], ed. I.T. Ker (Oxford: Clarendon Press, 1985), p. 177.

[13] Ibid., pp. 189–90.

[14] Wilfrid Ward, *The Life of John Henry Cardinal Newman, Based in His Private Journals and Correspondence* (London: Longmans, Green and Co., 1912), vol. 1, p. 58. See also Coulson, *Newman and the Common Tradition*, Appendix, 'How much of Coleridge had Newman read?', pp. 254–5.

Dietrich Bonhoeffer, a near contemporary at school. His father was a victim of Auschwitz and almost certainly his brother died under Stalin, the background to his profound sense of evil. Escaping to London Simon was baptized in 1934, and later ordained as a priest into the Anglican Church. Simon never minced his words. He described *Honest to God* (1963) as a 'mean little book' wherein John Robinson 'acted as a kind of catalyst for the religious dishonesty towards God which Bultmann's demythologization had begun'.[15] He vehemently hated what he regarded as the jargon of theory. The opening of Ulrich's lecture at the conference, later published as an essay in the proceedings, is utterly characteristic.

> Comparisons in literature are as common as they may be either odious or boring, or both. Despite Virginia Woolf's scathing caricature in *To the Lighthouse* we are still compelled to listen to learned papers on the Influence of Someone on Someone else. Perhaps there is some justification for this procedure, for it is not a wholly sterile endeavour to find out, say, for example, where Shakespeare got his material for *Troilus and Cressida* and why he departed from the conventional treatment.[16]

What then follows in his lecture are penetrating close readings of the Book of Job and Sophocles' *Philoctetes* as dark tragedies, brushing aside the claims of George Steiner for the death of tragedy in our time.[17] From the depths of tragic literature Simon gives his answer to the 'hopeless superficiality of contemporary Christian trends', (44) because for him theology deeply matters and without it there can finally be nothing, even when theology becomes impossible.[18] In Job it is the 'comforters'' attempt to take us on the road towards 'a harsh non-involvement in suffering' (47) that is unbearable, for suffering can only be defeated if it is faced out. In literature, the weapon must be the one with which Simon himself began his lecture – the *irony* that bars any escape from the cold truth. He concludes, returning to his own Jewish tradition:

> Here we come up against a problem which must concern all who care for Religion and Literature, and especially Christian traditionalists. If irony pertains to the legacy of the tragic victory how can it become enshrined and made fruitful in Christian life and worship? Is not the ironic an unwelcome alien in both? True, we detect traces of irony in some Biblical books, not only in Job, but also in the Lukan narrative. The Jewish genius adds its own special brand of irony to

---

[15] Ulrich Simon, *Sitting in Judgement: 1913–1963: A History of Interpretation* (London: SPCK, 1978), p. 118.

[16] Ulrich Simon, 'Job and Sophocles', in David Jasper (ed.), *Images of Belief in Literature* (London: Macmillan, 1984), p. 42.

[17] In this Simon is at one with and anticipates Terry Eagleton in his reading of the idea of the tragic in *Sweet Violence* (Oxford: Blackwell, 2003).

[18] For the development of this, see below Chapter 3.

the Greek heritage. But when all is said and done the Christian tradition does not grant ironic distance ... Perhaps the time has come when the tragic irony will liberate the stale religious positions of our time.(50)

Simon ends, characteristically, by returning in pity to Job and Philoctetes: '*sunt lacrimae rerum*' ... that is, inescapably, how the world is, only made bearable by heroism and compassion.

Simon's is a dark and sombre call, but never less than serious, and rooted in both literature, theology and in the dark places of the human world. Another Anglican priest who spoke at the conference, but of a very different nature, was the gentle Peter Walker, the Bishop of Ely. Walker had seen war service in the Royal Navy, at first as a rating, and once preached on the sinking of HMS *Broadwater*, a ship on which he should have been serving, 'with all the watch below' – a phrase repeated in his sermon.[19] Walker's lecture at the conference was on the vision of literature, and on the call to watch with the closest attention. The Bishop was almost the opposite of Simon in character. A fine classicist he wore his learning lightly, his lecture more than anything a slow meditation on W.H. Auden's poetic sequence *Horae Canonicae*. Walker loved poetry and personally knew Auden well, as he knew also Geoffrey Hill. For him 'the meaning was in the waiting', and the complex, classical cadences of his prose yield their meanings slowly, sometimes hesitatingly. But there was nothing hesitant in his faith, though it was understated and often deeply concealed. In his gentle manner and in his teaching Walker followed a *disciplina arcani* which drew him to Auden, as Auden, in his turn, was drawn to Walker's utterly self-effacing way of celebrating the Eucharist. In a quiet moment in his lecture, the bishop notes:

> Auden might not parade his devotion, but there are moments when, in terms of his own understanding of things, it must be remembered that he died a communicant member of his church, as I am humbled to remember recalling a Palm Sunday morning Holy Communion (his last) in Christ Church Cathedral, Oxford at which I was the celebrant.[20]

Walker's lecture refers in passing to a wide range of literature and reading, including George Steiner's 'brilliant recent exposition of Heidegger on the Fall', (58),[21] but it is to Charles Williams and his book *The Forgiveness of Sins* to

---

[19] Obituary by Richard Smail, *The Independent*, 24 February, 2011.

[20] Peter Walker, '*Horae Canonicae*: Auden's Vision of a Rood – A Study in Coherence', in David Jasper (ed.), *Images of Belief in Literature* (London: Macmillan, 1984), p. 59.

[21] See George Steiner, *Heidegger*, Fontana Modern Masters. Ed. Frank Kermode (London: Fontana, 1978).

which he returns most insistently, and to what he calls the 'feel' of Williams and his central theme of 'coinherence' and sacrifice.

In the end, in Walker's writing, the theology – and it is deeply felt, and it profoundly matters – is in the very words and in the manner. His style borders on the incoherent, but never quite so; rather it calls us back from the edge of chaos to a vision that is never less than accessible, even mundane, rather like the poetry of Auden himself. It might be said, in words of Alfred North Whitehead, which Auden liked to quote, that Walker's prose represents a civilization that is a 'precarious balance between barbaric vagueness and trivial order'.[22] Yet, in him, within such balance and vision there was nothing either barbaric or trivial.

The same might be said, though in a very different way, of Fr Martin Jarrett-Kerr, an unjustly forgotten scholar, a priest and monk of Mirfield whose work embraced 'the Christian presence in modern humanism'.[23] Jarrett-Kerr was a man of immense learning who was active for seven years in South Africa with Bishop Trevor Huddleston, and he was involved (though never called to witness) with the defence of D.H. Lawrence's literary freedom in the trial of Penguin Books in 1960 concerning *Lady Chatterley's Lover* under the Obscene Publications Act of 1959. He published in 1951, under the pseudonym 'William Tiverton', a book on Lawrence which remains one of the most insightful studies of his work.[24] His numerous writings on the relationship between literature and religion are largely in the form of conversations with great writers and they deliberately avoid being, in his words, 'too theological', though the theology is embedded in the wit and close attentiveness to text. Martin regarded Alessandro Manzoni as 'the last of the Christian humanists', comparing him with later Catholic novelists like François Mauriac and Graham Greene 'who have his convictions but none of his width of sympathy and fullness of human background.'[25] Continually he reminds us of the dangers of 'neglecting the power of symbolic thinking – the influence of imagination over fact',[26] and in his lecture at the 1982 conference he links this to the relationship between literature and commitment of which, prophetically, he fears the decay with the advent of deconstruction in debates which even then he remarks, with some justice, are 'very old, very confused, and

---

[22]   W.H. Auden, 'The Greeks and Us', in *Forewords and Afterwords* (London: Random House, 1973), p. 8.

[23]   M.A.C. Warren, General Introduction to Martin Jarrett-Kerr, *The Secular Promise* (London: SCM, 1964), p. 12.

[24]   Martin Jarrett-Kerr, *D.H. Lawrence and Human Existence*, with an Introduction by T.S. Eliot (London: Rockliff, 1951). It was published under a pseudonym, Jarrett-Kerr's superior at Mirfield being fearful of its outspokenness.

[25]   Martin Jarrett-Kerr, *Studies in Literature and Belief* (London: Rockliff, 1954), p. 78.

[26]   Jarrett-Kerr, *The Secular Promise*, p. 119.

perhaps by now very tedious.'[27] Beginning in philosophy with what he calls 'the Hegelian and the Paradoxical', (105)[28] Jarrett-Kerr's notion of commitment is broad, refusing simplified exclusions. His literary training (he taught literature in the United States and for over 10 years at the University of Leeds) was firmly in the school of F.R. Leavis, and he embraced a Christian *humanism* that is rooted in the living language of text and which excludes only 'the "safe" kind of commitment' (114). In terms which would have had more resonance in 1982 than today (the Church of England's Report *The Church and the Bomb* was published on 1 October 1982, one week after the Durham conference),[29] Jarrett-Kerr takes to task M.H. Abrams' writing on *The Prelude* Book III in his great study of English Romanticism *Natural Supernaturalism* (1971):

> Abrams says: 'God has not quite dropped out, but He is only mentioned after the fact, and given nothing to do in the poem … What does God do in the poem? … Nothing of consequence.' But even in the 1850 version, where the analogy with divine activity is made more explicit, Wordsworth still does not give God any more to 'do' in the poem. And he is right not to. The important feature of an analogy is that the two sides – the analogous and the analogate – must not cross. As well say 'Chess is like a military engagement', and then proceed to bomb the bishop.[30]

Jarrett-Kerr's inclusive frame of reference, though not his impish and sometimes labyrinthine sense of humour, characterizes also the father figure of the Durham conference, F.W. Dillistone. His writings have, perhaps, endured least successfully. Reading his books today one finds them loosely woven and often somewhat impressionistic, written in an elegant academic style which is more characteristic of the earlier part of the twentieth century. Dilly's mind (he was always affectionately known as Dilly) was too eirenic and too kindly to be truly critical, yet his two books on symbolism, *Christianity and Symbolism* (1955) and *The Power of Symbols* (1986), situate him within the same intellectual Coleridgean tradition as Jarrett-Kerr, Coulson and others. But if Jarrett-Kerr looks forward, Dillistone looks back with a degree of nostalgia to an age which

---

[27] Martin Jarrett-Kerr, 'Literature and Commitment: "Choosing Sides"', in David Jasper (ed.), *Images of Belief in Literature* (London: Macmillan, 1984), p. 105. He was referring to those who were even then jumping onto the bandwagon of the postmodern, rather than the serious philosophical questions being asked by Derrida and others.

[28] He compares this to the debates between 'the Essentialist and the Kierkegaardian', and finally 'the Structuralist and the Deconstructionist'.

[29] The Church of England's Board of Social Responsibility, *The Church and the Bomb* (London: Hodder & Stoughton, 1982).

[30] Jarrett-Kerr, 'Literature and Commitment', p. 117.

pre-dates what he calls the 'disengagement of theology from imagination'.[31] Like Simon and Jarrett-Kerr, Dillistone, who taught in the United States and knew both Tillich and Reinhold Niebuhr, was an Anglican priest whose life combined scholarship with a pastoral ministry, largely as Dean of Liverpool Cathedral before his return to Oriel College, Oxford – once the spiritual and intellectual home of Cardinal Newman. In his introductory lecture Dillistone quoted, perhaps surprisingly, Luther in defence of the theological combination of languages and letters: 'I am convinced that without the knowledge of the [Humanistic] studies, pure theology can by no means exist.'[32] In his book *Religious Experience and Christian Faith* (1981), which draws on a wide range of contemporary writers and thinkers including Arnold Toynbee, Julien Huxley, Wallace Stevens, T.S. Eliot, D.H. Lawrence, Paul Tillich and Karl Jaspers, Dillistone argues against all 'exclusivist claims' to truth: 'Is truth to be found in monologue, in uniformity, in the single vision, through the one-track mind? Or is it to be found through dialogue, through dialectic, through mutual interchange, even through the juxtaposition of contraries? All life, so far as we know, can be represented only in terms of structure *and* energy.'[33]

Along with such almost Blakean and universal hints in Dillistone's Introduction, the Durham conference, though deeply and more or less exclusively Christian, was conducted in this spirit of exchange and conversation. Dillistone, perhaps, was under no delusions about his own critical limitations. In a personal letter written to me on 25 January 1982, he admits that *Religious Experience and Christian Faith* 'is only a sketch and I have too sketchy an acquaintance with some of those I discuss. But my interest was awakened through my biographical studies'. He was, by instinct, a biographer and his interest was in the lives of people[34] who crossed boundaries of various kinds – between science and religion, in the mission field and its literature (like Jarrett-Kerr, who was one of the first to recognize the brilliance of the post-colonial novels of the Kenyan writer Ngugi Wa Thiong'o), and, above all in literature and theology. Dillistone's short study, *The Novelist and the Passion Story* (1960) remains valuable today as a *theological* study of fiction and a *literary* reading of the Passion narratives.

But after the broad and genial humanity of Dillistone, it was to John Coulson, the only Roman Catholic among these scholars, that the conference turned for a more precise and philosophical framework built upon his careful study of

---

[31]   F.W. Dillistone, Introduction to David Jasper (ed.), *Images of Belief in Literature* (London: Macmillan, 1984), p. 4.

[32]   *Luther's Works*, vol. 49, *Letters II*, ed. and trans. Gottfried G. Krodel (Philadelphia, PA: Fortress Press, 1972), quoted in Dillistone, Introduction, p. 4.

[33]   F.W. Dillistone, *Religious Experience and Christian Faith* (London: SCM, 1981), p. 116.

[34]   He wrote biographies of Charles Raven (1975), C.H. Dodd (1977), Max Warren (1980) and Joe Fison (1983).

the 'common tradition' of S.T. Coleridge and John Henry Newman. Coulson's life, like Walker's, was 'over-shadowed'[35] by the fighting of the Second World War, though he was in the army rather than the navy, and he emerged from it to study English Literature at Cambridge, where his teachers included F.R. Leavis and L.C. Knights in a tradition which was later to include Frank Kermode and such seminal books as *The Sense of an Ending* (1966) and *The Genesis of Secrecy* (1979). Of the importance of Leavis (so influential also, as we have seen, for Jarrett-Kerr) and the *Scrutiny* group after the 'withdrawal' of theology Coulson was in no doubt.

> Leavis belonged to the tradition of angry dissent. When he treated of religion he did so with reverence rather than with mere sympathy, but he treated all attempts to assimilate literature to conventional religious beliefs with the dismissive scorn of the evangelical preacher. It was he who put English literature into the gap left by the retreat of philosophy into linguistic analysis and by the withdrawal of theology into biblical exegesis. Those who in Europe would have studied theology or metaphysics, in England studied English Literature.[36]

He goes on to refer to the words of L.C. Knights and to truth as not something 'that we receive or acquire through logical demonstration, but something we live our way into through a complex, varying activity when we engage with formal verbal structures of a particular kind'. Coulson admits that the theological parallels were not immediately obvious to him, but they became so only later through his study of Blake, Wordsworth, Coleridge, the nineteenth century, and 'a romantic culture [that] expresses faith in a form which transcends itself, as in the case of *The Prelude*'.

Coulson's early book, *Newman and the Common Tradition* (1970) begins with giving attention to the Anglicanism of Coleridge and F.D. Maurice, and, through Newman and the Catholic Modernists, ends, on the one hand, in Vatican II (which is barely imaginable without the spirit of Newman), and, on the other, 'that theory of language which theologians now derive from the later Wittgenstein'.[37] In other words, we are now neatly brought back to the conference and to the guiding philosophical presence of D.Z. Phillips. The acknowledged origins of Coulson's book are significant. They lie in Newman's insistence on the role of the laity in the Church, that is, the voice of the 'common tradition' that resists the imposed claims of dogma and authority in religious matters. They emphasize also the fundamental role of education and the university, again

---

[35]   John Coulson, 'Faith and Imagination', *The Furrow*. Series on 'Belief and Unbelief' No. 7 (1983), p. 536.

[36]   Ibid., p. 537.

[37]   Coulson, *Newman and the Common Tradition*, p. v.

following in the steps of Newman. Coulson had already edited a Downside Symposium on *Theology and the University* in 1964, with interdisciplinary contributions from theologians like David Jenkins, the future Bishop of Durham, and literary scholars like L.C. Knights, and it is still worth reading, perhaps now more than ever in the current dark ages of our universities.[38] In his lecture to the Durham conference, just a year after the publication of his major book on Newman and T.S. Eliot, *Religion and Imagination* (1981), Coulson returned to the educational and pedagogical roots of his writing and to the degree of Religion with Literature, which he had initiated, with great daring and originality, at the University of Bristol. The importance of this was that it allowed us to see the intellectual structure and 'grammar' of his relating religion and the imagination.[39] Coulson writes of the 'imaginative forms' of literature in four phases: how they reinforce religious beliefs; where they 'testify to the beginnings of a dissociation of faith from belief, and culture from religion'; where 'culture is so violently disrupted that the imagination becomes "impaired"'; and 'where the imagination is engaged in a society which is constitutionally committed to a strict secularity'.[40] He, like Dillistone, was very conscious of living in a time of change and perhaps even the decay of culture after the dark days of the mid century. Thus, his project is essentially conservative, yet at the same time open to the future inasmuch as 'the traditional myths and symbols cannot simply be repeated' (15). In exploring a language which is 'irreducibly symbolic and metaphorical', Coulson recognized also the insistent need to change and grow, but only on the basis of careful and responsible foundations: 'older confessional forms (as Hopkins and Eliot testify) have not been superseded, but (as in the case of Eliot) they have been revived in new and original transfigurations' (22). From Coleridge and Newman, John learnt the value of what Newman, drawing on his own early Evangelical background, called 'the literature of religion' which led him back to the Fathers and to the Anglican Caroline Divines, as well as inspiring his own efforts as a novelist and a poet. Contemporaries of Newman like Thomas Mozley recognized the particular literary quality of the Oxford Movement with its background in Romanticism, as well as the fading of that quality in the theology which followed.[41] Behind this lay the disciplined 'system' of a rigorous classical education, and thus when Newman finally becomes a Roman Catholic and seeks a religious order, he avoids the Vincentians, in his

---

[38] John Coulson (ed.), *Theology and the University* (London: Darton, Longman & Todd, 1964).

[39] The lecture was published under the title 'Religion and Imagination (Relating Religion and Literature) – A Syllabus', in David Jasper (ed.), *Images of Belief in Literature* (London: Macmillan, 1984), pp. 7–23.

[40] Ibid., pp. 7–8.

[41] Thomas Mozley, *Reminiscences of the Oxford Movement*, 2 vols (London: Longmans, Green, 1882), vol. 2, pp. 422–3. See also John Coulson, *Religion and Imagination*, pp. 34–5.

words, on account of their not granting 'to theology and literature that place in their system which we wished'.[42]

In 1982 in Durham we were, I think, with varying degrees of consciousness, returning to the Coleridge, Kantian logic and 'sacerdotal principles' that, Mark Pattison noted, rather over-dramatically, were abandoned in Oxford after 1845 in 'a sudden withdrawal of all reverence for the past'.[43] It is easy to be scathing and dismissive of such matters in today's academic climate. At the same time, it needs to be remembered that the two subsequent conferences in 1984 and 1986 continued to focus upon the nineteenth century and Romanticism, its critical languages and its sense of religious withdrawal. And if it is the case that after them and by the end of the decade in 1990 a very different critical tone was being articulated and, as the twentieth century drew to a close, its demands, rather than those of the nineteenth century, were felt ever more insistently, then it is at least interesting that students of literature and religion today have returned once again, and insistently, to the writings and art of Blake, Coleridge and other voices in Romanticism, even while Christian theology appears to have largely lost its way in varying degrees of extreme conservatism or fundamentalism.[44] From the churches, it may be said, there seems little to be heard. There was, it has to be admitted, a certain, perhaps inevitable, parochialism in the discussions held in 1982 and amongst the authors in the conference proceedings there is only one woman, Ann Loades, whose essay on Simone Weil has 'dated' perhaps least of all. Her subtitle was 'a problem for theology', and she reflects most clearly the sense that Christian theology was threatened, above all, from within in a world which was beginning to change at a pace that was to carry critical thinking far beyond any restraining capacity of the will to believe. As modernism gave way to various forms of postmodernism, so literary and cultural theory moved on from classical traditions and the close attention to texts, while the wider world of varieties of liberation thought and the acknowledgement of other religious traditions took us into a world that consigned the books of the scholars who have been discussed in this chapter, by and large, to the upper, unread shelves of our libraries. Yet their roots are deep and their commitments remain of significance as universities struggle for critical identity and cultural relevance.

When the journal *Literature and Theology* first appeared in 1987 its founding editors were already of a different generation. Among them was John Milbank, to whom we shall return at the end of this book, and, from the United States, Robert Detweiler of Emory University. The early issues of the journal carried

---

[42]   P. Murray (ed.), *Newman the Oratorian: His Unpublished Oratory Papers* (Dublin: Gill & Macmillan, 1969), p. 81.

[43]   Mark Pattison, *Memoirs* (London: Macmillan, 1885), pp. 240, 160.

[44]   The point has been made also by Christopher Rowland, *Blake and the Bible* (New Haven, CT: Yale University Press, 2011).

the symbol of the cross on their covers, though this was quickly abandoned and its identity as a journal of 'critical theory' acknowledged in a self-defining paragraph on the inside page that was the result of many hours of editorial debate and soul searching. I think it is true to say, as Michael Kirwan has recently remarked, that the initial ebullience of the journal was gradually replaced by a much more low-key tone as confidence in the power of the study of literature and theology to establish itself began to wane.[45] At the same time, the life of the journal in its first 25 years falls clearly into three stages, broadly identified in the tenures of its first three Senior Editors, myself, Graham Ward and most recently Andrew Hass.[46] Although there has always been an American editorial presence, *Literature and Theology* has remained a British publication. The first 10-year stage remained still largely governed by the spirit of the early conferences and their founding fathers who have been the principal subjects of this chapter and those to follow. At the same time we benefited from the advice of such major intellectual figures as Nathan Scott in the USA and George Steiner in the UK in continual reflections on the nature of the study of 'literature and theology'. Under Graham Ward the turn was made to the theoretical, the postmodern and cultural studies. Increasingly papers expanded the range of subjects to other faith traditions and, occasionally, to the visual arts and music. In the last years, under Andrew Hass, the tone has been that of the complex and global cultural and intellectual environment of the post-postmodern world that is still difficult to define in both theological and literary terms. In many ways, the days of the 1982 conference in Durham now seem antique, remote and inaccessible. And yet its origins and preoccupations remain highly significant and perhaps never more so than at the present time as we continue to attempt to pursue the study of theology and literature. All too often that exercise comes across in publications as repetitive and uncreative, forgetting the deep and dramatic theological issues and imperatives that initiated our discussions more than 30 years ago. In an essay published in *Images of Belief in Literature*, which also has its beginnings as a lecture in the Durham conference, Dominic Baker-Smith examined the question of hermeneutics both 'literary and divine'. Like the scholars whom we have been considering, Baker-Smith's writing is rooted in a 'humanistic scholarship' and in 'Coleridge's alertness to the older hermeneutics [which] underlies his important remarks on imagination and the Bible in *The Statesman's Manual* (1816)'.[47] Such hermeneutics are deeply theological and deeply literary, both ancient and modern, marking:

---

[45] Michael Kirwan, 'Theology and Literature in the English-Speaking World', in Francesca Bugliani Knox and David Lonsdale (eds), *Poetry and the Religious Imagination: The Power of the Word* (Farnham: Ashgate, 2015), p. 11.

[46] The current senior editor is Professor Heather Walton of Glasgow University.

[47] Dominic Baker-Smith, 'Exegesis: Literary and Divine', in David Jasper (ed.), *Images of Belief in Literature* (London: Macmillan, 1984), pp. 172, 177.

... a return to the older monastic habits of reading ... The text is not treated as a store of isolated *dicta* suited to syllogistic elaboration but as a personal encounter which unfolds naturally as prayer and what can best be called imaginative participation. In consequence of this alertness to the nature of the text seen within its total context, the highly formalized four-fold exegesis of late medieval commentators gives way to a number of variants on what Jacques Lefèvre d'Etaples in his *Quincuplex Psalterium* of 1509 calls the *true* literal sense ... The result is an affective exegesis which works through imaginative response to establish a dramatic confrontation with the text.[48]

Behind such an imaginative response and participation is a highly disciplined project in both theology and literature. It was this project, driven by the weight of the times, which inspired the vision of the 1982 conference and the founding of the journal *Literature and Theology*. It remains our task both to sustain the vision and maintain the discipline in the terms set by contemporary conditions which are, perhaps, less propitious than those of 30 years ago, more challenging, yet still demanding that we listen to those founding voices and their wisdom. And so, in the next chapter we turn more specifically and in detail to the work of John Coulson.

---

[48]   Ibid., p. 173.

Chapter 2
A Habit of Mind:
Religion and Imagination –
John Coulson and John Henry Newman

The lecture with which John Coulson opened the 1982 conference seemed, at first hearing, rather too straightforward and simple, disappointing even. It was, in essence, an outline of the syllabus of the undergraduate degree he had developed at Bristol with the title 'Religion with Literature'. It seemed to me to be an unpromising beginning for a conference, but in fact we came to realize that it held the secret of the spirit of what we were doing – a spirit that has, sadly, died almost completely in the more recent study of literature and theology in our universities. Coulson, a mild mannered man for whom war service in the army could have been anything but congenial, was known as a distinguished scholar of the work of John Henry Newman and a Reader in Theology but initially, as we have seen in the previous chapter, he was educated at Cambridge in English literature. For him, the study of literature and theology began in education and teaching, and it lay not on the periphery but at the very heart of the intellectual life of a university. It is also deeply related to the idea of the Church. Coulson was a devout Roman Catholic. Rooted in the relationship between religion and the imagination Coulson's study of literature and religion was also profoundly theological, and herein, I think, lay the key to our whole enterprise. What we were engaged in was a deeply creative return to the discipline and the necessity of theology itself, an essential activity that was neither a throw-back to a former age (though, as with Newman, it demanded a beginning in the deep sense of history and tradition) nor an avoidance of the contemporary ethos and situation. In some ways, oddly, it was much more radical than the wave of theory and post-modernity that was to come and almost overwhelm us.

Thinking in retrospect, it was no accident that another key participant in the 1982 conference was the philosopher Dewi Zephaniah Phillips. His thought was grounded in the work of Ludwig Wittgenstein to whom Coulson, in his writings on Newman, continually refers. It was, we might claim, in their understanding of the nature of language that Newman and Wittgenstein were close. James Cameron describes the connection well, and it illustrates the energy present in our reaching out to the language of poetry and literature:

> Language ... for Newman is a set of tools well enough adapted to the furthering of
> particular practical or even speculative purposes, but compelled to strain itself to
> breaking point when it attempts to speak of God or the soul or faith. Language is
> framed to deal with our ordinary commerce with the world of things and persons,
> not with the subject-matter of theology. It is the tragedy of the vocation of the
> theologian – or the philosopher – that he must proceed by way of analysis and
> definition; but the nature of language is such that every comment he makes is an
> oblique one, every description a travesty, every definition a mutilation ... Newman
> has the view of language as a set of tools the function of which are determined by
> needs arising out of the way of life of those who use the language, and this view is
> close to that elaborated by Wittgenstein in his later work.[1]

Both Newman and Wittgenstein insistently deconstruct the theoretical
structures which serve only to cloud our quest for understanding. Furthermore,
as David Burrell has observed, Wittgenstein's reaching for 'philosophy as a way
of life' can 'facilitate a hermeneutical retrieval of classical texts'[2] just as Newman
leads us back to the classical literature of the Church Fathers and we, in the 1982
conference, were being led back to the great texts of our literary tradition. What
Phillips reminded us of at the conference was the need always to be exact in our
words and precisely alert to that exactitude in grammar that preserves us from
simply making nonsense – the exactitude that is demanded not by theory but by
the insistent actualities of the words we use and which are too often frustrated by
our tendency to abstraction and to decontextualize our words.[3] In other words,
Phillips reminds us, there must always be a deep commitment to the poetic
attention given to words and their living actuality required in any theological
exercise, a remembrance that it is finally more important (and more difficult) to
communicate with one person (human or divine) with the full resources of the
heart and mind than with ten thousand in trivial generalities. This is a mystery
known in poetry and in the life of prayer, but too often easily forgotten in the
counsels of the theologians.[4]

Wittgenstein clearly articulates the challenge here presented to us, calling us
back to our responsibilities to the 'soul' of words, our commitment to language

---

[1]   James Cameron, *Night Battle* (Baltimore, MD: Helicon Press, 1962), pp. 204–5.

[2]   David B. Burrell, 'Newman in Retrospect', in Ian Ker and Terence Merrigan (eds),
The Cambridge Companion to John Henry Newman (Cambridge: Cambridge University
Press, 2009), p. 264.

[3]   See D.Z. Phillips, 'Mystery and Meditation: Reflections on Flannery O'Connor and
Joan Didion', in David Jasper (ed.), *Images of Belief in Literature* (London: Macmillan, 1984),
p. 25, and above p. 22.

[4]   Phillips, from the works of Joan Didion, quotes the words of the singer Joan Baez
that 'The easiest kind of relationship for me is with ten thousand people ... The hardest is
with one'. Phillips, 'Mystery and Meditation', p. 32.

which offers deep objection to the tiresome and presumptuous habit of 'replacing one word by another arbitrary one of our own invention'.[5] The soul of words requires us to listen attentively even while acknowledging the 'tragedy' of the theologian who must (is this 'must' necessary?) proceed by way of analysis and definition. We will return to the deep tragedy of theology later in a consideration of the writings of Ulrich Simon in Chapter 3. Wittgenstein's distinction has to do with the very nature of understanding itself.

> We speak of understanding a sentence in the sense in which it can be replaced by another which says the same; but also in the sense in which it cannot be replaced by any other. (Any more than one musical theme can be replaced by another.)
>
> In the one case the thought in the sentence is something common to different sentences; in the other, something that is expressed by these words in these positions. (Understanding a poem)[6]

The same point, of course, had been made long before by S.T. Coleridge in his insistence on the resistance of all true poetry to paraphrase – its final *irreducibility*.[7] And, quite simply, it was Newman above all who reminded theology of this truth in its vocation of expressing the mystery of faith, in the best words in the best order, and our assent to that.

But to return now to John Coulson's degree syllabus in religion and literature, where for him the key word is 'imagination' in different modes of relationship between religion and the imagination. The history of the word begins most significantly for us in the familiar distinction between the Primary and the Secondary Imagination in Coleridge's *Biographia Literaria* (1817). But in literature we must go back much further than that and to that life in words which is far beyond any logic and is, in Coleridge's terms, a 'hovering between images', a fiduciary use of language which starts from a prior unity and yet brings diverse elements into one,[8] and whose energy 'is ... able to protect religious assent from cliché and over-simplification'.[9] Coulson's pedagogy in his degree syllabus separates (English) literature into four ages: the first is when imaginative forms and religious beliefs reinforce one another (Shakespeare to Jane Austen);

---

5   Ludwig Wittgenstein, *Philosophical Investigations*, 3rd edn, trans. G.E.M. Anscombe (Oxford: Basil Blackwell, 1981), para. 530, p. 143.

6   Ibid., para. 531, pp. 143–4.

7   See also John Coulson, *Religion and Imagination: 'In aid of a grammar of assent'* (Oxford: Clarendon Press, 1981), pp. 17–18. Coulson quotes Coleridge in *Table Talk* and *Shakespearean Criticism*, ed. T.M. Raysor (London: Everyman, 1960), i. p. 148, ii. p. 42.

8   This is what Coleridge calls the *adunating* power of language.

9   John Coulson, 'Religion and Imagination (Relating Religion and Literature) – A Syllabus', in David Jasper (ed.), *Images of Belief in Literature* (London: Macmillan, 1984), p. 9.

the second is that in which imaginative forms indicate the start of a dissociation of faith from belief (Coleridge and Newman to modernism); the third is when the imagination is 'impaired' by the violent disruption of culture (poets of the First World War); and finally, there is imagination when it is 'engaged in a society which is constitutionally committed to a strict secularity'. The last question which Coulson sets us is 'What is the place of the confessional imagination in a secular culture?'[10] I will return to the problem which this presents at the very end of this chapter.

There is, I think, a profound honesty here which subsequent times have been less than open to. It begins in the anxious questionings and restless debates over language of Coleridge and Newman (in their different ways) and was to be overshadowed (as Coulson's life was overshadowed by the Second World War) by the clever theorizing of more recent years and the generally conservative meanderings of Christian theology which have amounted to little beyond the increasingly irrelevant insistencies of ancient formularies that have accompanied the inevitable and rapid decline of the formal institutions of Western religion as they flex their wasted muscles in ever more pathetic attempts to attract public attention.[11] Their marginalization in our society (as of the universities understood properly within their ancient vocation) is deserved. Coulson expresses it bluntly for an age in which the religious imagination, properly expressed in living language, seems less and less plausible since what seems certain is that traditional myths and symbols cannot simply be repeated, since merely 'to enumerate old themes' is to discover, with W.B. Yeats, that they are but 'circus animals', whose desertion is inevitable:

> Now that my ladder's gone
> I must lie down where all the ladders start,
> In the foul rag-and-bone shop of the heart.
>   (W.B. Yeats, 'The Circus Animals' desertion')[12]

An example of this cultural (and theological) failure within the churches is described by Leslie Houlden in the context of the outburst of liturgical revision that happened in the aftermath of the Second Vatican Council and its failure to come to anything much beyond about 1980 (the time of the Durham conference).[13] Writing of the new Eucharistic liturgy proposed within the Church of England in the early 1970s, Houlden states bluntly:

---

[10]   Ibid., p. 8.

[11]   I am grateful to Richard Holloway for this image, which he used in his BBC series *The Sword and the Cross*, subsequently published by Saint Andrew Press, Edinburgh (2003).

[12]   Coulson, 'Religion and Imagination (Relating Religion and Literature)', p. 15.

[13]   In 1980 the Church of England published its *Alternative Service Book*, the first new authorized prayer book in England since 1662.

Its thought forms and theological assumptions are wholly traditional. Apart from a few traces of Reformation emphases, there is little sign of any development in Christian theology since patristic times, let alone in the last hundred years. Yet in that period both the achievements of, and challenges to, Christian thought have been, to say the least, substantial. That they find no echo in the words thought suitable may reflect an existing state of affairs – the virtual isolation of the great majority of believers from both the achievements and the challenges. That in itself is a matter worth pondering.[14]

The key word to note here is 'development', looking back to Newman and above all to his insistence upon it as a fundamental principle in theology in his key work of 1845, *The Development of Christian Doctrine*. And it was Newman, above all, who returned to patristic thought and theology and precisely linked it in a living tradition with the issues of contemporary belief and life within the Church and the world of his time.

It was in his *Apologia Pro Vita Sua* (1865) that Newman identified the key, if ambivalent role which Coleridge played in the principles of his thinking and his theology:

> While history in prose and verse was thus made the instrument of Church feelings and opinions, a philosophical basis for the same was laid in England by a very original thinker, who, while he indulged a liberty of speculation, which no Christian can tolerate, and advocated conclusions which were often heathen rather than Christian, yet after all installed a higher philosophy into enquiring minds, than they had hitherto been accustomed to accept. In this way he made trial of his age, and succeeded in interesting its genius in the cause of Catholic truth.[15]

In the early 1980s we were, I think, essentially a Coleridgean community in our concern for literature and theology, though we hardly knew it at the time, but we lacked, subsequently, anyone of the stature of Newman to give expression to the theology which we were struggling to recover through our sense of literature. Also the times were different. The Second Vatican Council, which was of Newman in mind and spirit, was already 20 years old, and neither the Church nor the world any longer heeded its wisdom and sense of movement. It was no accident that our second conference in Durham, held in 1984, celebrated the genius of both Coleridge and Schleiermacher, philosophically and hermeneutically, but even by then the new wave of theory in literature and

---

[14] J.L. Houlden, 'Liturgy and her Companions: A Theological Appraisal', in R.C.D. Jasper (ed.), *The Eucharist Today: Studies on Series 3* (London: SPCK, 1974), p. 174.

[15] John Henry Newman, *Apologia Pro Vita Sua*, ed. Ian Ker (London: Penguin, 1994), pp. 99–100.

culture was threatening to overcome the life of Christian theology, and the first fine immediacy of 1982 was beginning to be lost. Within the hermeneutical tradition it was Newman, the controversialist and above all in the *Grammar of Assent*, who anticipated Heidegger and Gadamer (and might therefore be seen as the real, and almost entirely unsuspected,[16] key to postmodern thinking) in his analysis of the fiduciary roots of inquiry which refuses to oppose knowing and believing, and his retrieval of Aristotle's analysis of *phronesis*. After the conference in Durham I had a brief but warm correspondence with Jacques Derrida. I could never persuade him to join us in our venture – he was, perhaps already too grand by then – but I regret now that I did not persist and I am presumptuous enough to think that things might have been very different for us (and perhaps for him) if he had joined in our deliberations.

But history cannot be changed and I must return to our, then, almost entirely English discussions. (It was this isolation, in the end, that was to prove fatal.) It was in 1970 that Coulson had published his book *Newman and the Common Tradition*, linking Church and society with the tradition that he traces through Coleridge to F.D. Maurice, Newman and finally the Wittgenstein of the *Philosophical Investigations*. We need to begin, with Coulson, with giving some further attention to what is meant by the *fiduciary* use of language. For Coleridge, quite simply, words and things cannot be directly equated, but understanding begins with a sense of the unity of all things rather than of things seen in isolation. It is this that governs not only the poetry of Wordsworth in *The Prelude*, the book which Coulson took to war with him and which he linked with Newman's understanding of the nature of assent,[17] but Coleridge's sense of the symbolic which is virtually the same as the sense of the sacramental. Thus the mind is capable of holding together opposites and contraries which defy analysis and reason's role is critical rather than foundational: or perhaps we are close here to something like the sense of Pascal's reasons of the heart. In the startling phrase which I have already referred to Coleridge, warns us against regarding language 'as a Chaos grinding itself into compatibility'.[18] Rather he appeals to the process in language of what he calls 'de-synonymization' whereby words become not a matter of closing up into meaning but rather in language that whereby 'in the progress of intellectual development new distinctions are

---

[16]   This, of course, is not quite the case. David B. Burrell has made a similar observation in his essay 'Newman in Retrospect', in *The Cambridge Companion to John Henry Newman*.

[17]   Coulson observed: 'The book I took to war with me was Wordsworth's *The Prelude*. Sub-titled "growth of a poet's mind" it deals with the restoration of his faith and of its transformation from what Newman terms notional assent into real assent: we move from the abstract and conventional to an awareness that we are inmates of an active universe'. 'Faith and Imagination'. *The Furrow*, Series on 'Belief and Unbelief' No.7 (1983), p, 538.

[18]   A.D. Snyder (ed.), *Coleridge on Logic and Learning* (New Haven, CT: Yale University Press, 1929), p. 138. See also the discussion above, p. 15.

brought into consciousness.[19] It is the differences between (and even within) words that are most significant. Within this living organism of language the past and present of a community are drawn into a vital unity and, as Coleridge writes in the Preface to *Aids to Reflection* (1825), which of all books can truly claim to be the true precursor of Newman's *Grammar of Assent*, words are 'LIVING POWERS, by which the things of most importance to mankind are actuated, combined and humanized'.[20]

Coulson suggests that Coleridge's original concerns with language were actually religious and that he failed, very significantly, inasmuch as he did not make sufficient distinction between the religious and the poetic:

> Obscurity arises because Coleridge fails to keep his literary and religious categories sufficiently separate, or to preserve a firm enough distinction between philosophy and theology; and he frequently weakens his theological arguments by grounding them on a particular form of idealist epistemology.[21]

This is, of course, essentially the same criticism as is made of Coleridge by Newman in the *Apologia*, though he would not have used Coulson's language. From Coleridge, whose 'conclusions were often heathen rather than Christian', Newman moves on to Southey and Wordsworth, two living poets in 'the department of fantastical fiction' and 'of philosophical meditation', before he returns to the theologians and the fathers of the Oxford Movement.[22] I think that in many ways we also failed to make the same distinction, and, lacking the genius either of Coleridge or another Oxford Movement, we finally suffered the same fate, and theology in any real sense vanished from our agenda. The consequences of this we will see in Chapter 6. As children of the modern (and postmodern) academy in which theology has no place and wherein departments of English Literature still almost seem to celebrate their sheer ignorance, of the magnitude of a Richard Dawkins, of theology and religion, we have not had the courage of our convictions. Perhaps things are changing a little now. But nor have we had the intellectual courage to distinguish within their unity between the realms of literature, philosophy and theology, rather muddling them (something very different) and failing to give them the close intellectual attention which they individually require.[23] The study of literature and theology, furthermore, has

---

[19] Ibid., p. 132. See also J. Coulson, *Newman and the Common Tradition: A Study in the Language of Church and Society* (Oxford: Clarendon Press, 1970), p. 17.

[20] S.T. Coleridge, *Aids to Reflection* (London: Bohn, 1904), p. xix.

[21] Coulson, *Newman and the Common Tradition*, p. 22.

[22] Newman, *Apologia*, p. 100.

[23] It is a pity that we did not have the benefit of the wisdom of Stanley Fish in his essay 'Being Interdisciplinary Is so Very Hard to Do', *There's No Such Things as Free Speech and It's a Good Thing Too* (New York: Oxford University Press, 1994), pp. 231–42. First published

not dedicated a conference to that key work, Newman's *Grammar of Assent*, and students, though well versed in the technical vocabulary of literary theory, have barely heard of the Illative Sense, which, as Coulson succinctly puts it (with echoes of Coleridge on the imagination), 'unifies the contradictory and separated images, and acts thereby as a power which realizes or forms ideas'.[24]

Newman's Illative (or Inductive) Sense, as the power to judge, is rooted in the *Nichomachean Ethics* and Aristotle's idea of *phronesis*.[25] Newman describes it as 'the sole and final judgement on the validity of an inference in concrete matters'.[26] He puts it even more precisely in a letter to a friend:

> There is a faculty of the mind which I think I have called the inductive sense, which, when properly cultivated and used, answers to Aristotle's *phronēsis*, its province being, not virtue, but the '*inquisitio veri*', which decides for us, beyond any technical rules, when, how, etc., to pass from inference to assent, and when and under what circumstances etc. etc. not.[27]

It is the Illative Sense that 'determines what science cannot determine, the limit of converging probabilities, and the reasons sufficient for a proof'.[28] Newman's sense of probability as 'the guide of life' begins with his early immersion in Bishop Butler's *Analogy of Religion*, read, so he recalls in the *Apologia* as far back as 1823 and a key work for him on the 'question of the logical cogency of Faith' though also, perhaps, it was at the root of what 'led to the charge against me both of fancifulness and of scepticism'.[29] I suppose those of us who have continued to pursue the study of theology and literature have grown used to similar charges: of *fancifulness*, or perhaps dilettantism, inasmuch as we have failed to continue to engage seriously enough with the tough, systematic business of the theologian; and of *scepticism* insofar as the reading of literature may quickly lead one into dangerous and unprincipled waters beyond the reach of true religion.

---

in *Profession* 89, 15–22. The same might be said of a great deal of the contemporary nonsense spoken about 'interdisciplinarity'.

[24]   Coulson, *Newman and the Common Tradition*, p. 60.

[25]   See further, Thomas J. Norris, 'Faith', in *The Cambridge Companion to John Henry Newman*, pp. 88–90.

[26]   John Henry Newman, *An Essay in Aid of a Grammar of Assent* [1870], ed. I.T. Ker (Oxford: Clarendon Press, 1985), p. 223.

[27]   Wilfrid Ward, *The Life of John Henry Cardinal Newman*, 2 vols (London: Longman, Green & Co., 1912), vol. 2, p. 589.

[28]   Newman, *A Grammar of Assent*, p. 228.

[29]   Newman, *Apologia*, pp. 30–31.

'Tell all the Truth, but tell it slant'.[30] The words of Emily Dickinson were a favourite expression of Bishop John Tinsley who for many years taught theology through literature at the University of Leeds. I do not think that anyone listened very seriously to him, least of all to the precision of what he was saying about the nature of theology and what Ian Ramsey would have called its 'odd' language of metaphor and symbol. While the 1960s and 1970s in Britain were embroiling themselves in the kind of theology that Newman above all despised, the 'liberal' theology of John Robinson's *Honest to God* (which Ulrich Simon, for one, as we have seen, loathed as a mean little book), the sharper, more epistemologically demanding forms of theological enquiry based on fiduciary premises were neglected or worse in the rush to relevance. This was partly, I now think, the anxiety of a dying Church that was forgetting its theology. I regret now that we did not give closer attention to those two fundamental works, Newman's *Development of Christian Doctrine* and his *Grammar of Assent*, both deeply literary in their assumptions and methods and sensitive to ways of reading texts in the delicate balance between text and reader as the very ground of proper theological thinking. Ultimately we held the reins too loosely and lost the tight control that was called for.

Perhaps we failed inevitably inasmuch as the Church and the modern university have also largely failed, and we were the children of both – each of us perhaps trapped by one or the other or both, for what were the alternatives? John Coulson's pedagogical instincts in Bristol were right, though no one really listened to him, and students of literature and theology know how difficult it is for them to get jobs – they have to become *either* theologians *or* literary critics – but not both. And, crucially for the narrative of this book, where we of my generation differed from people like Coulson and Simon is that our lives had not been 'overshadowed' by serious and dark events of history as theirs were. They were finally serious about theology and its profound difficulties, even impossibilities, in a way that we were not, and it only got worse. Looking back to the eighteenth century, Gerard Loughlin has written of the present crisis of identity in our universities:

> Theology has no place in the university of the twenty-first century. She is out of place in such a place, a pre-Enlightenment relic, an uncomfortable reminder of what the modern university was meant to abolish. As long ago as 1772, Baron d'Holbach, in *Le Bon sens*, declared the 'science' of theology to be 'a continual insult to human reason', and reason is the bedrock of the modern university,

---

[30] *The Complete Poems of Emily Dickinson*, ed. Thomas H. Johnson (London: Faber and Faber, 1970), p. 506.

which is home to all true science. Theology is no science at all but a chimera of
the imagination, an aberration in the place that banishes all such fantasies.[31]

This is, in fact, the judgement of the contemporary university on theology,
and in our response to it we need to return to the insights of Coleridge and to
the Newman of the *Discourses on the Scope and Nature of University Education*
(1852), lectures which he delivered in Dublin on the founding of his university
for Catholics in that city. Amongst Newman's reading for these lectures was
Coleridge's *Treatise on Method*, which was the Preface to his *Encyclopedia
Metropolitana*. (It ought to be remembered also that John Coulson edited
a Downside Symposium, very much in the spirit of Newman, under the title
Theology and the University in which L.C. Knights, the Regius Professor of
English Literature at Cambridge, brought alive Newman's contention that the
assent of faith must first be credible to the imagination.[32])

Newman, like Coleridge, saw university education as a balance between
functions within the society in which it is set, in what Coleridge might have
described as a 'unity in multeity'. A university, properly, allows autonomy for the
intellect within a balanced economy of disciplines all forming a whole. Within
this antecedent unity parts are abstracted for close consideration – Coleridge's
description of the Secondary Imagination in chapter 13 of *Biographia Literaria*
is a close description of this process. At the heart of it is the attempt to grasp and
articulate the 'idea': 'Excellence', writes Newman, 'implies a centre.'[33] Running
through all of Newman's writings on education is the distinction to be made
between intellectual and moral excellence (which, for him, leads us to the
difference between Nature and Grace).[34] It was through Coulson that we were
taken to a similar position – rather an old fashioned one today, it might seem,
until one recalls the turn in postmodern thinking much later towards the ethical,
a recalling of us to the responsibilities we hold as thinkers. And what of the place
of theology in the university, as a subject now at best on the outer periphery of
the curriculum where often today its place is taken by its chilly, soulless offspring
'religious studies'? Newman was quite clear that theology has a necessary and
distinctive place in the university though not in its ancient primacy as Queen of
the Sciences. Rather, in Coulson's words, 'theology regulates only to the extent

---

[31]   Gerard Loughlin, 'Theology in the University', in *The Cambridge Companion to John
Henry Newman* (Cambridge: Cambridge University Press, 2009), p. 221. Quoting Baron
d'Holbach, *Good Sense*, trans. Anna Knoop (New York: Prometheus Books, 2004 [1878]),
pp. 13, 14.

[32]   John Coulson, *Theology and the University* (London: Darton, Longman & Todd,
1964), pp. 207–18, and see above p. 23. At the time of the Symposium, Knights was
Winterstoke Professor of English in the University of Bristol.

[33]   J.H. Newman, *Historical Sketches*: 1872 (London: Pickering & Co., 1891), vol. 3, p. 16.

[34]   See Coulson, *Newman and the Common Tradition*, p. 89.

that it provides a true and unique account of Revelation: its power to regulate stems from its truth and not from any external coercion'.[35] Theology, in other words, takes its place within the careful critical exercises that direct the life and purpose of the university and must never, as Newman himself insisted:

> be excluded from the law to which every mental exercise is subject, namely, from that imperfection which must ever attend the abstract, when it would determine the concrete. Nor do I speak only of Natural Religion, for even the teaching of the Catholic Church ... is variously influenced by other sciences.[36]

This describes well what we were trying to do in the Durham conference. Ultimately ours was an attempt at a late exercise in theological recovery, a coming together of what Newman would have called an 'assemblage of sciences' (and more recently has been termed, with little actual understanding of its true nature, 'interdisciplinarity') within which the careful demands of literature offered the only way to theological utterance at a time when for the most part it had been stunned by the traumas of war and genocide, and was confirming its irrelevancy in both the churches (as increasingly anti-intellectual) and the academy by its claims to the absolute and the infallible. Like Newman later in his life when he was exercised by the issue of papal infallibility, we preferred at least to try to listen to the call of conscience heard, for us, in the voices of the poets.[37] Those of us at the conference in 1982 quickly realized that we were actually far from possessing a common language as academics – professors of English Literature found it hard or even impossible to communicate with professors of Theology as both were trapped in the defensive technical vocabulary beloved and fostered by the disciplinary barriers of the modern university which has abandoned the sense of necessary equilibrium of forms of enquiry for largely barren economic, shapeless and socially 'useful' models. Newman's view of the university was quite opposite:

> The assemblage of sciences ... may be said to be *in equilibrio*, as long as all its proportions are secured to it. Take away one of them, and that one so important in the catalogue as Theology, and disorder and ruin at once ensue. There is no middle state between the *equilibrium* and chaotic confusion; one science is ever

---

[35]   Ibid., p. 91.

[36]   J.H. Newman, *The Idea of a University Defined and Illustrated* [1873] (London: Longmans, Green & Co., 1925), III. 4, p. 52.

[37]   Newman famously remarked that he would drink 'to the Pope, if you please – still, to Conscience first, and to the Pope afterwards'. *Certain Difficulties felt by Anglicans in Catholic Teaching*, 2 vols (London: Longmans, Green & Co., 1876), vol. 2, p. 261.

pressing upon another, unless kept in check; and the only guarantee of truth is the cultivation of all of them. And such is the office of a University.[38]

Newman was, of course, arguing in the context of a Catholic university in Dublin, yet he is quite clear that his argument is far broader than that in his claim that theology is knowledge. If 'God' is understood as more of a question than an answer, then it is a name for the ultimate incomprehensibility of all things towards which we press with all the forms of enquiry at our disposal.[39] In Newman's words concerning the matter of truth:

> Not Science only, not Literature only, not Theology only, neither abstract knowledge simply nor experimental, neither moral nor material, neither metaphysical nor historical, but all knowledge whatever, is taken into account in a University, as being the special seat of that large Philosophy, which embraces and locates truth of every kind, and every method of attaining it.[40]

I wonder if, in fact, in Durham we were already too late. We were reaching for an 'idea' but by then our universities were without any Idea. We tried to give the study of literature and theology and religion a formal and recognized place within the academy and it was doomed to failure. In later times, as we shall see towards the end of this book, new, sometimes tentative but creative channels opened up for theology in ways we could not have anticipated 30 years ago. Then, too quickly, theology, already silenced by war and its unthinkable darkness, became ensnared on the thorns of postmodernity (see Chapter 6) and the economic demands and forms of assessment of our current institutions that have lost any notion of an Idea in the fruitless pursuit of what they call 'excellence'. We have always been, at best, on the edge, especially when we have tried to keep true to our principles.

The model we pursued, of course, had already even then been overtaken by the passage of time – we were at once, as I have already suggested, perhaps both too radical and too conservative. Not only were we committed to the idea of the University but also, in our way, to the idea of the Church. At the heart of literature and theology there certainly was an ecclesiology, or perhaps more precisely a clear Christian community which was sustained by the ways of thinking pursued by Coleridge and Newman, and behind them not only Kant (in Coleridge's odd reading of him) but the deep and finally mystical thought of the Caroline Divines and the Fathers of the Early Church. And so we come,

---

38   J.H. Newman, *Discourses on the Scope and Nature of University Education* (Dublin: James Duffy, 1852. Facsimile reprinted by Cambridge University Press, 2010), Discourse V, 'General Knowledge viewed as one Philosophy', p. 136.

39   See also Loughlin, 'Theology in the University', p. 229.

40   *Discourses on the Scope and Nature of University Education*, p. 153.

finally, to that other figure who spoke in Durham in 1982, Peter Walker, his life also 'overshadowed' by the part he had played in war – in his case at sea – and by now an Anglican bishop. Walker's lecture on W.H. Auden's sequence of poems *Horae Canonicae* exemplifies, or perhaps better embodies, much of what I have been trying to explore in this chapter. The lecture was almost one with the poems themselves, a riddling, complex meditation which almost seemed at times to 'topple over into prayer'.[41] His concern, as had been Auden's of his poetry, was whether its truthfulness would stand up,[42] and beneath the quiet, complex understatement of the poetic exchanges there is a toughness and an intellectual integrity that Newman would have understood and appreciated. There is also deep suffering – a profound belief in the goodness of all things, but also their fallenness, and the Cross, under whose shadow we stand. Walker's, and Auden's, sense of the sacred begins explicitly in 'the sphere of Coleridge's Primary Imagination'[43] – within the common tradition which we all felt in some way. Words here, too, are living things, reaching out to meaning yet somehow sufficient unto themselves so that they need no theology to *explain* them, for the theology is carried by them and within them. Auden, in the tradition of the *disciplina arcani*, disliked poets who make 'an admirable public object of one's feelings of guilt and penitence before God'.[44] He mentions Donne and Hopkins. For, 'Christ appears looking just like any other man'.[45] Walker (and Auden), like Newman (and, one may add Wittgenstein) is finally impatient with all 'philosophical accounts', particularly of reasoning. Things work, and are known in words, in their textures of thought and from a primary unity: and Auden, no more than Newman, is oddly not so far from postmodern forms of enquiry which rest on fiduciary premises.[46] Nor would Derrida, for whom it is not that there is no centre but rather the centre forever moves, have found so strange the idea of Charles Williams, that was so important for Auden (though in him it speaks of the Incarnation), that 'He became *everywhere* the centre of and *everywhere* energised and re-affirmed *all* our substitutions and exchanges'.[47] Not far away, too, is the theology of Duns Scotus, to which I will return in my final section of this book.

---

[41] Peter Walker, '*Horae Canonicae*: Auden's Vision of a Rood – A Study in Coherence', in David Jasper (ed.), *Images of Belief in Literature* (London: Macmillan, 1984), p. 72.

[42] Ibid., p. 52.

[43] Ibid., p. 53.

[44] W.H. Auden, 'Postscript: Christianity and Art', in *The Dyer's Hand and Other Essays* (London: Faber, 1963), p. 458.

[45] Ibid., p. 457.

[46] See David B. Burrell, 'Newman in Retrospect', p. 258, and above p. 32.

[47] Charles Williams, 'The Cross', in *The Image of the City and Other Essays* (Oxford: Oxford University Press, 1958), p. 137. Quoted in Walker, '*Horae Canonicae*', p. 70.

Yet for Walker, if his vision, like Auden's, is deeply theological, a vision of redemption in a fallen world that is yet good, it is also dark and overshadowed by the earlier years of the twentieth century. At the heart of his meditation Walker returns to Dietrich Bonhoeffer and his *Ethics*, which came from an 'abrupt and forcible alignment' of theology and the everyday world.[48] Walker reminds us of Auden's poem in memory of Dietrich Bonhoeffer, 'martyred at Flossenburg, April 9th, 1945'. His theology is clear, but it is a dark one: 'We cannot stay in Eden: we must carry responsibilities, sometimes dreadful, which will open with a new dawn.'[49]

I do not think that we quite realized how serious our business was in 1982. Certainly the academic concern for literature and theology has by and large failed since then to sustain the 'Idea' that was at the heart of our deliberations (as of our prayers). And there, I suppose, lies the rub, going back to John Coulson's question posed in his opening lecture: 'What is the place of the confessional imagination in a secular culture?' Rooted in the common tradition of Coleridge and Newman, in both theology and literature, and in this tradition they can never be separated or neither would make sense, we were not then embarrassed to say our prayers. That odd term 'spirituality' has to come into it somewhere. It was, indeed, a Christian vision, though with the potential to become more universal. Nor, in one sense, should we have been embarrassed, but neither Church nor University have survived in ways that can sustain the vision or open it up into the broader, more complex and intercultural, interfaith world in which we now live. And so we just fell into that world in a heap. At the end of his lecture Coulson returned to the poet, T.S. Eliot, for whom 'older confessional forms ... have not been superseded, but ... they have been revived in new and original transfigurations'.[50] I am not sure that this can be said now with such confidence. Perhaps Newman, even the Newman of *The Dream of Gerontius*, knew that the reciprocity between imaginative forms and the culture of belief was even then fracturing, and that to think otherwise was a delusion or, at best, a false Romanticism. If we were concerned with theology, then literature itself teaches us that at its heart lies the *irony* of faith. As Coulson himself was to put it at the end of his lecture given at the third of our conferences in 1986 (it was, I believe, the very last lecture he ever gave before he died):

> To restore the literary imagination to religion is to restore that theological virtue – the irony of faith – which keeps beauty from vanishing away and restores

---

48   Walker, '*Horae Canonicae*', p. 76.

49   Ibid., p. 77. On Bonhoeffer see also below Chapter 6, p. 94.

50   Coulson, 'Religion and Imagination (Relating Religion and Literature)', p. 22.

beauty to its rightful place with its companion transcendental attributes, truth and goodness.[51]

As we shall see in later chapters of this book, the theme of irony will not leave us alone; indeed, it becomes ever stronger until it breaks things apart. For when irony ceases to be ironic (or perhaps is perfected) then words simply express their own opposite and literacy descends into the abyss of literality. Against this background there is no hope for theology nor can it converse in any way, and a habit of mind that we tried to develop has no language with which it can express itself.

On that note we turn to the dark centre of all our deliberations, Ulrich Simon.

---

[51] John Coulson, 'Hans Urs von Balthasar: Bringing Beauty Back to Faith', in David Jasper and T.R. Wright (eds), *The Critical Spirit and the Will to Believe: Essays in Nineteenth Century Literature and Religion* (London: Macmillan, 1989), p. 231.

Chapter 3
Making the World Bearable: Ulrich Simon

This chapter is but a beginning, born of confusion, perhaps another stay against confusion as theology makes its demands in a world oppressed by overwhelming evil and darkness. We are still in 1982, and the focus now is upon the figure of Ulrich E. Simon, an unjustly neglected, idiosyncratic theologian, and the urgency that his words brought to our reflections on the task of literature and theology. A man of immense learning and culture, Ulrich could be difficult but never dismissive or self-absorbed, and his presence brought a seriousness to our discussions which we never finally understood. It was too dark, too engaged, too close to the heart of things. The title of this chapter is taken from the very last words of the lecture given by Ulrich Simon in Durham. The title of this lecture was 'Job and Sophocles' and it concluded with the words: '*Sunt lacrimae rerum* ... The world is like that, but heroism and compassion make it bearable.'[1] Its linking of the Sophoclean tragedy and the greatest poem of the Hebrew Bible will haunt much of the rest of this book.

As was noted in Chapter 1, Ulrich Simon was Jewish, born on 21 September 1913 in Berlin. As an adult in England and an ordained Anglican priest Simon eventually became Professor of Christian Literature at King's College, London and his three most beloved authors, he tells us, were Dante, Shakespeare and Dostoevsky. I often wonder how he could read the dreadful words of the enforced conversion of Shylock from *The Merchant of Venice*.

> *Antonio*: Two things provided more: that for this favour
> He presently become a Christian;
> The other, that he do record a gift
> Here in the court of all he dies possessed
> Unto his son Lorenzo and his daughter.
> ...
> *Portia*: Art thou contented, Jew? What dost thou say?
> *Shylock*: I am content.[2]

---

1   Ulrich Simon, 'Job and Sophocles', in David Jasper (ed.) *Images of Belief in Literature* (London: Macmillan, 1984), p. 51.

2   William Shakespeare, *The Merchant of Venice*, IV. i.

Of all the elder statesmen who were our first mentors in the study of theology and literature and who had endured the violence of war and conflict, none was more deeply scarred than Simon. In his book *A Theology of Auschwitz* (1967) he had entered in his own way into the fundamental problem of evil and the issues of conscience, responsibility and, hardest of all, forgiveness, haunted by the deaths of his father in Auschwitz and almost certainly at the hands of Stalin, his brother Jörn Martin, probably in 1937. Like his father, Ulrich was a fine musician, a violinist, and music was in the very fibre of his being. Indeed he believed that if you have no music in your soul you should leave theology alone.[3] (He more or less died while playing one of the late Beethoven string quartets, which, to him, were the portals of heaven.) When Simon spoke to us of suffering it was a terrible, tangible presence. Can we contradict the bitterness of his words on the guards of Auschwitz in his *Theology of Auschwitz*:

> The chant to the king of tremendous majesty for pity, for salvation, cannot be sung for them. No archangel descends to collect their souls in the world-wide offering of sacrifice and homage. In the darkness the shades blend with the blackness until complete indifference engulfs them.

> May they never rise again![4]

Within his own life and being Simon carried the ancient and bitter struggle between Jew and Christian in the history of Western society, a struggle which all too often reflects little credit on the Christian. He carried its contradiction and, as a Christian priest and theologian, in a sense, its resolution: except there is no resolution. *A Theology of Auschwitz*, and the books which followed it, up to the late work on Christianity and tragedy, *Pity and Terror*, which I edited in 1989 for the Macmillan series *Studies in Literature and Religion*, are beautiful and profoundly painful works of Christian theology written by a devout man who was, at heart and in his whole bearing, Jewish. His Christian theology, in so many ways deeply conservative, so thoroughly resonant with the theology of Karl Barth's *Der Römerbrief*, which he knew thoroughly, was, in the end, – and this was the tragedy – an impossibility. Even as we said our prayers in the college chapel in Durham, theology, so urgently necessary, lay in shreds – a theology of Auschwitz which took a generation, 20 years, to be uttered, so deep was the trauma, and then barely so. And we, who could never see so much nor live so long, and who had never lived through the years of the War and the nightmare of the Holocaust, could hardly begin to understand what was being breathed by those

---

[3]   See Colin Gunton, entry for Ulrich Simon in the *Oxford Dictionary of National Biography* (on line).

[4]   Ulrich Simon, *A Theology of Auschwitz* (London: Victor Gollancz, 1967), p. 75.

who had. That was, I think, why we turned to literature, for literature, at least, never dares to offer answers. It shows us, warns us and then lets us be. The poet does not presume to pursue what another Jewish post-Auschwitz theologian, Richard L. Rubenstein, has called the 'dissonance-reducing function' of theology. Rubenstein elaborates: 'a crucial function of theology is to foster dissonance reduction where significant items of information are perceived as inconsistent with established beliefs, values, and collectively sanctioned modes of behaviour'.[5] If theology does not attempt to explain, it at least endeavours to soften the blow, to make things better, to *salve* and heal our wounds of grief and conscience. But what of forgiveness and its possibility? In the presence of Simon the suffering and the guilt remained real, tangible. And the only voices which were, in any sense, eligible to be heard were those of the poets, who continued to sing in spite of all – from the tragedies of Sophocles, to Shakespeare, to Celan, even to Wilfred Owen, who wrote to his mother on 4 January 1913 in anticipation of the battlefield: 'I have murdered my false creed. If a true one exists, I shall find it. If not, adieu to the still falser creeds that hold the hearts of nearly all my fellow men.'[6] And in the Preface to his poems we are told by Owen – so soon to perish himself: 'The Poetry is in the pity. Yet these elegies are to this generation in no sense consolatory. They may be to the next. All a poet can do today is warn. That is why the true Poets must be truthful.'[7] In Durham in 1982 we were the next generation – after the Second World War, at a distance and at a cross-roads in which the voice of Christian theology might still speak with moving eloquence but perhaps with a claim to a regained coherence born only of a degree of forgetfulness and that was now, I begin to think, without sufficient compassion and which refused tragedy. And what of truth?

I do not think that then, or even now, we realized the radical nature of that moment and its call for heroism and compassion. Perhaps we were too quick to be consoled, and later too ready to forget and be taken up, in a short few years, with the intellectual seductions of such things as postmodernity and the turn to 'theory', or, later still, the claims and, I think, the moral vacuity of radical orthodoxies. No doubt they have their place for some, but I wonder now, as I think back to the time some 10 years after the Durham conference, if Terry Eagleton had it about right when he said of the postmodern turn, in all its intellectual cleverness, that it simply allowed us to ride a coach and horses through everyone else's position without burdening ourselves too much with

---

5　Richard L. Rubenstein, *After Auschwitz: History, Theology, and Contemporary Judaism*, 2nd edn (Baltimore, MD: Johns Hopkins University Press, 1992), p. 86.

6　Quoted by C. Day Lewis in the Introduction to *The Collected Poems of Wilfred Owen* (London: Chatto & Windus, 1963), p. 17.

7　Wilfred Owen, *The Collected Poems*, p. 31.

having to adopt one of our own.[8] The deeper problem we were facing in 1982 was not that of *dis*-continuity, as was to be found in the voice of Derrida, but the tragedy of a deep and inescapable *continuity*, in which we all played a part.

Let me try and explain what I mean. After the conference, the BBC wrote to me expressing an interest in what we were doing. David Craig, a producer in religious broadcasting, remarked that 'I think it is so important that the significance of religious thought is seen and attributed outside the traditional fields of accepted orthodoxy.'[9] But the real problem was that we were still very much, by and large, *within* the fields of accepted orthodoxy. That was the demon that Simon was wrestling with as an Anglican theologian. Going back to the Holocaust it was that logic of destruction in our culture and the inevitability of it within the cold reason of the Hitler regime and National Socialism in Germany that was the haunting presence. And if there was no rupture then we were left with the only possibility – that God not only allowed it, but, in accordance with the biblical tradition of divine instruments used as punishments against God's chosen people, Hitler was God's agent. Rubenstein puts the case succinctly:

> I have come to the conclusion that the Holocaust was not the complete rupture with the values of Western religion and philosophy depicted by [Emil] Fackenheim. On the contrary, given the radical demonization of the Jews in traditional Christian thought and the just-war tradition that legitimates whatever measures are necessary to combat a mortal enemy, once the Nazis succeeded in convincing a majority of Europeans that the Jews were a mortal threat to Christian civilization, it became morally acceptable for normal men and women to participate in the project of mass extermination *with a good conscience* and for the churches to remain silent and, in some cases, even to aid the perpetrators to escape after the war.[10]

If a pope, Pius XII, can stand condemned of not uttering a single explicit denunciation of the Final Solution, what does that say for our theology? After all, even in 1939, on the brink of war, T.S. Eliot could still make a claim for the idea of the Christian Society, remarking that 'we must treat Christianity with a great deal more *intellectual* respect than is our wont.'[11] I think that in Durham, in what was an academic conference, there was a deep intellectual distress, and that distress lay at the very heart of our turn to literature, above all the literature of tragedy. It has taken me a long time to begin to realize what we were facing in that lecture hall in Durham in 1982. I have only begun now to understand why

---

[8]   See Terry Eagleton, *Literary Theory: An Introduction*, 2nd edn (Oxford: Blackwell, 1996), pp. 200–204.

[9]   Personal letter dated 12 November 1982.

[10]   Rubenstein, *After Auschwitz*, p. 183.

[11]   T.S. Eliot, *The Idea of a Christian Society* (1939), in *Selected Prose*, ed. John Hayward (London: Penguin, 1953), p. 200.

I feel as angry as I do when I see yet another dutiful textbook and 'Reader' in the Bible and Literature (one more published already this year, as I write these words, with a clear conscience) – and stand condemned by myself as I teach a course of the same name in my university department. Because it is precisely the Bible which is the *problem* – that which tells us that it is because of the sins of Israel that God condemns them to exile. Or as we read in that truly ghastly book Hosea:

> My people are destroyed for lack of knowledge;
> I reject you from being a priest to me.
> And since you have forgotten the law of your God,
> I will also forget your children.[12]

As they were forgotten by God in the ovens of Auschwitz, one might add. And as the dissonance-reducing narratives of theology stumbled, so the pages of literature began to make a kind of sense to me. Now I saw the genius of Heinrich Böll in his fictional replication of the terrible, unanswerable dead language of Nazi logic and bureaucracy in such novels as *Gruppenbild mit Dame* (1971).[13] I realized the awful truth of the final page of Patrick Süskind's novel *Perfume*, and that it was a finger pointed at me as a Christian priest: as the demented crowd consume the body of Jean-Baptiste Grenouille – 'But to eat a human being? They would never, so they thought, have been capable of anything that horrible.' But then they realize the nature of their mysterious joy: 'When they finally did dare it, at first with stolen glances and then candid ones, they had to smile. They were uncommonly proud. For the first time they had done something out of love.'[14]

I am not exaggerating. It was some 20 years after the end of the Second World War before theologians could bring themselves to utter anything about the Holocaust. The first edition of Richard Rubenstein's book *After Auschwitz* was published in 1966, carefully articulating a Jewish 'death of God' theology which understood that death not as something that has happened to God but as a cultural event. Ulrich Simon's deeply troubling *A Theology of Auschwitz* was published a year later in 1967, followed in 1987 (after our conference) by *Atonement: From Holocaust to Paradise*. This latter book, though deeply theological, refers to almost no theologians but almost exclusively uses literature to propel its discussion (Goethe, Dostoevsky, but above all Shakespeare in *Measure for Measure*) in its concern with 'measures to comprehend guilt and

---

12 Hosea 4:6.

13 Translated into English as *Group Portrait with Lady* (1973).

14 Patrick Süskind, *Perfume*, trans. John E. Woods (London: Penguin, 1986), p. 263.

the possibilities of reconciliation.'[15] Relentlessly, even hopelessly, Simon clings to the Duke's lines to Angelo from Shakespeare's play, with his inner gaze on the butchery of the camps.

> Heaven does with us as we with torches do
> Not light them for themselves. For if our virtues
> Did not go forth of us, 'twere all alike
> As if we had them not.[16]

I remember thinking, as he spoke those desperate lines, of the counter lines from *King Lear*: 'As flies to wanton boys, are we to th'Gods; / They kill us for their sport.'[17] It is not only the Bible that can become a game of quote/counter quote.

But there were also Emil Fackenheim, Arthur A. Cohen and others. Yet I am thinking more of another voice that has haunted me for three decades – though recently a well-known English theologian (I will not mention his name) said to me rather pityingly that I was the only person on this side of the Atlantic who took Thomas Altizer seriously. The implication was clear. How quickly we forget. In 1966 – the same year as Rubenstein's book was published and a year before Simon's – appeared a book by Tom Altizer and William Hamilton entitled *Radical Theology and the Death of God*. Containing essays on, among other things, the work of Dietrich Bonheoffer (with whom Simon had attended Gymnasium), the book was dedicated to Paul Tillich – and its most important chapter by far, written by Altizer, was entitled 'William Blake and the Role of Myth in the Radical Christian Vision'. A brief quotation from this essay will illustrate why it has remained to haunt me, as does the spectre of Nietzsche and the Madman of the *The Gay Science*.

> Blake belongs to a large company of radical or spiritual Christians, Christians
> who believe that the Church and Christendom have sealed Jesus in his tomb and
> resurrected the very evil and darkness that Jesus conquered by their exaltation
> of a solitary and transcendent God, a heteronomous and compulsive law, and
> a salvation history that is irrevocably past. Despite its great relevance to our
> situation, the faith of the radical Christian continues to remain largely unknown,
> and that is so because that faith has never been able to speak in the established
> categories of Western thought and theology and because it has so seldom been

---

[15]   Ulrich Simon, *Atonement: From Holocaust to Paradise* (Cambridge: James Clarke & Co. 1987), p. 7.

[16]   Shakespeare, *Measure for Measure*, 1. i. Compare Paul S. Fiddes on human and divine judgement in 'Law and Divine Mercy in Shakespeare's Religious Imagination: *Measure for Measure* and *The Merchant of Venice*', in Francesca Bugliani and David Lonsdale (eds), *Poetry and the Religious Imagination: The Power of the Word* (Farnham: Ashgate, 2015), pp. 109–28.

[17]   Shakespeare, *King Lear*, IV. i.

given a visionary expression (or, at least, the theologian has not been able to understand the radical vision, or even perhaps to identify its presence)[18]

Tom Altizer and Richard Rubenstein have much in common – though a Jewish death-of-God theologian is very different, finally, from a Christian death-of-God theologian. Ulrich Simon, though he never for a moment would have admitted to the enormity of Altizer's sense of the death of God, and would have hated it, was both Jew and Christian, and under his gaze I felt at once abandoned and called to speak against the compulsive law, as did Blake, as did Joyce, or the Milton who was of the devil's party and therefore a true poet. Sadly, the pursuit of literature and theology in our time has in this respect entirely failed in its vision. We have not dared to be content to live with the Holy Nothingness of God[19] nor can our theology, before it can even begin or dare to be expressed, cultivate what I myself once described in an essay on Altizer as 'the isolation that – like that of the Desert Fathers – is deeply communal, unlike the terrible solitariness of the transcendent God of Christendom.'[20]

I cannot deny that there is another ghost that haunts us here. It is the ghost of Karl Barth's dialectical theology first heard in his Commentary on the Epistle to the Romans (*Der Römerbrief*) written in his utter despondency at the end of the Great War and translated into English in 1933 just as Nazism was coming to power in Germany. It is a conscious questioning of the relation of theology to the Church and that of the Bible to culture. We can easily forget that in his Preface to the Second Edition of his work Barth explicitly admits his debt to Kierkegaard and Dostoevsky, admits that he is a theologian and that is the problem. 'The point at issue [he remarks] is the kind of theology that is required.'[21] There is another searing passage in Tom Altizer's autobiographical memoir *Living the Death of God* (2006) that has terrible echoes of the Simon of *A Theology of Auschwitz*, to which I shall shortly return. Forgive me a lengthy quotation concerning what Altizer calls 'Barth's famous calling forth of that ultimate sin which is manifest in the betrayal of Judas Iscariot' in the *Church Dogmatics*. Altizer writes with an unbearable and awful persistence that I can hardly bear to read:

---

[18]   Thomas J.J. Altizer and William Hamilton, *Radical Theology and the Death of God* (London: Penguin, 1968), p. 182.

[19]   The phrase is not mine, but Richard Rubenstein's. See also Thomas J.J. Altizer, *Godhead and the Nothing* (Albany, NY: State University of New York Press, 2003).

[20]   David Jasper, 'In the Wasteland: Apocalypse, Theology and the Poets', in Lissa McCullough and Brian Schroeder (eds), *Thinking Through the Death of God: A Critical Companion to Thomas J.J. Altizer* (New York: SUNY, 2004), p. 186.

[21]   Karl Barth, *The Epistle to the Romans*, trans. Edwyn C. Hoskyns (Oxford: Oxford University Press, 1968), p. 4.

Barth is finally the radical Barth, and is so here by affirming that Judas is the 'holy' apostle, 'holy' in the old meaning of the term, one who is cursed, and the elect always occupy the place that was originally occupied by the rejected. And God in His burning wrath does to men what Judas did to Jesus. He takes their freedom from them and makes them totally powerless, just as God Himself is the One who hands over Jesus, and it was the divine omnipotence of which Jesus let himself be robbed, and did so by means of Judas. Nevertheless, Judas, in his concentrated attack upon Israel's Messiah, does only what the elect people of Israel had always done towards its God, and in Judas there lives again all the great rejected of the Old Testament, a people who are elected in and from its rejection, and in view of the act of Judas there can be no further doubt about the rejection of this people, and rejection of all those individuals within it. Yet Jesus Christ also dies for rejected Israel, and therefore even rejected Israel is always in the open, and the question of its future can never be put except in this situation.[22]

However we understand this, it cannot be without anger, degrees of confusion and a sense of the tragic. For, deep within the tragedy, is that profound continuity in division within which we are all both victims and perpetrators.[23]

As Jew and Christian we bear the curse, as Rubenstein observed, of sacrality, and of sacred traditions bearing the tragedy of a logic of destruction that only the true poet has known and uttered. Only a true poet could utter that 'the reason Milton wrote in fetters when he wrote of Angels & God, and at liberty when of Devils & Hell, is because he was a true Poet and of the Devil's party without knowing it'.[24] Only the true poet like Paul Celan could sing a Psalm in the words:

Niemand knetet uns wieder aus Erde und Lehm,
niemand bespricht unsern Staub.
Niemand.

Gelobt seist du, Niemand.
Dir zulieb wollen
wir blühn.
Dir
entgegen.

[22] Thomas J.J. Altizer, *Living the Death of God: A Theological Memoir* (New York: SUNY, 2006), pp. 63–4.

[23] It is a sense perhaps missing in Graham Ward's attempt at theological synthesis within the postmodern in his book *Barth, Derrida and the Language of Theology* (Cambridge: Cambridge University Press, 1995).

[24] William Blake, *The Marriage of Heaven and Hell*, in *Complete Writings*, ed. Geoffrey Keynes (Oxford: Oxford University Press, 1966), p. 150.

[No one moulds us again out of earth and clay,
no one conjures our dust.
No one.

Praised be your name, no one.
For your sake
we shall flower.
Towards
you.][25]

Where the poet begins, then perhaps, after all, the theologian shall follow – for surely it is in the worship of this Psalm of Celan that Richard Rubenstein speaks in admittedly inadequate language of the Holy Nothingness of God: God as Nothing that is superfluity not absence, yet distancing himself, as a Jew, from the Christian 'atheism' of Altizer, Hamilton, and, perhaps, Harvey Cox.[26] In Rubenstein there is a profound darkness – and that Ulrich Simon shares.

As Simon confronted us with the reality of evil in that chapel in Durham in 1982, one could only feel the shadow of the darkest tragedy: the death of God, the death of tragedy. My copy of George Steiner's book *The Death of Tragedy* (1961), bought when I was an undergraduate in 1971, is well worn to the point of disintegration. Steiner begins with a categorical statement: 'Tragedy is alien to the Judaic sense of the world.' For Steiner, the Western sense of tragedy, as the human encounter with blind necessity, begins in the Greek tradition, and only Job, a 'black fable that stands on the outer edge of Judaism' comes anywhere near to it, though even here there is justice not tragedy: 'Jehovah is just even in His fury.'[27] Ulrich Simon, though now far less well known, and far more modest, than Steiner, merges the Hellenic and the Hebraic in a complex, irrational vision that begins and ends in meaningless suffering. Even where the Christian tradition of atonement is shadowed forth it is rarely done in prose, and Simon offers here a connection between the dramatic poetry of Oedipus at Colonus and Job. The instruments, if you will, the environment, are literary – 'nor can we dispense [says Simon] with irony and all the tools of the literary task'. 'Theologians', he asserts, 'resent this richness of approach.'[28] Back to irony again.

As we return to *A Theology of Auschwitz* we cannot but be struck by its deep narrative structure. Following the awful journey to Auschwitz of the prisoners in the box cars we are led, with unspeakable honesty, as readers, to endure, a light only being offered not by explanation or analysis but by dramatic

---

[25]   Paul Celan, *Selected Poems*, trans. Michael Hamburger (London: Penguin, 1990), p. 175.
[26]   Rubenstein, *After Auschwitz*, pp. 298, 260.
[27]   George Steiner, *The Death of Tragedy* (London: Faber and Faber, 1961), pp. 4–5.
[28]   Simon, *Atonement*, p. 6.

comparison, placings alongside. The comparison is with the *via dolorosa*, and the narratives of the Passion. Theology has failed: in Simon's words, 'the failure of theology has been and remains at the root of our enslavement'.[29] Thus speaks the theologian in *A Theology of Auschwitz*. I think that that is what we faced in that conference – a stupid meeting of academics, at least free from the nonsensical and trivial competitiveness of so much life in the contemporary university – but confronted with a question and a dilemma that we have failed, by and large, to pursue in the years since. Nor can the Church claim any more, as the faith which restores sight to the blind is rendered dim by that which prefers to lay claim rather to a stake in the historical compulsiveness of things.[30]

That faith is only finally shown us in the creative and unprovable forms of the poetic. Let me try and explain if I can. It is clear to me that Simon, Karl Barth and Tom Altizer, an unlikely trinity, have one great thing in common. They are storytellers. (You might say so were Hegel, Freud and Nietzsche and all the other great prophets of modernity). At the end of Simon's theology of Auschwitz there is not even a proposition, much less a conclusion, but a demand, and a call – 'What then shall we do?'[31] Faced with the Nothingness of God we have a choice – as did Job. I remember once saying to Altizer that he was a storyteller, hardly, at times, in control of what he said with such great precision, and needing interpretation – as does all great literature, as does Barth. And so we come to Simon's 1982 lecture entitled 'Job and Sophocles'.

Its opening sentence is worthy of Jane Austen in its humour and its irony: 'Comparisons in literature are as common as they may be either odious or boring.'[32] The essay then proceeds precisely to make a comparison by laying alongside one another two great texts from two traditions – the book of Job and Sophocles' tragedy *Philoctetes*. Job is not a tragedy in the sense understood by Aristotle and the Greek stage. There is no change and no action. Yet the infinite hospitality of literature brings these texts together in forms of mutual recognition, and in a sense of the ultimately universal nature of the human condition. Questions remain unanswered at the very end, for Fate, or God, can (can they?) be avoided or elided. There must be a touch of irony, which, as the poet D.J. Enright once remarked, does not cast out seriousness.[33] In both Job and Sophocles there is a touch also of the parable or the riddle, and the point of the parable and the riddle is that we are caught by them first, before we try to understand them: 'What then shall we do?' Thus to return to a book of the Bible in company with a Greek play is to remember that actually theology is pretty

---

[29]   Simon, *A Theology of Auschwitz*, p. 138.
[30]   Ibid., p. 143.
[31]   The question forms the title of the final chapter of Simon's book.
[32]   Simon, 'Job and Sophocles', p. 42.
[33]   D.J. Enright, *The Alluring Problem: An Essay on Irony* (Oxford: Oxford University Press, 1986), p. 56.

remote from the Bible – at least in the first instance – and becomes malignant if it is introduced too soon into our readings as a putative solution or, worse still, an answer. Answers are not what we are looking for. Job *refuses* the answers of his so-called friends. He throws his fist in the face of God.

> See, he will kill me; I have no hope;
> but I will defend my ways to his face.
> This will be my salvation,
> That the godless shall not come before him. (NRSV 13:15–16)

Though God slay him, yet he will trust in him, in spite of all contradictions. He is like his younger brother Kafka's K in *The Trial*, about whom someone must have been telling lies, except K does not believe in God. He is not one of God's people. But Job conquers the enemy Satan through his endurance, his heroism. Is glory inevitably linked to such suffering for which there is no reason, an admission that Job will never make?

And what of Philoctetes about whom Aeschylus, Euripides and Sophocles wrote plays, though only the last has survived? Like Job he is cast away – in his case literally on an island – the victim of a festering ulcer, and he rages against those who cast him adrift, offended by the stench of his wound. Heracles can promise that there will be 'through suffering glory in life', yet the offence remains and the narrative of the play, its irony again, points, perhaps, to some redemption even though the future beyond remains dark. And there is pity felt for Philoctetes by the Chorus, and in the famous hymn to sleep: 'Sleep that knows not suffering or pain ... Spread your enveloping radiance, as now, over his eyes Come, come, Lord Healer.'[34] And at the end of the play – for it is but a play – Philoctetes begins the journey home with the words, 'I had never hoped for this'.[35] There is hope: and if there is a seeming resolution – though the future always remains unknown – there is in both Job and the Greek tragedy the presence of the last trope of rhetoric, irony, a smile, a possibility, that does not yet cast out seriousness. For we have seen too that there is heroism, and there is pity and compassion – which make the world bearable. The point about irony, a literary trope, of course, is that it can never be pinned down. A weapon against compliancy it also poses the question, refuses the iron fist of settlement, disturbs and reassures. Meaning is not nailed down but sense arises and walks away with the nail.

---

[34] Sophocles, *Philoctetes*, trans. David Grene, in *The Complete Greek Tragedies*, ed. David Grene and Richmond Lattimore, *Sophocles II* (Chicago, IL: University of Chicago Press, 1969), p. 228.

[35] Ibid., p. 252.

As I have mentioned earlier, it was some years later, after the conference in Durham, that I edited what I think was Ulrich's last published book, *Pity and Terror: Christianity and Tragedy* (1989). After he retired in 1980 he wrote little, being content to purse his love of music, especially Bach and Mozart. Indeed, it was on the day before he died, on 31 July 1997, that he bought a new set of strings for his beloved violin. In some respects, then, this book was his final word. Of it may be said what was once written of his autobiographical, idiosyncratic book *Sitting in Judgement* (1978), that it is 'dazzling in its virtuosity, devastating in its accusation, yet offering hope and not despair'.[36] Sadly I think that few people read *Pity and Terror* and it remains a largely unheard voice. By then, at the end of the 1980s, the world was moving on and the stark message of the Durham conference was already lost and the study of literature and religion already becoming too self-preoccupied and professional in its ambitions. The old men had died and language was changing. Literary people, it seemed, preferred theory to literature and I wonder how many people could actually appreciate a lecture on *Philoctetes* outside a Classics Department – or even within one.

The thesis of *Pity and Terror* is that Christianity, in its preaching of the cross, has denied the tragic reality of the human condition. I think that what Simon *wanted* to do in his book was to move towards a synthesis between Christian existence (and its theology) and tragic involvement. The power of the book lies in his failure to achieve this. *Anna Karenin*, described as 'a tragedy in prose', has at its centre a 'sublime' figure who cannot imagine a life that is not a torment. True, at her death beneath the wheels of the train, Anna makes the sign of the cross and asks the Lord for forgiveness, but her death is a punishment for those whom she hates, above all herself, and, in Simon's words, 'deceit governs all, everything is evil'.[37] The end is futility. Time and again, throughout his book, Simon returns to the unbridgeable divide, the rift in the human suffering of the great figures of Western tragedy, that theology cannot heal: the problem of suffering and evil remains, the cross itself, perhaps, its greatest example. For even after the promise of the resurrection, literature still insists on the theme of abandonment and even the quiet of Colonus cannot finally wipe away the terror of Oedipus' guilt. Simon will never let us forget the terrible figure of Michael Henchard, of whom there is something in all of us, and whose last Will ends with the words, '& that no man remember me'. Simon's words are telling:

> Job recompensed and Oedipus at Colonus are superseded by Henchard, poor, guilty, repentant, unwise. His is the tragedy of love, falsely begun, betrayed, lost and needed. He is a traveller on the road of class distinction without awareness of

---

[36]   *Expository Times*, 1978, 288.

[37]   Ulrich Simon, *Pity and Terror: Christianity and Tragedy* (London: Macmillan, 1989), p. 87.

political ends. He moves in a universe of Biblical imagery without the demands and consolations of religion. Like Hardy, Henchard is his own man in an alien land, a man whom God has forgotten and abandoned.[38]

Pity and Terror ends with a strange sentence: 'Christianity is tragic because of the Cross, and tragedy becomes Christian through the Resurrection.'[39] The uncertainty, the embarrassment, remains clear. In literature, Colonus is no resurrection. At the end of *King Lear* there is a resolution of sorts, a paying of debts, yet we exit the theatre to the dead beat of a death march and in our ears are Edgar's final words on our necessary obedience to the weight of this sad time and the realization that we that are young shall never see so much nor live so long. It is as if literature, in its wisdom, has never been quite persuaded and our willing suspension of disbelief never quite can amount to the coherence, or even just the dissonance reduction, of an admitted faith. Simon finally refuses to accept George Steiner's thesis on the death of tragedy, and if literature since 1961 – in a Solzhenitsyn or a Mandelstam – has continued its tragic search for redemption, the evils of which they write remain in a continued response to the insights of Miguel de Unamuno in his work of 1913, *The Tragic Sense of Life*.

I see little redemption in the works of Solzhenitsyn, except that he continued to write. He did not give up. Perhaps that is, finally, the message of the Durham Conference. There is no resolution between literature and theology. Standing before the people of Ulrich Simon's generation we that were then young realized that we would never see so much, we would be spared that, and that our impossible task was to acknowledge their profound, genuine and painfully expressed piety (I prefer that word to theology, though a theology without piety is not worth the paper it is written on) and at the same time the literary necessity that could not rest in much more than the heroism and the pity and compassion of Job and Philoctetes. The one without the other becomes either trivial or barbaric.

Another figure at that conference was Professor Ann Loades, then my PhD supervisor in Durham. When I was organizing the conference it was Ann who gave me the wise advice that we needed a philosopher to keep all these theologians and literary critics on the rails. That is why we invited the distinguished, if, it must be admitted, somewhat maverick, philosopher D.Z. Phillips of Swansea University, a man whose very name had a suitably prophetic resonance to it. Phillips began his lecture to us with a reference to Simone Weil (of whom a word more in a moment), 'at a time [he said] when professions of faith are made in a muted voice, or with a deadening insensitivity to difficulty and application in

---

[38] Ibid., p. 118.
[39] Ibid., p. 145.

human life'.[40] Phillips, as a philosopher schooled in the writings of Wittgenstein, constantly reminded the professors of English and theology that they needed to watch their grammar, to be precise in their words and language if they were to avoid speaking nonsense. Looking back to Weil and to the philosopher M.O'C. Drury, Phillips reminded us that 'the dialectic must work from within': that is – from within the text. I wonder if we have sustained that painful degree of honesty or responsibility for what we say and think, inasmuch as we can think at all in the benighted world of the contemporary academy. It was Ann Loades herself, a lonely female voice in the male-dominated world of our conference, who contributed an essay on Simone Weil – another voice of articulate suffering in the twentieth century suspended between the claims of the Hebraic and the Christian. Weil is presented by Ann as 'a problem for theology'. A sacrificial offering in her death, perhaps, Simone Weil died in England in 1943 as a result of *anorexia nervosa* (or maybe it was just her refusal, out of a sense of compassion, to eat anything more than was given to her compatriots in Occupied France). Ann ended her lecture to us with the deliberately more familiar and painful image of an old woman in a nursing home being spoon fed by a young nurse:

> 'Eat up your nice porridge.' The woman sat unspeaking while the nurse tried to push the spoon into the unwilling mouth. The ward was quiet, the helpless looked away while the helper forced in the porridge. The woman turned her head, wordlessly, tears streaming down her face. The nurse momentarily defeated, angrily turned to the helpless for support, 'She's got to eat, it's good for her.' Simone Weil didn't, and the result was inevitable, whatever she intended.'[41]

'It's good for her': but what of her dignity, her memory, herself? I have thought often since then that that is what religion and theology so often can feel like. Something good for us, spooned into our unwilling mouths by the impatient and the well-intentioned to ensure eternal life, but finally an affront to our sense of self. While the truth is so much more complicated – the images laid alongside one another in hopeless disparity. 'Whatever she intended': Weil must have looked like the starving corpses in Auschwitz, like Simon's father and brother in their deaths, those who were robbed of all intention – victims, sacrificial victims, the hated Jews. Literature does not presume to give us answers.

I end with one last image, and in my mind as well is one of Ulrich's Simon's most often quoted books, Part I of Goethe's *Faust*, which he refused to de-couple

---

[40]   D.Z. Phillips, 'Mystery and Mediation: Reflections on Flannery O'Connor and Joan Didion', in David Jasper (ed.), *Images of Belief in Literature* (London: Macmillan, 1984), p. 24.

[41]   Ann Loades, 'Simone Weil – Sacrifice: A Problem for Theology', in David Jasper (ed.), *Images of Belief in Literature* (London: Macmillan, 1984), pp. 135–6. Quoting from J. Campling (ed.), *Images of Ourselves: Women with Disabilities Talking* (London: Routledge & Kegan Paul, 1981).

from Christopher Marlowe's *Dr. Faustus*, a dramatic figure whom not one drop of Christ's blood as it streams in the Firmament could save from hell. It is the famous scene in which Faust, with Mephistopheles in the form of a great poodle at his side, is studying the beginning of the Fourth Gospel. 'In the beginning was the Word.' But he translates afresh, with terrible consequences for Europe: 'In the beginning was the Deed.'[42] Here is the Affidavit of SS Grüppenführer Otto Ohlendorf, signed on the 5 November (to those of us who are English, Bonfire Night) 1945 in Nurnberg, Germany:

> The men, women and children were led to a place of execution which in most cases was located next to a more deeply excavated antitank ditch. Then they were shot, kneeling or standing, and the corpses thrown into the ditch. I never permitted the shooting by individuals in the group D, but ordered that several of the men should shoot at the same time *in order to avoid direct, personal responsibility*. The leaders of the unit or especially designated persons, however, had to fire the last bullet against those victims which were not dead immediately. I learned from conversations with other group leaders that some of them demanded that the victims lie flat on the ground to be shot through the nape of the neck. I did not approve of these methods.[43]

I sometimes wonder how we can presume to go on doing what we do – in the study of theology and literature.

We turn now to a very different teacher, to Fr Martin Jarrett-Kerr CR.

---

[42] Goethe, *Faust/Part One*, trans. Philip Wayne (London: Penguin, 1949), p. 71.

[43] Simone Gigliotti and Berel Lang (eds), *The Holocaust: A Reader* (Oxford: Blackwell, 2005), p. 182 (emphases added).

Chapter 4

Choosing Commitment:
Martin Jarrett-Kerr CR

By the time of the third Durham Conference on Literature and Religion in 1986 the mood of our meetings was already changing and becoming a little theologically 'softer', less anxious and more historical. The overriding theme of the volume of essays from that conference, entitled *The Critical Spirit and the Will to Believe*, edited by myself and T.R. Wright, was that of Victorian doubt, with attention also given to issues in aesthetics and the nineteenth-century debate between science and religion. In some ways the key essay from that conference was Nicholas Sagovsky's discussion of Von Hügel and 'the will to believe', though it is another, more eccentric contribution from another of the older generation of scholars, Martin Jarrett-Kerr, that will occupy us more fully for the greater part of this chapter.

But first we must turn to Baron von Hügel. I think that Sagovsky's lecture was, perhaps, the last serious moment in our conferences which expressed that which drove us at the beginning – the will to believe. As he analysed the mind and heart of von Hügel, he was, in effect, pointing a dagger at the heart of many of us. Sagovsky begins with the recognition of the Baron's complexity – that is his care for both the concrete and the abstract in life and criticism combined with his profound adherence to prayer and the sacramental life. He quotes Josef Sauer, writing after von Hügel's death:

> He was one of the most remarkable of men, and, in consequence, not to be understood by such as knew him not intimately. I have seen him, after the sharpest critical argument, or after slashing away at some abuse or faultiness in clerical or Church questions, go into the nearest Church and pray, rapt and absorbed like a saint – or a child.[1]

Only as a Catholic layman and an aristocrat von Hügel, perhaps, 'avoided condemnation' in his pursuit of critical thought, especially in biblical criticism,

---

[1] B. Holland (ed.), *Selected Letters of Baron Friedrich von Hügel* (London: J.M. Dent & Sons, 1927), pp. 48–9. Quoted in Nicholas Sagovksy, 'Von Hügel and the Will to Believe', in David Jasper and T.R. Wright (eds), *The Critical Spirit and the Will to Believe: Essays in Nineteenth-Century Literature and Religion* (London: Macmillan, 1989), p. 207.

while at the same time maintaining his preparedness to leave questions of orthodoxy to 'God and the Church authorities'.[2] His 'taxonomy of life' he owed to his study of Augustine, Blondel and, most significantly, to John Henry Newman, with whom he shared a necessary sense of the importance of the historical which yet never abandons the 'reality, distinctness, provenience of God, our Home'.[3] But what was finally in Newman a complex unity of being wrought in the heat of a battle waged in the combination of intellect, spirit, conscience and will, in von Hügel was a fragile structure fraught with tensions, dangerous even, and perhaps especially, when positive in their effects. In Sagovksy's words:

> von Hügel never believed that these elements of religion lived in peaceful coexistence. He believed that they set up constant 'tension' and 'friction' (both of which were favourite words) and that this tension was spiritually beneficial ... He constantly tried to restrain himself and his friends from precipitate action springing from a need to resolve painful tensions ... [T]his was precisely the way in which von Hügel used his own, deep 'wish to believe': he did, in fact, resolve painful tension prematurely thereby.[4]

In his attention to von Hügel, Sagovsky was, I believe, searching out a tension that was in many of us in 1986 in Durham. We were finally losing sight of Newman and the common tradition that was bound together by a language of ultimate concern, a fiduciary language that was now cracking and becoming disjointed. Thus losing sight of questions of ultimate concern, we were also losing our grip on the theological vision, or perhaps better horizon, that presented the possibility (even in its impossibility) of an articulation in a unified poetics that was at once intelligent and devout. As in von Hügel, the will to believe remained for some of us, and we might, with him, have looked back to William James' *The Will to Believe*, though without quite appreciating the Baron's hesitation before that work: 'he regretted James' concentration on the conative aspect of religion in isolation from the mystical and intellectual elements with which, for von Hügel, it was inextricably linked'.[5]

Those elements were with us, the intellectual perhaps too strongly, the mystical barely appreciated (and to this we must return, if often only by implication) – but they were dislocated and finally failed to hold together. Our beginnings, we might have claimed, were with the careful taxonomy of the *Grammar of Assent*,

---

2   Sagovsky, 'Von Hügel and the Will to Believe', p. 210.

3   Gwendolen Green (ed.), *Letters from Baron Friedrich von Hügel to a Niece* (London: J.M. Dent & Sons, 1928), p. 49.

4   Sagovsky, 'Von Hügel and the Will to Believe', p. 214.

5   Ibid., p. 213.

which later in von Hügel, though more loosely, becomes a central concern within the nature of religious intuition. As he wrote to Wilfrid Ward:

> How are we ever to show that where we pass beyond the bounds of verbal logic we do not come into the region of mere rhetoric or poetry? What is the guarantee? We know it; but how can it be presented as we know it?[6]

Was that, then, the choice? Were we, at a conference on literature and theology, consigned to fall back upon 'mere poetry' in matters of faith? Sagovsky left us with a von Hügel who was finally a self-deceiver, lacking the courage and genius of a Newman who would drink 'to the Pope, if you please – still, to Conscience first, and to the Pope afterwards'.[7] Von Hügel never allowed that the magisterium should set limits on critical thought yet worked within the limits he had set himself, and thus he lived within a tension, believing in its ultimate resolution: 'despite his acceptance at one level of evidence critically sifted, at another level he simply *chose* to believe the Catholic faith as a whole'.[8]

If Sagovsky reveals the vulnerability of von Hügel's faith – to historical criticism, to psychology and to sociology – and portrays him as a man who looks back to the example of Newman but, it might be said, from a later and more brittle age, then our own plight, we might say, was infinitely worse. By 1986 (unlike 1982), we were no longer saying our prayers in the chapel at the beginning of each day of the conference, though perhaps some of us might still have said them in the privacy of our rooms. In our claims for literature and theology were we, by then, deceiving ourselves, and had theology, in fact, become so remote that we were left with 'mere poetry'? Sagovsky employs a dramatic image for von Hügel – which might have applied to us of the younger generation as we moved further away from the heat of the real battle, from the dark immediacies of Simon.

> In practice, however, he was like an officer who recognizes the reality of the fighting and has, from time to time, committed himself to the battle, but because of the larger perspective given to him in staff college has never had to involve himself hand-to-hand, blinded by sweat and smoke.[9]

And finally, perhaps von Hügel was important in another way. In his work *The Mystical Element of Religion as studied in St. Catherine of Genoa and her*

---

6   Von Hügel to Wilfrid Ward, undated (St Andrews University Library, MS vii, 318a[6]).

7   J.H. Newman, *Certain Difficulties Felt by Anglicans in Catholic Teaching* (London: Longmans, Green & Co., 1876), vol. 2, p. 261.

8   Sagovsky, 'Von Hügel and the Will to Believe', p. 215.

9   Ibid., p. 215.

Friends (1908) he progresses through three stages in the religious life. The first, connected to the needs of the child, is that of authority, institution and tradition. The second, linked to the enquiring mind of youth, relates to thought and philosophy. The final element he calls the 'Experimental and Mystical', and this is within the domain of maturity. It is to this element that we shall finally return in due course at the end of this book.

Perhaps the term 'experimental' well describes one of the early fathers of our conferences, the now unjustly forgotten scholar and churchman Martin Jarrett-Kerr CR. An Anglican monk of the Community of the Resurrection, Mirfield, by 1982 Martin had long been an Associate Lecturer in Theology and English at the University of Leeds. Diminutive in stature and in all other respects larger than life, with an impish sense of humour, Martin, as I noted in Chapter 1, had fought alongside Bishop Trevor Huddleston in South Africa (until he was thrown out), had defended *Lady Chatterley's Lover* (and written a fine book on D.H. Lawrence under the pseudonym of 'Father Tiverton'), and was a close associate and friend of the formidable doyen of religion and literature in the United States (and also an Anglican priest), Nathan Scott Jn. of the University of Chicago. Jarrett-Kerr was born into a military family and had read both English and theology at Oxford, where Austin Farrer, with his deep sense of poetry and philosophical theology, was a powerful influence upon him. During his seven years in South Africa Martin taught, among others, Desmond Tutu and, apart from his political activism, worked tirelessly to promote theatre and music in Soweto (where he was Anglican chaplain to the Baragwanath Hospital) and the black townships. He was a man to be reckoned with.

Yet, sadly, Martin's voluminous writings are not read today. They are, undeniably, dated in style and approach, but he deserves to be remembered for two reasons. First, he was a man of the book. He seemed to have read everything, and he knew literature and the history of ideas from the inside and with an independence of mind that gave no grounds to school or party. Critically he was his own man. Second, although he could hardly be called, in any strict sense, a theologian, he understood the nature of religious commitment, and by the end of the 1980s that was beginning to be a rare commodity in the university, and perhaps also within the Church.

Martin's first lecture to the conferences in 1982 was entitled 'Literature and Commitment: "Choosing Sides"'. He was, by nature, a storyteller, and he began with a story of an exchange between Reinhold Niebuhr and William Temple on the question of paradox, giving little credit to Temple and his Hegelianism. In the story Niebuhr ends with the 'ultimate paradox of existence', which Temple 'blandly' dismisses with the remark that surely Dr Niebuhr 'does not expect us to imagine that the Blessed Trinity suffer from eternal perplexity in their contemplation of One Another?' There is no recorded answer by Niebuhr to this put-down, and so Jarrett-Kerr supplies one himself, putting words into

Niebuhr's mouth: 'Ah, William: but you see only a Hegelian like you could find the doctrine of the Blessed Trinity non-paradoxical.'[10]

The relevance of Martin's stories to his theme was always at least twice removed – he left it to his audience to make the connections. And here his theme was the relationship between literature and commitment, which, true to the atmosphere of the 1982 meeting, required some kind of philosophical basis (hence the connection, at the outset of his lecture, with Temple and Hegel). His point in his story about the debate between the Hegelian and the Paradoxical (his terms), we eventually worked out was that all great literature or reflections on literature is linked to a sense of commitment, or even didacticism, and the philosophical assumptions that lie behind it. As Ezra Pound once said, 'I am perhaps didactic; so in a different sense, or in different senses are Homer, Dante, Villon and Omar … A revelation is always didactic. Only the aesthetes since 1880 have pretended to the contrary, and they aren't a very sturdy lot.'[11] In literature, people of the generation of Martin Jarrett-Kerr and John Coulson fell under the influence of a guiding spirit who now seems very distant from us, though even I can remember his last lectures in Cambridge when I was an undergraduate in the late 1960s. It was, of course, F.R. Leavis, and his place in the development of the study of literature and theology and behind the Durham conferences should not be underestimated. Martin quotes Leavis on literature: 'When I say that a great work will inevitably have a profound moral significance I am thinking of such a significance as will need to be described as religious too.'[12] I am perfectly well aware how old fashioned this now must sound. But we should not forget the importance of Leavis and the periodical *Scrutiny* for the post-War generation. Coulson remarked that it was Leavis and his associate Professor L.C. Knights who brought the reading of literature back to the sense of 'commitment', 'that of the whole man, so that in discovering something about the text, the reader was discovering something about himself'.[13] Furthermore, it was training in this school that developed in students a sense of the necessary imaginative response to literature in a manner close to something like the sense of 'faith'. Jarrett-Kerr points us back to a book by Roger Trigg, *Reason and Commitment* (1973) and to

---

[10]   Jarrett-Kerr, 'Literature and Commitment: "Choosing Sides"', in David Jasper (ed.), *Images of Belief in Literature* (London: Macmillan, 1984), pp. 104–5.

[11]   Ezra Pound, *Letters, 1907–1941*, ed. D.D. Paige (London: Faber and Faber, 1951), p. 248.

[12]   F.R. Leavis, *Times Literary Supplement*, 19 September, 1958. Quoted in Martin Jarrett-Kerr, 'Literature and Commitment: "Choosing Sides"', in David Jasper (ed.), *Images of Belief in Literature*, p. 111. John Coulson remarked of Leavis, that 'when he treated of religion he did so with reverence rather than with mere sympathy, but he treated all attempts to assimilate literature to conventional religious beliefs with the dismissive scorn of the evangelical preacher'. 'Faith and Imagination', *The Furrow*, Series on 'Belief and Unbelief', no. 7 (1983), p. 536.

[13]   Ibid., p. 536.

D.N. Morgan in an article in the *Journal of Aesthetics and Art Criticism* written in 1967:

> Why, to put the point incisively, if painfully, should we demand a birth certificate of Jesus of Nazareth, any more than of Odysseus or Buddha or Hamlet? Why can we not live and grow in these beings imaginatively, without feeling any nagging guilt because we cannot recite their social security numbers? Are they not in human terms more important than they would be if they were merely literal and historical?[14]

Roger Trigg responds to this, seeing it as 'a failure to differentiate between propositional belief and the commitment which is the normal response to it ... If all our attention is diverted to the fact of commitment and none to the importance of certain beliefs, it becomes unimportant why someone rejects Christianity'.[15]

But Trigg, at least in the context of our conference, misses the point. For people of Jarrett-Kerr's generation (such as Coulson and Ulrich Simon), theology was of fundamental importance, but its resources had been rendered almost impossible by the first-hand experience of war or conflict. Literature, it seemed, offered a way back, and the language of Leavis, as well as his commitment to the great tradition of English literature, was, for them, both intelligent and seductive. In its shadow a way back might be found, making a circuit back to the nineteenth century, through the idea of the university and eventually to the poetics of Keble and Newman.[16] It was John Coulson who asked the crucial question:

> Newman's question became mine: how does an impression on the imagination become a system or creed in the reason? In other words, how do you make the transition from poetry and imagination to fundamental theology?[17]

With Jarrett-Kerr we had not quite reached that stage of transition to 'fundamental theology'. His 1982 lecture was, in a quirky way, beginning to construct a language for us in our own time. It was the language of imagination, intuition, mysticism – and commitment. It was only a step, but an important one, and it was not entirely safe. Martin with his often confused, encyclopaedic

---

[14]   D.N. Morgan, 'Must Art Tell the Truth?', in *Journal of Aesthetics and Art Criticism*, 26 (1967), 26. Quoted in Jarrett-Kerr, 'Literature and Commitment', p. 112.

[15]   Roger Trigg, *Reason and Commitment* (Cambridge: Cambridge University Press, 1973), pp. 82–3.

[16]   I will return to Keble's *Lectures on Poetry, 1832–41*, in Chapter 12, in a discussion of contemporary Australian literature.

[17]   John Coulson, 'Faith and Imagination', *The Furrow*, p. 540.

knowledge and his experience of Africa and what was then called 'Third World Literature', opened up new vistas for us, and new ways of thinking.

In the final analysis, for Martin, the only 'safe' commitment is to language, and in that context we needed to take seriously the emerging literatures of Africa and East Asia within our common humanity. We were returning in the end to the 'word' and to the stories we tell in words, and through them coming back to the issue of religion and its 'spiritual urgency'.[18] It is on this note that I turn to the lecture which Jarrett-Kerr delivered to the third of our conferences in 1986, a typically eccentric conversation with Christian missionary hermeneutics in nineteenth-century Africa entitled 'Victorian Certainty and Zulu Doubt'.[19] In it Jarrett-Kerr returns to Africa and to his own involvement in its politics as a priest and teacher that had clearly deeply scarred him, though he was not one to show it. He returned to the case of Bishop Colenso of Natal,[20] a bye-word in Victorian England for the doubting cleric such that even Renan could speak of 'les doutes de Colenso'.[21] Undeniably John William Colenso, as a scholar, was of a plodding critical nature, lacking in imagination and thus all too easily became the butt of Matthew Arnold's criticism when he launched into the bishop's mathematical calculations about the books of the Pentateuch.[22] Colenso was perfectly well aware that his critical attack on biblical fundamentalism (what Coleridge would, perhaps, have called 'bibliolatry') leaves him with an 'aching void' in his bosom, but therein lies the matter of Martin's essay. It was the acute observing mind of the Zulus, those for whom the truth of the Gospel was being carried by the 'superior' intellectual and spiritual hand of the white missionaries, that was leading the good bishop towards a critical spirit to the point where he asked

---

[18]   Martin Jarrett-Kerr, *The Secular Promise* (London: SCM, 1964), p. 119.

[19]   In David Jasper and T.R. Wright (eds), *The Critical Spirit and the Will to Believe* (London: Macmillan, 1989), pp. 145–57.

[20]   See for further literary and witty insights into the influence of Bishop Colenso see Anthony Trollope's essay 'The Clergyman who Subscribes for Colenso', the last of his essays in *Clergymen of the Church of England* (London: Chapman and Hall, 1866. Facsimile edition reprinted in The Victorian Library, Leicester University Press, 1974), pp. 119–30. Originally published in the *Pall Mall Gazette* (1865–66), the essays were first entitled 'The Zulu in London' and purported to be by a foreign observer of the idiosyncrasies of the Church of England, one of Colenso's Zulu friends.

[21]   See Wyn Rees, *Colenso's Letters from Natal* (Pietermaritzburg, SA: Shuter & Shooter, 1958), quoted in Martin Jarrett-Kerr, 'Victorian Certainty and Zulu Doubt: A Study in Christian Missionary Hermeneutics from Shaka to Colenso', in David Jasper and T.R. Wright (eds), *The Critical Spirit and the Will to Believe*, p. 145.

[22]   Matthew Arnold, 'The Bishop and the Philosopher', in *Lectures and Essays in Criticism*, ed. R.H. Super (Ann Arbor, MI: University of Michigan Press, 1962), vol. 3, pp. 415ff.

himself, 'Shall a man speak lies in the Name of the Lord?'[23] Writing of Colenso's Zulu interpreter and critic, William Ngidi, the *Times*, with appalling racist sarcasm, notes: 'This *enfant terrible*, a sort of coloured Spinoza ... began asking impertinent questions, which Dr. Colenso found a difficulty in answering ... Instead of Dr. Colenso converting the Zulu, the Zulu converted Dr. Colenso.'[24]

Why was Martin Jarrett-Kerr telling us of this somewhat remote Victorian episode in missionary and biblical critical history? I think, in fact, that there were profound issues being explored – though I suspect as we smiled at the tone of the lecture, we were not fully aware of them at the time. Before I attempt to unpack these we need to return for a moment to the final paragraphs of Martin's essay. It is easy to belittle Colenso and present him as a rather wooden figure who led honest Victorian believers into doubt and uncertainty as to the truths of scripture and the faith. Indeed, even Bishop Colenso's wife, after his death, places him, with sadness, outside the pale of 'clever men' like F.D. Maurice or Ernest Renan. Yet she protested, with nice irony, in his defence: 'He never ventilated doubts! He always believed in God, but it seems as if many of the clever men thought that impossible in one who maintained the in-authenticity of histories of Abraham, Isaac and Jacob.'[25] And perhaps this best prepares us for the final powerful and moving image of Colenso with which Jarrett-Kerr leaves us in his lecture. It concerns the bishop's remarkable sermon preached on 12 March 1879, the 'Day of Humiliation', in the cathedral of Pietermaritzburg following the crushing defeat of Lord Chelmsford's army by King Cetshwayo two months before, in which 1,600 British soldiers died. Jarrett-Kerr describes Colenso's words as 'one of the great sermons of the world', spoken with a 'rhetoric of integrity' that literary criticism would do well to attend to.[26] With enormous courage the bishop asked a congregation which was bent on revenge on the Zulu peoples, 'What doth the Lord require of thee, but to do justice, and to love mercy and to walk humbly with thy God.' (Micah 6:6). He bid them recall not only the British losses but also the Zulus who 'have bravely and nobly died in repelling the invaders and fighting for their king and fatherland'.[27]

---

23   Quoted in Jarrett-Kerr, 'Victorian Certainty and Zulu Doubt', p. 146.

24   *The Times*, 16 February, 1863. Quoted in Super, *Matthew Arnold: Lectures and Essays in Criticism*, vol. 3, pp. 415–16.

25   Wyn Rees, *Colenso's Letters from Natal*, quoted in Jarrett-Kerr, 'Victorian Certainty and Zulu Doubt', p. 145.

26   Jarrett-Kerr, 'Victorian Certainty and Zulu Doubt', pp. 154, 155.

27   W.G. Cox, *Life of Bishop Colenso*, 2 vols (London: W. Ridgway, 1888), vol. 1, pp. 491–9. Cox reprints the text of the entire sermon. More contemporary with us in Durham was the sermon by the Dean of St Paul's Cathedral preached after the war with Argentina over the Falkland Islands, with not dissimilar overtones of warning against hatred of enemies in war.

Why does Jarrett-Kerr call us back to the brave moral passion of Bishop Colenso in this context, spoken against the huge weight of British imperial pride? There was a pattern being examined here that at the time we should have felt was familiar. Colenso, an emblem of Victorian doubt, was, in his quiet way, a man of religious passion for whom, in his own time, the Church's Christological teaching and conservative biblical interpretation were becoming matters of pain and theological anxiety. Faced by the task set upon the white Christian missionary in Africa Colenso found himself displaced by 'Victorian certainty' and he struggled with a kind of integrity that the political and religious tenor of the times made almost impossible. Colenso's Pietermaritzburg sermon was his literary moment – and Martin's response in his lecture to it clearly reflects his own later experience of South Africa under apartheid, made the more painful by his distance from home. Once again theology was both the problem and the necessary and only answer – but theology could only find utterance in terms of that 'rhetoric of integrity' such as was found in the words of Colenso's sermon in words which rise at times to a pitch that cannot be avoided or denied – almost, indeed, they are the words of the poet when all else are silent.

Jarrett-Kerr's last words to our conferences were spoken in 1988, at our fourth meeting in Durham, when he spoke of the now almost forgotten novelist and critic Wyndham Lewis on the subject of time. Beginning with the work of Henri Bergson on time, Martin moves on in his lecture to Lewis's *Time and Western Man* (1927), published only four years before his notorious praise of the rise of Hitler's Germany in *Hitler* (1931).[28] It was an odd and rather rambling lecture, not altogether coherent or clear in its final purpose. As it recalls the theological approval given to Lewis by writers as eminent as the Jesuit Fr Martin D'Arcy and Jarrett-Kerr's colleague in the Community of the Resurrection in Mirfield, Lionel Thornton, it seems to celebrate Wyndham Lewis's desire to 'crystallize that which (otherwise) flows away'[29] – to seek for permanence in the face of flux and dissolution. But in his conclusion – Jarrett-Kerr's last words to the conferences on literature and religion – he reflects the ageing Lewis's late, too late, turn towards God. Lewis's projected four-part work *The Human Age* remained unfinished at his death in 1957. Its projected fourth part, *The Trial of Man* would have reflected the realization that '"God values man: that is the

---

[28]   It was a position which Lewis repudiated later in *The Hitler Cult* (1939) and the pro-Jewish *The Jews: Are They Human?* (1939).

[29]   Wyndham Lewis, *Paleface: The Philosophy of the Melting Pot* (London: Chatto & Windus, 1929), p. 255. Lewis is quoting from the Thomist Père Rousselot, without giving any references. See also Martin Jarrett-Kerr, 'Wyndham Lewis on Time', in David Jasper and Colin Crowder (eds), *European Literature and Theology in the Twentieth Century* (London: Macmillan, 1990), p. 60.

important thing to remember." But due to declining health, he was never able to write the volume.'[30]

Somehow these words reflect the spirit of the 1988 conference, a voice at the end of the decade in which the conferences began. It had a faltering note from which the discipline of theology was somehow absent. Martin Jarrett-Kerr, for all that he was remarkably learned in theology, was a literary critic rather than a theologian, and there is actually little theology in his voluminous and often brilliant writings. Certainly Martin was a man of strong convictions – brought early to a belief in Christian socialism and (by Dick Sheppard)[31] to pacifism and the simple life of the monastic tradition at Mirfield. 'Commitment' was a key word for him, as most clearly evidenced in his political activity in South Africa, described most vividly in his book *African Pulse* (1960). But it was his work on D.H. Lawrence that suggests, finally, where the issue lay in Martin's close attention to literature and religion. His book, *D.H. Lawrence and Human Existence* (1951), published under the name of 'Father Tiverton' at the express wish of his superior at Mirfield, attracted considerable comment in its reading of Lawrence as a religious writer and *Lady Chatterley's Lover* as 'a book for which we ought to be profoundly grateful'. Ten years later it was republished (under Jarrett-Kerr's real name) and after the *Lady Chatterley* trial, at which Martin had agreed to be a witness for the defence.[32] It was in the Introduction to this later edition that Martin asserted that:

> Christians who are not prepared to sit down and learn from great non-Christian artists – from Homer, Sophocles, Virgil, Ovid, Lucretius, Kalidisa, Goethe, Thomas Mann, W.B. Yeats, D.H. Lawrence, and the remaining cloud of witnesses – are cutting themselves off from some truth about the world. And if all truth comes ultimately from God, that means depriving themselves of some knowledge of God.[33]

But most significant, I think, is the brief Foreword written for the 1951 edition by T.S. Eliot which describes the book as 'a serious piece of criticism of Lawrence, of a kind for which the time is now due'.[34] In some ways, Eliot's description of Lawrence might almost do as well for Jarrett-Kerr – 'a man of fitful and

---

[30]   Jarrett-Kerr, 'Wyndham Lewis on Time,' p. 66. Quoting from Hugh Kenner, Appendix to *Malign Fiesta*, vol. 3 of *The Human Age* (London: Calder & Boyers, 1955).

[31]   Sheppard (1880–1937) was vicar of St Martin-in-the-Fields, and for brief periods towards the end of his life Dean of Canterbury and a Canon of St Paul's Cathedral. He was a noted pacifist.

[32]   He was, in fact, never called.

[33]   Martin Jarrett-Kerr, *D.H. Lawrence and Human Existence*, 2nd edn (London: SCM, 1961), p. 22.

[34]   T.S. Eliot, Foreword to Jarrett-Kerr, *D.H. Lawrence and Human Existence*, p. 9.

profound insights, rather than of ratiocinative powers'. But of Lawrence Eliot concludes that:

> No Christian ought to feel sure that he is religious-minded enough to ignore the criticism of a man who, without being a Christian, was primarily and always religious.[35]

Certainly it could not be said of Jarrett-Kerr that he was not a Christian, but his mind was religious rather than theological. Thus his commitment to literature relates to religion and belief rather than to the tough matter of theology, and his radicalism was of a nature that prompted action rather than reflection on the nature of evil or the possibility of salvation. Sadly, for all his brilliance and wit, his energy and learning, and above all his sense of commitment, it was in Jarrett-Kerr that we began to lose our theological way in the conferences.

It was in 1964 that Martin published his book *The Secular Promise* with its embracing of humanism, and it was written in the light of his close relationship with Nathan A. Scott Jr of the University of Chicago, with whom Jarrett-Kerr taught for a semester in the Chicago Divinity School. Like Jarrett-Kerr, Scott was vastly learned and passionately principled, but not, in the end, a theologian. I could never persuade Nathan, whom I liked immensely, to join our conferences, for I think that he perceived that the pursuit of religion and literature in the United States, largely under his ample tutelage, was just that – the study of literature and religion and not literature and *theology*. At the heart of our literary concerns as we have been following them in the early conferences were profound and often dark questions of sin and redemption – whereas Scott's imagination was ultimately civic and Heideggarian in addressing the question of Being from 'the ontic evidence upon which the ontological analysis will build'.[36] The same might have been said of Robert Detweiler, as evidenced in his last book *Uncivil Rites: American Fiction, Religion, and the Public Sphere* (1996), and, finally, it was true of Jarrett-Kerr also. (To Robert we will later return in Chapter 6.) The consequence for our study was well summarized by an American pupil of Scott, Giles Gunn, in his book *The Interpretation of Otherness: Literature, Religion and the American Imagination* (1979) in words that have haunted me for years:

> discussion of the relations between literature and religion, between culture and belief, has taken a fresh turn in recent years and ... it is now necessary to widen the terms in which it is conducted: to reconstitute the discussion on the plane of

---

[35]   Ibid., p. 10.
[36]   George Pattison, *The Later Heidegger* (London: Routledge, 2000), p. 196.

the hermeneutical rather than the apologetic, the anthropological rather than the theological, the broadly humanistic rather than the narrowly doctrinal.[37]

In our case these terms should have been reversed. As with von Hügel and, perhaps, in his way, Heidegger, there was a turn towards the mystical, and I will later acknowledge this[38] and I am perfectly well aware of its tone in some of my own writings such as *The Sacred Desert* (2004), but that was not the underlying imperative in 1988. Rather, it was then the deeply serious call of the theological rather than the anthropological, the doctrinal deep within the heart of the human as it struggled with the darkness of its own nature under God.

Jarrett-Kerr read literature, in the words of the obituary written by Alan Wilkinson in the *Guardian*, in his 'vocation as a synthesist', while for Simon, Coulson, Loades and others of our early speakers, there was a more urgent note that took the narratives of literature back to questions of a different kind. It was not that Jarrett-Kerr was not committed – very far from it. But his voice took us in a different direction, and ultimately away from the central task of literature and theology, which had a closer focus and was, perhaps, less easily defensible in a world that was rapidly moving away from the Church and its traditional language. An illustration of what I mean may be taken from Jarrett-Kerr's book on the impact of Christian missionary work, *Patterns of Christian Acceptance* (1972). In his account of Christians in China, Jarrett-Kerr devotes considerable space to General Feng Yü-Hsiang (c. 1880–1948). Involved in the revolution of 1911, Feng was appointed battalion leader in 1912 when Yüan Shih-kai became president of China. Converted to Christianity in 1913 by the preaching of the American John R. Mott, Feng was baptized in 1914 by a Chinese pastor of the Methodist Episcopal Church. As a military leader under Sun Yat-Sen, Feng attained considerable prestige and standing so that by 1925, after Sun's death, he was appointed Governor of the North-West.

Feng's increasing opposition to Chiang Kai-shek led him, by 1945, to withdraw to America. Although he never returned to China, by then the People's Republic, in 1953 his ashes were given honourable burial and Chairman Mao sent a funeral scroll. Whether his being taken into the roll of honour of the People's Republic of China constituted a betrayal of his Christianity, or what exactly his Christian profession amounted to – was finally of relatively little importance to the Christian socialist mind of Martin Jarrett-Kerr. He wrote of Feng:

---

[37] Giles Gunn, *The Interpretation of Otherness* (New York: Oxford University Press, 1979), p. 5.

[38] See below, pp. 223–4.

His was, in fact, an honest-to-God,[39] uncomplicated soldier's view of a fundamentalist version of Christianity ... The fact that the People's Republic of China later honoured him (as they also did Sun Yat-Sen) may be taken by some as proof of his betrayal of Christianity. I prefer to take it as proof of the genuineness of Feng's continuous and often compassionate concern for the welfare of the *lao-pai-hsing*.[40]

Commitment comes in many forms. Jarrett-Kerr was, I think, the odd man out in our early conferences, but precisely because of his broad humanity and finally un-theological mind he missed the keynote of the impetus to pursue the study of literature and theology, its particularity and its inherent difficulty. It is for the same reason that in China today the study of literature and theology has re-emerged in the new energies of Chinese theological thinking and the development of Sino-Christian theology.[41] In some ways, Martin also looked forward to the later period of 'cultural studies' and theory – though he abhorred theoretical cant as much as Ulrich Simon, believing, with some justification, that most academic debates and theories are 'very old, very confused, and perhaps by now very tedious'.[42] At the same time, his extensive writings in literary criticism have not stood the test of time well, lying too close to the text and without the underlying 'theory' that was, for us, theology. Our commitment was of a different kind from his – perhaps less socially aware, certainly more historically grounded, perhaps more conservative, more enmeshed in the Western crisis of metaphysics, certainly less sure of itself. It is with this sense that we turn to the last of the figures drawn from our early conferences, this time a man of my own generation and today a major theological figure, Werner G. Jeanrond.

---

[39] *Patterns of Christian Acceptance* was published nine years after John Robinson's *Honest to God*. Bishop Robinson, unlike Jarrett-Kerr, had refused to be called as a defence witness in the *Lady Chatterley* trial.

[40] That is 'the common people'. Martin Jarrett-Kerr, *Patterns of Christian Acceptance: Individual Response to the Missionary Impact, 1550–1950* (London: Oxford University Press, 1972), p. 282.

[41] See below, Chapter 13. An important mouthpiece for such studies is the Chinese *Journal for the Study of Christian Culture*, edited from Renmin University of China in Beijing.

[42] Jarrett-Kerr, 'Literature and Commitment: "Choosing Sides"', p. 105.

Chapter 5
Finding the Otherness of God in Literature: Werner G. Jeanrond

This chapter represents a slight detour from those that have preceded it. Before we finally leave the Durham conferences, we need to pay attention to Werner Jeanrond's contribution as it sounds a new note in the eventual return to theology in the study of literature and religion. Jeanrond, another early speaker at the conferences, was not one of the older generations of scholars. Rather he was at that time a rising star in the academic world, a German who had earned his doctorate at Chicago University under the tutelage of David Tracy, and was then teaching at Trinity College, Dublin. I was looking for someone to speak about Friedrich Schleiermacher, and Stephen Sykes, then Van Mildert professor of theology at Durham, assured me that Werner was just the right person. He was quite correct.

And so I first met Werner, and we have since remained close friends and colleagues, in September 1984 in Durham University when he spoke at the second of our conferences. That conference was specifically concerned with issues in English and German Romanticism, and Werner's lecture, which was subsequently published, in the book that I edited entitled *The Interpretation of Belief* (1986), explored the impact of Schleiermacher's hermeneutics on contemporary interpretation theory. This book as a whole was constructed around Caspar David Friedrich's remarkable painting of 1808, *The Cross on the Mountains*, and the way in which it presents a series of contrasts or ambivalences which prompt reflection, as I put it: 'not simply the perception of the sacred in the real world, but the stark contrast between the central image of the Cross and the background of the twilight, between the massive created earth and the sun-shot sky, within one of whose beams rises Christ crucified, interceding between earth and heaven'.[1]

Such ambivalences, set between heaven and earth, lie at the heart of the hermeneutical task, and *hermeneutics* as the theory of interpretation, was a new theme that had so far not been given the proper attention in our study of

---

[1]   David Jasper, Preface to *The Interpretation of Belief: Coleridge, Schleiermacher and Romanticism* (London: Macmillan, 1986), p. vii.

literature and theology.[2] To such a task, caught between two realms, Jeanrond returned in his conference paper as he sought a critical theory of interpretation. In his reading of Schleiermacher he rejects that 'sympathetic congeniality' between text and reader that is found in Gadamer, but rather, drawing upon Schleiermacher himself, insists upon 'the difference between the individuality of the text and the individual reader [that] can only be minimised through efforts of approximation, but never sublated in Hegel's sense'.[3] Schleiermacher's term 'divination' describes the risk involved in an inevitably preliminary and approximate grasp of the meaning of the text, and the process of reading as an enterprise which risks 'again and again a deeper grasp of sense in history'.[4] Every act of reading is new, preliminary and risky, and although the grammatical structure of the text remains constant the mystery of its sense is appropriated anew time and time again. Thus we can never be said to have moved beyond the 'always preliminary divination of the sense' of the text – the hermeneutical task of interpretation is always incomplete and provisional.

What does this mean for the theological dimension within the texts of literature? The recent Papal Encyclical of Pope Francis, *Lumen Fidei* (*The Light of Faith*), makes a brief reference to the passages in Dostoevsky's *The Idiot* that reflect upon the painting by Hans Holbein the Younger (1497–1543) entitled *The Body of the Dead Christ in the Tomb*. The reference gives us a good example of theology's tendency and unwillingness to remain open and unresolved in the face of the undetermined mystery of literature. Early in Dostoevsky's novel Prince Myshkin had attempted unavailingly to speak of the same picture. Later he sees a reproduction of it in Rogozhin's house and 'struck by a sudden thought' he exclaims, 'Why, some people may lose their faith by looking at that picture.'[5] Much later in the novel, the minor character Ippolit gives an extended account of Holbein's painting which concludes with a question:

> The picture seems to give expression to the idea of a dark, insolent, and senselessly eternal power, to which everything is subordinated, and this idea is suggested to you unconsciously. The people surrounding the dead man, none of whom is shown in the picture, must have been overwhelmed by a feeling of terrible anguish and dismay on that evening which had shattered all their hopes and almost all their

---

[2]   In 1991, Jeanrond published his important book *Theological Hermeneutics: Development and Significance* (London: Macmillan) as a volume in the Macmillan series Studies in Literature and Religion.

[3]   Jeanrond, 'The Impact of Schleiermacher's Hermeneutics on Contemporary Interpretation Theory', in David Jasper, *The Interpretation of Belief: Coleridge, Schleiermacher and Romanticism* (London: Macmillan, 1986), pp. 85–6.

[4]   Ibid., p. 86.

[5]   Fyodor Dostoevksy, *The Idiot*, trans. David Magarshack (Penguin: Harmondsworth, 1955), p. 251.

beliefs at one fell blow. They must have parted in a state of the most dreadful terror, though each of them carried away within him a mighty thought which could never be wrested from him. And if, on the eve of the crucifixion, the Master could have seen what He would look like when taken from the cross, would he have mounted the cross and died as he did? This question too, you can't help asking yourself as you look at the picture.[6]

Here is no conclusion or consolation, but rather the incompletion and provisionality that Jeanrond ascribes to the hermeneutical task. By contrast, *Lumen Fidei* offers a theological resolution to the painting that is quite other from the never-ending challenge of Dostoevsky's novel. In the Encyclical it is clearly stated that 'it is precisely in contemplating Jesus' death that faith grows stronger and receives a dazzling light; then it is revealed as faith in Christ's steadfast love for us, a love capable of embracing death to bring us salvation.'[7]

The more unresolved encounter with Holbein's painting in *The Idiot* is the subject of an essay by Julia Kristeva to be found in her book *Black Sun: Depression and Melancholia* (1987, trans. 1989). Placing it within the context of the image of death in the Renaissance, Kristeva offers a very different vision from that of Pope Francis, nearer to that of Dostoevsky, and linked with Desiderius Erasmus' *In Praise of Folly* (1511). Erasmus and Holbein, it should be noted, were close friends. Acknowledging his folly, writes Kristeva, man looks death in the face, 'absorbing it into his very being, integrating it not as a condition for glory or a consequence of a sinful nature but as the ultimate essence of his desacralized reality, which is the foundation of a new dignity ... man achieves a new dimension. Not necessarily that of atheism but definitely that of a disillusioned, serene, and dignified stance.'[8]

What Kristeva describes as this 'humanization', 'devoid of pathos and Intimist on account of its very banality'[9] in Holbein, and in Dostoevsky's reading of Holbein, links closely with Jeanrond's description of Schleiermacher's term 'divination' which 'describes the courageous risk of an always preliminary grasp of the text's sense. Understanding is a never-ending task and challenge.'[10] Literature and theology are drawn closely together, and in this provisionality and uncertainty, as we face the deliberate openness of the literary text, its immediate question as we face the reality of death as a cadaver which seems to shatter all our hopes and religious beliefs, is 'Where is God?' Or, more precisely, where in

---

[6]   Ibid., p. 447.

[7]   *Lumen Fidei* (*The Light of Faith*), Encyclical Letter of the Supreme Pontiff Francis (Dublin: Veritas Publications, 2013), p. 18.

[8]   Julia Kristeva, 'Holbein's Dead Christ', in *Black Sun: Depression and Melancholia*, trans. Leon S. Roudiez (New York: Columbia University Press, 1989), pp. 118–19.

[9]   Ibid., p. 115.

[10]   Jeanrond, 'The Impact of Schleiermacher's Hermeneutics', p. 86.

our human being is there space for God in our absorption of death as an end? For here the ready resolution of *Lumen Fidei* is an unwelcome, too ready, presence, without the patience of the necessary dignity of irresolution to be found in the space of literature. It is not that resolution is not to be hoped for, but rather that it cannot be found too quickly or too suddenly. As Maurice Blanchot reminds us, in the space of literature, the work must allow death its space, the divine must allow the human its dignity as the story awaits its end, and God remains 'other' in the uncertainty of our imperfect understanding.[11] Dostoevsky acknowledges this supremely in the conclusion of *Crime and Punishment* as the murderer Raskolnikov waits in the living death of his punishment in Siberia with the hope of a possibility that is the condition of his 'gradual regeneration'. But, in the last words of the book, 'that might be the subject of a new story – our present story is ended'.[12]

Theology and its reassurances, then, must await the painful, necessary dignity of the human, known in the unending, unresolved hermeneutical challenges of literature, challenges which remain even yet when the light of faith begins to shine more brightly. In George Steiner's words in his book *Real Presences* (1989), caught in the space between Good Friday and Easter Sunday, we must patiently traverse the paradoxes of the terrible beauty as 'ours is the long day's journey of the Saturday. Between suffering, aloneness, unutterable waste on the one hand and the dream of liberation, of rebirth on the other.'[13] It is art and literature that teach us the immensity of waiting, the beauty of suffering though not without hope. Only here can we enter, with stumbling steps, the shocking intimacy of human experience that is not yet ready – if it ever will be, perhaps – for the narrative of promise that leads to the end. As Jacques Derrida has reminded us we must not omit to undertake the human, liberating work of mourning in the face of death.[14]

In what sense can we even begin to grasp the agonizing, even shocking, ending of the Hungarian writer Imre Kertész's autobiographical novel *Fateless*? In this 'fiction' we seem to be back with Ulrich Simon's unresolved agony and sense of evil as a young Jewish boy endures and survives the horrors of Auschwitz, where so many others died, finally returning home to Budapest and his mother and family. 'My mother was waiting and would no doubt greatly rejoice over me.'[15] But neither his mother nor the rest of his family can possibly

---

[11]   Maurice Blanchot, 'The Work and Death's Space', in *The Space of Literature*, trans. Ann Smock (Lincoln: University of Nebraska Press, 1982), pp. 85–159.

[12]   Fyodor Dostoevsky, *Crime and Punishment*, trans. David Magarshack (Harmondsworth: Penguin, 1966), p. 559.

[13]   George Steiner, *Real Presences* (Faber and Faber: London, 1989), p. 232.

[14]   Jacques Derrida, *The Work of Mourning*, ed. Pascale-Anne Brault and Michael Naas (Chicago, IL: University of Chicago Press, 2001).

[15]   Imre Kertész, *Fateless*, trans. Tim Wilkinson (Vintage Books: London, 2006), p. 262.

understand the change that has taken place in him, nor the full nature of the experiences that have prompted it. He speaks in a language that lies outside the structures and categories of those who can only look upon the Holocaust from the outside with horror. And only he, from the inside, knows fully that to live at all, even in a manner that to the rest of us is unimaginable, entails the recognition that nothing is impossible:

> there is nothing impossible that we do not live through naturally, and keeping a watch on me in my journey, like some inescapable trap, I already know there will be happiness. For even there, next to the chimneys, in the intervals between the torments, there was something that resembled happiness. Everyone asks only about the hardships and the 'atrocities,' whereas for me perhaps it is that experience which will remain the most memorable. Yes, the next time I am asked, I ought to speak about that, the happiness of the concentration camps.
>
> If indeed I am asked. And provided I myself don't forget.[16]

As with the Holbein painting, it is almost impossible for us to look death in the face, but that is exactly what the young boy, Gyuri, has necessarily done, and in this utterly desacralized reality is found a new dignity and even 'something that resembled happiness'. As one reads this passage the attempt to understand and make sense of it is almost defeated. Indeed, we, though bystanders, are almost offended, were it not that Gyuri alone has permission to enter the dark truth of his sayings. And where are God and those patterns of religious thought and belief that try vainly to comprehend the nature of such evil? Perhaps we might put it this way: that God is wise enough to know when to leave the space clear, the unresolved *espace littéraire* which allows the foundation of a new human dignity held within the fragility of memory and wise enquiry.

The Jewish tradition, perhaps more than any other, knows of the divinity of the text, its garments the ink and paper that hold it before us, challenging our attempts at interpretation, yet sustaining our hope against the blackness of night. As Susan A. Handelman has written of Torah, 'every crownlet of every letter is filled with significance, and even the forms of letters are hints to profound meanings. To understand creation, one looks not to nature but to the Torah; the world can be read out of the Torah, and the Torah read from the world.'[17] Another survivor of the Holocaust, the Italian writer Primo Levi, while he was a prisoner in Auschwitz, received the precious gift of a letter from home, and he wrote, 'that piece of paper in my hands, which had reached me in such a

---

[16]   Ibid., p. 262.

[17]   Susan A. Handelman, *The Slayers of Moses: The Emergence of Rabbinic Interpretation in Modern Literary Theory* (Albany, NY: State University of New York Press, 1982), p. 38.

precarious way and which I would destroy before nightfall, represented a breach, a small gap in the black universe that closed tightly around us, and through that breach hope could pass'.[18]

From the reading of the text flows a stream of possibilities as, in Schleiermacher's words, 'the hermeneutical task moves constantly'[19] in never-ending, always-preliminary acts of understanding that have their beginning in the dignity of human nature in the face of all that life can suffer. In her essay on Holbein's *Dead Christ*, Julia Kristeva writes of the 'Protestant affliction' of Calvin and Luther whereby the human will is enslaved to God and the devil.[20] Rather, she suggests, Holbein is closer to the Occamist position of his friend Erasmus whereby human free will provides a way of access to salvation. It is this way which I am identifying here with the space of the text in which the will and imagination of the human enable a process by which God, in God's otherness and in a glimpse of the theological, may yet be hoped for. At the end of *In Praise of Folly*, Erasmus writes of the imaginative world – the world of the poet and writer – whereby we can deliberately look upon the face of death and yet live, even in happiness, in spite of all. Erasmus writes of the theology and religious vision that look to articulate the 'future life of heaven toward which the pious aspire with so much endeavour'.[21] Yet it is Folly herself who leads some, the poets and artists, to find such a transformation in the foretaste of the present: 'They are very few, [and] suffer from something akin to madness. They speak in a manner that is not quite coherent, not in the ordinary manner but with meaningless sounds.'[22] Such a one may indeed be Kertész's survivor Gyuri, as we seek to interpret his words – not quite meaningless sounds but yet, calling from the depths of Gyuri's tormented spirit, such as are almost beyond our comprehension – about the happiness of the concentration camps. And still, as Simon expresses it as he intones his terrible litany of damnation on the *via dolorosa* of the death camps,[23] 'between us and Auschwitz lies a wide gulf' even as 'the Church has throughout the ages endeavoured to mitigate the harshness of the condemnation'.[24]

---

[18]   Primo Levi, 'A Disciple', in *Moments of Reprieve*, trans. Ruth Feldman (Abacus: London, 1987), p. 54.

[19]   Friedrich D.E. Schleiermacher, 'General Hermeneutics', in Kurt Mueller-Vollmer (ed.), *The Hermeneutics Reader: Texts of the German Tradition from the Enlightenment to the Present* (Oxford: Blackwell, 1986), p. 73.

[20]   Kristeva, 'Holbein's Dead Christ', pp. 119–20.

[21]   Desiderius Erasmus, *The Praise of Folly*, in *The Essential Erasmus*, trans. John P. Dolan (New American Library: New York, 1964), p. 172.

[22]   Ibid., p. 172.

[23]   See above, p. 44.

[24]   Ulrich Simon, *A Theology of Auschwitz* (London: Victor Gollancz, 1967), pp. 28, 69.

I have made the reference to *In Praise of Folly* quite deliberately, for it is hard in reading that work, especially in translation, to catch the tone and levels of irony (that term again) which are employed throughout it. Erasmus is of the company of literary men and women who is most serious when he flicks words at his reader as challenges, as does Kierkegaard or Kafka, whom Blanchot once compared with the poet Hölderlin: 'Kafka's passion is just as purely literary, but it is not always only literary. Salvation is an enormous preoccupation with him, all the stronger because it is hopeless, and all the more hopeless because it is totally uncompromising.'[25] Always in Kafka's writings, God is ever near, but never stated, always 'other'. Another of this company of literary figures is the unjustly forgotten French writer André Schwarz-Bart, if only for his extraordinary novel *The Last of the Just* (1959). In the last pages of this book, Ernie Levy, the last of the just, that is those 36 Jews in every generation whom God has chosen to bear the burden of the suffering of the world, is travelling in a box car to the death camp with some other adults and a group of frightened children. Setting a little girl on his knees he tells them of the joys in store when they will reach the Kingdom of Israel on their arrival the next day.

> There children can find their parents, and everybody is happy. Because the country we're going to, that's our kingdom, you know. There, the sun never sets, and you may eat anything you can think of. There, an eternal joy will crown your heads; cheerfulness and gaiety will come and greet you, and all the pains and all the moans will run away ...[26]

An older woman, a doctor, in the box car, rails at Ernie for telling lies to the children who, she knows, will only face such appalling sufferings and finally a terrible death when they reach their journey's end.

> Rocking the child mechanically, Ernie gave way to dry sobs. 'Madame,' he said at last, 'there is no room for truth here.' Then he stopped rocking the child, turned, and saw that the old woman's face had altered.
> 'Then what is there room for?' she began. And taking a closer look at Ernie, registering all the slightest details of his face, she murmured softly, 'Then you don't believe what you're saying at all? Not at all?'[27]

This is literature, where there is no truth but only the telling of stories. Here the truth claims of theology have no part, at least in the first instance and for the

---

[25]   Maurice Blanchot, 'Kafka and the Work's Demand,' in *The Space of Literature*, p. 57.

[26]   André Schwarz-Bart, *The Last of the Just*, trans. Stephen Becker (Secker & Warburg: London, 1961), p. 396.

[27]   Ibid., pp. 397–8.

moment, and there is no place yet for God, but there are only stories to comfort the children on their journey to a terrible death the next day. There is only what Jeanrond, writing of Schleiermacher's term 'divination', calls the 'courageous risk' of the one who, even without belief, dares to search for some preliminary grasp upon sense – the making of meaning in an utterly meaningless world. And in this space of fiction may be sensed, even experienced, an absent presence – the otherness of God in literature, the future hope in the darkness of the present, the beginnings again, perhaps, of theology. Jacques Derrida describes this insistently present hope as a *trace* and as an experience that is itself eschatological.

> But this future, this beyond, is not another time, a day after history. It is *present* at the heart of experience. Present not as a total presence but as a *trace*. Therefore, before all dogmas, all conversions, all articles of faith or philosophy, experience itself is eschatological at its origin and in each of its aspects.[28]

In *The Last of the Just* Ernie Levy, of course, dies, 'dead six million times', a character in fiction who yet remains to haunt our imagination. The novel ends on the same extraordinary note as Kertész's *Fateless* as it speaks in a doxology of the happiness of the concentration camps:

> And praised be Auschwitz. So be it. Maidanek. The Eternal. Treblinka. And praised be Buchenwald. So be it. Mauthausen. The Eternal. Belzec. And praised be Sobibor. So be it. Chelmno. The Eternal. Ponary. And praised be Theresienstadt. So be it. Warsaw. The Eternal. Wilno. And praised be Skarzysko. So be it. Bergen-Belsen. The Eternal. Janow. And praised be Dora. So be it. Neuengamme. The Eternal. Pustkow. And praised be ...[29]

In literature this grotesque, never-ending doxology before death itself is finally sanctified and made possible by the figure of Ernie Levy, the teller of children's stories, 'disillusioned, serene and dignified'.[30] And so the novel's narrator concludes, with the hope of Dostoevsky:

> Yesterday, as I stood in the street trembling in despair, rooted to the spot, a drop of pity fell from above upon my face; but there was no breeze in the air, no cloud in the sky ... there was only a presence.[31]

---

[28]   Jacques Derrida, 'Violence and Metaphysics', in *Writing in Difference*, trans. Alan Bass (Routledge & Kegan Paul: London, 1981), p. 95.

[29]   Schwarz-Bart, *The Last of the Just*, p. 408.

[30]   Kristeva, 'Holbein's Dead Christ', p. 119.

[31]   Schwarz-Bart, *The Last of the Just*, p. 409.

And in this trace of a presence, even in the lies of fiction, the uncertainties of sense and the endless search for meaning which is the task of hermeneutics and before that of poetics itself, whose vocation is to find the silence at the heart of all language, is finally to be realized what the death of God theologian Thomas Altizer has termed a total presence: 'That silence [which] is the silence of a new solitude, and absolute solitude which has finally negated and reversed every unique and interior ground of consciousness, thereby releasing the totality of consciousness in a total and immediate presence ... for the only true joy is the joy of loss, the joy of having been wholly lost and thereby wholly found again. Not only is the true paradise the paradise that we have lost, but the only regained paradise is the final loss of paradise itself.'[32]

When the 'new atheist' Richard Dawkins was read the story of Ernie Levy's 'lies' to the children in the box car he was asked, 'What would you have said to them?' He replied that he would have said the same thing. He would have told them stories of heaven.[33]

Reading, interpreting, now and then grasping some sense, often in spite of all, in the endless search for meaning in texts, perhaps alone can prepare us for the claims of theology and its language. It is only when, perhaps illicitly, we find innocence and beauty in the darkest places, where neither innocence nor beauty can *be* found, that spaces open up for the impossible. If Ernie's story, and the novels of Dostoevsky, are concerned with the nature of truth, what then of that greatest of all religious virtues, love? George Steiner has written of a late poem on love and freedom, with a glance at the comedic in Shakespeare, by another Holocaust survivor, Paul Celan:

> The innocence of obscenity has moved into the last total embarrassment available to us, which is that of prayer. We know this if only by virtue of a supreme word-play and finding at the climax of one of Celan's late poems. He says to, he says of the beloved that she 'beds and prays him free'. The pun does not translate: *bettest/ betest*. But the wonder of the congruence is plain. The commerce of love finds the as-yet unspoken. Privacy is made new, Eros translates (as in Bottom) into *Logos*. And this translation speaks freedom.[34]

The obscene is found both within the public and the intimate, private lives of people and nations. In the paradoxes of literature and language even this can become the space in which a divine otherness suggests light and love.

---

[32] Thomas J.J. Altizer, *Total Presence: The Language of Jesus and the Language of Today* (The Seabury Press: New York, 1980), pp. 107–8.

[33] I was told this by Richard Holloway.

[34] Steiner, *Real Presences*, p. 195.

In his lecture at our conference and in the essay in *The Interpretation of Belief*, Werner Jeanrond reflects upon what he calls the absurdity of Gadamer's accusation of a theological bias in Schleiermacher's hermeneutical reflection. Certainly, of course, we may agree that it is the theological need to interpret texts that constitutes Schleiermacher's hermeneutical point of departure. Yet, as Jeanrond recognizes, 'he always insists that the theological interpreter has no prerogative when he tries to understand texts'.[35] Theology, in other words, must be neither hasty nor arrogant in its claims, but await the otherness of God in the textures and imaginings of the textual, literary world. Schleiermacher maintained that the final goal of interpretation was 'to understand the text at first as well as and then even better than its author'.[36] Yet, as Manfred Frank has pointed out, this constitutes no arrogant claim upon superior competence, 'but it means for the interpreter to risk again and again a deeper grasp of sense in history. The components of the text, its grammatical structure, remain the same, but their sense has to be appropriated anew in every act of reading.'[37]

It is our story-shaped world[38] that affirms the power of human dignity – a profound humanism that radiates from Holbein's almost unbearable painting of Christ's dereliction which, in *The Idiot*, is known and held up as a challenge to theological expectation and its consolations. Perhaps, reflects Ippolit, if Christ had known what horror his followers would have to face as they see his cadaver after the crucifixion, would he even have died as he did? Yet, it is our task to watch, and to persist as patient interpreters in a vocation that seeks to bind earth with heaven, just as Hermes, the messenger of the gods, 'bridged the gap between the divine and the human realm'.[39]

This chapter in our story has deliberately sounded a slightly different note and opened a door, if only hesitantly, upon theological possibilities in the study of literature and theology. Our conferences, as they progressed towards the end of the century and into a new millennium, failed, at least for a while, to follow this suggested path. With Werner Jeanrond its tone was rather different from what had gone before and we were not ready for it and moved, with literature, in a rather different direction, one haunted not so much by the past but by the future and by different kinds of theory. I began this chapter with a reference

---

[35]   Jeanrond, 'The Impact of Schleiermacher's Hermeneutics', p. 85.

[36]   Schleiermacher in his lectures on hermeneutics, in Mueller-Vollmer, *The Hermeneutics Reader*, p. 83.

[37]   Manfred Frank, *Das individuelle Allgemeine: Textstrukturierung und interpretation nach Schleiermacher* (Frankfurt am Main, 1977), p. 361, quoted in Jeanrond, 'The Impact of Schleiermacher's Hermeneutics', p. 86.

[38]   See Brian Wicker, *The Story-Shaped World: Fiction and Metaphysics: Some Variations on a Theme* (London: The Athlone Press, 1975).

[39]   Werner G. Jeanrond, *Theological Hermeneutics: Development and Significance* (London: Macmillan, 1991), p. 1.

to Caspar David Friedrich's painting *The Cross on the Mountains*. Perhaps the picture and its angel hovering over us was the *Angelus Novus* of the painting by Paul Klee, so powerfully described by Walter Benjamin in the ninth of his *Theses on the Philosophy of History*. Even as his face, as the angel of history, is turned towards the past:

> The angel would like to stay, awaken the dead, and make whole what has been smashed. But a storm is blowing from Paradise; it had got caught in his wings with such violence that the angel can no longer close them. The storm irresistibly propels him into the future to which his back is turned, while the pile of debris before him grows skyward. This storm is what we call progress.[40]

And with that image we move to Part II and to the figure of Robert Detweiler.

---

[40]   Walter Benjamin, *Illuminations*, ed. Hannah Arendt (London: Fontana Press, 1992), p. 249.

PART II
The Loss of and the Return to Theology

Chapter 6
'A Tone Born out of the World of Ruins':
Robert Detweiler

The apocalypse transformed the living. What was before this time is no longer comprehensible, and appears like a fairy tale, sunken and silent. Another tone determines life, a tone born out of the world of ruins.[1]

These words of Hans Werner Richter were written in 1947. A year later Paul Tillich, in *The Protestant Era*, wrote: 'A new element has come into the picture, the experience of the "end". Something of it appeared after the First World War; but we did not feel it in its horrible depth and its incredible thoroughness.'[2] This was the darkness of absolute evil and the 'over-shadowing' felt by Ulrich Simon and John Coulson – that sense of an ending which cried out for, and still knew in a way, the comfort of the language of theology and yet also somehow made that theology impossible and inaccessible. Perhaps, after all, Theodor Adorno was right, though his axiom has been described as hackneyed, though painfully so, and now only silence was possible. Any words would be simply barbarous.[3] And yet out of the very depths of Auschwitz and the Holocaust the poets and writers – Celan, Levi and others – somehow have spoken with an almost unbearable eloquence, often using the language of a faith and a sacred literature that, for many of them, had been lost but yet remained a haunting presence.

Both Tillich and Richter were quoted by Robert Detweiler in the opening of his lecture at the fourth of our conferences in Durham in September 1988. Borrowing from the title of the 1972 book by the historian Theodor Roszak, highly popular in its time but now almost wholly forgotten, the conference was entitled 'Where the Wasteland Ends: European Literature and Theology in the Twentieth Century'. It was, for me, a turning point in our meetings –

---

[1]   Hans Werner Richter, quoted in Robert Detweiler, 'Apocalyptic Fiction and the End(s) of Realism', in David Jasper and Colin Crowder (eds), *European Literature and Theology in the Twentieth Century* (London: Macmillan, 1990), p. 153.

[2]   Paul Tillich, 'Religion and Secular Culture', in *The Protestant Era*, trans. James Luther Smith (Chicago, IL: Chicago University Press, 1948), p. 59.

[3]   Rowan Williams, who described Adorno's axiom as 'most challenging and – painfully, the most hackneyed example', has recently pointed out that it is more strictly the 'barbarity' of writing poetry after Auschwitz that Adorno speaks of. *The Edge of Words: God and the Habits of Language* (London: Bloomsbury, 2014), p. 159.

historically we had begun at the end of the eighteenth century, with the birth of Romanticism, and now we had reached an end in the present time, and it proved to be a bleak place. Robert's lecture was entitled 'Apocalyptic Fiction and the End(s) of Realism'. (It was fashionable then to put brackets around parts of words.) His was the last essay to be published in the conference volume and at its very end we find these words:

> I believe that over much of the globe we are already *living* the unthinkable, to the extent that my freedom to think the unthinkable at a literature and religion conference is a First--World luxury.[4]

There was a deep irony in these words that none of us, Detweiler least of all, could have imagined then. For around midnight on 27 March 1995, Robert suffered a massive stroke from which he never fully recovered. He did, indeed, come not only to think but also to live the unthinkable. For me, as his friend, the return to his writings and the writing of this chapter have been, perhaps, the most difficult parts of this book, an over-shadowing that is profoundly personal and deeply human. In the Preface to the 1995 Westminster John Knox edition of his prize winning book *Breaking the Fall* (the first edition of which I myself edited),[5] Robert speaks of three things: suffering, prayer and irony. The last is a theme and a trope in rhetoric to which I keep returning in this book.

As I re-read Robert's writings now, some years after his death, I realize that the predominant theme in them is indeed theological, but that it is held at the very edge of theology, perhaps even beyond its edge, at the moment when theology is most necessary and already, perhaps, utterly impossible or even worse, finally corrupted. Detweiler was of a slightly younger generation than Coulson, Walker or Simon, but older than myself, and his youth had been spent in Germany helping with the clearing up of the mess and massive human displacement after the Second World War. He was also trained in German theology and was, in his particular and idiosyncratic way, a deeply devout Christian. The key word in *Breaking the Fall* is taken from Meister Eckhart (and after him Heidegger – whom Robert understood profoundly). It is *Gelassenheit* – which means, in Detweiler's words, something like 'abandonment, nonchalance, relaxation'.[6] More eloquently and acutely Bob describes it as 'the ability – and it may be a gift – to move gracefully through life's fortunes and accidents, or to wait out its calamities'.[7] This he was

---

[4]   Detweiler, 'Apocalyptic Fiction and the End(s) of Realism', p. 181.

[5]   Like Jeanrond's *Theological Hermeneutics*, for the Macmillan series Studies in Literature and Religion, of which I was the general editor.

[6]   Robert Detweiler, *Breaking the Fall: Religious Readings of Contemporary Fiction* (Louisville, KY: WJK Press, 1995), p. ix.

[7]   Ibid., p. 35. See also John D. Caputo, *The Mystical Element in Heidegger's Thought* (Athens, OH: Ohio University Press, 1978), pp. 173–83.

to know so painfully in his own life after his stroke, and it is linked closely to his sense of what it means to pray, which is, for him, an emptying out of the self (a *kenosis*) to God in a combination of reason and intuition. Prayer is, in his words, 'conversation with God in which the prayee can pour out one's heart, can empty oneself. In prayer, by a combination of reason and intuition, one focuses on feeling, a stance not unlike *Gelassenheit*'.[8] Newman would, I think, have understood at least something of this combination of reason and intuition – of prayer as a driven necessity that is yet wholly a part of our intellectual being.

Suffering, prayer and irony: for Detweiler theology was absolutely necessary but its necessity arose not from the Church and its establishments, nor even, I think, from the revelation given in Christ. It is necessitated by the death, or perhaps the disappearance, of God and prayer is all that we have after God has disappeared. Perhaps, in the end, those two 'events' should be clearly separated – the *death of God* which is present in Hegel and dramatically announced in Nietzsche's *The Gay Science* (1863); and the *disappearance of God* in Victorian literature,[9] which may be in the end the more tragic event and condition for it is nothing less than the being condemned to live with a religious sense in a world where belief is no longer possible.[10] It may be that this was the final tragedy of our early enterprise in theology and literature, or, at least, its own deep irony. If there was a death it was that of the Church, which was, for Newman, utterly central. And after the Church's demise God disappears, no longer accessible through a theology that has ceased to make any sense, for it was a theology that finally could not be prayed, a theology without a true community or ecclesia. Could literature and its communities of readers, then, move to save our souls and somehow articulate faith? That, perhaps, was Robert's hope as he wrote:

> Above all, narrative theology and its relationship to irony is key to the irony of death. I exist and yet I do not. I exist as ironic. That is why we tell our stories.
>
> Narrative fiction, not all that secular to many, explores this relationship. Story is redemptive by nature, hoping against hope that one will yet be saved by and through the telling.[11]

Yet this, for all of its irony, is deeply and terribly fragile. How much more fragile than the cries and prayers of Newman's Gerontius that are uttered from deep

---

8   Detweiler, *Breaking the Fall*, p. ix.

9   See J. Hillis Miller, *The Disappearance of God: Five Nineteenth century Authors* (Harvard University Press, 1963).

10   'It was said that one of the worst tragedies of the spirit was to be born with a religious sense into a world where belief was no longer possible. Was it an equal tragedy to be born without a religious sense into a world where belief *was* possible?' Julian Barnes, *Staring at the Sun* (1986), quoted in *Breaking the Fall*, p. xviii.

11   Ibid., p. ix.

within the traditions of the Church and its liturgy, profoundly within the biblical tradition of the Psalms.

> Sanctus fortis, sanctus deus
> De profundis, oro te ...
> (From *The Dream of Gerontius*)

Perhaps closer to Detweiler, in his way, and I even like to think so, is the later Gerard Manley Hopkins in his anguish at the hiddenness of God in the 'Terrible Sonnets', written in despair, yet in faith:

> And my lament
> Is cries countless, cries like dead letters sent
> To dearest him that lives alas! away.[12]

Behind Newman (and through him Bishop Butler) there was the exercise of the will and the conscience – but now we were not so sure any more of either.

Detweiler's best book, though it is uneven in its quality, is the award winning *Breaking the Fall*, published a year after our Durham conference of 1988, and therefore it was being written more or less while the conference was taking place. Its central and most important chapter is the second, entitled 'What is Reading Religiously?' At its heart is the notion of the community very much as it is found in the literary work of Stanley Fish in his understanding of the 'interpretative community'.[13] Close to the surface of Detweiler's text is the later thought of Martin Heidegger (and behind Heidegger the poetry of Hölderlin) in which our reaction and response to text moves beyond interpretation, with its stress on meaning and power, to what Heidegger calls the 'conversation' that we have been.[14] Another way of putting this idea of conversation is, in Robert's words, our 'allowing the text to be its multifold articulation that is the object of our communal curiosity'.[15] It is in the relaxation of such reading that we come close to realizing the sense of the two German terms that are near to the heart of all of Detweiler's concerns; Eckhart's *Gelassenheit*, and the word *Geselligkeit*, which is close to the idea of 'sociability', though with a closeness and even intimacy that

---

[12] G.M. Hopkins, 'I wake and feel the fell of dark, not day', *Poems of Gerard Manley Hopkins*, ed. Robert Bridges (London: Oxford University Press, 1931), p. 65.

[13] See Stanley Fish, *Is There is Text in This Class? The Authority of Interpretive Communities* (Cambridge, MA: Harvard University Press, 1980).

[14] Martin Heidegger, 'Hölderlin and the Essence of Poetry', trans. Douglas Scott, in *Existence and Being* (Chicago, IL: Henry Regnery, 1949), pp. 277–8. *Breaking the Fall*, pp. 34–5.

[15] Detweiler, *Breaking the Fall*, p. 34.

the larger term does not quite convey.[16] In a highly dramatic sentence, Robert defines the practice of 'reading religiously' as that of 'a group of persons engaged in gestures of friendship with each other across the erotic space of the text that draws them out of their privacy and its stress on meaning and power'.[17] Yet, for all its seductiveness, there is a liberalism here that is at once attractive but yet has its own dangers and even holds a deeply tragic tone.

For as 'reading religiously' moves the community towards some form of condition of belief, and as form intensifies in the space of the text, even as the drive to control and find meaning reasserts itself, we still find that confusion is not far distant and 'the reading community's participation in the construction of myths and rituals *against impending chaos*'.[18] In something close to what we have seen as Maurice Blanchot's sense of the space of the text must be held the belief, even desperately, that the world is finally not uninterpretable and that the 'grand narratives' that support our culture are, at least in some sense, sustainable. Detweiler draws at length upon Clifford Geertz's 1965 essay 'Religion as a Cultural System' – but as one reads further in his chapter on religious reading there grows the dark sense that all of this is, in the end, just language 'about something', a description of words and their task which has lost the deep symbolic life and even the sacramental reverberations of theology and the practice of liturgy. If religious reading is about celebration it is, it might seem after all and for all its forms and meanings, somehow nothing much more than a game, and often a desperate one at that, and, to borrow from Robert Frost, no more than a momentary stay against confusion.[19] It is not that the ludic is not important and that playing games, as we know from Gadamer and others, is not important in human life. But there is a sense of deep anxiety in Detweiler and a sense that we are trying to read *into* belief in a way that is the very opposite of Newman's profoundly serious position in writings like *On Consulting the Faithful in Matters of Doctrine*. Something serious has been lost.

That position is far being resolved by any faithful resort to the testimony of the apostolical tradition or merely the judgement of the infallible Church.[20]

---

[16] See Samuel Weber, 'Ambivalence, the Humanities and the Study of Literature', in *Diacritics*, vol. 15, no. 2 (1985), 19, on *Geselligkeit* in Kant.

[17] Detweiler, *Breaking the Fall*, pp. 34–5.

[18] Ibid., p. 36 (emphases added).

[19] Frost writes that a poem 'begins in delight and ends in wisdom, it inclines to the impulse, it assumes direction with the first line laid down, it runs a course of lucky events, and ends in a clarification of life – not necessarily a great clarification, such as sects and cults are founded on, but in a momentary stay against confusion '. Preface to Robert Frost, *Collected Poems*, quoted in Ron Hansen, *A Stay against Confusion: Essays on Faith and Fiction* (New York: Perennial, 2002), p. xvii.

[20] J.H. Newman, *On Consulting the Faithful in Matters of Doctrine* [1859 and 1871], ed. John Coulson (London: Geoffrey Chapman, 1961), p. 67.

Perhaps the most significant of the five characteristics of the consent of the faithful in Newman is found in the term *phronema* – that is a kind of instinct which is lodged at the very heart of the mystical body of Christ.[21] This is a sort of communal counterpart to the *phronesis* or Illative Sense which governs the giving of real, as opposed to notional assent. If this is a deeply theological moment in Newman, I am left uneasy that Robert's argument does not even begin to move towards it and beyond the anthropological in Geertz or the literary critical in Fish. As Detweiler puts it: 'Belief does not mean faith, and community here does not mean *koinonia*'.[22] In other words, in religious reading we are, at best, responding to the human need to interpret via belief and only moving, if at all, in the direction of faith by means of myth and ritual impulse. There is here a note of desperation which is quite different from the dark, theological seriousness that underlay the earlier Durham conferences on literature and religion.

I am not in any way wishing to underestimate the power of Detweiler's argument in *Breaking the Fall*. But I see it now as a book written at and for the end of time, a work that already knew itself as too late. If we had been serious in our regard to theology and its recovery after the traumas of the mid-twentieth century, measuring the deep literary insights of the later theologians of the Western Church and their patterns woven into the literature of English and German Romanticism and post-Romanticism, such seriousness was evaporating inasmuch as the only *forms* left to us were in fictive texts written in our literature or on the body in pain. The 'intensity of form' sought by reading religiously would detach liturgical ritual from the theology which was its heart and consign the theological, finally, to a purely intellectual pursuit that could in the end answer nothing. In Detweiler's words:

> A religious reading could, by the process of playing with form, become the only approach to take it seriously. Christian myth and ritual, in celebrating the Incarnation and Resurrection, hint at a far stronger commitment to form than Christian theology has seemed to recognize.[23]

This fails to acknowledge that the terrible experience of the death of God is itself a profoundly *theological* moment – as some, like Thomas J.J. Altizer, who are in a deeper continuity within the Christian faith than is often thought, have indicated within the deeply Catholic poetics of Dante, and even Milton, Blake and Joyce. For many of us at the end of the 1980s there seemed to be, at best, a hovering between the expressible and the inexpressible, the thinkable and the unthinkable with a renewed Kierkegaardian sense of the discontinuity

---

[21]   Ibid., pp. 73–4.
[22]   Detweiler, *Breaking the Fall*, p. 42.
[23]   Ibid., p. 44.

of existence (as opposed to the tragedy of continuity found in the writings of Ulrich Simon and Richard L. Rubenstein)[24] and only the oh so fragile texts of so-called postmodernity between us and the final silence. Theology itself seemed silent or at best outdated. Yet there was something more than that, a sense of what Detweiler called a 'foundational mystery'[25] that was at the heart of the recovery of a sense of apocalyptic, against the demythologizing tendencies of the age, and it brought us to the brink of a Christian recovery that we never quite had the courage to grasp or perhaps even insightfully to recognize. And anyway, was there anyone even willing to listen? Or perhaps we had lost the deep sense of theological hermeneutics that we have seen Jeanrond draw from Schleiermacher. Detweiler's instinct was to link religious reading with the apocalyptic and with the anticipation of Revelation 22:20 – the Eucharistic prayer '*maranatha*', 'come, Lord Jesus'[26] – together with liturgical texts, but it ended in a loss of nerve. Liturgy can, in the end, Bob wrote, only learn to 'practise playful experimentation'[27] with a lack of the serious discipline that forgets its true shape and its deep continuity with the worship of earlier ages, offered, finally, by all people and everywhere.

In the conference volume published after the 1988 conference, edited by Colin Crowder and myself, there remained only two voices of the first generation of scholars in literature and religion – Martin Jarrett-Kerr and Peter Walker. Robert Detweiler was the bridge with the newer age. The tone of the conference and the volume of essays was predominantly negative, moving from forms of nihilism and Thomas Mann (George Pattison's essay) to Eliot's *The Wasteland* (Michael Edwards), visions of hell in Malcolm Lowry and Beckett (Francis Doherty and Marius Buning) and finally Detweiler's sense of the end(s) of realism in apocalyptic fiction. But before turning to Robert's essay more particularly we should dwell for a moment with the paper offered by Bishop Peter Walker entitled 'T.S. Eliot: Poetry, Silence and the Vision of God'. It was the last time Bishop Walker was to address our conferences and the difference in tone, when set beside his first address on W.H. Auden's *Horae Canonicae*, given six years earlier, is significant. In this later paper we are given readings of the *Four Quartets* as a mystical vision and 'silence in the presence of the ultimate, as before the vision of God'.[28] It is a typical paper from the bishop – slow and labyrinthine in its form of words, careful and occasionally hovering

---

[24]   See above, pp. 46–7.

[25]   Ibid., p. 54.

[26]   See G.B. Caird, *A Commentary on the Revelation of St. John the Divine* (London: Adam & Charles Black, 1966), p. 288.

[27]   Ibid., p. 59.

[28]   Peter Walker, 'T.S. Eliot: Poetry, Silence and the Vision of God', in David Jasper and Colin Crowder (eds), *European Literature and Theology in the Twentieth Century* (London: Macmillan, 1990), p. 88.

on the brink of incoherence in its anxiety to be precise. Walker describes it as a 'theological appreciation', but one that is not so much a moving away from the world into mystical solitude, yet rather 'one of outreach towards the world, and as such, the present writer would maintain, a rediscovery of a primary Christian perception'.[29] It comes across in its written form as the last faint utterance of the churchman seeking a place and relevance 'within the substance of actual living in the "available" world of the temporal'.[30] Yet if the world is available is it also receptive to such a voice? The fragility, the uncertainty here, is all too present.

> Upon whether *Four Quartets* may be so read, the validity of this paper will depend. The danger is that, to some degree unwittingly, we shall in the event have done no more than shake the poem down to fit a scheme.[31]

This is the danger of all exercises in interpretation and all literary criticism. The poem has not been allowed to speak for itself but rather shaped and interpreted, shaken down, to 'fit a scheme' – that is the scheme of Christian belief and doctrine, to support a given position which is not, finally, part of the substance of our actual living any longer. I remember once being asked at an interview in a Cambridge college (it was for the position of dean) if I thought that it was necessary to be a Christian to read the *Four Quartets*. I did not, perhaps could not, answer the question – and did not get the job either!

Peter Walker's essay ends with a brief Postscript that was not part of his lecture at the conference. It concerned the meeting between Dietrich Bonhoeffer and the saintly George Bell, Bishop of Chichester, in Sweden, an inter-church initiative, when Bonhoeffer disclosed to Bell the secrets of the plot to assassinate Hitler. Walker notes, a fact omitted in the official biography of Bell,[32] that Eliot was also present at the meeting, though there is no reason to believe that he was privy to the assassination plot. When Bonhoeffer was finally being led to his execution in Flossenburg he sent his final message to Bell: 'Tell him that for me this is the end, but also the beginning'.[33] Walker notes (as he had with Auden) his own personal friendship with Bell. But it was a dark note to end on – another ethically unresolved over-shadowing from the violence of 1945. And as that note sounds, I turn now to Detweiler's essay in the book, with its sense of an ending but now none of any new beginning.

Walker's readings of the poets starts, always, with the voice of the theologian, who, through the poetry of Auden and Eliot, he believed, found utterance

---

[29] Ibid.

[30] Ibid., p. 93.

[31] Ibid., p. 94.

[32] The biographer was, as it happens, my own father, R.C.D. Jasper.

[33] R.C.D. Jasper, *George Bell, Bishop of Chichester* (Oxford: Oxford University Press, 1967), p. 279.

again in our time. Detweiler, on the other hand, begins with the critics, a harsher and less creative voice and a bleak place to start: 'Critics of twentieth-century literature and its poetics such as Patricia Waugh and Brian McHale distinguish between modernist and postmodernist on the basis of epistemology and ontology.'[34] (I cannot help thinking back to the resounding insults flung between Estragon and Vladimir in Samuel Beckett's *Waiting for Godot*, 'Curate! Cretin! Crritic!'.[35]) Thus we are held – in suspension between epistemology and ontology – that is between 'modes of knowing and being exercised in modes of revelation and destruction'.[36] The keynotes are provided by Derrida (*trace*)[37] and Baudrillard (*simulacrum*), and they are both in their different ways here sad and lonely, speaking in Detweiler of unreality and absence – inscriptions, perhaps, but cold comfort for what may once have been, possibly, a real presence. And so we move from poetry to contemporary fiction, Detweiler's preferred milieu.

I find it hard now to write about Detweiler's work. He was a close friend and an incomparably warm and generous human being, and yet there is a thinness now about his writing and his literary preferences, often works of genuine creativity that somehow celebrate nothing, indeterminate in their readings, perhaps in the end too honest, giving us too much to carry and to bear. They evidence a mixture of sexuality and violence, written at too many removes, with too many sleights of hand – as at the critical, almost cynical end of the last novel he refers to, Margaret Atwood's *The Handmaid's Tale* (1986) as Professor Pieixoto's speech examining the question of the validity of Offred's narrative concludes with the question to his academic audience, 'Are there any questions?'[38] What, then, is the nature of the community of readers who meet in these texts, and in what sense can the reading of them be understood as 'religious', an engagement in gestures of friendship with each other across the erotic space of the text? Of *The Handmaid's Tale* and Russell Hoban's *Riddley Walker* (1980), Robert writes:

> Although these fictions of cataclysmic waste are, in part, less postmodernistically experimental and thus, superficially, more realistic, they turn out to be as elusive as those employing intertextual overkill. These, too, by demonstrating how simulation finally only simulates itself, leave us endlessly reflected and reflective. But whereas according to Baudrillard such hypperreality should implode into a dense nothing, these novels show instead a vast messiness. Nothingness is revealed, but not as a tidy abstraction. It translates into chaos, which translates into waste.[39]

---

34   Detweiler, 'Apocalyptic Fiction and the End(s) of Realism', p. 155.

35   Samuel Beckett, *Waiting for Godot*, 2nd edn (London: Faber, 1965), p. 75.

36   Detweiler, 'Apocalyptic Fiction and End(s) of Realism', p. 156.

37   See in a more positive sense, above p. 80.

38   Margaret Atwood, *The Handmaid's Tale* (London: Virago, 1987), p. 324.

39   Ibid., p. 181. We might compare Rowan Williams' more recent, and much more up-beat, reading of *Riddley Walker* in his Gifford Lectures, *The Edge of Words: God and*

There can be here no revealed religion in what is a final return to the beginning, Genesis 1:1 – the chaos and waste that can only wait for the creative word of God to speak order into being. What future can there be for a conference on religion and literature that ends with the unthinkable, that which is without words?

We had reached here, it seems to me, a new sense of apocalypse. If Christianity, as poets and theologians from Blake to Altizer have shown us anew, is at its very heart, indeed, an apocalyptic religion, then this was clearly not it. This was rather a dark and unfathomable abyss that Derrida's bleak sense of a trace *aufgehoben* – in a perpetual suspension – could do little to lift us from.[40] Returning again to Detweiler's writings some 20 years on has been difficult. He was a man of great learning and devoted to life, and, I think, wanted to be a person of faith. I co-edited with Mark Ledbetter his festschrift volume, entitled *In Good Company* (1994),[41] and in the 'Conversation' with Sharon Greene published there Robert made clear his high sense of the nature of the university as a place of humanity and proper sociability. For him, in many ways, it replaced the Church in its vocation in a kind of twentieth century version of Coleridge's 'clerisy'. But he admitted, with typical wry humour, that he had been working in universities for almost four decades and the world, far from being better, was a worse place than when he had begun, and he took it as a personal insult! One rather knows what he means. Detweiler had a profound sense of the sacred – within the sense of place, the sense of the body, and the capacity of the human mind. But I think, finally, and in spite of his attempt to create a real sense of reading religiously, he missed the theological and hermeneutical tone that was at once and at the same time an articulation and a sacramental reality within the corporate body. His literary preferences, therefore, moved from the almost desperate to the despairing – stories told 'against the End'.

Detweiler concludes his book *Breaking the Fall* with a chapter that refers back to the tales of Scheherazade. It opens with words from Francesco Alberoni's *Falling in Love*: '… a mutilated, incomplete self, composed of nostalgia and a sense of guilt'.[42] The chapter proposes to develop the discussion of community, or communities in works of fiction that 'function in "postchirographic" societies

---

the Habits of Language (London: Bloomsbury, 2014), pp. 140–2. I am less than persuaded by this.

[40] Jacques Derrida, 'No, Apocalypse, Not Now (full speed ahead, seven missiles, seven missives)', *Diacritics*, vol. 14/2 (1984), 20–31.

[41] The phrase was taken from the poet Cecil Day Lewis' poem *The Magnetic Mountain*. 'Then I'll hit the trail for that promising land; May catch up with Wystan and Rex, my friend, Go mad in good company, find a good country, Make a clean sweep, or make a clean end.' The references are, of course to W.H. Auden (Wystan) and Rex Warner, the classicist and novelist, best remembered for his novel *The Aerodrome* (1941).

[42] Francesco Alberoni, *Falling in Love*, trans. Lawrence Venuti (New York: Random House, 1983), p. 94.

and depend crucially on religious ritual that is at least in part reinforced by spurious theology'. Theology, in such dystopic fiction has become a negative force, perpetrated only by narrators who 'tell corrective stories that constitute much of the narratives' substance'.[43] Such stories become mere stays against execution, theology, meanwhile, hardened into repressive and moribund dogmas that have little continuity with the living past within which living doctrines may develop. Indeed, religion itself here is a deathly element in the community instead of its necessary and living heart: finally, in the endless retelling of stories, this is the utter separation of literature and theology which stand henceforth over against each other as enemies.

At the end of his book Detweiler returns us to Mikhail Bakhtin and the carnivalesque world of Rabelais via the conclusion of Paul Ricoeur's *Time and Narrative*. Ricoeur writes of the 'distance of fiction' that is:

> the representation of a reality in full transformation, the painting of incomplete personalities, and the reference to a present held in suspense, 'without any conclusion' – all this requires a more rigorous formal discipline on the part of the creator of tales than on the part of the storyteller of a heroic world that carries with it its own internal completion.[44]

Ricoeur is, of course, thinking back to Bakhtin's distinction between the epic and the novel. But perhaps we are in danger here of forgetting the ultimately heroic world and the 'grand narrative' of Christianity that develops, for us, through its doctrines, however hardly won. Milton knew this, and even Blake knew that in apocalyptic Christianity there is, finally, an internal completion, though always anticipated, yet acknowledged and believed in. In such a tradition, with its careful rituals and liturgy, there is no creation of tales as mere stays against confusion or daily dissolution. In the end, perhaps even Heidegger is not enough and he becomes yet another over-shadowing, another grey banality in his refusal to change. The community of religious reading, in Detweiler's terms, has finally never quite grown into maturity, has never truly acknowledged, with full seriousness, the dark and unspeakable shadow of evil that halts all utterance but from which the poet alone must speak and the theologian follow in a voice known only to later ages.

This has been a desperate chapter to write. I want to believe that Robert Detweiler was teaching us a way forward in the final decade of the twentieth century. After his stroke in 1995 he wrote more deeply on the subject of irony

---

[43]   Detweiler, *Breaking the Fall*, p. 160.
[44]   Paul Ricoeur, *Time and Narrative*, trans. Kathleen McLaughlin and David Pellauer (Chicago, IL: Chicago University Press, 1985), vol. 2, p. 156. See also Mikhail Bakhtin, *Rabelais and His World*, trans. Hélène Iswolsky (Bloomington, IN: Indiana University Press, 1984).

and, for the first time in a new reprint of *Breaking the Fall*, of prayer, which yet, it seems, has only Heidegger and not the ecclesial community of the ages to fall back on. 'The story of life [Bob writes] is that death constantly negates our hopes and expectations. These hopes we have come to take for granted, so that we are encouraged to nurture faith in the face of negative situations.'[45] I am not sure that I recognize this sense of hope as that which has come to be taken for granted. It is not taken for granted in St Paul – and hope is only truly meaningful in the face of hopelessness. It is only powerful when it becomes, seemingly, an impossibility. The faith and hope which remain alive against all possibility are the very ground of a form of language which the true poet knows and theology, in its deepest recesses and most careful, painful articulations, gently sustains.

If prayer, for Detweiler, is that 'conversation with God in which the prayee can pour out one's heart, can empty oneself',[46] then it is possible only because God has already emptied himself out in Christ and faced the dark pit of hell itself with something like *Gelassenheit*. Such profound Christocentricity is found in the works of Blake and Milton, and hinted at in the hermeneutical recoveries of Coleridge and Schleiermacher – the dark, hidden centres of our early conferences that were now dissolving into something finally more sadly pathetic rather than tragic, an apocalypse from which there was no resurrection and a tone born out of a world of ruins.

---

45 Detweiler, *Breaking the Fall*, p. ix.
46 Ibid.

Chapter 7
Returning to Theology: Nijmegen, 2000

> With hands outstretched towards the old places, with sorrowing hearts, – with
> hearts which still love the old teachings which the mind will no longer accept, –
> we, too, cut our ropes, and go out in our little boats, and search for a land that will
> be new to us, though how far new, – new in how many things, we do not know.
> Who would not stay behind if it were possible to him?[1]

Times were changing for the conferences on literature and theology. They were growing and becoming less domestic. In 2000 the conference, by now under the auspices of the International Society for Religion, Literature and Culture, met in the Dutch University of Nijmegen, within the interdisciplinary Heyendaal Institute for Theology, Science and Culture, and under the watchful eye of Eric Borgman. It proved to be a meeting that, in a way, recovered some of the original theological, intellectual and indeed spiritual energies of the earliest conferences, perhaps a sign of hope for the new millennium, although I doubt that the indicators which it suggested to us have been properly recognized, acknowledged or built upon in the 15 years since then.

One of the key issues raised at this conference was described by one of the participants (a faithful attendee at our meetings), the feminist philosopher Pamela Sue Anderson of the University of Oxford, as the 'ethics of memory' within which is to be sought an ethics of forgiveness (the old theme going back to Ulrich Simon and the first conference),[2] but specifically, for Anderson, a feminist ethics of forgiveness.[3] Insistent within these themes of memory and forgiveness remains the haunting, inescapable horror of the two great wars of the twentieth century, whose shadow is cast over almost every page of the present book. In another, almost contemporary essay, Anderson writes:

> Storytelling is a significant form of memory; it shapes remembering. However,
> early in the twentieth century Walter Benjamin expressed regret for the loss of our
> ability to tell or write stories about our lives. Benjamin experienced the shattering

---

[1]   Anthony Trollope, *Clergymen of the Church of England* 1866 (Leicester: Leicester University Press, 1974), pp. 128–9.

[2]   See also below, Chapter 8, pp. 112–14.

[3]   Pamela Sue Anderson, 'Ethics and Hermeneutics: A Question of Memory', in Erik Borgman, Bart Philipsen and Lea Verstricht (eds), *Literary Canons and Religious Identity* (Aldershot: Ashgate, 2004), pp. 79–96.

of European memory in the two world wars, when the moral and political agreements, or mutual promises which had shaped the Western Enlightenment were tragically broken down. My essay builds critically on this profound sense of loss and presents a reconsideration of three acts of memory: promising, forgiving, and yearning.[4]

This loss, and with it the failure of any theology of forgiveness, and its undermining of those elements in human life which are at the heart of both literature and theology – narrative and remembering – gives rise to that form of disillusionment or disenchantment which we broadly call postmodernism. This is nothing less than what David E. Klemm, another faithful companion of the conferences, has called 'the shattering of an age' which has its origins in the trauma such as was felt when Karl Barth read the names of his professors of theology on the petition supporting the war policy of Kaiser Wilhelm II, and wrote, 'For me, at least, nineteenth century theology no longer held any future.'[5]

In this is expressed the paradox of my central argument. From the beginning, in our conferences on literature and theology in the early 1980s, we found the way back to theology barred, and yet there was no other way: the very impossibility of the theological task took us back to our very roots, yet with no illusions. This impossibility is well expressed by David Klemm inasmuch as 'the postmodern world picture is neither the image of the sacred cosmos nor the loss of that image. It is rather the image that there is no image of the whole of things'.[6] And it was with this formless despair that we returned to the space of literature with a sense that Maurice Blanchot so acutely attributes to Kafka, whose passion was literary but not just purely literary, yet its expression is within the conflict between a literature that is felt to be a means to an end though it never consents to become only a means: I mean his concern with the matter of salvation and the capacity of literature itself to open a path to salvation, even if that is felt, finally, to be hopeless.[7] I am perhaps here becoming too personal when I admit to finding myself drawn with Blanchot to the sense of the spiritual which, in Kevin Hart's words in his book *The Dark Gaze* (2004), 'restores the category of

---

4   Pamela Sue Anderson, 'An Ethics of Memory: Promising, Forgiving, Yearning', in Graham Ward (ed.), *The Blackwell Companion to Postmodern Theology* (Oxford: Blackwell, 2001), p. 233.

5   David E. Klemm, Introduction to *Hermeneutical Enquiry*, vol. 1: *The Interpretation of Texts* (Atlanta, GA: Scholars Press, 1986), p. 19. For the link between Barth and post-modernity, see also Graham Ward, *Barth, Derrida and the Language of Theology* (Cambridge: Cambridge University Press, 1995).

6   Klemm, Introduction to *Hermeneutical Enquiry*, vol. 1, p. 22.

7   Maurice Blanchot, 'Kafka and the Work's Demand', in *The Space of Literature*, trans. Ann Smock (Lincoln, NE: University of Nebraska Press, 1982), p. 57, and see above, p. 79.

the sacred in the very gesture in which the possibility of faith in God is rejected',[8] a spirituality which would be, this time in Blanchot's own words as recorded by his friend Georges Bataille, a 'contestation of itself and non-knowledge [*non-savoir*]'.[9] With Blanchot I return, above all, to Meister Eckhart for whom such non-knowledge affirms nothing less than the impossible. But I am getting ahead of myself, into deep and dark waters that challenge the sense. And our present way, by an unlikely route enough, is one in which we will find ourselves finally back in the continuities of the literature and theology of the nineteenth century.

Before we return to the Nijmegen conference of 2000 we need to admit that our project in literature and theology began to offer, so it seemed, a recovery of the theological through an engagement with texts and reading, and yet this promise has never been fully realized, perhaps through a loss of nerve, or maybe because the task was finally simply beyond us, intellectually, spiritually and even, it may be, ecclesiologically. In this chapter, and again at the conclusion of the book (Chapter 15), I will briefly indicate our differences from, and therefore why most of us never espoused, the theological project of Radical Orthodoxy in England, or the broader and often contradictory claims of various post-modern theologies or a-theologies. Had we stuck to our task things might now have been different, but we did not. Yet, in 2000 in Nijmegen, for a moment or two, things seemed to me to be possible. Somehow, though in a different way, we were back on track and picking up the theological threads from the first Durham conferences.

The key voice in Nijmegen was the formidable Dutch professor of the Theory of Literature, Mieke Bal. Bal admits that she is not religious, and does not even really comprehend what 'religion', broadly understood, might be. Yet she acknowledges that religion cannot be avoided or neglected, though literature, and its broad, undefined canon, necessarily destabilizes any possible and particular religious identity precisely through the proposing of a literary identity which 'is connected to representation as a form of *incarnation* or embodiment', and such identity 'infuses' the canons of religion in various ways.[10] Bal is never afraid to confront the enemy on his own ground. But having established this incarnational tendency in literature, at the same time she calls upon it to face up to its own tendency to *ethical indifference*, much of it born of a gender bias that awaits the attention of a feminist critique. The contest is fought out within the space of literature and the struggle towards 'ethical non-indifference' that

---

8   Kevin Hart, *The Dark Gaze: Maurice Blanchot and the Sacred* (Chicago, IL: University of Chicago Press, 2004), p. 223.

9   Georges Bataille, *Inner Experience*, trans. Leslie Anne Boldt (Albany, NY: State University of New York Press, 1988), p. 102. Quoted in Hart, *The Dark Gaze*, p. 223.

10   Mieke Bal, 'Religious Canon and Literary Identity', in Erik Borgman, Bart Philipsen and Lea Verstricht (eds), *Literary Canons and Religious Identity*, p. 11.

can be achieved only through close attention to and detailed conversation with the text. Bal offers a close reading of the narrative of Joseph and Potiphar's wife as retold by Thomas Mann in his great biblical tetralogy of novels *Joseph and His Brothers* (1933–42) – a reading that is sensitive at once to both the presences and absences in the text, and finally to the 'body' which becomes, paradoxically, Bal suggests, actually an 'unexamined term' within Christianity. Proceeding from Mann to the body in the history of *Pietà* imagery, Bal recovers the task and the necessity of mourning as a reckoning with the dead, a recovery she shares with Jacques Derrida in *The Politics of Friendship* (1994) and *The Work of Mourning* (2001).

According to Bal, in the interplay between religious and literary canons, the former with their 'oppressive power in that they police boundaries',[11] close attention to the looser and changeable canon of literature begins to break down the barrier between them, allowing new freedoms to the religious canon in the play of the literary that lies within it. Yet this only happens within the act of reading and then the almost impossible task of re-reading the religious canon. But then, as Bal suggests: 'This gesture opens up the tight boundaries that separate and thus protect from each other the distinct domains of religion and literature on the level not of their texts or their functions, but of their *readings*.'[12] And it is in this task and art of reading that the work of mourning for the past, for dead friends, for the irrecoverable which is beyond ready forgiveness or reconciliation (like the lost person whose fate remains unknown) that we might begin again to reconstruct a possibility of salvation and a living theology. Reading and the landscape of literature thus comes to resemble, to return to Proust and the *Remembrance of Things Past* (which has haunted so much of this present book), 'a huge cemetery in which on the majority of the tombs the names are effaced and can no longer be read'.[13] Yet in reading and in the sometimes painful acts of deciphering and interpretation, in the words of the Editors' Introduction to Derrida's *The Work of Mourning*, 'some of the names are nonetheless still legible because of these acts of mourning and friendship, even if these names mask or refer to others that have long been obscured'.[14] Such reading might become, in Bob Detweiler's terms, an act of reading religiously as we stretch out to one another and to the past 'in gestures of friendship with each other across the erotic space of the text'.[15]

---

[11] Ibid., p. 22.

[12] Ibid.

[13] Marcel Proust, *Remembrance of Things Past*, trans. C.K. Scott Moncrieff, Terence Kilmartin and Andreas Mayor (New York: Random House, 1981), vol. 3, p. 940.

[14] Pascale-Anne Brault and Michael Naas, Introduction to Jacques Derrida, *The Work of Mourning* (Chicago, IL: University of Chicago Press, 2001), p. 4.

[15] Robert Detweiler, *Breaking the Fall: Religious Readings of Contemporary Fiction* (Louisville, KY: WJK Press, 1995), pp. 34–5. See also above, p. 91.

In its recovery of the body, a body that is lost and yet somehow found again, impossibly, in a resurrection of reading, we sense a sacramental presence, even if unwillingly admitted, in acts of reading literature wherein forgiveness might become possible as the ideological is gradually fragmented into the necessary particularity which each body demands.[16] We return, inevitably and always, to the haunting presence of the Holocaust and the feminist readings in the work of Thomas Mann and the Bible of Mieke Bal. In her book *Reading Rembrandt* (1991), Bal writes:

> While Nazism, with its neurotic ideology of maleness, was beginning to make the limits between groups of subjects so absolute as to become those between life and death, the ambivalence, both sexual and ethnic, of the encounter between two ambivalent subjects became an acutely necessary alternative, an opportunity to dramatise the intensity of emotional community.[17]

It is this necessary alternative, which leads us back, whether we like it or not, to something like a kind of ecclesial community wherein might reside the hidden, unverifiable presence of a literary identity which, so the story goes, sustained the victims of the death camps in their silent recitation of poetry.[18] It was in this hidden, remembered literature, recited in the face of unimaginable suffering and evil, that life might yet be found, identified and pursued. And unknown even to ourselves, we who are on the outside of the death camp walls, begin to read between the lines as a form of prayer. As the Christian Russian poet Irina Ratushinskaya wrote from her solitary prison cell in Mordovia to her husband in a poem scratched on a tiny scrap of paper that has miraculously survived:

> I know it won't be received
> Or sent. The page will be
> In shreds as soon as I have scribbled it.
> Later. Sometime. You've grown used to it,
> Reading between the lines that never reached you,
> Understanding everything.[19]

---

[16]   It is such mazy meditations that led me, much later, to edit, alongside colleagues in the University of Glasgow (Ramona Fotiade and Olivier Salazar-Ferrer), a book of essays on the body in text within the work of J.-L. Nancy, Michel Henry, J.-L. Marion and others, entitled *Embodiment: Phenomenological, Religious and Deconstructive Views on Living and Dying* (Farnham: Ashgate, 2014).

[17]   Mieke Bal, *Reading Rembrandt: Beyond the Word-Image Opposition* (Cambridge: Cambridge University Press, 1991), p. 117.

[18]   Bal, 'Religious Canon and Literary Identity', p. 27, quoting also J.H. de Roder, *Het schandaal van de poëzie: Over taal, ritueel, en biologie* (Nijmegen: Vantilt/De Wintertuin, 2000).

[19]   Irina Ratushinskaya, *Pencil Letter* (Newcastle-upon-Tyne: Bloodaxe Books, 1988), p. 13.

Words are hard to erase. Men and women, faced with what Bal calls 'semiotic incapacitation', the incapacity to frame identity into a meaningful coherence, and physical death in the camps, instead found such literary identity as literally a matter of life and death. Ulrich Simon would have known exactly what Bal meant, though he might have expressed it in other ways. And it was what Elisabeth Jay, in her lecture in Nijmegen in 2000, was reconstructing through reading and through literary identity – nothing less than a theology of salvation. Elisabeth reminded her audience of a question that I myself had asked her once at a conference some years before, oddly, in the University of Durham, as it happens. (I had forgotten the occasion myself.)

> A couple of years ago David Jasper, responding to a lecture I was giving, asked whether I was in the process of developing a new theology of salvation through reading. At the time I was taken aback by this question. Two years later, I think I would agree with him that this is precisely what I am engaged in: though I would want to qualify his phrase by suggesting that it is by reading in, with and across the communities we inhabit that we may find a route to salvation.[20]

I began this chapter with an acknowledgement of the sense of theological *discontinuity*, after Karl Barth, that we experienced in the twentieth century, later the postmodern recognition after Walter Benjamin and others of the 'shattering of European memory in the two world wars',[21] and yet also Kafka's hopeless literary obsession with salvation, and now we have come back to this theme. Lis Jay refers us back to an article of her colleague in Oxford, Valentine Cunningham in the journal *Literature and Theology*, which insists that there is only one reading of the Bible and that is the contemporary one, which 'occurs at the intersection of perpetually shifting canons'.[22] We are back to the issue of canons again. But, asks Jay, 'have we so lost touch with the roots of our religious identity that the project is in danger of becoming pointless?'[23] The tradition and the memory of the past continues to be insistent, and we are back also with the matter of identity, religious identity or, as Bal would have us think, literary identity – that which saved, perhaps, the inmates of the camps who were 'denied access to frames, including, importantly, those frames that shape canons'.[24] Literary identity is closely linked to religious identity and it is finally

---

[20]   Elisabeth Jay, 'Why "Remember Lot's Wife"? Religious Identity and the Literary Canon', in Erik Borgman, Bart Philipsen and Lea Verstricht (eds), *Literary Canons and Religious Identity*, p. 46.

[21]   Anderson, 'An Ethics of Memory', p. 233.

[22]   Valentine Cunningham, 'The Best Stories in the Best Order? Canons, Apocryphas and (Post)modern Reading', *Literature and Theology*, vol. 14, no. 1 (2000), 69.

[23]   Jay, 'Why "Remember Lot's Wife"', p. 34.

[24]   Bal, 'Religious Canon and Literary Identity', p. 28.

the former that grants a space for readings of the Bible, and of other texts, that are, perhaps, capable of overcoming the shattering of religious memory, the loss of faith, and its particular narratives, and continue even and perhaps especially in the counter-coherences of readings in the lives of communities that, as the Holocaust indicates, can be extraordinarily tenacious in the face of the darkest pain and evil.

I am reminded that the community of our earlier conferences was extremely diverse and included many who were outside the walls of the academic world, which is always, as Jay reminds us, 'in danger of creating a Levitic priestly élite with its own exclusive vocabulary and sense of identity'.[25] And any such élite or 'self-appointed Levitic cohort', whether it be in the Church or in the university, must sooner or later face the question posed by John Henry Newman in 1833: in what, then, does your authority lie?[26] Churches and their theologies, academies and their theories, may have their day, but memory persists within the darkness of the tragedy (with its heroism and compassion) even of our unrightable personal pasts[27] such as haunt the ageing Thomas Hardy in the *Poems of 1912–13*, or linger in the dying lament of the abandoned Dido in Purcell's *Dido and Aeneas* (1689). Within the memory of the reader, Jay concludes:

> Dido ... becomes the progenitor of those alternative heroines like Bertha Mason, stigmatised as antisocial, etching their memory by way of a flaming pyre upon the mind of a departing hero, now bent on following the mores and religious identity of a society busy reinventing itself. It is Dido's dying lament that dominates the opera, refusing to be smoothed away or tidied up in a celebration of history's heroes.[28]

Memory, then, can be counter-cultural, standing over against a diminished and diminishing world and in spite of all.

I would need to distinguish these tentative remarks, both intellectually and spiritually from other theological 'projects' of the time, though a number of people like Graham Ward may be associated both with the history of the conferences and the project known as Radical Orthodoxy. First of all, the theological framework known as Radical Orthodoxy is quite different in spirit from our enterprise inasmuch as 'in the face of the secular demise of truth, it

---

25   Jay, 'Why "Remember Lot's Wife"?', p. 35.

26   J.H. Newman, *Thoughts on the Ministerial Commission, Respectfully Addressed to the Clergy* (London: J.G. and F. Rivington, 1833), quoted in Jay, p. 35.

27   The phrase is Jay, 'Why "Remember Lot's Wife", p. 40.

28   Ibid., p. 40. At the outset of her lecture, Jay played us a recording of Dido's Lament from Purcell's opera. It was a haunting experience.

seeks to reconfigure theology'.[29] In one sense I am offering nothing as substantial as this, less scholastic, perhaps more radical, in a way, certainly less 'orthodox' yet finally more sustaining of religious continuities. Radical Orthodoxy has a quite different sense of the present times, and also a sense of theology that is finally rooted much more deeply in a tradition that refuses to acknowledge the disruptions of the Enlightenment and its tragic consequences in the twentieth century. Newman and the nineteenth century were nothing if not heirs of the Enlightenment, and therefore prepared us for the dislocations of modernity and postmodernity that radical orthodoxy refuses, finally, to acknowledge. As Don Cupitt has put it, writing of John Milbank, perhaps the most public figure among the Radical Orthodox theologians:

> in Milbank's own scheme of thought, nihilism is regarded as a very bad thing. Only theology (and an eclectic sort of catholicized neo-Calvinism at that) can deliver us from it. To speak more plainly, only God can conquer the Nihil at which Western thought has arrived. *Fiat lux*, say God: 'Let there be light.' So God will reinstate the old discriminations, and bring back the good old days.[30]

But actually it is only by entering into the Nihil, by refusing this sense of the secular in the face of the theological, by being prepared utterly to lose God, in Meister Eckhart's words, by taking leave of God for God's sake, that we can begin to trace deeper coherences in a politics of incoherence and counter-coherence. Even the varieties of the postmodern God seem too insistent, too burdened still with metaphysical possibilities and traces of a past that was simply inconceivable and too ready to be reconstructed, too *priestly*. Postmodern theologies, by and large, at once go too far and not far enough, generally too careless of the community and its ecclesiology, perhaps still tainted with the vestiges of utopianism.

And the word made strange in John Milbank's vocabulary, which is anything but postmodern, has yet to remain familiar in the insistencies of reading. I have repeatedly in this book gone back to our own roots in Cardinal Newman and the Oxford Movement, and it is there that we can find both the literary and the theological foundations that sustain continuity in discontinuity and the theological in traditions of reading and the imagination that requires and provides a model for the urgent task of theology and literature. It is theology, that is the insistent call, together with an insistent sense of poetry, that offer together possibilities that go beyond, in their toughness and promise, the liberal

---

29   John Milbank, Graham Ward and Catherine Pickstock, Introduction to *Radical Orthodoxy: A New Theology* (London: Routledge, 1999), p. 1. See also below, chapter 15, on Radical Orthodoxy.

30   Don Cupitt, 'Anti-Discrimination', in Graham Ward (ed.), *The Blackwell Companion to Postmodern Theology* (Oxford: Blackwell, 2001), p. 486.

arguments for religion to be found in many of the writings of our American colleagues at the time such as Nathan A. Scott Jr. Scott, in what I think was his last completed book, *The Poetics of Belief* (1985). Scott rightly takes us back to the tradition of S.T. Coleridge but reads him far too constructively and immediately in the process of the formation of belief. Newman, as ever, concedes the central importance of Coleridge and the Romantic tradition, but precisely *because* Coleridge, to Newman, was also intolerable, acknowledges, thereby, both the necessity and the impossibility of theology. Of Coleridge Newman wrote in his *Apologia*, as I have had occasion to note earlier:

> While history in prose and verse was thus made the instrument of Church feelings and opinions, a philosophical basis for the same was laid in England by a very original thinker, who, while he indulged a liberty of speculation, which no Christian can tolerate, and advocated conclusions which were often heathen rather than Christian, yet after all installed a higher philosophy into inquiring minds, than they had hitherto been accustomed to accept. In this way he made trial of his age, and succeeded in interesting its genius in the cause of Catholic truth.[31]

For Newman there was an insistent and deep symbiosis between the Church and poetry:

> Her [the Church's] very being is poetry; every psalm, every petition, every collect, every versicle, the cross, the mitre, the thurible, is a fulfillment of some dream of childhood, or aspiration of youth. Such poets as are born under her shadow, she takes into her service; she sets them to write hymns, or to compose chants, or to embellish shrines, or to determine ceremonies, or to marshal processions; nay, she can even make schoolmen of them, as she made St Thomas, till logic becomes poetical.[32]

But Newman, the Catholic churchman, is ultimately deriving this from Coleridge and the fiduciary sense of language, which perceives within the very form of the words themselves the impulse of theology. Thus it is in the very act of reading that one embarks again and again on a theology of salvation, taken in finally, for Newman to the profound continuities of the Church. Such a sense of theology not only tolerates but insists upon the complexity of contested interpretations and open-ended conversations whereby alone 'the internal flux

---

[31] John Henry Newman, *Apologia Pro Vita Sua* [1864], ed. Ian Ker (Harmondsworth: Penguin, 1994), pp. 99–100.

[32] J.H. Newman, *Essays Critical and Historical*, 3rd edn, 2 vols (London: Basil Montagu Pickering, 1873), vol. 2, p. 243. See also Geoffrey Rowell, 'Europe and the Oxford Movement', in Stewart J. Brown and Peter B. Nockles (eds), *The Oxford Movement: Europe and the Wider World, 1830–1930* (Cambridge: Cambridge University Press, 2012), p. 155.

of death and procreation at work in the Old Testament narrative' is prevented from collapsing 'into a simpler dichotomy of death and resurrection'.[33] Yngve Brilioth in his classic work on the Oxford Movement, *The Anglican Revival* (2nd edn, 1933) correctly finds its roots in the literary currents of the age and the Romantic Movement, but profoundly underestimates the deep and complex *literariness* of the theological processes most evident in the work of Newman up to, and culminating in the *Grammar of Assent* (1870), but also in his own poetry, above all *The Dream of Gerontius* (1865) with its roots in Dante and Christian eschatology.[34]

But how can this take us back to Mieke Bal in Nijmegen in 2000? In *The Idea of a University* (1873) Newman does not avoid acknowledging, with ironic insight, even in his own day, the plight of theology in the university in an age of scepticism.[35] Nor is he unaware that theology in the university must take its place within the fields of critical discourses that comprise the lush growth of knowledge and humanistic learning. It has no peculiar privileges or protections. And it is only through reading and profound engagement with texts within the literary canon that identity can begin to become religious identity. It cannot be imposed or commanded, nor can it be taken for granted – but its deep continuities must be endlessly rediscovered in the exchanges with the text that are involved in close, insistent reading. It was Coleridge who struggled with Christian theology as it encountered the inescapable demands of Enlightenment criticism,[36] never avoiding the critical issues but rooted in the deeps of poetic language and their sustaining spirit.

It was this sustaining spirit that flickered again for a moment in Nijmegen in 2000. It shone through the darkest of theological failures and false claims to coherence. It was kept alight in the close readings of literary texts and in the haunted phrase 'Remember me' of Dido, words that are a memorial to those whom history and its religious continuances have forgotten, or else have chosen to forget. This is a spirit that cannot be imposed but must be realized and nurtured with liturgical patience, with endless repetitions and stories that do not frame but enable us to live again with compassion and hope. It is nothing less than a theology of salvation. Perhaps our universities have indeed now become, in Lis Jay's term, too Levitic and élitist, speaking a language that is not

---

[33]   Jay, 'Why "Remember Lot's Wife"?', p. 44.

[34]   See further, Michael Wheeler, *Death and the Future Life in Victorian Literature and Theology* (Cambridge: Cambridge University Press, 1990), pp. 305–39.

[35]   See further, Gerard Loughlin, 'Theology in the University', in Ian Ker and Terrence Merrigan (eds), *The Cambridge Companion to John Henry Newman* (Cambridge: Cambridge University Press, 2009), p. 227.

[36]   See Elinor Shaffer, *'Kubla Khan' and* The Fall of Jerusalem: *The Mythological School in Biblical Criticism and Secular Literature, 1770–1880* (Cambridge: Cambridge University Press, 1975), p. 32.

merely technical, but, it might seem, designed to exclude the common man or woman. While the Church has fallen back into moribund hierarchies, Newman was celebrated for a brief moment in the Second Vatican Council in the middle years of the twentieth century, but forgotten all too quickly, and is now again largely unread as a writer of literature.

In Nijmegen we returned to the Bible, forgetting the obvious questions related to its, at least, partial status 'as literature', but reading it in its oddities and incoherences before they became ironed out by the simplifying demands of the theology of the tradition and the Church. Elisabeth Jay addresses this process of transformation that takes place from the enigmatic figure of Lot's wife in Genesis 19:26 ('But Lot's wife, behind him, looked back, and she became a pillar of salt.') to her becoming a 'monument of an unbelieving soul.' (Wisdom of Solomon 10:6–7). It is in the daring to be caught again in that shift and transformation, as in Job, between the impossibility of ever making sense of the story and its causalities, and yet the need to trust God and believe that there *is* a story of which we are a meaningful part. Our task can only be to go on reading in faith, caught in this caesura between enigma and monument, without forgetting those who have gone before, and in the spirit of forgiveness.

This could never constitute a radical *orthodoxy*, but it might be in the form of theological reflection within a religious humanism that is directed towards the future, yet with a sense of the past, a proper sense of mourning, and with realism and in hope. In the Preface to the volume of essays published after the second conference in 1984 entitled *The Interpretation of Belief* (1986), as I noted in Chapter 5,[37] I drew particular attention to Caspar David Friedrich's painting of 1808, *The Cross on the Mountains*. I suggested that it presented a series of contrasts or ambivalences not as a statement of the sacred but caught in the contrast made in the intersections of the Cross with the fading light, the earth and sky – Christ in this intersection as intercessor between earth and heaven.[38] I did not attempt to explain more. In these contrasts and intersections we remain and only there, where it is already in the process of disintegration, and with the closest attention, can theology begin again.

---

[37] See above, pp. 73, 83.

[38] David Jasper, *The Interpretation of Belief: Coleridge, Schleiermacher and Romanticism* (London: Macmillan, 1986), p. vii.

Chapter 8

Seeking Forgiveness and Retrieving a Theological Sense of Being Human: Leuven, 2014

Vladimir: We'll hang ourselves tomorrow. (Pause.) Unless Godot comes.
Estragon: And if he comes?
Vladimir: We'll be saved.[1]

This, the last chapter of this part of the book, represents a kind of summing up of all that has gone before. It began life as my own lecture to the most recent of the literature and theology conferences which took place in the University of Leuven in 2014. For me, and for one or two others, that conference was a revisiting of the spirit of Durham in 1982, an occasion haunted by many figures now gone and an attempt to recover the seriousness of their concerns for theology after the twentieth century. For this reason I have omitted reference to the meetings that took place between 2000 and 2014, at which I was (with one exception) present, though I took relatively little part in them.

The shadow of war hung over our first meetings. And so where better now, in the year that saw the centenary of the outbreak of the First World War, to begin my story again than with Proust, a year before the beginning of that terrible conflict, reading in bed in 1913? 'I had been thinking all the time, while I was asleep, of what I had just been reading, but my thoughts had run into a channel of their own, until I myself seemed actually to have become the subject of my book.'[2] In the years since 1982 I had thought so long upon the issues opened up there, that I could no longer separate them from myself. And the reasons for addressing those issues continue to unsettle and perplex me. In a sense the subject was myself, and it is now so long ago and so much a part of me that I am not now sure how much of what I remember is just a story, my story, and something I have made up. But, as Isak Dinesen once said, 'All sorrows can be

---

[1]   Samuel Beckett, *Waiting for Godot* (London: Faber and Faber, 1956), p. 94.
[2]   Marcel Proust, *Swann's Way*, Part One (1913), trans. C.K. Scott Moncrieff (London: Chatto & Windus, 1966), p. 1.

borne if you put them into a story or tell a story about them.'[3] And that is what I am doing.

It seems clear to me that these conferences were, I think, begun in great sorrow, though perhaps we were hardly aware of it ourselves, and the study of literature and theology has subsequently become less serious, certainly in its address to theological questions. How easy it is to forget. Ulrich Simon is now largely forgotten, with his brooding, complex presence, his memories of Auschwitz and his deep sense of tragedy in pity and terror. A year before the first Durham conference, in 1981, Simon had published an essay entitled 'Samson and the Heroic' which looks back to the earlier conflict of August 1914 in which, he wrote, the soldiers 'suffered a spiritual shock from which they could not recover again. There were no heroes, no bloody heroes, and if you wanted to be one you were a crazy idiot. Yet ... [the literature about the war] bears witness to the astounding deeds of self-sacrifice ... [and] without that brand of godly heroism a race is doomed.'[4] The literary critic and professor of English at the University of Sussex, Gabriel Josipovici, later dismissed Simon's words on heroism as 'the pious remarks of [a] theologian,' rousing stuff which is good for sermons but little else.[5] But we should not be too hasty and never forget that the Greek word 'hero' in Homer means originally no more than every human being who fought against Troy, and even more broadly, refers to any free-man of Greece of whom a story may be told, even those anonymous and unknown soldiers whom war robs of their identity and human dignity.

Above all, for Simon (and he was not alone), war can rob us of the capacity to forgive in the face of what Hannah Arendt called the 'sheer thoughtlessness' of evil.[6] In his book *A Theology of Auschwitz* (1967) the Christian priest and theologian, remembering his own father, writes of the camp guards that, for them there should be no pity or forgiveness, no salvation and the dark hymn is sung that they may never rise again.[7] Throughout the literature after the Second World War the same sad note is sounded again and again – forgiveness is impossible. Peter, the young boy abandoned at the end of the war on the railway station by his mother in Julia Franck's novel *The Blind Side of the Heart* (2007) asks: 'Did she by any chance want to ask him to forgive her? Was he supposed to forgive her? He couldn't forgive her, he'd never be able to do that. It wasn't

---

[3]   Quoted in Hannah Arendt, *The Human Condition*, 2nd edn, (Chicago, IL: Chicago University Press, 1998), p. 175.

[4]   Ulrich Simon, 'Samson and the Heroic', in Michael Wadsworth (ed.), *Ways of Reading the Bible* (Brighton: The Harvester Press, 1981), pp. 165, 166.

[5]   Gabriel Josipovici, *The Book of God: A Response to the Bible* (New Haven, CT: Yale University Press, 1988), p. 125.

[6]   Hannah Arendt, *Eichmann and the Holocaust* (Harmondsworth: Penguin, 2005).

[7]   Ulrich Simon, *A Theology of Auschwitz* (London: Victor Gollancz, 1967), p. 75. See above, p. 44, for the full quotation.

in his power; even if he had wanted to.'[8] And where forgiveness is impossible, theology necessarily falters and remains silent. We have reached here that rarity and deep mystery in human affairs which George Steiner once called 'absolute tragedy'. That was in an essay of the same title that was published in the journal *Literature and Theology* in 1990 in an issue which I myself edited with Terry Wright on tragedy and reflecting upon the tone of our meetings. Steiner writes there that 'an absolutely tragic model of the condition of men and women views these men and women as unwanted intruders on creation, as being destined to undergo unmerited, incomprehensible, arbitrary suffering and defeat. Original sin, be it Adamic or Promethean, is not a tragic category.'[9] Such absolute tragedy moves beyond the reach of theology and its articulations, though tragic drama is almost inseparable from religion. But we have met the dead silence of the absolutely tragic in our own time as during the Holocaust, the Gypsy or the Jew died simply for committing the crime of being. It was this silence that brooded over our first conference of 1982 and echoed even to the deliberations in 2014. We met to talk of theology and literature precisely because of the failure, even the impossibility, of theology, its silence in the face of absolute tragedy, and, as Simon himself wrote, 'the failure of theology has been and remains at the root of our enslavement'.[10] That is why we turned, and still turn, to literature. It is a serious matter.

Later, as we have already seen in Chapter 3,[11] Simon himself was to write a book on tragedy and Christianity entitled *Pity and Terror* (1989) in which he acknowledged that Christianity, in its preaching of the cross, has finally denied the tragic reality of the human condition. I suggested that the power of that book lies in its failure to achieve what it set out to do. There is, it would seem, no synthesis between Christian existence (and its theology) and tragic involvement. Theology remains, in the end, silent, arrested by the impossibility of forgiveness in the face of utter evil. Hannah Arendt has suggested, without apparent irony, that 'the discoverer of the role of forgiveness in the realm of human affairs was Jesus of Nazareth'.[12] But forgiveness implies change and progression, and how could this be enacted in the face of a logic of destruction that represented not a rupture with the values of Western religion and philosophy, as suggested by Emil Fackenheim, but on the other hand a deadly and immoveable continuity. As Richard Rubenstein has written, it was such continuity in the traditional

---

[8]   Julia Franck, *The Blind Side of the Heart*, trans. Anthea Bell (London: Vintage Books, 2010), p. 422.

[9]   George Steiner, 'A Note on Absolute Tragedy', *Literature and Theology*, vol. 4, no. 2 (July, 1990), 147.

[10]   Simon, *A Theology of Auschwitz*, p. 138.

[11]   See above, pp. 54–5.

[12]   Arendt, *The Human Condition*, p. 238.

Western Christian attitude towards the Jews that allowed mass extermination to be carried out while 'normal men and women' maintained clear consciences.[13]

The silence of such people is profound, and theology remains arrested. Speaking against the scribes and Pharisees, Jesus is clear that it is not only God who has the power to forgive but, in Arendt's words, the power of forgiveness 'must be mobilized by men towards each other before they can hope to be forgiven by God'.[14] Reconciliation, atonement, begins deep in the human condition, in the heroism of the human heart and its pity and compassion. And even as we grasp for the spirit of theological humanism, for the ability to put an end to something, to put it behind us, change the way things are and move on, we are yet haunted by the sin that, in the Rabbinic phrase, 'hath not forgiveness for ever', the sin against the Holy Spirit 'that will not be forgiven, either in this age or in the age to come'.[15] And for us, too, struggling to speak again with a voice of hope, it was as if we were dispossessed of all power for there are some crimes and a radical evil that somehow remain beyond our reach and articulation, and, as Arendt says, 'we can neither punish nor forgive such offences and ... they therefore transcend the realm of human affairs and the potentialities of human power, both of which they radically destroy wherever they make their appearance'.[16] Is this, too, a death of God, or yet more?

For such sterility transcends even the theological enterprise, a darker event even than the death of God (which is a theological event), but is, rather, the utter disappearance of God, God's vanishing and withdrawal not at a point of creation as in the Kabbalistic *Zim zum*, but as a departure and a desertion: God the traitor. What undermines faith ultimately is neither atheism nor materialism but the doubts and despair of the genuinely religious concerning the possibility of salvation in the face of God's desertion – the final horrible absurdity of everything that is left.

These were the dark undercurrents of our early conferences on literature and theology, and, although they were later forgotten or buried, they never finally left us. Their theological hauntings remained with us in Leuven in 2014. Such hauntings were not, strictly speaking, academic, but born of a profound existential panic and a hope that there might be another way through in the ancient mysteries of story and poem. In both the public and the private realm, in both Church and university, if we were honest, theology was either silent or dangerous. Faced with the absolute tragedy of the Holocaust we were forced to admit the truth of Machiavelli's teaching, that good works are finally not

---

[13]   Richard L. Rubenstein, *After Auschwitz: History, Theology and Contemporary Judaism* 2nd edn. (Baltimore, MD: Johns Hopkins University Press, 1992), p. 183, and see above, p. 46.

[14]   Arendt, *The Human Condition*, p. 239.

[15]   Matthew 12:32 NRSV.

[16]   Arendt, *The Human Condition*, p. 241.

of this world, that prudence teaches us 'to know how to do wrong',[17] and that religious teaching in schooling people to be good and not 'to resist evil' results in the condition that 'wicked rulers do as much evil as they please'.[18] At the same time, the roots of dehumanization are both religious and secular. At the heart of European anti-Semitism (a term first used only in 1860 by the Jewish scholar Moritz Steinschneider when he spoke of Ernest Renan's 'anti-Semitic prejudices', and used popularly in Germany by the 1870s) is the ancient Christian denunciation of the Jew as a Christ killer and a denier of God's truths, a religious hostility which quickly acquired racial overtones.[19] This becomes even more deadly when coupled with the ancient classical concept of the *animal laborans*, explored by Arendt in *The Human Condition* and Rancière in his book *The Philosopher and His Poor*,[20] as one excluded from the conditions of human life. In the Greek tradition of the non-human condition of the slave it was the fate of the slave labourer to share a manner of life that is to be found in all other forms of the animal existence without exhibiting that which alone characterizes the human. Thus Euripides calls all slaves 'bad' because they only think in terms of their stomachs, like animals. Aristotle, however, who on his deathbed freed his slaves, at least recognized the capacity of the slave to *become* human when freed from the 'necessity' of labour. This tradition was, in the twentieth century, radicalized by the Final Solution, the slogan over Auschwitz, *Arbeit macht frei* (drawn from the title of a popular novel of 1873 by Lorenz Diefrenbach), all the more profoundly ironic. The ghastly ontology, searingly portrayed in Art Spiegelman's story of cats and mice which is prefaced with words of Adolf Hitler that 'the Jews are undoubtedly a race, but they are not human',[21] is relentlessly present in the dead logic of Nazi writings. Heinrich Himmler in 'Some Thoughts on the Treatment of the Alien Population in the East' writes on the 'sub-human people' of Eastern Europe:

> This population will be available as a leaderless labouring class and provide Germany with migrant and seasonal workers for special work projects (road building, quarries, construction); even then they will get more to eat and have more from life than under Polish rule and, while lacking in culture themselves, under the strict, consistent and fair leadership of the German people will be called

---

[17]   Nicolo Machiavelli, *The Prince*, trans. W.K. Marriott (London: J.M. Dent, 1908), p. 122.

[18]   Nicolo Machiavelli, *Discourses*, Book III, ch. 1, quoted in Arendt, *The Human Condition*, pp. 77–8.

[19]   See Bernard Lewis, *Semites and Anti-Semites: An Inquiry into Conflict and Prejudice*, 2nd edn (New York: Norton, 1987).

[20]   Jacques Rancière, *The Philosopher and His Poor*, trans. John Drury, Corinne Oster and Andrew Parker (Durham NC: Duke University Press, 2003).

[21]   Art Spiegelman, *Maus: A Survivor's Tale*, 2 vols (New York: Pantheon Books, 1986).

upon to participate in their eternal cultural deeds and monuments and, in view of the amount of heavy labour required to produce them, may even make them feasible at all.[22]

I found that reading this, even in English rather than German, to a silent audience in Leuven, my own voice took on a deadness, caught like a virus from the very words themselves: words as contamination. But strangely, it was in the dark abysses of such language that we sought recovery – in the capacity of language itself to find new birth and possibilities in the spaces of literature. In the early 1980s in England we had begun to be aware of the writings of Henrich Böll in such novels as *Gruppenbild mit Dame* (*Group Portrait with Lady*) (1971. Trans. 1973), with its parody of Nazi documentary style, and the counterpointing of living voices of the imagination with the terrible dead language of Nazi bureaucracy.[23] If theology was immobilized and forgiveness – atonement – impossible, words still called to us to be spoken and written to be held in our memory. The story not to be told or passed on, is written and remembered. As Elie Wiesel, writing contemporary with our first conference, in *The Testament* (1981) writes of his dead father, 'even though he is no longer living and no gravedigger will ever lower him into the ground because the ground is cursed and so is heaven', yet 'I will implant in you his memory and mine, I must ... you understand, I must. Otherwise ...'.[24] So the book ends. Any alternative is, indeed, unthinkable. The writer is like the Just Man who comes to Sodom to save its people from sin and punishment. It is the voice of the child, moved by compassion, who finally tells him that this is a hopeless task, and the Just Man replies that he knows it is, but by speaking, though he cannot change man (there is no forgiveness), yet I may 'prevent man from ultimately changing me'.[25] The poet continues to speak – Wiesel, Celan, Levi and others – as the poet always does in all conflicts that are hopeless, or seemingly so. I move for a moment to the novelist André Brink in South Africa, writing in 1979 in his denunciation of the apartheid regime, *A Dry White Season*, who concludes his novel with these words: 'Perhaps all one can really hope for, all I am entitled to, is no more than this: to write it down ... So that it will not be possible for any man ever to say

---

[22]　Heinrich Himmler, 'Some Thoughts on the Treatment of the Alien Population in the East', in Simone Gigliotti and Gerel Lang (eds), *The Holocaust: A Reader* (Oxford: Blackwell, 2005), p. 169.

[23]　See the review in the *Guardian* of Heinrich Böll, *Group Portrait with Lady* (Harmondsworth: Penguin, 1976), quoted in the Penguin edition.

[24]　Elie Wiesel, *The Testament*, trans. Marion Wiesel (Harmondsworth: Penguin, 1982), p. 295.

[25]　From Wiesel's book *One Generation After* (1970), quoted as a preface to Wiesel, *The Testament*.

again: *I knew nothing about it*.[26] We cannot claim the protection of innocence, and that, at least, is a start.

I mention the conflict over race in South Africa and this takes us back again to Father Martin Jarrett-Kerr, who had, you will recall,[27] worked tirelessly as an Anglican chaplain in Soweto, promoting theatre and music in the black townships before he was finally expelled from the country. And there were all the others mentioned in this book – Bishop Peter Walker who served in the Battle of the Atlantic, and the gentle John Coulson whose life, he says, was 'overshadowed by war and by life in the war-time army, from which [he] emerged with a two-fold conviction: to make education my profession and to pursue the study of English Literature'.[28] We younger ones, whose lives were virtually unaffected, at least at first hand, by war and conflict, would learn that for these people literature was vital, the only possible space and a way forward, even and perhaps especially when prayer falls silent. One of the most influential English novels of recent years, not the work of a believer, sums up well the framework of our initiative in literature and theology. Ian McEwan's book *Atonement* (2001) concludes with the final reflections of the younger sister Briony Tallis, the 'betrayer' of her sister Cecilia and her lover Robbie:

> The problem these fifty-nine years has been this: how can a novelist achieve atonement when, with her absolute power of deciding outcomes, she is also God? There is no one, no entity or higher form that she can appeal to, or be reconciled with, or that can forgive her. There is nothing outside her. In her imagination she has set the limits and the terms. No atonement for God, or novelists, even if they are atheists. It was always an impossible task, and that was precisely the point. The attempt was all.[29]

'Even if they are atheists': there is no escape. And yet it just may be that the theological truth that is finally realized in *Atonement* is that the narrative can, perhaps, offer atonement and even salvation – call it what you will – for those about whom it speaks, for those 'outside', even if it is only finally constructed within the fiction. Yet that is not the final point. If it were, then theology itself would be only another form of escapism and fantasy. Of her sister and Robbie, the narrator, Briony can say, within the fiction, 'I gave them happiness, but I was not so self-serving as to let them forgive me.'[30] And so the dilemmas of theology only then begin again, in the unforgiven-ness, when the willing suspension of

---

26   André Brink, *A Dry White Season* (London: Minerva, 1992), p. 316.

27   See above, p. 62.

28   John Coulson, 'Faith and Imagination', *The Furrow* Series on 'Belief and Unbelief', no. 7 (1983), 536.

29   Ian McEwan, *Atonement* (London: Vintage Books, 2002), p. 371.

30   Ibid., p. 372 (emphases added).

disbelief in the narrative is itself suspended and we ask the question – 'and for us?' And yet, perhaps, the attempt is all.[31]

Maurice Blanchot, as I have already noted, starts an essay on Kafka with the words, 'Someone begins to write, determined by despair.' Kafka's passion (like that of Hölderlin), according to Blanchot, is 'purely literary', but his preoccupation is with salvation and it is 'hopeless, and all the more hopeless because it is totally uncompromising'.[32] In Kafka, who certainly knows imaginatively exactly what it is for the human being to be reduced to the bestial and the condition of the insect, this preoccupation with salvation is for a long time sustained through literature, but in the end it no longer blends with literature – in Blanchot's words, 'it tends rather to use literature'.[33] But literature can never be simply a means to an end, and Kafka knows this perfectly well. It cannot be that simple and literature on its own cannot 'save our souls and heal the State'.[34] We are close to the very heart of the troubled relationship between theology and literature, and a lesson to us that perhaps we expect too much too quickly. For Kafka, especially in his early years, the effort of writing becomes something like a means of psychological, but not as yet spiritual, salvation. It is, for him, nothing less than a fight for survival – as Blanchot puts it: 'At such moments writing is not a compelling call; it is not waiting upon grace, or an obscure prophetic achievement, but something simpler, more immediately pressing: the hope of not going under.'[35] But at least that is a start, providing a space in which things might change and from which at last we can move on, perhaps, even, one day find forgiveness. Blanchot recognizes that the danger even, or perhaps especially, in Kafka is found which describes well the imperatives and perhaps results of our conferences, that is 'a tendency at first to let literature's demand *relieve* religion's and then, especially toward the end, an inclination to allow his religious experience to take over from his literary one'.[36] But here is no recipe for a happy marriage. Literature has its limits.

This tendency and this inclination are both present in Ulrich Simon's book *Atonement: From Holocaust to Paradise* (1987), which offers a theological narrative from guilt to heaven using almost entirely literary resources from Marlowe to Shakespeare, and Dostoevsky to Kafka.[37] Simon ends between

---

[31] I am drawing here upon my own essay 'Reading Texts Theologically', *Yearbook of English Studies*, vol. 39, nos 1 and 2 (2009), 7–19, 16.

[32] Maurice Blanchot, 'Kafka and the Work's Demand', in *The Space of Literature*, trans. Ann Smock (Lincoln, Nebraska: University of Nebraska Press, 1982), p. 57. See also above, pp. 79, 100–101.

[33] Ibid., p. 58.

[34] George Gordon, early professor of English Literature at Oxford, quoted in Terry Eagleton, *Literary Theory: An Introduction*, 2nd edn (Oxford: Blackwell, 1996), p. 20.

[35] Blanchot, 'Kafka and the Work's Demand', p. 63.

[36] Ibid., p. 83 (emphasis added).

[37] See also above, p. 47.

hope and despair, but a journey has been made, or at least started, its value to be found not in any final word spoken, as if the pain of the crucifixion is somehow resolved by the promise (in another life) of the resurrection. There is no conclusion, as there is none in the text of the Gospel of Mark, yet in the words of Stewart Sutherland in the issue of *Literature and Theology* on tragedy to which George Steiner also contributed (and they are Sutherland's words, not mine): 'Even so that the cry of dereliction is uttered by the founder of Christianity is a vindication of the presence of Truth within the tragic vision of human life.'[38] Perhaps Simon's dependence on literature rather than formal works of theology in tracing his journey towards paradise should remind us of the ancient relationship between art and truth. It is Iris Murdoch, writing as a novelist rather than as a philosopher, who reminds us that 'The writer has always been important, and is now *essential*, as a truth-teller and as a defender of words.' She goes on to affirm the primitive force of stories as the preservative of our culture and language: 'The story is almost a fundamental a human concept as the thing, and however much novelists may try, for reasons of fashion or art, to stop telling stories, the story is always likely to break out again in a new form.'[39] Yet she warns us, time and again, against trusting to form and its consolations, for the story, like theology, can be 'an expert fantasy-monger'.[40] Ever fearful of its conclusions, we must yet remain open to the presence of truth in art, for, as the tricksy 'Editor's Postscript' to Murdoch's novel *The Black Prince* (1973) states, rather alarmingly: 'Art is not cosy and it is not mocked. Art tells the only truth that ultimately matters. It is the light by which human things can be mended. And after art there is, let me assure you all, nothing.'[41]

Let us not be naïve,[42] yet at the same time acknowledge the possibility for change present in narratives. As we have seen, the hero of the story needs no heroic qualities, but only, perhaps the capacity for a certain unpredictability that offers the suggestion of forgiveness, the impossible duty to forgive precisely *because* 'they know not what they do'. Overburdened by the weight of the times and their absolute tragedy in the frailty of human affairs, we retreat into the poetry of the chorus, which resists reification or submergence into the plot, and plays with irony and all other devices of literary craft which, as Simon once reminded us (Josipovici pay attention!), theologians resent 'as if novelists

---

[38]   Stewart R. Sutherland, 'Christianity and Tragedy', *Literature and Theology*, vol. 4, no. 2 (1990), 165.

[39]   Iris Murdoch, quoted in A.S. Byatt, *Iris Murdoch* (London: Longman, 1976), p. 15.

[40]   Iris Murdoch, 'Existentialists and Mystics', in W.W. Robson (ed.), *Essays and Poems Presented to Lord David Cecil* (1970), quoted in Byatt, *Iris Murdoch*, p. 16.

[41]   Iris Murdoch, *The Black Prince* (Harmondsworth: Penguin, 1975), p. 415.

[42]   Rowan Williams reminds us that it is in *The Black Prince* that Murdoch reminds us of the way in which language, in its restlessness, 'makes jokes in its sleep'. Rowan Williams, *The Edge of Words: God and the Habits of Language* (London: Bloomsbury, 2014) , p. 146.

provided an escape mechanism from serious issues'.[43] For, in spite of all, literature is very serious and has an enormous capacity for regeneration and for providing a space for the ungraspable and the forgotten truth that lies behind the error of the imaginary.[44] It may indeed be that any possible refashioning of theology and belief, vetoing all 'easily won and stated patterns of reconciliation and redemption,' will necessarily proceed by some form of the *via negativa*,[45] but though literature may give us a *Timon of Athens* and a *Mayor of Casterbridge*, such examples of absolute tragedy, as Steiner has suggested, are rare. And occasionally in theology, especially in the theology born from defeat, we find a narrative pattern which breaks indifference and inevitability. In Karl Barth's *Römerbrief* of 1918 and 1921, in Ulrich Simon's *A Theology of Auschwitz*, in the whole and as yet incomplete oeuvre of Thomas Altizer, we recognize that we are in the presence of story-tellers that present themselves to theology, in Steiner's words, preserving it 'from some unsparing humiliation inside theology itself, from some naked acquiescence in defeat'.[46] In such theologians there is found the narrative instinct that well knows the fallacy of the suggestion that story works by discernible cause and effect, and acknowledges, as Aristotle did, that a likely impossibility is always preferable to an unconvincing possibility.

And so are we content, we who cannot forgive, simply to read the story, a supreme fiction, turning it page by page perhaps with the madness of the old gentleman of La Mancha?[47] Jacques Rancière, in his reading of Cervantes' novel, asks:

> ... what does this 'madness' consist of, if we are not content to divide it, in the Romantic manner, between the representation of the ideal confronting reality and the creative 'fantasy' surrounding that opposition? In the interpretation of the relationship between the madness of the character and the 'fantasy' of the author, the whole question of the 'theological-poetical' nature of the novel is at stake.[48]

The point is, of course, as I have pointed out elsewhere,[49] that Don Quixote, in his madness, never for one moment falls into the error of *mistaking* 'the green cheese of reality for the moon in a book', but wholly *imitates* 'the act that the

---

[43]   Ulrich Simon, *Atonement: From Holocaust to Paradise* (Cambridge: James Clarke & Co, 1987), p. 6.

[44]   See Blanchot, *The Space of Literature*, p. 83.

[45]   Sutherland, 'Christianity and Tragedy', p. 166.

[46]   Steiner, 'A Note on Absolute Tragedy', p. 156.

[47]   See further, David Jasper, *The Sacred Community: Art, Sacrament and the People of God* (Waco, TX: Baylor University Press, 2012), pp. 36 -7.

[48]   Jacques Rancière, *The Flesh of Words: The Politics of Writing*, trans. Charlotte Mandell (Stanford, CA: Stanford University Press, 2004), p. 87.

[49]   Jasper, *The Sacred Community*, p. 36.

book makes a duty.' In short, the Don is mad out of duty to the truth of the book, and to this Rancière makes the following response, which seems obvious enough until we make the mistake of taking it too seriously in the wrong way:

> Finally, it is the social body of the readership of the fiction, which validates the impossible nature of the madness as psychologically plausible, yet belonging to the category of what happens only in fiction. The social body itself is fictionalized as a condition of the poem. The poet represents himself as in the privileged position of a story-teller who is addressing a literate audience.[50]

Thus we are drawn back into the supreme fiction and this takes me back to the beginning of this chapter – to asking myself if this is just a story, just my story that is spun from the tangled web of my memory. Or is this the whole point? What we were searching for in 1982 was a way beyond the impasse of absolute tragedy that allows no progression or atonement, or even the attempt made. What we began to find (though few took us very seriously, hardly surprisingly) was the importance of a duty to the truth of the book and the imitation of the action that that requires. Hannah Arendt, who has been a presence with us for much of this chapter, reminds us that since Galileo our capacity to adopt a cosmic, universal standpoint without actually moving suggests to us that we are not, finally, of this world even though we spend our life here, and we do not any longer need theology to tell us this.[51] Thus, the modern loss of faith is not religious in origin, but, at least since Descartes, springs from an almost exclusive concern with the self – that is the self as distinguished from the soul or the self in general – thus reducing all conversation finally to pure solipsism and a talking to oneself. Already theology is rendered silent, its narratives enslaved to form and its false, helpless, even pointless consolations. Confronted with the brutal, pure logic of the Final Solution and its absolute demands, theology simply ceases to exist. And there is nothing to fall back on when we remember that Descartes' famous *cogito ergo sum* was but a mere generalization of a *dubito ergo sum*. As he writes: '*Je doute, donc je suis, ou bien ce qui est la même chose: je pense, donc je suis.*'[52]

Yet the corrosion of doubt is not the only conclusion of religious belief. Clearly there are forms of agnosticism that are deeply religious as much in art and literature knows. We might recall the remark of Dostoevsky's Prince Myshkin as he reflects upon the image of the dead Christ in the painting of Hans Holbein the Younger and that 'some people may lose their faith by looking at

---

[50]   Ibid., p. 88.

[51]   Arendt, *The Human Condition.*, p. 270.

[52]   From the dialogue *La recherché de la vérité par la lumière naturelle*, quoted in Arendt, *The Human Condition*, p. 279.

that picture!'[53] And yet still, theologians of the death of God are often among the most God-haunted of all beings. Tom Altizer's recent work on *The Apocalyptic Trinity* (2012) recognizes in the absolute self-negation of the tragic Trinity a transfiguring action – a form of tragedy that is not the absolute negation of Steiner but can confess, in Altizer's words, 'a divine suffering and death that can realize atonement or ultimate reconciliation'.[54] But in my experience it is literary scholars rather than the theologians who have bothered to read Altizer carefully and understand him in his paradoxes that take us to the very edge of meaning in words, to the hope that is found at the very limit of despair. Blanchot wrote of Kafka: 'There he is, then, obliged to live off his death and constrained in his despair, and in order to escape despair – immediate execution – to make of his condemnation the only road to salvation.'[55] Thus we come to lose ourselves in the story, not seeking sense through the story, but from our sense of duty to its truth. And so Blanchot can say: '... in the time of distress which is ours, the time when the gods are missing, the time of absence and exile, art is justified, for it is the intimacy of this distress: the effort to make manifest, through the image, the error of the imaginary, and eventually the ungraspable, forgotten truth which lies behind this error'.[56]

It is only thus, in such ungraspable truth, that we can begin to make any sense of narratives of the Holocaust in the face of which there are no bloody heroes, no reconciliations, and the one who moulds us again out of earth and clay is No one – *Niemand*. Yet the poet sings – 'Praised be your name, No one,'[57] and André Schwarz-Bart sings his unbearable litany and hymn of praise to the death camps at the end of *The Last of the Just* (1959).[58] The hymn is, of course, almost unreadable, beyond the daring of negation, an enormity that yet releases us from the dead language of Himmler and the Reich. Words, as living things, begin the transfiguration of that suffering which stops language. And so it is that the end of his narrative of Auschwitz, Kertész's survivor, the boy Gyuri, through his torments, can speak of the happiness of the concentration camps – provided he himself does not forget.[59]

For me the study of literature and theology is the most serious thing I have ever been engaged in. It has been a task of retrieving a theological sense of being

---

[53]   Fyodor Dostoevsky, *The Idiot*, trans. David Magarshack (Penguin: Harmondsworth, 1955), p. 251, and see above, p. 74.

[54]   Thomas J.J. Altizer, *The Apocalyptic Trinity* (New York: Palgrave Macmillan, 2012), p. 133.

[55]   Blanchot, *The Space of Literature*, pp. 82–3.

[56]   Ibid., p. 83.

[57]   Paul Celan, 'Psalm', in *Selected Poems*, trans. Michael Hamburger (Harmondsworth: Penguin Books, 1990), p. 175.

[58]   See above, p. 80.

[59]   See above, p. 77.

human, but before one can even begin to do that one must begin by retrieving a sense of being human at all, without which we are nothing. Before we can recover any sense of God (whatever that might mean or in whatever language), we must elect to engage in a constant mutual release in forgiveness of one another in order to remain free. My old friend Bob Detweiler, may he rest in peace, a man who knew profound suffering in illness, once described this release as best found in what he called religious reading, that stretching out in gestures of loving friendship across the space of the text. Then one must go further, though such gestures at least draw us out of solipsisms and privacies, and out of all deadly obsessions with power and meaning to something far more profound. And it is in this space that we might begin to find the consolations of religion speaking again, grasped in those words of Meister Eckhart, and taken up by Heidegger – *Gelassenheit* and *Geselligkeit* – accepting the gift of moving gracefully through life's accidents and calamities with a sociability within which forgiveness can begin afresh.[60]

Reading together texts which resist all attempts to simplify and manipulate we may learn again to live *through* a religious tradition into a form of theological humanism which has recently been outlined by David Klemm and William Schweiker in which it is neither God's will nor human flourishing that alone offer any sufficient measure for human life. Yet brought together they offer guidance in the human responsibility for integrity of life. I am not sure that we have succeeded very far in persuading anyone in either Church or academy of the profound importance of what we have tried to do. But, in our various ways, we must keep trying. I return sometimes to the end of book of Job and try to place myself in Job's position: 'I had heard of you by the hearing of the ear, but now my eye sees you; therefore I despise myself and repent in dust and ashes.'[61] The point of God's great outburst to Job is not that there is no meaning, or even that meaning is a human category,[62] but that it is beyond our reach, only to be accepted as a gift of grace. The end of Job, as Muriel Spark well understood in her novel *The Only Problem* (1984), is neither a frame nor a finished form but a story that holds its secrets and hides its causal links, a story not to be accepted simply nor refused, but one which prompts endless questions to God and to ourselves. If it pains it also restores, and it enables us to move on, to craft our own story from memory, in Kierkegaard's phrase in the *Concluding Unscientific Postscript*, it keeps 'the wound of the negative open'.[63]

---

[60]   Robert Detweiler, *Breaking the Fall: Religious Readings of Contemporary Fiction* (Louisville, KY: WJK Press, 1995), pp. 34–5, and above, pp. 88–9, 90.

[61]   Job 42:5b–6.

[62]   *Contra* Susan Neiman in *Evil in Modern Thought* (Princeton, NJ: Princeton University Press, 2002).

[63]   Quoted in Josipovici, *The Book of God*, p. 290. The phrase reminds us also of the title of Rowan Williams' book on Christian Spirituality from the New Testament to St John of the Cross, *The Wound of Knowledge* (London: Darton, Longman & Todd, 1979).

After the primarily historical course of the first two parts of the book, some attention will now be given, in Part III, to primary underlying themes and directions in which the study of literature and theology is now moving.

PART III
Themes and the Wider World

Part III of this book represents a change of direction from Parts I and II. So far we have broadly followed the history of the conferences on literature and theology since 1982 up to 2014. Part III sets out to do two things. Chapters 9–11 are thematic, exploring three foundational areas for the study of literature and theology: poetry (with specific concern for the poetry of the Oxford Movement, and Newman and John Keble in particular); the sacrament of the Eucharist and its central place within the Christian tradition; and the Bible, seen through a brief review of the study of the Bible as literature from the end of the nineteenth century and concluding with some contemporary questions in such study through the writings of such scholars as Robert Alter and Meir Sternberg, and the criticism of them by the by-now familiar figure of Mieke Bal.

Chapters 12 and 13 open up the discussion from the primarily North American and Eurocentric focus of the conferences to date. The first focuses on Australia by means of a kind of dialogue with the novelist and poet David Malouf, and the second acknowledges the growing significance of the study of religion and literature in China through the hugely significant work of Yang Huilin of Renmin University of China in Beijing. These chapters can only act as indicators and much more could be said about important new scholarship in Taiwan, South Korea, Japan and elsewhere.

Chapter 9
Poetry: The Poetry of the Oxford Movement

The Oxford Movement, whose theology and ethos as the foundation for contemporary interest in literature and theology has been with us for so much of this book, was born in the spirit of poetry. John Keble's poems known as *The Christian Year* were published in 1827, six years before he preached the Assize Sermon, and the guiding spirits of the Movement, with the exception of E.B. Pusey, were poets or novelists of more than modest competence. Between the years 1832–41, Keble held the Chair of Poetry in Oxford, as a result of which he published his lectures, in Latin (as was the custom until Matthew Arnold), as *De poeticae vi medica* (1844), which he dedicated to William Wordsworth and which, though largely neglected for more than a century and not translated into English until 1912, were described by M.H. Abrams in 1953 as:

> the most radically sensational criticism of their time. They broach views of the source, the function, and the effect of literature, and the methods by which literature is appropriately read and criticized, which, when they occur in the writings of critics schooled by Freud, are still reckoned to be the most subversive to the established values and principles of literary criticism.[1]

It was while writing his review of John Gibson Lockhart's *Memoirs of the Life of Sir Walter Scott* (1838) that Keble first clearly expressed his sense of poetry as *catharsis*: 'the indirect expression in words, most appropriately in metrical words, of some overpowering emotion, or ruling taste, or feeling, the direct indulgence whereof is somehow repressed'.[2]

The burden of this statement, in its careful reserve and sense of the indirection of literature and poetry catches very precisely the beginnings of our study of literature and theology some one hundred and fifty years later and characterizes the spirit and sense of the scholarship of John Coulson and that 'old Anglican,

---

[1]   M.H. Abrams, *The Mirror and the Lamp: Romantic Theory and the Critical Tradition* (New York: W.W. Norton & Company, 1958), p. 145.

[2]   John Keble, Review of *Life of Scott* (1838), in *Occasional Papers and Reviews* (Oxford: James Parker and Co., 1877), p. 6.

patristic, literary, Oxford tone'[3] with which, in many ways, we began. It was a tone which avoided exaggerations, was redolent of the *via negativa* – and in Manning's words, 'it is worldly Catholicism'. Behind it also lies a tradition, at once intellectual and religious, that includes Samuel Taylor Coleridge, Bishop Butler, Pascal, and the Christian humanism of Erasmus. Its sense of language, particularly for John Henry Newman, draws most immediately upon the heritage of Coleridge and the old tradition of the organic sense of language as drawing together the past and present into one, the response to which is, as we have seen[4] in Coulson's word, 'fiduciary', that is, requiring a 'complex act of inference and assent ... [in which] we begin by taking *on trust* expressions which are usually in analogical, metaphorical or symbolic form'.[5] For Coleridge words are living things and language is a living organism, and it is this sense of the power of language which underlies all of Newman's thinking on the imagination and the Illative Sense which lies at the heart of religious belief in his *Essay in aid of a Grammar of Assent*. It was what we picked up again later.

Working in the field of literature and religion at the end of the twentieth century, John Coulson taught us from his study of Coleridge and Newman the value of what Newman, drawing on his own Evangelical background as a young man, called 'the literature of religion'. It is this that led Newman back to study the texts of the early Church Fathers and to the English Caroline Divines, as well as inspiring his own writings as a novelist and poet. Contemporaries of Newman like the journalist and clergyman Thomas Mozley also recognized the particular literary quality of the work of the Oxford Movement and its background in Romanticism, as well as the fading of that literary quality in the theology which followed it.[6] Behind this lay the disciplined 'system' of a rigorous classical education, and thus when Newman becomes a Roman Catholic in 1845 and seeks a religious order, he avoids the Vincentians, in his words, on account of their not granting 'to theology and literature that place in their system which we wished'.[7] The fading of this quality in theology was to be enormously significant for the study of literature in the twentieth century, for what has its roots in Newman's insistence on the role of the laity in the Church, that is, the voice of the 'common tradition' that resists the imposed claims of dogma and authority

---

[3]   Cardinal Manning on Newman, in a letter to George Talbot, February 1866. See above, p. 13.

[4]   See above, Chapter 1, pp. 15–16.

[5]   John Coulson, *Newman and the Common Tradition: A Study in the Language of Church and Society* (Oxford: Clarendon Press, 1970), p. 4.

[6]   Thomas Mozley, *Reminiscences of the Oxford Movement* (London: Longmans, Green, 1882), vol. 2, pp. 422–3. See also Coulson, *Religion and Imagination: 'in aid of a grammar of assent'* (Oxford: Clarendon Press, 1981), pp. 34–5.

[7]   Placid Murray (ed.), *Newman the Oratorian: His Unpublished Oratory Letters* (Dublin: Gill & Macmillan, 1969), p. 81.

in religious matters, emerges in the middle years of the century in Cambridge literary studies in the secular spirit of F.R. Leavis, L.C. Knights, and later Frank Kermode who, in such works as *The Sense of an Ending* (1966) and *The Genesis of Secrecy* (1979), gave particular attention to the literary forms of the Bible in the context of contemporary literature.[8] Coulson never underestimated the importance of Leavis and the *Scrutiny* group and its critical roots that were filtered through the decay of theology. He recognized Leavis' contempt, in the 'tradition of angry dissent', for all attempts to align literature with conventional religious belief and his sense of the importance of the study of literature at a time when theology seemed to retreat into little more than biblical exegesis.[9] Oddly, and writing before the melancholy, long nineteenth-century withdrawal of the sea of faith and the seeming decay of theology, Newman would perhaps have recognized a kindred critical spirit in Leavis and the common tradition. Indeed, he would possibly have recognized it even more so in L.C. Knights, who wrote as then Winterstoke Professor of English at the University of Bristol on theology and poetry in John Coulson's Downside Symposium *Theology and the University* (1964).[10] For Knights, Coulson suggests, truth is not something 'that we receive or acquire through logical demonstration, but something we live our way into through a complex, varying activity when we engage with formal verbal structures of a particular kind'.[11] In short, truth has much to do with poetry.

It was just such an approach to truth and such engagement that Newman found in S.T. Coleridge and others among the Romantics, in reaction to 'the dry and superficial character of the religious teaching and literature of the last generation, or century'. As he might surely have felt of Leavis, Newman spoke, as we have seen, of Coleridge in the *Apologia Pro Vita Sua*, quoting himself in an article in the *British Critic* of April 1839 entitled 'The State of Religious Parties', that although his 'liberty of speculation' took him beyond Christian limits, yet his philosophical genius instructed thinking people and worked, in the end, towards the 'cause of Catholic truth'.[12] (In this defence of the philosophical roots of the enterprise we might recall, without too much stretch, the role of D.Z. Phillips in our early conferences.) In the same passage in the *Apologia* Newman refers to five other figures and their influence upon the Oxford Movement. First, and foremost, is Sir Walter Scott who 're-acted on his readers,

---

[8] See further below, Chapter 11.

[9] See also above, p. 22, and John Coulson, 'Faith and Imagination', *The Furrow* Series on 'Belief and Unbelief', no. 7 (1983), p. 537.

[10] L.C. Knights, 'Theology and Literature – A Reply', in John Coulson, *Theology and the University: An Ecumenical Investigation* (London: Darton, Longman & Todd, 1964), pp. 207–18.

[11] Coulson, 'Faith and Imagination', p. 537.

[12] J.H. Newman, *Apologia Pro Vita Sua* [1864], ed. Ian Ker (London: Penguin, 1994), pp. 99–100.

stimulating their mental thirst, feeding their hopes, setting before them visions, which, when once seen are not easily forgotten, and silently indoctrinating them with nobler ideas, which might afterwards be appealed to as first principles'.[13] To the concept of the 'idea' we will return a little later. Then there are the English poets Southey and Wordsworth (who, for Keble also, was a 'true philosopher' as well as an 'inspired poet ... by the special gift and calling of Almighty God')[14] as they 'addressed themselves to the same high principles and feelings'. Finally, to these literary figures, Newman adds two churchmen, Alexander Knox (1757–1831) and 'a much venerated clergyman of the last generation', almost certainly Thomas Sikes, rector of Guilsborough (d.1834).[15] Knox was a clergyman of Coleridgean turn of mind, while Sikes looked backward in the Church and then to a time when 'those great doctrines, now buried, will be brought out into the light of day, and then the effect will be fearful'.[16] In the essentially conservative revitalizing of the riches of the past lies the dynamism of the future, a principle worked out in Newman most fully in the *Essay on the Development of Christian Doctrine* (1845).

But it was from Coleridge that Newman, as he moved away from the principle of the *via media* as early as in the 1838 *Lectures on Justification*, drew the sense of the unity of opposing forces which underlies the dynamic quality of all life, that sense of 'polarity' or 'two forces of one power'.[17] What in Coleridge's thought is described as the symbolic, in Newman becomes the sacramental rooted in the history of the Church. Furthermore, although Newman does express some qualifications with regard to the Romantic claims of the poetic imagination,[18] nevertheless it is this faculty and activity from which religious belief originates, and Coleridge's classic statement regarding the primary and secondary imagination in chapter 13 of the *Biographia Literaria* (1817) is quite specific in its use of religious terms: that the primary imagination is 'a *repetition* in the finite mind of the eternal act of creation in the infinite I AM'.[19]

---

[13] Ibid., p. 99.

[14] Dedication to the Oxford *Lectures on Poetry, 1832–1841* (*Praelectiones Academicae*). In 1839 Keble delivered the Creweian Oration in Oxford in honour of Wordsworth on the conferment of an honorary degree. G.B. Tennyson, *Victorian Devotional Poetry: The Tractarian Mode* (Cambridge, MA: Harvard University Press, 1981), p. 17.

[15] Tennyson, *Victorian Devotional Poetry*, p. 15.

[16] Newman, *Apologia*, p. 100.

[17] Owen Barfield, *What Coleridge Thought* (Middletown, CT: Wesleyan University Press, 1971), p. 11.

[18] See David Newsome, *Two Classes of Men: Platonism and English Romantic Thought* (London: John Murray, 1972), ch. 4, 'Coleridge and Newman', pp. 57–72.

[19] S.T. Coleridge, *Biographia Literaria* (1817), ed. James Engell and W. Jackson Bate, *The Collected Works*, vol. 7 (2 vols), (Princeton, NJ: Princeton University Press, 1983), vol. 1, p. 304 (emphasis added).

That is, through the imagination the human mind actually participates in the divine creative activity, the finite engaged with the creative act of the infinite in sacramental form.

In his Oxford *Lectures on Poetry* Keble is broadly consistent with Newman in his writings on poetics and aesthetics. In the *Apologia*, Newman describes Keble's *The Christian Year* (1827) in fulsome terms as 'one of the classics of the language', written at a time when 'the general tone of religious literature was so nerveless and impotent'.[20] If, for Keble, it is poetry that 'gives healing relief to secret mental emotion',[21] it is its divine nature that is the basis for all his reflections. His response to nature, as for Newman, owes as much to Bishop Butler's *Analogy of Religion* (1736) as it does to the poetry of Wordsworth, and Keble's work as a literary critic stems almost entirely from his calling as a theologian. If Coleridge is a literary critic writing in religious terms, then Keble is a theologian addressing literary questions, and if Newman can write of the dry and superficial character of the religious teaching of the previous generation, Keble is clearly aware of how easily in theology ideas can become dead and inert, only to be brought to life in the language of poetry and aesthetics. Indeed for him poetry is consistently referred to more or less in sacramental terms, its veiled expressions to be compared to that instinct of reserve in the Church Fathers who take care 'lest opponents and mockers should attain knowledge of sacramental mysteries and the keywords of the faith'.[22] What in Keble was a sacramental mystery, a *disciplina arcani*, later as the century wore on into doubt, in Tennyson's *In Memoriam* (1850) was to become an image of a darkened Church:

> And then I know the mist is drawn
> A lucid veil from coast to coast,
> And in the dark church like a ghost
> Thy tablet glimmers to the dawn. (LXVII, 13–16).[23]

The English poets to whom Keble refers most often are Shakespeare (pre-eminently), Spenser, Herbert and Milton, and as for Newman, it was Walter Scott who was the primary poet amongst his near contemporaries, 'the noblest of all poets in our own day'.[24] In Scott he was attracted to 'the tenets of the presence of good and evil angels ... the power of the sacramentals ... unencumbered of

---

[20]   Newman, *Apologia*, p. 36.

[21]   John Keble, *Lectures on Poetry, 1832–1841*, trans. E.K. Francis (Oxford: Clarendon Press, 1912), vol. 1, p. 22.

[22]   Ibid., pp. 13, 74.

[23]   See further, W. David Shaw, *The Lucid Veil: Poetic Truth in the Victorian Age* (London: The Athlone Press, 1987).

[24]   Keble, *Lectures on Poetry, 1832–1841*, vol. 2, p. 148.

Romanism'.[25] Of Byron and Shelley, Keble was dismissive on the grounds of their *inconsistency* – that is that, as poets, unlike Wordsworth, they failed to recognize that their gift was of God for they shared rather 'the wild dreams of those who, whether or not they really believe that either no Supreme Power, or, if any, a Malignant Power, rules the universe, at any rate wish that it were so'.[26] In short, for Keble poetry and religion are inseparable, and in the poetic there is no place for the irreligious or the atheistical.[27]

For Coleridge, as we have seen, language is a living organism linking together and reconciling the past and present of the community. Thus, both poetry and religion are living and have at their centre the principal of development and growth that is yet consistent with itself. Wordsworth's great autobiographical poem *The Prelude* was never so named by himself yet as early as 24 December 1804 he described it in a letter to Sir George Beaumont as 'a Poem ... on my earlier life or the growth of my own mind'. During the final revisions to the poem, on 11 April 1839 he described it in a letter to T.N. Talfourd as 'a long poem upon the formation of my own mind'.[28] Its full title, *The Prelude: or, Growth of a Poet's Mind*, was suggested by Mary Wordsworth for the final edition of 1850. Some five years earlier, between March 1844 and September 1845, Newman had written his *Essay on the Development of Christian Doctrine* as 'a hypothesis to account for a difficulty'.[29] That is, it sought to account for the consistency of Christianity through the changes and growth in doctrine and worship that are apparent through its history of 1,800 years. In a sense, Wordsworth and Newman were engaged on the same task; that is, to establish the principal of consistency in change. Newman's answer is essentially simple and one with the principals of Coleridgean and Romantic poetics – that Christianity is a

---

[25]   Keble, *Occasional Papers and Reviews*, p. 76.

[26]   Keble, *Lectures on Poetry, 1832–1841*, vol. 2, p. 339.

[27]   The close affinity between Wordsworth and Keble as poets might be identified in Wordsworth's *Essay, Supplementary to the Preface* to the *Lyrical Ballads* (1815): 'The commerce between Man and his Maker cannot be carried on but by a process where much is represented in little, and the Infinite Being accommodates himself to a finite capacity. In all this may be perceived the affinity between religion and poetry; between religion – making up the deficiencies of reason by faith; and poetry – passionate for the instruction of reason; between religion – whose element is infinitude, and whose ultimate trust is the supreme of things, submitting herself to circumscription, and reconciled to substitutions; and poetry – ethereal and transcendent, yet incapable to sustain her existence without sensuous incarnation.' William Wordsworth, *Poetical Works*, ed. Thomas Hutchinson, revised by Ernest de Selincourt (Oxford: Oxford University Press, 1969), p. 744.

[28]   See J.C. Maxwell, Introduction to *The Prelude: A Parallel Text* (London: Penguin, 1971), p. 17.

[29]   J.H. Newman, *An Essay on the Development of Christian Doctrine* (1845), ed. J.M. Cameron (London: Penguin, 1974), p. 90.

single, living and organic 'idea', instantiated solely not within Protestantism but within the consistency of the Roman Catholic Church in which, in Stephen Prickett's words, 'developments of doctrine are, therefore, not difficulties to be accounted for, but what we should expect'.[30] Or, as Newman himself expressed it more precisely:

> If Christianity is a fact, and impresses an idea of itself on our minds and is a subject matter of exercises of the reason, that idea will in course of time expand into a multitude of ideas, and aspects of ideas, connected and harmonious with one another, and in themselves determinate and immutable, as is the objective fact itself which is thus represented.[31]

The process of the development of an idea, that is, 'the germination, growth and perfection of some living, that is, influential truth',[32] takes place in the complex movements of the minds and institutions within both the individual and the corporate, historical life of humanity. These early passages on the idea of Christianity from Newman's *Essay* bear a remarkable comparison with Coleridge's celebrated words on the 'living educts of the Imagination' in Scripture in *The Statesman's Manual* (1815) with their insistence on reason, permanence, harmony and the life of the imagination moving forward on the wheels of the 'living chariot' of the first chapter of Ezekiel:

> of that reconciling and mediatory power, which incorporating the Reason in Images of the Sense, and organizing (as it were) the flux of the Senses by the permanence of self-circling energies of the Reason, gives birth to a system of symbols, harmonious in themselves, and consubstantial with the truth, of which they are the *conductors* ... The truths and the symbols that represent them move in conjunction and form the living chariot that bears up (for *us*) the throne of the Divine Humanity.[33]

Read side by side one is struck by the similarity both of diction and resonance in the styles of Newman and Coleridge – in their complex language they seem to share a common 'grammar' so that language itself becomes the 'conductor' and words the embodiment of the thought. Furthermore, in chapter two of his *Essay*, and with a remarkable anticipation of the reader-response criticism of the twentieth century in Michael Riffaterre, Georges Poulet, Wolfgang Iser

---

[30] Stephen Prickett, *Romanticism and Religion: The Tradition of Coleridge and Wordsworth in the Victorian Church* (Cambridge: Cambridge University Press, 1976), p. 154.

[31] Newman, *Development of Christian Doctrine*, p. 148.

[32] Ibid., p. 99.

[33] S.T. Coleridge, *Lay Sermons*, ed. R.J. White, *The Collected Works*, vol. 6 (Princeton, NJ: Princeton University Press, 1972), p. 29.

and others, Newman suggests how the Holy Scriptures initiate or create (in Coleridge's words, 'give birth to') an idea 'and that idea is not in the sacred text, but in the mind of the reader; and the question is, whether that idea is communicated to him in its completeness and minute accuracy, on its first apprehension, or expands in his heart and intellect, and comes to perfection in the course of time'.[34] It is thus the growth of the mind and the organism that is Newman's concern, the 'idea' being a living energy that grows into reason, the Pascalian reasons of the heart.[35] Like the older Coleridge who had roused his reader to abandon dry evidences and 'feel the *want*' and need of Christianity,[36] so Newman, as he had done in *The Tamworth Reading Room* (1841), insists in the *Grammar of Assent* (1870) that 'man is not a reasoning animal; he is a seeing, feeling, contemplating, acting animal'[37] who, from the impressions made by the events of history upon the imagination grows into reason, and thus the idea lives and grows to maturity. As he says in the last of his *University Sermons* of the processes in the development of an idea: 'this process is its development, and results in a series, or rather body of dogmatic statements, till what was at first an impression on the Imagination has become a system or creed in the Reason'.[38]

In his 1845 *Essay* Newman proposes seven tests for the 'true development' of an idea: (1) preservation of type; (2) continuity; (3) power of assimilation; (4) early anticipation; (5) logical sequence; (6) preservative additions; (7) chronic continuance.[39] What is conspicuous by its absence here is any reference to the idea of progress. Like both Coleridge as religious thinker and Wordsworth as poet, Newman was essentially conservative, at once both modern and traditional, the principal critical difference between them being that his mind was essentially historical and the poets' minds were not.[40] The *Essay on the Development of Christian Doctrine* was based ultimately, as Owen Chadwick long ago pointed out, upon an historical investigation of the ancient Church.[41] However, Chadwick also notes rather disapprovingly (being a professional historian himself) that a

---

[34]   Newman, *Development of Christian Doctrine*, p. 149.

[35]   On the comparison with Pascal, see J.M. Cameron, 'Pascal and Newman', *University of Leeds Review*, vol. 12, no. 2, (1969). For a meditative extension of this, see John S. Dunne, *The Reasons of the Heart* (London: SCM Press, 1978).

[36]   S.T. Coleridge, *Aids to Reflection* (1825) (London: G. Bell & Sons, 1913), p, 272.

[37]   J.H. Newman, *An Essay in Aid of a Grammar of Assent*, ed. I.T. Ker (Oxford: Clarendon Press, 1985) p. 67.

[38]   J.H. Newman, *Fifteen Sermons Preached before the University of Oxford, between 1826 and 1843* (London: Longmans, Green & Co., 1900), p. 329.

[39]   Newman, *Development of Christian Doctrine*, pp. 122–47.

[40]   See further, Joel Harter, *Coleridge's Philosophy of Faith* (Tübingen: Mohr Siebeck, 2011).

[41]   Owen Chadwick, *From Bossuet to Newman: The Idea of Doctrinal Development* (Cambridge: Cambridge University Press, 1957), p. 144.

significant omission from the revised essay of 1878 is the comparison 'between early Christian historiography and the work of secular historians like [Connop] Thirlwall',[42] weakening the appeal to history in Newman's argument. What is interesting, therefore, is the insistence and durability in the revised edition of the essentially literary rather than historical, or perhaps better, *poetic* themes of the *Essay*, based upon two proposals. First, that 'the Christian revelation is an *idea* which impressed itself upon the corporate mind of the Church'.[43] Second, a proposal which became clearer in his later defence of the *Essay* rather than in the *Essay* itself: that is, that there is, in Chadwick's words 'a valid analogy between the Church's appropriation of her faith, and the individual Christian's appropriation of his faith'.[44] It was a principle that was dear to the minds of Wordsworth and Coleridge. For the latter a symbol is that which is found in the binding together of the individual and the universal, the individual or specific being that which 'enunciates the whole, [while it] abides itself as a living part in that Unity, of which it is the representative'.[45] Thus, we might say by extension, the Church abides in the individual and the individual is a living part of the Church that it represents. Furthermore, in his emphasis upon the role of the laity, Newman is never far from the faith of the child, the illiterate and the poor – those whose faith may be sure yet whose access to the processes of reason is limited. Faith is, in the first instance, a loving and moral assent to revelation,[46] just as for Wordsworth, in the *Lyrical Ballads* and elsewhere, the idea of childhood lay at the centre of his 'serious philosophic purpose of formulating a concept of the moral consciousness based on the relation between Nature and the poetic self'.[47]

And so we turn now to Newman and Keble as poets. If the Oxford Movement might be said to have been born in the poetic and liturgical spirit of John Keble's *The Christian Year*, then its poetic nature, its strengths, weaknesses and ambivalences, find their fullest poetic expression in the collection called the *Lyra Apostolica*, published nine years later in 1836 and the work of six poets, chiefly Newman, who is the collection's presiding spirit. Of the 179 poems in the collection Newman wrote 109, Keble wrote 46 and the other four (Isaac Williams, Hurrell Froude, John William Bowden and Robert Isaac Wilberforce) 24 between them. When the book appeared in 1836 neither the title nor the poems were original. They had been appearing in the *British Magazine* since 1833, edited by Hugh James Rose, in whose rectory in Hadleigh, Suffolk a meeting took place in July 1833 that might be taken as the true initiation of the

---

[42]   Ibid., p. 149.

[43]   Ibid.

[44]   Ibid., p. 151.

[45]   Coleridge, *The Statesman's Manual*, in *Lay Sermons*, p. 30.

[46]   Chadwick, *From Bossuet to Newman*, p. 151.

[47]   Peter Coveney, *The Image of Childhood: The Individual and Society – A Study of the Theme in English Literature*, revised edn (London: Penguin, 1967), p. 69.

Oxford Movement.[48] It was Isaac Williams, writing on Newman as a poet in the *Lyra Apostolica*, who described poetry as cathartic and that which 'Providence seemed to have designed as a natural vent to ardent and strong feelings'.[49] At the same time Newman's verse gives evidence of his deeply theological and doctrinal sensibility – the poetry and the doctrine occasionally blending in a liturgical moment as in at least some of the verses of the angelic hymn of praise in the much later *The Dream of Gerontius* (1865), 'Praise to the holiest in the height'.[50] It remains as one of the greatest of all Victorian hymns still sung in churches today.

From its title the *Lyra Apostolica* is a blending of the religious and the Romantic. The image of the lyre, the inspiration of the song of the poet, looks back to Shelley's 'Ode to the West Wind' and Coleridge's 'The Aeolian Harp', though without the ambiguity of Coleridge's poem, which itself looks back to Jacob Boehme's *Aurora* (1634) and in its central lines which begin 'O! the one Life within us and abroad'[51] blends Trinitarian theology with a pantheism which is utterly absent from Newman.[52] In his poetry, the inspiring breeze which sounds through the Aeolian harp is purely Christian and apostolic, the breath or the spirit of God.

In all his works Newman is never purely the historian or the theologian, though his preoccupations are necessarily deeply of both. As we have seen in his *Essay on the Development of Christian Doctrine* in which the appeal to history is weakened in the 1878 revision, and in the style of his prose, Newman, it might be said, is poetic in his sensibility, or better his aesthetic sense of the devotional, a poet in the first instance with deep theological and apostolic preoccupations rather than a theologian who has recourse to the language of poetry. The fourteenth poem of *Lyra*, entitled 'The Cross of Christ' is prefaced by a Latin epigraph from Tertullian's *De Corona*, its first four lines employing the scansion of the far better known poem No. XXV, 'Lead, Kindly Light', in each case the second and fourth lines dramatically slowing the tempo:

---

[48]   For further details of the history of the origins of *Lyra Apostolica*, see G.B. Tennyson, *Victorian Devotional Poetry*, pp. 115–16.

[49]   Isaac Williams, *The Autobiography of Isaac Williams*, ed. Sir George Prevost (London: Longmans, Green & Co., 1892), p. 69.

[50]   It is difficult to separate this poem from Sir Edward Elgar's musical setting and it says much for the inspiring power of Newman's poetic culminating drama of the human soul that Elgar wrote at the conclusion of his score, 'This is the best of me.'

[51]   Actually these eight lines were not part of Coleridge's original poem of 1795, but were added in the later version of 1817.

[52]   See further, David Jasper, *Coleridge as Poet and Religious Thinker* (London: Macmillan, 1985), pp. 35–40; Thomas McFarland, *Coleridge and the Pantheist Tradition* (Oxford: Clarendon Press, 1969).

> Whene'er across this sinful flesh of mine
>> I draw the Holy Sign,
>> All good thoughts stir within me, and collect
> Their slumbering strength divine.[53]

The making of the sign of the cross, a 'Romish' practice that would give offence to Low Churchmen, becomes a slow, devotional action, as does its effect in releasing the 'strength divine' and its consequence felt in the last two lines of the first stanza:

> Till there springs up that hope of God's elect
>> My faith shall ne'er be wrecked.

Thus the poetry becomes the vent to ardent and strong feelings experienced in a profoundly theologically rooted devotion. At this stage Newman can still rage against the Roman Catholic Church, as in the poem 'The Cruel Church':

> O Mother Church of Rome! Why has thy heart
>> Beat so untruly towards thy northern child?
>> Why give a gift, nor give it undefiled,
> Drugging the blessing with a step-dame's art?[54]

Yet there is also a sense of longing which almost even now at this early date finds a home in the Mother Church. And in the poem which immediately follows this outburst, the Church of Rome becomes the Good Samaritan (the title of the poem) and the place which resolves and calms the passions – if only the doctrinal and creedal difficulties could be resolved. Poetically and aesthetically, it could be said, Newman is already home:

> O that thy creed were sound!
> For thou dost sooth the heart, Thou Church of Rome,
>> By thy unwearied watch and varied round
> Of service, in thy Saviour's holy home.
>> I cannot walk the city's sultry streets,
> But the wide porch invites to still retreats,
>> Where passion's thirst is calmed, and care's unthankful gloom.[55]

---

[53] J.H. Newman, *Lyra Apostolica* [1836], 4th edn (Derby: Henry Mozley & Sons, 1840), p. 14.

[54] Ibid., p. 234.

[55] Ibid., p. 235.

Already Newman has found apostolic consistency ('thy unwearied watch') and integration ('varied round of service'), and the necessary *Essay on the Development of Christian Doctrine* is not so far away, a confirming theological meditation on an achieved poetic sensibility.

In many ways, if not precisely in poetic genius, Newman as a poet looks back to the seventeenth century, to George Herbert and even John Donne. From Herbert there is the echo of the yearning for the life of devotion that is inextricably, grammatically and structurally, embedded in Christian doctrine and liturgical practice. There are echoes of Herbert's 'Love (III)' on the Eucharist, its images of unworthiness and consumption of the Flesh of Christ (echoes of the line, 'So I did sit and eat'),[56] but little of Herbert's gentle pastoral kindliness and Anglicanism, even now. Already Newman has moved beyond the Anglican *via media* and its reasoned ambiguities, though poetically he remains within the common tradition:

> Whene'er I seek the Holy Altar's rail,
> > And kneel to take the grace there offered me,
> It is not time to ask my reason frail,
> > To try Christ's words, and search how they may be;
> Enough, I eat his Flesh and drink his Blood,
> More is not told – to ask it is not good.[57]

As we move backwards in time by about a decade from the *Lyra Apostolica* and turn to Keble's *The Christian Year*, we encounter poetry for the Anglican liturgical Calendar that was almost, if not quite, universally praised by the Victorians, and yet has not stood the poetic test of time particularly well, with the exception of the few poems that are now still sung as hymns in churches.[58] Wordsworth, who is the greatest poetic influence on Keble, especially in his 'Immortality Ode', catches both the strength and weakness of Keble as a poet when he famously remarked that the poetry of *The Christian Year* is so good that he wished he had written it himself so that it might have been better.[59]

But behind Wordsworth lay another intellectual figure who is at the very heart of Keble's poetry (as it was of Newman's thought) – Bishop Joseph Butler and his *Analogy of Religion*. As W.J.A. Beek has remarked, 'Keble saw his fundamental

---

56   George Herbert, 'Love (III)', *The English Poems of George Herbert*, ed. Helen Wilcox (Cambridge: Cambridge University Press, 2007), p. 661.

57   Newman, *Lyra Apostolica*, p. 37.

58   For example, verses from the second half of the Morning hymn, 'New every morning is the love'; verses from the hymn for the Purification of the Blessed Virgin Mary, 'Blessed are the pure in heart'; verses from the Evening hymn, 'Sun of my soul! Thou Saviour dear '.

59   Mary Moorman, *William Wordsworth: The Later Years, 1803–1850* (Oxford: Oxford University Press, 1968), pp. 479–80.

religious principle, which was philosophically based on Butler's theory of analogy, confirmed by Wordsworth's poetic principle.'[60] Above all, perhaps, it is Butler's idea of the relation between sensation and reflection that bears close comparison with Wordsworth's notion of 'emotion recollected in tranquillity' and finally the state of reflection throughout *The Christian Year*.[61] Butler remarks early in the *Analogy* that 'our external organs of sense are necessary for conveying in ideas to our reflecting powers ... yet when these ideas are brought in, we are capable of reflecting in the most intense degree, and of enjoying the greatest pleasure, and feeling the greatest pain, by means of that reflection, without any assistance from our senses'.[62] Just as Butler begins with the external organs of sense, so Wordsworth, in his 1800 Preface to the *Lyrical Ballads*,[63] insists on the power of objects in nature rather than abstractions, and Keble draws his devotional reflections from nature, by recourse to analogy. For example, in the poem for the 'Sunday called Septuagesima', one of the most familiar in the collection, Keble writes of nature:

> There is a Book, who runs may read,
> > Which Heavenly Truth imparts,
> And all the lore its scholars need,
> > Pure eyes and Christian hearts.

> The works of God above, below,
> > Within us and around,
> Are pages in that Book, to shew
> > How God Himself is found.
> ...
> Two worlds are ours: 'tis only Sin
> > Forbids us to descry
> The mystic heaven and earth within,
> > Plain as the sea and sky.

> Thou, who hast given me eyes to see
> > And love this sight so fair,
> Give me a heart to find out Thee,
> > And read Thee everywhere.[64]

[60] W.J.A. Beek, *John Keble's Literary and Religious Contribution to the Oxford Movement* (Nijmegen: Centrale Drukkerij N.V., 1959), p. 85.

[61] See further, Brian W. Martin, *John Keble: Priest, Professor and Poet* (London: Croom Helm, 1976), pp. 121–2.

[62] Bishop Butler, *The Analogy of Religion, Natural and Revealed* (1736) (London: J.M. Dent, 1906), p. 16.

[63] Much enlarged in 1802.

[64] John Keble, *The Christian Year* (London: Longmans, Green & Co., 1909), pp. 49–51.

Newman in his *Apologia*, for whom 'Keble struck an original note and woke up in the hearts of thousands a new music'[65] in his poetry, draws from this sense of sensation and reflection in Butler and in Keble's verse what he calls 'the Sacramental system':

> That is, the doctrine that material phenomena are both the types and the instruments of real things unseen, – a doctrine which embraces, not only what Anglicans, as well as Catholics, believe about Sacraments properly so-called; but also the article of 'the Communion of Saints' in its fullness; and likewise the Mysteries of the faith.[66]

The 'second intellectual principle' which Newman claims to have gained from Keble, and again drawing on Butler's *Analogy*, is that 'probability is the guide of life'. The danger of the doctrine of probability is its 'tendency to destroy in [many minds] absolute certainty'. In Keble this difficulty is met, Newman affirms, 'by ascribing the firmness of assent which we [Roman Catholics] give to religious doctrine, not to the probabilities which introduced it, but to the *living power of faith and love which accepted it*. In matters of religion, he seemed to say, it is not merely probability which makes us intellectually certain, but probability as it is put to account by faith and love.'[67]

In such reflections we can perceive clearly the affinities and differences between Keble and Newman, as men and as poets: Newman – sharper edged, doctrinal, uncompromising; Keble – putting all to account by faith and love, gentler, quieter, perhaps humbler. The taste of the twentieth century has not been kind, on the whole, to Keble as a poet. Owen Chadwick, as a historian, is far enough out of touch with the spirit of Romantic poetry to make little of *The Christian Year*. Of the poetry of the Oxford Movement and Keble in particular he wrote, in a style more of the nineteenth than the twentieth century, admitting to the limitations of 'personal taste' in poetry:

> In order to share in this poetry, it is necessary not to shrink from the Romantics as though they were harlots, but to engage them with head and heart as true lovers. It is necessary, perhaps, to be capable of pleasure in Wordsworth, or parts of Wordsworth. I will confess that I can only understand, with a bare assent of the intellect, the influence exerted by *The Christian Year*. Keble has moments of grandeur, moments of deep sincerity and simplicity; but the moments of bathos, or of superficiality, bring you down again to the dust too soon after you have soared above it. To read *The Christian Year* feels like seeing an honest and

---

65   Newman, *Apologia*, p. 36.
66   Ibid., p. 37.
67   Ibid. (emphases added).

moral play where the illusion is often being broken. I give this only as a reflexion of personal taste. Perhaps there are men who still, like their forefathers, elevate *The Christian Year* to the level of *Pilgrim's Progress* or *The Imitation of Christ*.[68]

Yet the judgement of Keble's contemporaries seems clearer, more insightful and less judgemental, perhaps because they were themselves, in their different ways, part of that deeply *literary* common tradition of the language of Church and society which we glimpsed again in the 1982 Durham conference on literature and theology. Certainly neither Keble nor Newman was among the greatest of poets, yet, each in his own manner, carried the poetic genius of the Romantics into their theology and devotion so that finally the two elements could not be disentangled. In the Postscript to Newman's letter of 1875 that prefaces Keble's *Occasional Papers and Reviews*, Pusey quotes Sir John Coleridge's comment on Keble's preaching, its humility, diffidence and yet 'the very quietness, the almost tearful monotony of his delivery became extremely moving, when you recollected how learned, how able, how moved in his own heart, and how earnest was the preacher'.[69]

To this voice of Keble[70] we add that of Newman and, in John Coulson's words, his grammar of imagination and belief. The *Grammar of Assent* finally, can only be fully understood when read within a 'common tradition' of poetry that moves, for us, from Coleridge to Matthew Arnold and T.S. Eliot.[71] It is the engagement with this tradition that is the key to this grammar of assent, and at the same time it is the assent itself – that which Coleridge described in the *Biographia Literaria*, writing of the work of Wordsworth, as 'these shadows of imagination, that willing suspension of disbelief for the moment, which constitutes poetic faith'[72] – which teaches us the grammar. Through Coleridge is maintained the adherence to an essentially conservative tradition of language which regards the present through a sense of the past through a fiduciary rather than an analytic response to language. It is such a perspective that Newman developed in the 1850s in his lectures on the *Scope and Nature of University Education*, later revised and expanded into his work *The Idea of a University Education* (1873), which were quite different from the speculative tone of the later

---

[68] Owen Chadwick (ed.), *The Mind of the Oxford Movement* (London: Adam & Charles Black, 1960), Introduction, p. 63.

[69] Keble, *Occasional Papers and Reviews*, p. xxi. See also Brian W. Martin, op. cit., pp. 116–17.

[70] The closest to it in the twentieth century was, perhaps, that of Bishop Peter Walker. He was a gentle and a deeply learned man who wore his learning lightly and loved poetry, especially that of W.H. Auden. In his celebration of the liturgy he almost vanished behind the mystery of words.

[71] See Coulson, *Religion and Imagination*, p. 47.

[72] Coleridge, *Biographia Literaria*, vol. 2, p. 6.

Lux Mundi essays of 1889 under the editorship of Charles Gore, whose purpose was 'to put the Catholic faith into its right relation to modern intellectual and moral problems.' There was nothing of such liberalism in theology, or indeed speculation, in Newman, and yet he was open to the advancement of knowledge and the contemporary world in his sense of the role and nature of the university. Such is exactly the tone of Coulson's symposium on *Theology and the University*, and it deeply undergirded the return to the study of literature and theology in the last two decades of the twentieth century in England, profoundly present even as the tides of continental philosophy and postmodernism swept over later discussions at the end of the century.

Thus, to neglect the poetry of the Oxford Movement is to miss a living sense of the vibrant and organic link between theology and literature in the life of the Church, a sense of the unity of all things in the dynamic and creative response to words and the Word that is at once scriptural, historical, sacramental and, in the best sense of the word, devotional.[73] It lies at the very heart of the spirit of our enterprise, even though it was a voice that was lost as the years went by and we lost our theological nerve, to our own cost.

---

[73] The term is taken from the title of Stephen Prickett's book *Words and the Word: Language, Poetics and Biblical Intepretation* (Cambridge: Cambridge University Press, 1986), which draws a tradition of the 'poetic' through Vico, Herder, Coleridge, Arnold and Hopkins, up to the figures of Austin Farrer and Paul Ricoeur.

Chapter 10
Sacrament: The Eucharistic Body

This chapter might seem to represent a change of direction from the tone of this book so far. Its hinge, however, will become clearer towards the end when we return to the work of S.T. Coleridge and his understanding of the living power of language, and this takes us back to the underlying sacramental quality of our reflections on literature and theology as they are rooted in Romanticism and the theology and writings of the Oxford Movement. Of necessity this brief study of the Christian Eucharist will have deeper historical roots, but will also relate closely to my own recent writings on literature and theology in my books *The Sacred Body* (2009) and *The Sacred Community* (2012), and also the sense of the liturgical foundations of theology as recently explored in the phenomenological (and deeply literary) work of French scholars like Jean-Yves Lacoste and Jean-Luc Marion.

And so we go back to beginnings. The earliest accounts that we have of the Eucharist strive to indicate the legitimate and proper character of Christian worship in the face of pagan suspicions. From the writing of St Paul and in the gospels of Mark, Matthew and Luke we learn that on the night of his betrayal, Jesus, in the context of a meal and in the presence of his disciples took bread and wine and pronounced, 'this is my body' and 'this is my blood of the covenant'.[1] In his *First Apology* (*c.*150 CE), written in Rome and within a well-established tradition of Eucharistic practice, as well as the earlier *Dialogue with Trypho* (*c.*135), Justin Martyr is clearly uncomfortably aware of the accusation that Christians drank human blood and he makes it plain that the bread and wine over which thanks have been given are not 'common' but by 'a word of prayer' are the 'flesh and blood of [the] incarnate Jesus'. But this is quite different, Justin insists, from the practices of the 'evil demons' of the mysteries of Mithras who 'commanded the same things to be done' but who engaged in false and lurid imitations of the action of Jesus.[2] Justin is perfectly well aware that here is a particular, dynamic and transformative use of language as the 'word of prayer'. He makes no further comment as to *how* the bread and the wine become the

---

[1]   Mark 14:22–4, Matthew 26:26–9, Luke 22:7–13, I Corinthians 11:23–5.

[2]   See R.C.D. Jasper and G.J. Cuming, *Prayers of the Eucharist, Early and Reformed*, 3rd edn (New York: Pueblo Publishing Company, 1987), pp. 25–30; Elaine Pagels, *Beyond Belief: The Secret Gospel of Thomas* (London: Macmillan, 2003), pp. 19–20; L.W. Barnard, *Justin Martyr: His Life and Thought* (Cambridge: Cambridge University Press, 1966), pp. 147–8.

body and blood of Christ. Some 50 years later in Carthage, North Africa, in his *Apologeticum*, written in defence of Christian morality, Tertullian offers a satirical and sarcastic account of pagan reaction to the Eucharist. He is perfectly well aware of the power of irony:[3]

> No doubt [the Christian] would say, 'You must get a child still very young, who does not know what it means to die, and can smile under your knife; and bread to collect the gushing blood ... Come, plunge your knife into the infant ... Or, if that is someone else's job, simply stand before a human being dying before it has really lived ... Take the fresh young blood, saturate your bread with it, and eat freely.[4]

Tertullian is using the power of words to attack pagan superstition, from the Word made flesh to the flesh made word written in defence of the Eucharist within which, as Justin Martyr expresses it, '[God] is well pleased with all the sacrifices in his name, which Jesus the Christ handed down to be done, namely in the eucharist of the bread and the cup'.[5] Yet the offence and enormity stubbornly remains that Christianity is a religion of the 'Word made *flesh*', insisting upon the sacrifice of the real human flesh of the incarnate God.[6] Probably contemporary with Tertullian is the enormously influential work, the *Apostolic Tradition* of Hippolytus (*c*.215) which claims to reflect in Rome the liturgical 'tradition which has remained until now' and which begins the anaphora with a statement asserting belief in the Word who 'was made flesh and demonstrated to be Thy Son', rehearsing again the words 'Take eat: this is my Body which is broken for you' and 'This is my Blood which is shed for you.'[7]

The key biblical verse regarding the incarnation of the Word is John 1:14, 'And the Word became flesh [ὁ λογος σαρξ ἐγενετο] and lived among us' (NRSV). As C.K. Barrett has pointed out, the verb here cannot mean simply 'became' as the Word continues to be the subject of further statements, and he suggests that

---

3   On literary irony and Ulrich Simon, see above, p. 51.

4   Tertullian, *Apologeticum* 7, quoted in Elaine Pagels, *Beyond Belief*, p. 18.

5   Justin Martyr, *Dialogue with Trypho*, 117.1, quoted in Jasper and Cuming, *Prayers of the Eucharist*, p. 28.

6   See Margaret R. Miles, *The Word Made Flesh: A History of Christian Thought* (Oxford: Blackwell, 2005).

7   Gregory Dix, *The Treatise on the Apostolic Tradition of St Hippolytus of Rome*, ed. Henry Chadwick (London: SPCK, 1968), pp. 7–8. Dix agrees with the earlier edition in English, edited by Burton Scott Easton, in translating the first statement as a present tense: 'My Body which is broken for you.' (See *The Apostolic Tradition of Hippolytus*, trans. Burton Scott Easton (Cambridge: Cambridge University Press, 1934), p. 36). More recent English editions read this as a future tense. See Jasper and Cuming, *Prayers of the Eucharist*, p. 35, which has, 'which shall be broken for you'. This point, as we shall see, is of some importance.

a closer rendering would be 'the Word came on the (human) scene – as flesh'.[8] The Word, or *Logos*, remains as the eternal Word in the mysterious paradox of the particularity of the incarnation. Thus our engagement with the Eucharistic body in an act of consumption and what Charles Williams in *The Descent of the Dove* (1939) called 'co-inherence',[9] a term to which I have already referred to in relation to Bishop Peter Walker,[10] is a moment of eternity in time, at once the result of an event already found in history and yet always experienced in anticipation. This eschatological dimension of the Eucharistic meal is fundamental to our understanding of its fleshly nature. As Rowan Williams has said of its 'shape', referring specifically to Gregory Dix's great work of liturgical imagination, *The Shape of the Liturgy* (1945):

> Its central theme is the single movement of the Son to the Father, in eternity and in time: the outpouring of the Son to the Father in the Trinity ... with the great pivotal sign of the Lord's Supper summing up and holding the meaning of that journey and opening out on to the perspective of eternity again.[11]

It is this present and anticipatory nature of the Eucharistic body, spoken in word and known only in the mystery of the sacrament that enables the Fathers of the early Church to assert that we already live the life of the resurrection by virtue of baptism, in which we have already passed through the waters of death into new birth, and participation in the Lord's Supper. St Maximus the Confessor (*c.*580–662) gives more generous corporeal shape to the ancient Platonic sense of this life understood as a preparation for death and the next, more spiritual, manner of existence.[12] For, like St Paul, St Ambrose, St John Chrysostom and others before him, Maximus proclaims that by passing through the waters of baptism the Christian has already journeyed upon the path through death to the life beyond, emerging, like Christ at his Passion, with the resurrected body

---

8   C.K. Barrett, *The Gospel According to John: An Introduction* (London: SPCK, 1955), p. 138.

9   See Charles Williams, *The Descent of the Dove: A Short History of the Holy Spirit in the Church* (London: Longmans, Green & Co., 1939), p. 1. 'The visible beginning of the Church is at Pentecost, but that is only a result of its actual beginning – and ending – in heaven.'

10   See above, Chapter 1, pp. 18–19.

11   Rowan Williams, Foreword to Gregory Dix, *The Sacramental Life*, ed. Simon Jones (Norwich: Canterbury Press, 2007), p. ix.

12   See Adam G. Cooper, *The Body in St Maximus the Confessor: Holy Flesh, Wholly Deified* (Oxford: Oxford University Press, 2005), ch. 5, 'Corporeality and the Christian', pp. 206–50. Also Edward Yarnold SJ, *The Awe-Inspiring Rites of Initiation: Baptismal Homilies of the Fourth Century* (Slough: St. Paul Publications, 1971). The same theme is found also in the work of the ninth-century theologian John Scotus Eriugena. See Christopher Bamford, *The Voice of the Eagle* (Great Barrington, MA: Lindisfarne Books, 2000).

that is nothing short of the Eucharistic body, consumed and being consumed in the Spirit. In short the Christian already lives the resurrection life which is yet to come, in both body and spirit, baptism made complete at the final resurrection when our mortal bodies will be raised from the dead.[13] We live thus on a dual level, corporeal and spiritual, in the present and in anticipation: and so, in the anaphora of Hippolytus, by an act of remembrance [ἀναμνησις] we have become one with the body and blood of Christ and then immediately follows the epiclesis in which we pray for the longed-for coming of the Holy Spirit whereby all the saints will be united finally with God.[14] There is a remarkable parallel to this shape of the early liturgy at the end of Jean-Luc Marion's book, both a philosophical and a literary reflection on the nature of love, *The Erotic Phenomenon* (2003), when the experience of the flesh (the σαρξ of the John 1:14) anticipates the child that is both witness and guarantee of the lovers' faithfulness – the seal of the Spirit that also stands in judgement. Thus, in the echoes of Trinitarian modes of thoughts that are to be found in Marion's narrative, paralleling those of the Eucharistic prayer, the child as third party actually precedes us and guarantees, in spite of all fleshly weakness, the perfected end of the endless repetitions of love, pronouncing upon a last judgement.[15]

The members of the congregation of the Eucharist participate in the fleshly being of God incarnate, yet, like the community of readers, readily cross the boundaries of time and space. From the sixth century in the East and a little later in the West, the story of St Mary of Egypt circulated in monastic communities. Her life as told by St Sophronius (*c.*560–638) is racy, multilayered and focused upon the semi-mythical Mary as at once the Eucharistic body and the body of flesh.[16] Read at one level it is a love story as the mysterious figure of Mary, the repentant prostitute and desert ascetic entrances the priest Father Zossima for

---

[13]　This anticipatory image is graphically discovered in St Bernard of Clairvaux's sermons for the Feast of All Saints, and his description of the saints who wait on their beds of rest, their souls longing for the glorified body which will join them at the great final day when their bliss will be glorified and they will take their places at the great Messianic feast. See Anna Harrison, 'Community among the Dead: Bernard of Clairvaux's *Sermons for the Feast of All Saints*', in Caroline Walker Bynum and Paul Freedman (eds), *Last Things: Death and the Apocalypse in the Middle Ages* (Philadelphia, PA: University of Pennsylvania Press, 2000), pp. 192–4.

[14]　Gregory Dix, *On the Apostolic Tradition*, p. 9.

[15]　See Jean-Luc Marion, *The Erotic Phenomenon*, trans. Stephen E. Lewis (Chicago, IL: Chicago University Press, 2007), p. 198. See further, David Jasper, *The Sacred Body: Asceticism in Religion, Literature, Art, and Culture* (Waco, TX: Baylor University Press, 2009), pp. 179–84.

[16]　*The Life of St. Mary of Egypt* is reprinted in English in Benedicta Ward SLG, *Harlots of the Desert: A Study of Repentance in Early Monastic Sources* (Kalamazoo, MI: Cistercian Publications, 1987), pp. 35–56. See also Virginia Burrus, *The Sex Lives of the Saints:*

whom she is a dream woman finally absorbed into the mystery of the sacrament as she eats but three grains of the lentils that he has brought for her sustenance as, for her, 'the grace of the Holy Spirit is sufficient to keep whole the substance of the soul'.[17] A story both of divine miracles and human fascination, the narrative recounts the life of Mary from prostitute to saint living in the wilderness and 'waiting for my God'.[18] As her story draws to a close, she sends Father Zossima away for a year, bidding him meet her on the banks of the Jordan and bringing with him the Eucharistic elements. In their final meeting, Mary approaches the priest by crossing the Jordan in the manner of Jesus, walking on the water, begs his blessing and receives the sacrament and disappears again as she came. A year later again, the priest comes again only to find Mary lying dead with words written above her head giving instructions for her burial, the more remarkable as Mary, who literally 'lives' and embodies the texts of Scripture, is illiterate. In her the Word is made flesh as flesh becomes word, the text incarnate. The priest realizes also that the journey that had taken him 20 days, Mary had completed, after receiving the sacrament, in but one hour 'and then at once passed on to God'.[19] As in all fictions, time and space are relativized.

Mary's story, which in later tellings such as is to be found in Jacobus de Voragine's thirteenth century *Golden Legend*, becomes over-burdened with fantasy and miracle, in Sophronius' fine narrative is clearly a meditation on the Eucharistic body, the body of flesh and spirit that is capable of deep attractions yet which draws us into a sense of a present that is most profoundly characterized by divine anticipation. For her earthly 'lover', Father Zossima, there only remains the necessary word of proclamation to his brothers so that 'all marvelled to hear of God's wonders and kept the memory of the saint in fear and love'.[20]

It has been said that 'reading the Lives of Harlots with unrepentant pleasure is risky business'.[21] The point is obvious, and not a new one. Indeed, such risk attends the wider exercise of literature and theology as the imagination of the poet and writer is uncircumscribed by the careful demands of theology. At the beginning of the third century Origen wrote a commentary on the Song of Songs which he read as a song 'recited in the character of a bride who was being married and burned with a heavenly love for her bridegroom, who is the Word of God',[22] and he was perfectly well aware of the risks involved in reading

---

An Erotics of Ancient Hagiography (Philadelphia, PA: University of Pennsylvania Press, 2004), pp. 147–54. Jasper, *The Sacred Body*, pp. 69–80.

[17]   Ward, *Harlots of the Desert*, p. 54.

[18]   Cf. Psalm 55:6–8. 'Truly, I would flee far away; I would lodge in the wilderness.'

[19]   Ward, *Harlots of the Desert*, p. 55.

[20]   Ibid., p. 56.

[21]   Burrus, *The Sex Lives of Saints*, p. 155.

[22]   Origen, *The Prologue to the Commentary on the Song of Songs*, trans. Rowan A. Greer (Mahwah, NJ: The Paulist Press, 1979), p. 217.

such spiritual texts to those still subject to 'the vexations of flesh and blood'. Some of the greatest texts of literature should be restricted only to those who have 'attained a perfect and mature age'.[23] Yet, the risk that is inherent in the Eucharistic body is precisely the point, the paradox of the 'Word made flesh'. It is this that drives the erotic language of the *Canción de la subida del Monte Carmelo* of St John of the Cross, the dramatic and fleshly night visions of Dame Julian of Norwich, and the sermons, in his turn, of St Bernard of Clairvaux on the Song of Songs.[24] The Eucharistic body is '*con ansias en amores inflamada*' ('inflamed by love's desires'), language drawn from the experience of erotic anticipation, yet, in St John of the Cross' poem such desires are actually the entrance to the dark night of sensory purification in which 'the soul sings of the path she followed as she left behind attachment to herself and to created things'.[25] In the writings of St John of the Cross, of Meister Eckhart, of Teresa of Avila and of all the late medieval Christian mystics we enter a profoundly Trinitarian world of which the energies are not motivated by the theological world of the creeds and councils of the Church, but they are rather found in the form of a reverent experiment and a seeking to express the inner dynamism of the Divine life with all its forces, its potential, its dangers, and its mystery.[26] The language used to express such Trinitarianism must of necessity be inconsistent, incomplete, and finally *poetic*.[27] But such mystical writing shares liturgical roots with the shape and even the language of the earliest Eucharistic liturgies, a connection that has not so far been adequately recognized, and which finds its focus in the great moment at the heart of the Eucharistic prayer when the congregation, together with angels and archangels and the whole company of heaven, in a moment of eternity lost in time, utter the Sanctus, the ancient great hymn of praise that has its origins in the vision of the Lord that is granted to Isaiah in the Temple (Isaiah 6:1–3). The liturgical scholar E.C. Ratcliff argued that in Hippolytus's *Apostolic Tradition* the anaphora originally ended with the Sanctus. Few have accepted his insight, but it seems theologically to be profoundly correct as the Eucharist reaches its conclusion in the merging of the energies of the human, the spiritual and the

---

[23]   Ibid., p. 218.

[24]   For a modern instance of this 'paradox' of spirituality and the Eucharistic body see the novel by Ron Hansen, *Mariette in Ecstasy* (1991).

[25]   St John of the Cross, *Song of the Ascent of Mount Carmel*, reprinted in Don Cupitt, *Mysticism after Modernity* (Oxford: Blackwell, 1998), pp. 72–3; *Dark Night of the Soul*, trans. Mirabai Starr (London: Rider, 2002), p. 33.

[26]   See Bernard McGinn, *The Mystical Thought of Meister Eckhart* (New York: Crossroad Publishing, 2001), p. 90.

[27]   The use of the word 'poetic' here is quite deliberate. When Jesus utters the words to his disciples, 'Do this in remembrance of me' (I Corinthians 11: 24), the verb which he uses is 'ποιεῖτε'.

divine in words of supreme poetry that celebrate the final flooding of heaven and earth with the glory of God.[28]

It is this supreme moment of praise that encapsulates in language the mystical tradition and its sense of the body. In a very real manner the Sanctus is pure 'language', making it nonsense to speak of the 'mystical experience'. There is no experience prior to language, nothing anterior that we strive to put into words. The Word is all. As Don Cupitt has expressed it:

> St John of the Cross did not first have a language-transcending experience and then subsequently try to put it into words. On the contrary, the very composition of the poem was *itself* the mystical experience. The happiness is *in the text*; it lies in the fact that John, in prison, has been able through the imagery of the poem to make religious happiness out of the various conflicting forces bearing upon him and the personal suffering he is undergoing. *Writing* is redemption ...[29]

We are close here to the heart of the serious fascination and necessity of the study of literature and theology. Participating in the liturgy is an utterance of words, a *poiesis* or making, which is the realization not of the Word *made* flesh, for it is, in the Prologue of St John's Gospel, the Word who 'dwells among us' and whose glory 'we beheld': and it is the Word which comes to us as flesh in the incarnation and in the sacrament. Thus in the twelfth century, Arnold of Bonneval (d. after 1156) is very precise in his description of the identification of the Eucharist and the Church, writing that 'Christ calls this sacrament sometimes flesh and blood, sometimes bread, and sometimes his body ... By his body he meant to indicate both himself and his church, of which he is the head, and which he unites by the communion of flesh and blood.'[30] It is what Christ *says* and the meaning of his words that is important. But this does not imply that for the medieval Christian the Word is not also felt and known in the body. In the form of the bread and wine within the narrative of the Eucharistic liturgy the Word 'becomes' (ἐγένετο) flesh in miracles of consecrated wafers dropping blood, actually and creepily, as Caroline Walker Bynum describes it:

---

[28]   E.C. Ratcliff, 'The Sanctus and the Pattern of the Early Anaphora', *Journal of Ecclesiastical History*, vol. 1, no. 1 (1950), 29–36, vol. 1, no. 2 (1950), 125–34, reprinted in E.C. Ratcliff, *Liturgical Studies*, ed. A.H. Couratin and D.H. Tripp (London: SPCK, 1976), pp. 18–40.

[29]   Don Cupitt, *Mysticism after Modernity*, p. 74. Denys Turner in *The Darkness of God* (1995) goes even further and denies that there is any such thing as mystical 'experience'. Rather, through language there is only realized a silence or negativity which is the darkness of God.

[30]   Jean Leclercq, 'Les Meditations eucharistiques d'Arnauld de Bonneval', *Recherches de théologie ancienne et médiévale*, 13 (1946), 53. See also Caroline Walker Bynum, *Holy Feast and Holy Fast: The Religious Significance of Food to Medieval Women* (Berkeley, CA: University of California Press, 1987), pp. 62–4.

Miracles of bleeding hosts, which proliferate from the twelfth century on, sometimes have sinister overtones. The host becomes flesh to announce its violation; the bleeding is an accusation. When the nun Wilburgis (d.1289) took the host to her enclosure to help her avoid sexual temptation, it revealed itself, in a quite common miracle, as a beautiful baby who spoke the words of the Song of Songs. But when another nun hid a host that she dared not swallow because she was in mortal sin it turned into flesh. The second miracle sounds a threatening note not present in the first.[31]

Certainly the increasingly graphic and bizarre forms of especially women's Eucharistic piety in the twelfth and thirteenth centuries can and should be linked to various kinds of psychosomatic conditions, yet, nevertheless, theologically they remain to a degree at least consistent with the doctrinal insistence on the reality of the incarnation and the paradox of the Word made flesh, the word, and words, made real in human fleshly experience. Certainly many thirteenth century theologians, such as James of Vitry and Thomas of Cantimpré endorsed such graphic Eucharistic piety as evidence of the falsity of the heretical claim that God was not present in the matter of human flesh.[32] In literature, and art, we find celebrated that which has been described by Leo Steinberg as the 'incomprehension' and 'oblivion' of the Church and so much of its theology, an oblivion that is 'profound, willed and sophisticated. It is the price paid by the modern world for its massive historic retreat from the mythical grounds of Christianity.'[33] It was a price felt so keenly by those scholars and theologians we have been returning to in our discussions of the early conferences and their turn to literature.

Nor is such extreme and complex Eucharistic 'devotion' limited to the medieval period. A twentieth century thinker as sophisticated as Simone Weil, who very likely died as a result of anorexia nervosa, found it quite reasonable when she was told by her doctor of the nun who had nourished herself for an extended period on the holy Eucharist. One thinks again of the story of St Mary of Egypt. Weil's doctor is well aware of the dilemma, probably unwittingly using the ancient language of the (saving) wounds of Christ: 'I had the sensation that I was both giving her pleasure and doing her *harm*. This was how it was with this creature who was at war with her own life. If you did one side of her good,

---

[31]   Bynum, *Holy Feast and Holy Fast*, p. 63.

[32]   For more arguments for the 'fleshly' and miraculous experience of the Eucharist as a guard against heresy, see Ernest W. McDonnell, *The Beguines and Beghards in Medieval Culture, with Special Emphasis on the Belgian Scene* (New Brunswick, NJ: Rutgers University Press, 1954), pp. 310, 315, 330, 415.

[33]   Leo Steinberg, *The Sexuality of Christ in Renaissance Art and in Modern Oblivion*, 2nd edn (Chicago, IL: Chicago University Press, 1997), p. 106.

you wounded the other side.'[34] At her most extreme, Weil monstrously identifies wholly with the sacrificial flesh of the incarnate Lord, describing herself as a form of nourishment for soldiers dying at the front in the Second World War. She prays (and her words were read to us by Ann Loades, painfully, in her paper of 1982):

> That I may be unable to will any bodily movement, or even attempt at any movement, like a total paralytic. That I may be incapable of receiving any sensation, like someone who is completely blind, deaf, and deprived of all the senses. That I may be unable to make the slightest connection between two thoughts ... devoured by God, transformed into Christ's substance, and given for food to afflicted men whose body and soul lack every kind of nourishment. And let me be a paralytic – blind, deaf, witless, and utterly decrepit.[35]

Appalling though this may be, Weil is, in fact, in a tradition of both men and women who identify utterly with the Eucharistic body, a tradition that finds its origins in the Christ of the Passion and the Suffering Servant of the text of the deutero-Isaiah.[36] It is closely connected with the idea of the body, beginning with Christ's body on the cross, as a text to be read for our salvation – reading as salvation.[37] In the fourteenth century the English poet and mystic Richard Rolle wrote in his work *Meditations on the Passion*, having compared Christ's body with the starry heaven, a net, a dovecot and a honeycomb: 'More yet, Sweet Jesu, thy body is like a book written all in red ink; so is thy body all written with red wounds.'[38]

Simone Weil's figure as the Suffering Servant who is read and devoured, is present everywhere in the literature of the lives of the early saints. In the fourth century *Lausiac History* we find the story of the mad kitchen-maid who is the 'sponge of the monastery' upon whose (non)existence the community feeds and by which it is nourished. Providing food for others 'not one ever saw her chew anything during the years of her life ... without speaking little or much, though

---

[34] S. Pétrement, *Simone Weil: A Life*, trans. E. Crauford (London: Mowbray, 1977), p. 178.

[35] Quoted in Ann Loades, 'Simone Weil – Sacrifice: A Problem for Theology,' in David Jasper (ed.), *Images of Belief in Literature* (London: Macmillan, 1984), p. 126.

[36] Isaiah 53:1–12. 'Surely he has borne our infirmities and carried our diseases; yet we accounted him stricken, struck down by God, and afflicted' (v. 4).

[37] See above on Blanchot and Kafka, p. 79.

[38] Quoted in Finaldi, *The Image of Christ*. Catalogue of the exhibition *Seeing Salvation*, National Gallery, London, February–May, 2000 (London: National Gallery, 2000), p. 148. We might compare such 'reading of the body' to Isaac Watt's (1674–1748) great hymn, 'When I survey the wondrous Cross', based on Galatians 6:14.

she was beaten with blows, insulted, laden with curses, and treated with disgust'.[39] And when it is finally revealed that upon her the well-being of all others depends, she disappears into the desert and is lost.

Theologically and within the Church this Eucharistic tradition changed and very largely decayed after the Reformation and with the advent of modernity, to the extent that one notable Roman Catholic liturgical scholar, Louis Bouyer, in his influential book *Eucharist* (1966) entitles his penultimate chapter 'Modern Times: Decomposition and Reformation', writing of the 'un-eucharistic eucharist of the Reformers'.[40] Yet it was never entirely lost, within even the secular traditions of art and literature and in their recognition of the power of the image and of the word. We need only return again to the by now familiar example of Coleridge on the power of language to see the close relationship between the Eucharistic body of the sacrament and the Romantic sense of the immense power of the symbol in language and poetry, partaking of the reality which it seeks to render intelligible and present. In *The Statesman's Manual* Coleridge describes the words of Scripture as 'the living *educts* of the Imagination'. The imagination he regards as incorporating reason with 'Images of the Sense' and as giving birth to a system of symbols which are 'consubstantial with the truths, of which they are the conductors.' Then, writing of the words of Scripture themselves, he affirms that:

> These are Wheels which Ezekiel beheld, when the hand of the Lord was upon him, and he saw visions of God as he sate among the captives by the river of Chebar. *Whithersoever the Spirit was to go, the wheels went, and thither was their spirit to go: for the spirit of the living creature was in the wheels also.* The truths and the symbols that represent them move in conjunction and form the living chariot that bears up (for *us*) the throne of the Divine Humanity. Hence, by a derivative, indeed, but not a divided, influence, and though in a secondary yet in more than a metaphorical sense, the Sacred Book is worthily intitled [*sic*] *the* WORD OF GOD.[41]

Coleridge's sense of the living power of language is clear, and in particular the power of the words of Scripture to carry us as in a living chariot into the presence

---

[39]   Text reproduced in Michel de Certeau, *The Mystic Fable*, vol. 1: *The Sixteenth and Seventeenth Centuries*, trans. Michael B. Smith (Chicago, IL: Chicago University Press, 1992), pp. 32–3. See also Edith Wyschogrod, *Saints and Postmodernism* (Chicago, IL: Chicago University Press, 1990), ch. 1, 'Why Saints?', pp. 1–30.

[40]   Louis Bouyer of the Oratory, *Eucharist: Theology and Spirituality of the Eucharistic Prayer*, trans. Charles Underhill Quinn (Notre Dame, IN: University of Notre Dame Press, 1968), pp. 380–442.

[41]   S.T. Coleridge, *Lay Sermons*, ed. R.J. White, *The Collected Works*, vol. 6 (Princeton, NJ: Princeton University Press, 1972), p. 29. See also above, p. 133.

of the Word made flesh, the Divine Humanity.[42] In the nineteenth century it is very evident how such a sense in Romanticism of the powerful capacity of language to realize 'in more than a metaphorical sense' had not only a profound influence on the renovation of Eucharistic devotion of the Oxford Movement, but also the liturgical recovery prompted by Dom Prosper Guéranger's refounding of the Benedictine Abbey of Solesmes in 1832 which formed the true beginning of the Liturgical Movement, and through the theology of Newman who was, in many ways, the guiding spirit behind the Second Vatican Council in the century after his death, to the composition and promulgation of the first of the Constitutions of the Council, on the Sacred Liturgy (*Sacrosanctum Concilium*) on 4 December 1963.

In drawing towards a conclusion in this chapter, therefore, it is fitting to refer briefly to that Council, which took place in Rome between 1962 and 1965, and its stress on the central importance of the liturgy known as 'something profound rather than merely external'.[43] What is emphasized in the documents of the Council is the corporate nature of the Eucharist, stressing like the medieval Church the elements of bread and wine, the body and blood of Christ, as symbols not just of humankind but of the whole mystical body which is the Church. Throughout there is the presence of Christ. Christ is present in the 'sacrifice of Mass' in the person of the priest, in the 'Eucharistic species', in word and sacrament, Christ speaking when Holy Scripture is read in the church and, finally but not least, present in the community of those gathered as the Church.[44] Furthermore, the importance of the eschatological dimension of the Eucharistic body is clear, as in the ancient tradition inhabited by St Maximus the Confessor and others, wherein the sense of anticipation sustains the life of the Eucharistic prayer as the celebration of the narrative of the Last Supper with its imagery of fleshly consumption is followed by the invocation of the Holy Spirit in the epiclesis and the consummation of all things as we finally enter into our heritage in the company of the Virgin Mary, all the saints and our brothers and sisters living and departed.[45] The 'Pastoral Constitution on the Church in the Modern World' from the documents of Vatican II states:

---

[42] See further, Emerson R. Marks, *Coleridge on the Language of Verse* (Princeton, NJ: Princeton University Press, 1981). Compare also the great poem of the English-born early American poet, Edward Taylor (*c.*1644–1729), 'The Joy of Church Fellowship rightly attended'. 'For in Christ's Coach they sweetly sing, As they to Glory ride therein', *The Oxford Book of American Verse* (New York: Oxford University Press, 1950), p. 15.

[43] *The Documents of Vatican II*, ed. Walter M. Abbott SJ (London: Geoffrey Chapman, 1972), p. 138.

[44] Ibid., pp. 140–41.

[45] I am drawing here from the wording of the 1982 Scottish Liturgy of the Scottish Episcopal Church.

> The Lord left behind a pledge of this hope and strength for life's journey in that sacrament of faith where natural elements refined by man are changed into His glorified Body and Blood, providing a meal of brotherly solidarity and a foretaste of the heavenly banquet.[46]

The issues in literature and theology with which we have been involved have led to the formulation of such eschatological, theological language, rooted in liturgical practice.

Writing only one year after the conclusion of the Council, Louis Bouyer indicates in detail the continuity between the post-Vatican II Eucharistic liturgies, both Catholic and Protestant, and the earliest liturgical texts that we have alluded to, Hippolytus' *Apostolic Tradition* in particular.[47] The anaphora, as the great act of thanksgiving for creation and redemption, contains the form found in Hippolytus with the mention of the body 'which will be given for you'[48] as a deliberate anticipation of the Passion to come, an event which has now taken place in history involving the broken flesh of the incarnate Lord, and an anticipation of the banquet which is to come and guaranteed by the coming of the Holy Spirit.

The dependence of contemporary Eucharistic formulations on the formulas of the early Church in the Roman rite and the Mozarabic and Gallican tradition sustains the early dynamic and necessary interplay between Word, words and flesh. As in the literature of the mystical tradition, and indeed poetry more generally, the word is not dependent upon experience but the other way around. The Word (and therefore words with their capacity for reference) are creative of the real presence of Christ in the Eucharistic body in a paradox that sustains the miracle of the incarnation and is empowered by the dynamism of the inner life of the Trinity. In the words of Edward Schillebeeckx, like Bouyer writing immediately after the conclusion of Vatican II:

> The real presence of Christ in the Eucharist can therefore only be approached by *allowing* the form of bread and wine experienced phenomenally to *refer to* this presence (of Christ and of his Church) in a projective act of faith which is an *element of and in* faith in Christ's Eucharistic presence. The event in which Christ, really present in the Eucharist, appears, or rather, offers *himself* as food and in which the believer receives him as food therefore also includes a projective act of faith. This act does not bring about the real presence, but presupposes it as a

---

46   *The Documents of Vatican II*, pp. 236–7. See also E. Schillebeeckx OP, *The Eucharist*, trans. N.D. Smith (London: Sheed & Ward, 1968), pp. 150–51.

47   See Louis Bouyer, *Eucharist*, pp. 448–61.

48   See above, note 6.

metaphysical priority.[49] Thus the 'sacramental form' is really the 'body of the Lord' proclaiming itself as food. Christ really gives himself as food for the believer. This 'sacramental form' only reaches its fulfilment in the meal in which we nourish ourselves on Christ to become a believing community.[50]

'Christ really gives himself as food for the believer.' The sentence captures well the paradox of the Eucharist body – a fleshly scandal entered into through the Word only by a willing suspension of disbelief.[51] It can be argued that as heirs of the Enlightenment and the primacy of instrumental reason, today we have inherited an attenuation of those forms of embodiment and somatic experience that are to be found only in engagement with text, ritual and liturgical sacramentality.[52] In secular forms of reflection from the Romantics to Zygmunt Bauman and Michel Foucault, what can be broadly called 'modernity' has found its critics, a constant theme being that of disembodiment and with it the devaluation of ritual and liturgical participation (one might add, in a largely post-literate age). In such modernity we have lost the sense of a world that is created and given and replaced it with one that is without any doctrine of creation (known so profoundly in Milton and Blake) but perceived as commodity, to be used and rebuilt in a descending spiral of ecological decay. It reaches its apex, perhaps, in the nihilist social theory of Jean Baudrillard on commodity consumption and the reduction of the body to an object of 'consumerist desire'.[53] We move from the dishonesty of *dissimulation*, which is the first step in sacramental decline, the point at which we can no longer believe what is still present, to 'feign not to have what one has',[54] to the deceit of *simulation*. If the first yet implies a presence, the second admits to an absence. Simulation, a deceit of words, inevitably follows when the order of things in the world is no longer taken as 'given'. To simulate an illness is not simply to pretend, but actually to produce symptoms that were not previously present.

Herein lies the departure of the modern (and postmodern) world of simulacra and simulations from the creative reality of the Eucharistic body. It is

---

[49]   Newman would have deeply approved of this with its sense of the close relationship between faith and human culture.

[50]   Schillebeeckx, *The Eucharist*, p. 150.

[51]   The phrase 'willing suspension of disbelief' is taken from S.T. Coleridge and his description of 'poetic faith' as he reflects upon his and Wordsworth's plan for *Lyrical Ballads*, in *Biographia Literaria* [1817], ed. James Engell and W. Jackson Bate, *The Collected Works*, vol. 7 (Princeton, NJ: Princeton University Press, 1983), vol. 2, p. 6.

[52]   See also David Torevell, *Losing the Sacred: Ritual, Modernity and Liturgical Reform* (London: T&T Clark, 2000), ch. 3, 'Modernity and Disembodiment', pp. 80–115.

[53]   Torevell, *Losing the Sacred*, p. 115.

[54]   Jean Baudrillard, 'Simulacra and Simulations', in *Selected Writings*, ed. Mark Poster (Cambridge: Polity Press, 1988), p. 167.

a pattern of loss that is present also in the decline that we have discussed in our reflections upon literature and theology in Chapter 6. From the very beginning, in Christian witness, faith and participation in the breaking, the death – and resurrection – of the body of the Word made flesh, the scandal which was recognized by St Paul and after him Justin Martyr and Tertullian, the shocking mystery of the invitation to eat flesh and drink blood – symbolically? actually? – was the necessary heart of the matter of being human. In human flesh and the language and poetry of humanity, the Word lives, and we thus exist dynamically in the sensation of the present and the hope of the future. This mystery necessitates a language that is finally beyond our understanding, for what can these words possibly mean: 'Those who eat my flesh and drink my blood have eternal life, and I will raise them up on the last day; for my flesh is true food and my blood is true drink'?[55] Hardly surprisingly Jesus' disciples respond to them with incomprehension: 'This teaching is difficult; who can accept it?'

It is no accident that in the stumbling beginnings of the modern science of anatomy, the cadavers used for dissection were those of criminals, often tortured to death before they become objects for examination on the dissecting table.[56] One of the great early examples of this in art is Rembrandt's painting *The Anatomy Lesson of Dr. Nicholas Tulip* (1632), in which the enquiring Dr Tulip invades the side of the dead body on the table just as Thomas the doubter was invited to penetrate the wounded side of Jesus, now the Jesus of the resurrection body (John 20:24–5). Later the nightmare of Mary Shelley's *Frankenstein* (1818) sees the haunted and godless mind of science seeking to reanimate the dead criminal body, snatched from the grave, with ghastly consequences. It was a nightmare awaiting the renovations in literature and theology that we have been exploring. And it is the Christian tradition that supplies the perfect exemplar to science in the Eucharistic body, the notion of the resurrection of the flesh in the word made flesh of liturgical celebration. Modern science, caught in its own ambivalences and still the child of Enlightenment reason, has perhaps missed the necessary paradox and true scandal of the sacrament, born upon the chariot of language. As David L. Martin has written:

> Marked within the very discursive structures of modern observational science seems to be an irresolvable ambivalence: on the one hand there is the desire to homogenize the difference of knowledge production through the one-to-one subject-object relationships of scientific classification; yet, on the other, there

---

[55]   John 6:54–5.

[56]   See further, David L. Martin, *Curious Visions of Modernity: Enchantment, Magic and the Sacred* (Cambridge, MA: The MIT Press, 2011), ch. 2, 'Bodies', pp. 55–111.

is the constant failure of these efforts to fully erase the heterogeneous from knowledge production.[57]

Such heterogeneity remains, insistently and in spite of all efforts to erase it or deconstruct it from within, in the insistence of the Church and its texts from the very beginning to find human life and hope in the divine, kenotic movement of the Word found in the medium of the flesh, a journey which embraces the full humanity of the body and raises it so that it becomes what it is by virtue of what it shall be. The liturgical scholar, and, one may say, poet, Dom Gregory Dix was thus led to speak of us as *homo eucharisticus*, defined and ever renewed in and through the Eucharist.

I have deliberately, in this chapter, tried to bind more closely together the field of literature with a sacramental theology that was inherent in our deliberations in Durham from the very beginning, above all in the key figure of Newman. In the next chapter I will address the third 'theme' within the study of literature and theology: after poetry and sacrament, we turn now to the central texts of the Bible, read as literature.

---

[57] Martin, *Curious Visions of Modernity*, p. 179.

Chapter 11

The Bible: The Bible as Literature – *Parergon*

Part One: The Bible as Literature

This chapter will be in two parts. The first will be a fairly brief review of the project of studying the Bible as literature since the end of the nineteenth century, and why, on the whole, we avoided it in our conferences. In short it was too *literary*, and elided or avoided the problem of literature and theology as we found ourselves addressing it. The second part will return to the figures of Ulrich Simon and Mieke Bal as they, in their very different ways, unpick the literary readings of the Bible and expose their theological fallacies and dangerous coherences. They thus re-route the study of literature and theology as we understood it.

Although the phrase 'the Bible as Literature' first appeared in Matthew Arnold's *Isaiah of Jerusalem* (1883), twentieth-century study of the Bible as literature truly begins with the work of Richard Green Moulton, Professor of Literary Theory and Interpretation at the University of Chicago.[1] Beginning with *The Literary Study of the Bible* (1895), Moulton (with others) published a collection of essays under the title *The Bible as Literature* (1899), and, more popularly *A Short Introduction to the Literature of the Bible* (1901). His work, though idiosyncratic, remains valuable and even prophetic, David Norton describing him as 'a structuralist before his time'.[2] Moulton was, above all, a literary critic with essentially no concern for theology, his interest focusing almost entirely on literary morphology and form. In his treatment of verse and the Psalms Moulton looks directly back to the eighteenth century and Robert Lowth's *Lectures on the Sacred Poetry of the Hebrews* (1753) with their 'discovery' of literary parallelism, and his work, like Lowth's, following the words of the latter's translator into English,[3] Richard Gregory, is 'more calculated for persons of taste and general reading, than for what is generally termed the learned world'.[4]

---

[1]   See David Norton, *A History of the Bible as Literature*, vol. 2: *From 1700 to the Present Day* (Cambridge: Cambridge University Press, 1993), pp. 277–85.

[2]   Ibid., p. 277.

[3]   Lowth, as was the custom for the Oxford Professor of Poetry even until John Keble's time, lectured in Latin, his work being translated into German before appearing in English in 1787, more than 30 years after their first publication.

[4]   Richard Gregory, quoted in John Drury, ed. *Critics of the Bible, 1724–1873* (Cambridge: Cambridge University Press, 1989), p. 70.

Moulton was only concerned with the English Bible, and, oddly, specifically the Revised Version (1881–85) rather than the 1611 King James Bible, yet his work contains valuable insights, not least in the sense of the wholly unclear distinction between poetry and prose in Hebrew literature.[5] It was a point picked up much later by James L. Kugel in his book *The Idea of Biblical Poetry* (1981). Although Moulton spawned no immediate successors in his field, the purely literary interest in the Bible continued into the earlier part of the twentieth century in such works as Sir James George Frazer's *Passages of the Bible Chosen for Their Literary Beauty and Interest*, first published in 1895, but reprinted in an enlarged form in 1909 and frequently thereafter. Frazer's interest in the English Bible as 'pure literature' was aesthetic and unscholarly. He seeks to render a 'service to lovers of literature' and picks out the 'gems' of the Bible in order to 'delight, to elevate and to console'.[6] Yet some 30 years later it was a major poet, T.S. Eliot, in an influential essay entitled 'Religion and Literature' (1935) who summarily dismissed all such claims for 'the Bible as literature', *fulminating*, in his word, against such claims inasmuch as, he suggests, 'the Bible has had a *literary* influence upon English literature *not* because it has been considered as literature, but because it has been considered as the report of the Word of God. And the fact that men of letters now discuss it as "literature" probably indicates the *end* of its "literary" influence'.[7] But there was also a third and middle path, though it will not concern me here: that of literature as a devotional aid. A year before Eliot's essay appeared, William Ralph Inge, Dean of St Paul's, published *Every Man's Bible: An Anthology Arranged with an Introduction* (1934), a literary anthology without scholarly notes or commentary, designed for 'those who wish to use the Bible as their chief devotional book'.[8]

By the middle years of the twentieth century literary scholarship began to focus firmly and critically on the Hebrew Bible, and the interest was clearly literary rather than theological. Perhaps still the most quoted example of this is the first chapter of Erich Auerbach's great work *Mimesis: The Representation of Reality in Western Literature* (1946) which compares the Hebrew and Greek literary traditions in readings of Genesis 22, the sacrifice of Isaac, and the return of Odysseus in Homer's *Odyssey*. Later books such as *The Bible as Literature* by T.R. Henn, a Cambridge literary scholar noted for his work on W.B. Yeats, are virtually devoid of any religious concerns and paved the way for such books as Robert Alter and Frank Kermode's *The Literary Guide to the Bible* (1987)

---

[5]   R.G. Moulton, *The Literary Study of the Bible: An Account of the Leading Forms of Literature Represented in the Sacred Writings* (London: Isbister and Co., 1896), pp. 113–14.

[6]   Sir James Frazer, *Passages of the Bible Chosen for their Literary Beauty and Interest*, 2nd edn (London: Macmillan, 1909), p. viii.

[7]   T.S. Eliot, *Selected Essays*, 3rd edn (London: Faber and Faber, 1951), p. 390.

[8]   William Ralph Inge, *Every Man's Bible: An Anthology Arranged with an Introduction* (London: Longmans, 1934), p. ix.

which understands the books of the Bible primarily in terms of their 'literary qualities ... in the virtues by which they continue to live as something other than archaeology'.[9] Frankly such approaches were of little interest to us in our concerns for the study of literature and theology. Perhaps it was the very *division* between the Bible 'as literature' and the Bible as what Eliot called 'the report of the Word of God' that was the point for us.

Long ago it was C.S. Lewis who made the reasonable point that those who call themselves professional biblical critics may not be best qualified as literary critics.[10] He warned also, with some justification, in his 1950 essay 'The Literary Impact of the Authorised Version' that the influence of the King James Bible on English literature should not be overestimated, and he reminds his reader, rather in the manner of T.S. Eliot, that when William Tyndale was working on his English Bible his considerations were not literary: 'the matter was much too serious for that: souls were at stake. The same holds for all translators'.[11] In their essay 'To the Reader', the translators of the King James Bible regard its books as, first and foremost 'a fountain of most pure water springing up unto everlasting life'.[12] In short, literature and its study do not necessarily relate easily to the matter of the Bible and its more religious and even theological concerns. Yet such uneasiness remains of profound importance.

Still, the attention of serious literary critics was not to be silenced. It is important to note that it was largely from Jewish critics in the early 1980s that the Bible *as* literature was taken seriously, its literary genius held by them as an intrinsic part of its religious message. Furthermore, the re-emergence of rabbinic interpretation in the business of modern literary theory, as proposed by scholars such as Susan A. Handelman,[13] brought the study of the Bible – and in particular the Hebrew Bible – into close touch with the radical theoretical shifts in literary study associated with philosophical thinkers such as Derrida and Levinas. It cannot be denied that some of the most brilliant contemporary readings of the texts of the Bible are found in Jacques Derrida's 'glosses' on the stories of Babel and Abraham (after Kierkegaard and Kafka), on Tobias and in

---

[9]   Robert Alter and Frank Kermode, General Introduction to *The Literary Guide to the Bible* (London: Collins, 1987), pp. 1–2.

[10]   C.S. Lewis, *Fern-Seed and Elephants*, ed. Walter Hooper (Glasgow: Fontana, 1975), pp. 104–25.

[11]   C.S. Lewis, 'The Literary Impact of the Authorised Version', in *They Asked for a Paper* (London: Bles, 1962), p. 34.

[12]   *The Bible: Authorized King James Version with Apocrypha*, ed. Robert Carroll and Stephen Prickett (Oxford: Oxford University Press, 1997), p. lvi.

[13]   See Susan A. Handelman, *The Slayers of Moses: The Emergence of Rabbinic Interpretation in Modern Literary Theory* (Albany, NY: State University of New York Press, 1982); S.A. Handelman, *Fragments of Redemption: Jewish Thought and Literary Theory in Benjamin, Scholem and Levinas* (Bloomington, IN: Indiana University Press, 1991).

his essay 'Shibboleth'.[14] This latter, originally given as a lecture at a conference on the works of the poet Paul Celan, was reprinted in a volume entitled *Midrash and Literature* (1986), edited by Geoffrey H. Hartman and Sanford Budick, which examines the burgeoning interest among literary theorists at the time in midrash, or 'the rabbinical exegesis of Old Testament writings,' and brings together literary readings of texts as diverse as the book of Genesis, kabbalah, Milton and Kafka. Hartman, in the opening essay on Genesis 32:1–22, the narrative of wrestling Jacob, offers a close reading of the text (with clear deference to Auerbach) that begins with the question, 'is there a basis to the distinction between fiction and scripture?'[15] At the centre of Hartman's literary analysis is the 'struggle for the text', for a supreme fiction that the 'accreted, promissory narrative we call Scripture'[16] offers. Reading the Bible is necessarily a struggle in the 'frictional' encounter with the religious mystery that remains 'baffling on the level of narrative which cannot be smoothed over or harmonized without further redactional or interpretive moves'.[17]

The necessary ambivalence of any answer to the question of the uniqueness of the Bible is reflected in the persistent yet uneasy tradition of poetic and fictive writing from Scripture, with its great example of John Milton's *Paradise Lost* (1667), about which Milton's fellow poet expressed the fear of the 'ruin of sacred truths to fable and old song'.[18] Regarding the Bible as literature can never be a simple, or even safe, matter. Yet in the twentieth-century novelists and creative writers have continually returned to the literary genius of the narratives of the Old Testament for their themes, perhaps the greatest being Thomas Mann's *Joseph und seine Brüder* (1933–42) drawing on Genesis 12–50, and exploring the beginnings of religion and the emergence of the God of Israel.[19] One of the possibilities of such fictional inter-texts with Scripture is the giving of voices to biblical characters who are silent in the Bible itself, a fine example being the Swedish novelist Torgny Lindgren's *Bathsheba* (1984, trans. 1988), written in the rhythms and cadences of the Hebrew original, and subtly developing the

---

[14]   See John D. Caputo, *The Prayers and Tears of Jacques Derrida: Religion without Religion* (Bloomington, IN: Indiana University Press, 1997), p. xxvi.

[15]   Geoffrey H. Hartman, 'The Struggle for the Text', in G.H. Hartman and S. Budick (eds), *Midrash and Literature* (New Haven, CT, and London: Yale University Press, 1986), p. 3.

[16]   Ibid., p. 17.

[17]   Ibid., p. 12.

[18]   Andrew Marvell, 'On Mr Milton's *Paradise Lost*'. Harold Bloom adapted the phrase for the title of his Charles Eliot Norton Lectures (1987–88), *Ruin the Sacred Truths: Poetry and Belief from the Bible to the Present Day* (Cambridge, MA: Harvard University Press, 1989).

[19]   More recent, and slighter examples, include Howard Jacobson, *The Very Model of a Man* (1992), which explores the figure of Cain; Frederick Buechner, *The Son of Laughter* (1993), retelling the story of Jacob; and Joseph Heller, *God Knows* (1984), an irreverent first person narrative account of the life of King David.

shadowy figure of the original biblical figure of Bathsheba. Novelists and writers have also contributed to creative readings of the Old Testament, notably in the collection of Jewish authors entitled *Congregation* (1987), edited by David Rosenberg, in which the novelist Isaac Bashevis Singer writes movingly on the early effect on him as a writer of the book of Genesis.

> I have heard Bible critics maintain that the Book of Genesis was written not by one person but by many, who pieced various legends together. Yet I am sure it was the same master writer, who knew exactly where his pen was leading him. I feel the same way even now, some sixty or seventy years later ... In our times, Tolstoy was a writer of such calibre, and so was Dostoevsky, and so were, to a lesser degree – such remarkable talents as Sholem Aleichem, Peretz, Knut Hamsun, Strindberg, and many others whose books I read in Yiddish or Polish translation and admired immensely.
>
> I am still learning the art of writing from the Book of Genesis and from the Bible generally.[20]

Other contributors to *Congregation* include Elie Wiesel and the novelist Cynthia Ozick.

But where, in this, can we find theology? In his now classic, and much debated, book *The Eclipse of Biblical Narrative* (1974), Hans Frei recounts the rise of historical criticism of the Bible in the eighteenth and nineteenth centuries, and the critical fading of what he calls 'strongly realistic' readings of biblical stories: 'Most eminent among them were all those stories which together went into the making of a single storied or historical sequence'.[21] Literary readings, it might seem, are in danger of ironing out the problems of theology, and it is precisely for this reason that the study of literature and theology, especially when it gives its attention to the Bible, can sometimes be seen as a cheap way into the difficult business of theology, and thus, all too often, we have not been taken seriously by the real, systematic scholars of theology. Thus, in an essay in the Report of the Doctrine Commission of the Church of England, *Believing in the Church* (1981), John Barton and John Halliburton attempt to recover the category of 'story' in the study of theology and liturgy, seeking 'to show that it

---

[20]   Isaac Bashevis Singer, 'Genesis', in David Rosenberg (ed.), *Congregation: Contemporary Writers Read the Jewish Bible* (San Diego, CA, and New York: Harcourt Brace Jovanovich, 1987), p. 7.

[21]   Hans Frei, *The Eclipse of Biblical Narrative: A Study in Eighteenth and Nineteenth Century Hermeneutics* (New Haven, CT, and London: Yale University Press, 1974), p. 1. See also M.H. Abrams, 'The Design of Biblical History', in *Natural Supernaturalism: Tradition and Revolution in Romantic Literature* (New York: W.W. Norton, 1971), pp. 32–7: 'The design of Biblical history constitutes a sharply defined plot with a beginning, a middle, and an end ...' (p. 35).

can be used in a positive way, to describe the way in which much of the Bible, and of other traditions and formularies of Christian faith, actually function in the life of the Church ...'.[22] 'Story', in other words, can be a nice short cut to practical understanding, the Bible being neatly shaped for easier digestion. In the same year, Robert Alter's widely read book *The Art of Biblical Narrative*, building on the work of such theoreticians as Tzvetan Todorov and essays in the journal *Semeia*, suggested that it is 'not presumptuous' to analyse the narratives of the pre-exilic literature of the Pentateuch and the early Prophets with the critical tools used on the novels of Flaubert, Virginia Woolf, Tolstoy or Henry James. Employing a structuralist approach to examine such elements as narrative pace and the use of dialogue and imagery, Alter defends such attention as leading not 'to a more "imaginative" reading of biblical narrative but to a more precise one; and since all these features are linked to discernible details in the Hebrew text, the literary approach is actually a good deal *less* conjectural than ... historical scholarship'.[23] Thus literary critics make a strong claim to serious interpretations of the Bible read *as* literature, releasing themselves from the criticisms of historical anachronisms. The dangers of this we will examine in more detail in the second part of this chapter through the voice of Mieke Bal. In the field of New Testament scholarship, Frank Kermode reinstated the biblical work of the Oxford theologian Austin Farrer when even Farrer himself had largely abandoned his theories:

> He himself altered them, and then more or less gave them up, partly persuaded, no doubt, by criticisms of them as farfetched, partly disturbed by the imputation that a narrative of the kind he professed to be discussing would be more a work of fiction than an account of a crucial historical event. Neither of these judgements seems to me to be well founded.[24]

I think, now (though I did not in the past)[25] that Kermode was wrong and that Farrer was wise enough to perceive the theological dangers of what he was doing

---

[22] John Barton and John Halliburton, 'Story and Liturgy', in *Believing in the Church: The Corporate Nature of Faith* (A Report by the Doctrine Commission of the Church of England) (London: SPCK, 1981), p. 79.

[23] Robert Alter, *The Art of Biblical Narrative* (London: George Allen & Unwin, 1981), p. 21.

[24] Frank Kermode, *The Genesis of Secrecy: On the Interpretation of Narrative* (The Charles Eliot Norton Lectures, 1977–78) (Cambridge, MA: Harvard University Press, 1979), p. 61. To remain for a moment with the New Testament, the critical reading of the Bible as 'fiction' continues to flourish. See, for example, Douglas A. Templeton, *The New Testament as True Fiction* (Sheffield: Sheffield Academic Press, 1999).

[25] See my chapter on Farrer's *Glass of Vision* (1948) in *Coleridge as Poet and Religious Thinker* (London: Macmillan, 1985), pp. 145–52.

in his literary studies of the New Testament in such books as *A Rebirth of Images* (1949) and *A Study in Mark* (1951).

Actually it was the Hebrew Bible rather than the New Testament that yielded the richest fruits of critical attention to the structural forms of narrative and the genres of literature.[26] Furthermore, Jewish critics, their critical souls steeped in the midrashic tradition, have been pre-eminent in close critical readings from the perspective of biblical narrative poetics. Meir Sternberg, a professor of poetics and comparative literature at Tel Aviv University and to whom I shall return more critically in a while, published *The Poetics of Biblical Narrative* in 1987 which focuses on the omniscient biblical narrator who 'concretizes the opposition to the human norm ... in the form of dramatic irony that no character (and, to rub it in, no reader) escapes'.[27] With this omniscience (and the emphasis is deeply patriarchal) the biblical narrator has insight into the minds of his *dramatis personae*, including that of God himself – a tale told like no other. Furthermore, the telling of the biblical story is uniquely rhetorical – a narrative constructed to persuade. Like other biblical literary critics, Sternberg draws on the work of Auerbach, who compares biblical rhetoric with that of Homer – who seeks to enchant us, while the Bible claims our subjection. Sternberg is clear about the unique status of the Bible – but that uniqueness is rooted in literary and rhetorical origins, which are also universal:

> Like all speakers ... the biblical storyteller is a persuader in that he wields discourse to shape response and manipulate attitude. Unlike most speakers, however, his persuasion is not only geared to an ideology but also designed to vindicate and inculcate it. Even among ideological persuaders, he has a special claim to notice, due less to the theology preached than to the rules and rhetoric of its preaching.[28]

For Sternberg, then (and we shall see how Bal profoundly questions the seeming literary bases of his criticism), the Bible is unique not so much for its theological as for its literary quality, its narrator suspended, trickily, between heaven and earth – both human and divine. The literary dilemma originates in the status of the figure of God who is both a subject of representation – a dramatic figure in the poetics of biblical narrative – and its 'inspiring originator'. The narrator is, then, both master and subject of his own narrative, a dilemma shared by no

---

[26]   For example, Adele Berlin in *Poetics and Interpretation of Biblical Narrative* (Sheffield: The Almond Press, 1983) explores character and multiple narrative perspectives in the books of Samuel and Kings. J. Cheryl Exum recovers the tragic vision of Judges, Samuel and Kings in *Tragedy and Biblical Narrative* (Cambridge: Cambridge University Press, 1992).

[27]   Meir Sternberg, The *Poetics of Biblical Narrative: Ideological Literature and the Drama of Reading* (Bloomington, IN: Indiana University Press, 1987), p. 85.

[28]   Ibid., p. 482.

other literature, as Sternberg observes, from Petronius to Joyce.[29] In the Bible, literature and theology blend, for Sternberg, in a unique way.

Thus the poetics of biblical narrative are both universal and unique, a tension described by Harold Fisch in his book *Poetry with a Purpose* (1990) that is caught between the aesthetic and the non-aesthetic modes of discourse within biblical literature. Do the biblical books offer instances of literary art – or is such art subsidiary to their real business, which is religious? The answer must be both affirmative and negative – for their real business, which is beyond the literary, can only be conducted through literary means. Citing both Christian and Jewish authorities, Fisch argues that the Bible is both literature and, in his term, 'anti-literature' – and it is the latter precisely because it is the former. Appealing to Milton, Blake and after them the critic Northrop Frye, Fisch acknowledges the 'mythopoeic power of the biblical narratives', and yet from St Augustine, the medieval Jewish philosopher Yehuda Halevi, to Dr Samuel Johnson it has been argued that, in Johnson's categorical words, 'the intercourse between God and the human soul cannot be poetical'.[30] Theology and literature remain utterly distinct. Yet for Sternberg the Bible contains poetry with a purpose, theological poetry – in his term, it is an 'ideological literature'.

The form and structure of biblical poetics has been the subject of a number of studies in the later twentieth century, notably Robert Alter's *The Art of Biblical Poetry* (1985) and James L. Kugel's *The Idea of Biblical Poetry* (1981). Both look back (Alter more critically) to the seminal work of Robert Lowth in the eighteenth century and his Oxford Lectures on the *Sacred Poetry of the Hebrews* (1853) which, with its 'discovery' of parallelism, brought Hebrew poetry back into the mainstream of English verse in, for example, the poetry of Christopher Smart, who praised Lowth's work for 'its elegance, novelty, variety, spirit and (I had almost said) divinity',[31] and above all in the poetic forms of William Blake who, in the introduction to *Jerusalem*, left the 'monotonous cadence' of English blank verse for 'a variety in every line, both of cadences and number of syllables'.[32] The implication is that poets could share their vocation with the psalmists and prophets and dare to articulate what Alter calls 'the intricate substantive links between the poetic vehicle and the religious vision of the poets, and the crucial

---

[29]   Ibid., p. 155.

[30]   Harold Fisch, *Poetry with a Purpose: Biblical Poetics and Interpretation* (Bloomington, IN: Indiana University Press, 1990), p. 1.

[31]   Christopher Smart, *Universal Visiter*, January/February 1856, quoted in John Drury (ed.), *Critics of the Bible, 1724–1873* (Cambridge: Cambridge University Press, 1989), p. 70.

[32]   William Blake, *Complete Writings*, ed. Geoffrey Keynes (Oxford: Oxford University Press, 1972), p. 621.

place of the corpus of biblical poetry in the complex growth of the Western literary tradition.'[33]

The capacity for literary readings of the Bible to 'open' the text to reveal what is hidden and therefore too often forgotten below its surface can, for some people, be an emancipatory experience that may be either liberating or threatening. The study of literature in the twentieth century saw a shift of attention away from merely the text itself towards the response of the reader[34] – and nowhere has this been more apparent than in feminist revisionary readings of the Bible. In her book *God and the Rhetoric of Sexuality* (1978), and continuing in the literary tradition of structuralist readings, Phyllis Trible opens her discussion of the book of Ruth with a search for the 'deep structures' which underlie its 'surface design'.[35] Trible's reading of the story of Naomi and Ruth 'as they struggle for survival in a patriarchal environment' begins with an observation of the power of the *grammar* of the text: 'The story begins in the tension of grammar (vv. 1–5). Third-person narration names the characters, specifies their relationships, and describes their plight, but it does not allow them to emerge as human beings.'[36] It is precisely this hiddenness that feminist interpretations have sought to bring to the surface in readings which do not so much apply any critical theory to the text, but bring the biblical text into conversations with theoretical approaches which oblige it to speak, sometimes against itself, in ways hitherto rendered inaudible within the traditions of 'patriarchal' interpretation.[37] Alicia Suskin Ostriker writes of 'the buried woman in biblical narrative' who remains 'out of my sight' until readings of the text effect an emancipation and a challenge to the politics of interpretation which have for so long deliberately effected such burials.[38] Cheryl Exum has, more recently, taken in cultural studies to the task in her book *Plotted, Shot, and Painted: Cultural Representations of Biblical Women* (1996), using the lens of film and the images of the visual arts

---

[33]   Robert Alter, *The Art of Biblical Poetry* (New York: Basic Books, 1985), p. 214. Such 'substantive links' were famously acknowledged by S.T. Coleridge in his definition of the Primary Imagination in *Biographia Literaria* [1817], ch. 13, as 'the living Power and prime Agent of all human Perception, and as a repetition in the finite mind of the eternal act of creation in the Infinite I AM'.

[34]   For a discussion of the move towards 'reader-response' in biblical studies, see Mark G. Brett, 'The Future of Reader Criticism?', in Francis Watson (ed.), *The Open Text: New Directions for Biblical Studies* (London: SCM, 1993), pp. 13–31.

[35]   Phyllis Trible, *God and the Rhetoric of Sexuality* (London: SCM, 1978), p. 166.

[36]   Ibid., pp. 166–7.

[37]   Mieke Bal describes this encounter as 'transgressive': '... the very dialogue between narrative theory and a body of biblical texts leads to a transgression of disciplinary boundaries'. 'Dealing/with/Women: Daughters in the Book of Judges', in Regina Schwartz (ed.), *The Book and the Text: The Bible and Literary Theory* (Oxford: Blackwell, 1990), p. 16.

[38]   Alicia Suskin Ostriker, *Feminist Revision and the Bible* (Oxford: Blackwell, 1993).

to reveal the hidden lives of such women as Bathsheba, Naomi and Delilah, and claiming critical importance for the 'cinematic power and interpretive genius' of Cecil B. de Mille in his Oscar-winning film *Samson and Delilah* (1949).[39] These are powerful readings, but how do they relate to the deep questions of theology?

The anger which is so often a characteristic of such feminist readings of the Bible is rooted in the felt need to unpick the *coherence* of the Bible as this is imposed by certain demands of history and theology. In short, there are different stories to be found within the narratives of the texts, and thus, in her study of the book of Judges, *Death and Dissymmetry* (1988), Mieke Bal seeks to establish a *counter-coherence* against the grain of the patriarchal stories and politics that have dominated its readings (and, indeed, its very writing). This necessarily deconstructive exercise begins with a creative moment that finds a voice to address the issue of women's anonymity in Judges (specifically the cases of Jephthah's daughter, the Levite's concubine and Samson's bride). Bal gives them names:

> No names; no narrative power. They are subjected to the power of, mostly named, men. The first act that awaits us, then, is to provide the victims with a name. A name that makes them into subjects, that makes them speakable. Naming the victims is an act of insubordination to the text. Is it a distortion? In fact, the problem of naming is a useful way to become aware of the need of readerly activity. But the goal is not to embellish the text; only to account for its effect.[40]

The responsibility of the reader against the grain of the politics of patriarchal interpretation is clearly asserted – reading as creative as well as critical in order to rewrite those forgotten by history into history. This is a form of aggressive reading that rescues characters within the text from becoming mere textual objects and perhaps from the 'purpose' of the poetry. Implicit within it is the possibility that biblical texts may finally be irrecoverable (a conclusion reached, for example, by Daphne Hampson), and that the book of Hosea, for example, may finally be irredeemably a work of 'prophetic pornography'.[41] But this is merely to place the Bible into the context of *all* other literature, which must take its chance unprotected by the odour of sanctity that surrounds the 'sacred text'. Yet is it that simple?

The *politics* of 'emancipatory' readings have not been limited to issues of feminism and gender. As novelists like Howard Jacobson have given dramatic readings of the figure of Cain, so the critic Regina Schwartz has given detailed

---

[39]　J. Cheryl Exum, *Plotted, Shot, and Painted: Cultural Representations of Biblical Women* (Sheffield: Sheffield Academic Press, 1996), p. 236.

[40]　Bal, 'Dealing/with/Women: Daughters in the Book of Judges', p. 19.

[41]　A term used by Cheryl Exum in *Plotted, Shot and Painted*, pp. 101–28.

readings to expose the 'violent legacy of monotheism' in her book *The Curse of Cain* (1997), with its focus on the city (Babel), the possession of the land and the identity of nationhood. The beautifully ironic opening paragraph of Jacobson's novel *The Very Model of a Man* (1993) best expresses the essence also of Schwartz's concerns:

> The Lord was our shepherd. We did not want. He fed us in green and fat pastures, gave us to drink from deep waters, made us to lie in a good fold. That which was lost, He sought; that which was broken, He bound up; that which was driven away, He brought again into the flock. Excellent, excellent, had we been sheep.[42]

This familiar pastoral (and patriarchal) image from Psalm 23 resonates throughout R.S. Sugirtharajah's work on biblical interpretation and postcolonial criticism.[43] His revisioning of biblical hermeneutics begins with the critical role played by creative literature as a precursor of current postcolonial thinking. In the Ugandan author's Akiki Nyabongo's novel *Africa Answers Back* (1936), the Bible comes under critical scrutiny in the scene when the missionary Abala Stanley Mujungu reads from the Bible the story of the Israelites' crossing of the Red Sea to the King of Buganda, who relates immediately to the 'White man's mythology', remarking: 'Hm, that's just like our story, because when the Gods came from the north they reached the River Kira and the waters stopped flowing, so that they could get across. Isn't it strange that his story and ours should be the same.'[44] The Bible, as a text of Western imperial authority becomes, in the novel, a place of 'hermeneutical contestation'.[45]

The 'postmodern condition' which is heralded by Jean-François Lyotard in his much quoted *Report on Knowledge* of 1979 has, arguably, had little lasting effect on biblical criticism. Indeed, the fact that most of the books so far referred to in this chapter were published some 30 years ago might suggest that, apart from a few ripples on the surface, the reading of the Bible has gone on much the same way, if anything critically even more conservative, in the present century even while 'literary approaches' to Scripture have continued with little of profound effect on the fading but still formidable citadel of biblical authority. To some extent this might account for the relatively small part played by the Bible in our study of literature and theology. In 1988, Edgar V. McKnight published his *Postmodern Use of the Bible*, a work which does not go much further than reflect upon the shift of critical attention from text to reader-response criticism

---

[42]   Howard Jacobson, *The Very Model of a Man* (London: Penguin, 1993), p. 1.

[43]   R.S. Sugirtharajah, *Postcolonial Criticism and Biblical Interpretation* (Oxford: Oxford University Press, 2002).

[44]   Akiki Nyabongo, *Africa Answers Back* (London: George Routledge & Sons, 1936), p. 10.

[45]   Sugirtharajah, *Postcolonial Criticism*, p. 19. See also above on Martin Jarrett-Kerr on the Bible and Western colonialism, pp. 65–7.

and the movement away from historical methods of criticism. A.K.M. Adam, in *What is Postmodern Biblical Criticism?* (1995) suggests, more broadly, that postmodernism is little more than a revising of earlier bad habits and that 'most intellectuals and academies continue to function along typically modern lines'.[46]

But this is entirely to miss the point that at the heart of Lyotard's *Report* is essentially a *literary* observation: 'Simplifying to the extreme, I define *postmodern* as incredulity towards metanarratives'.[47] Linking postmodernism with poststructuralism, Stephen D. Moore focuses on the Derridean relationship of speech with writing in the biblical texts in his book *Poststructuralism and the New Testament* (1994), locating the history of Western 'logocentrism' in Genesis 3:18: 'They heard the sound of the Lord God walking in the garden at the time of the evening breeze, and the man and his wife hid themselves from the presence of the Lord God,' and Moore quotes the Jewish poet Edmond Jabès, 'The garden is speech'.[48] Derrida carries Jabès' comment on language beyond the Fall: 'God no longer speaks to us; he has interrupted himself: we must take words upon ourselves. We must ... entrust ourselves to traces ... because we have ceased hearing the voice from within the immediate proximity of the garden ... The *difference* between speech and writing is sin ... lost immediacy, work outside the garden.'[49] Such work, then, is the work of literature, its contours in the context of readings of the Bible examined at length by Stephen Moore and other members of the so-called 'Bible and Culture Collective' in the volume entitled *The Postmodern Bible* (1995).

It is easy now to see why such enterprises very largely passed us by as we gradually began to turn back to *theology* and literature as our serious concern at the very end of the last century. Certainly we had concerns in common with the Bible and Cultural Collective, but they missed the central point, I think. Their concern was not with salvation and the ends of theology. True, setting themselves in direct opposition to Robert Alter and Frank Kermode and the *Literary Guide to the Bible*, the Collective sought to deconstruct the 'institutionalizing and normative effects' of the work of Alter, Kermode and others, finding 'central and energizing' what Alter and Kermode dispatch to the margins, including the 'literary criticism' of feminism, ideological readings, psychoanalytic and Marxist approaches.[50] Like Mieke Bal, they seek to read politically, against the grain of

---

[46]   A.K.M. Adam, *What is Postmodern Biblical Criticism?* (Minneapolis, MN: Augsburg Press, 1995), p. 4.

[47]   Jean-François Lyotard, *The Postmodern Condition: A Report on Knowledge*, trans. Geoff Bennington and Brian Massumi (Manchester: Manchester University Press, 1986), p. xxiv.

[48]   Edmond Jabès, *Le Livre des questions* (Paris: Gallimard, 1963), quoted in Jacques Derrida, 'Edmond Jabès and the Question of the Book', in *Writing and Difference*, trans. Alan Bass (London: Routledge, 1981), p. 68.

[49]   Derrida, 'Edmond Jabès and the Question of the Book',, p. 68.

[50]   Ibid., p. 7.

both biblical texts and the institution of biblical scholarship, and they, too, begin, at least, not with theory, but with close and creative readings of particular texts in acts of 'consciousness-raising about our own reading experiences'.[51] It thus seems appropriate that when *The Postmodern Bible Reader* appeared in 2001, deliberately dedicated to 'our friends and colleagues' of the Bible and Culture Collective, its focus was firmly on the writings of literary critics and writers from Umberto Eco to Roland Barthes, Hélène Cixous, J. Hillis Miller, Mieke Bal, Terry Eagleton and Jacques Derrida. Not one theologian was in their midst.

But as one brief example of 'postmodern' and creative biblical criticism we might turn to the joint work of a poet and a literary critic, David Rosenberg and Harold Bloom's *Book of J* (1990). Rosenberg and Bloom begin with the critical tradition which suggests that the Pentateuchal literature is a composite work from a number of different 'authors' or strands – and identifying the so-called 'J' author, they claim to have recovered a literary and religious masterpiece from some of the oldest elements of the Hebrew Bible. My own reading of Bloom's introductory essay to the *Book of J* suggests that this is a masterpiece of post-modern irony – deconstructive, playful, oblique – and literary to the highest degree, positively antagonistic to any theological concerns. Bloom plays the game of Old Testament criticism to perfection. Yet his tone from the outset is deliberately that of the story teller – the maker of fictions: 'In Jerusalem, nearly three thousand years ago, an unknown author composed a work that has formed the spiritual consciousness of much of the world ever since.'[52] He (ironically?) assumes, of course, without comment, the proposal of the scholarly authorities that subscribe (as a clearly established fact) to the 'four author' hypothesis – the strands in the narrative of the Pentateuch known as J E P and D. As the biblical scholar Gerhard von Rad confidently states: 'The books Genesis to Joshua consist of several continuous source documents that were woven together more or less skilfully by a redactor'.[53] Deliberately, and with delicate irony, following the historical methods of von Rad, Bloom concludes that the author of 'J' was a woman of high birth 'and that she wrote for her contemporaries as a woman, in friendly competition with her only strong rival among those contemporaries, the male author of the court history narrative in 2 Samuel'.[54] Building upon an understanding of humour and an analysis of literary sophistication 'as knowing as Shakespeare or Jane Austen',[55] Bloom meets biblical critics on their own turf, and establishes 'J' as the 'ultimate ancestor of *The Canterbury Tales* as well as of

---

[51]   Ibid., p. 23.

[52]   Harold Bloom, Introduction to *The Book of J*., trans. David Rosenberg, interpreted by Harold Bloom (London: Faber and Faber, 1991), p. 9.

[53]   Gerhard von Rad, *Genesis: A Commentary*, trans. John H. Marks, 3rd revised edn (London: SCM, 1972), p. 24.

[54]   Bloom, Introduction to *The Book of J*., p. 9.

[55]   Ibid., p. 12.

Tolstoy's fictions and Kafka's parables'.[56] His ultimate purpose in 'scrubbing away the varnish' seems to be anything but religious:

> I do not think that appreciating J will help us love God or arrive at the spiritual or historical truth of whatever Bible. I want the varnish off because it conceals a writer of the eminence of Shakespeare or Dante, and such a writer is worth more than many creeds, many churches, many scholarly certainties.[57]

Bloom's 'commentary' on J is unsettling and destabilizing, serious and mocking, irreligious yet, to the canons of literature, reverent. It poses the problem of the Bible *as* 'pure' literature while daring as an outsider to enter the camp of biblical criticism which is concerned, in some sense, with the Bible as a sacred text. It also enters the Derridean world of 'the adventure of the text as weed, as outlaw far from "*the fatherland of the Jews*," which is a "*sacred text surrounded by commentaries*".[58] In this postmodern and Kafkaesque world (though Kafka never writes 'pure' literature)[59] writing and the Bible as the Book become the problem, the way of God being the way of detour. Derrida again quotes Jabès, both of them Jewish writers, looking back to the figure of Jacob: '*Reb Jacob, who was my first master, believed in the virtue of the lie because, he said, there is no writing without a lie and writing is the way of God*'.[60] I wish now that Derrida could have been with us in our early days in Durham, before we (and he?) lost our way in writing.

The English Bible, as Harold Bloom notes, looks back to two literary geniuses, William Tyndale and Miles Coverdale, though their purpose as translators (contra the scholarship of Bloom himself) was certainly not to create literature but entirely to seek the salvation of souls. Bloom regards the great King James Bible of 1611 as 'essentially a correction'[61] of Tyndale–Coverdale.[62] In their introduction to the Oxford World Classics text of what they entitle the *Authorized King James Version*, Robert Carroll and Stephen Prickett introduce the Bible as a work of literary, religious and cultural importance:

---

[56]   Ibid., p. 25.

[57]   Ibid., p. 44.

[58]   Derrida, 'Edmond Jabès and the Question of the Book', p. 67, quoting Jabès, *Le Livre des questions* (Paris: Gallimard, 1963), p. 109.

[59]   See above p. 79, on Blanchot and Kafka.

[60]   'Edmond Jabès and the Question of the Book', p. 68, quoting *Le Livre des questions*, p. 92.

[61]   David Daniell in his book *The Bible in English* (2003), with better reason, suggests that the KJV, as the work of a committee, is more of a diminution from the brilliance and genius of the earlier translators.

[62]   Bloom, Introduction to *The Book of J*, p. 45.

The Bible is the basic book of our civilization. It holds a unique and exclusive status not merely in terms of the religious history of the western world but also in literary history and even in what might be called our collective cultural psyche.[63]

But their interest is in the rather simpler notion of the Bible *and* literature rather than the Bible *as* literature. As the four hundredth anniversary of the publication of the King James Bible, 2011 saw a large number of publications, the majority of which were not by biblical scholars as such, but by authors concerned with its place in Western literature and culture. One of the more scholarly of these books, Hannibal Hamlin and Norman W. Jones' *The King James Bible after 400 Years* (2010) opens with attention given to the *language* of the King James Bible and the 'literary power' of the Hebrew original. Robert Alter states in his essay in this book: 'Much of the literary power of the ancient Hebrew texts derives from their terrific compactness of formulation. This quality often cannot be readily conveyed in English because English is an analytic language and biblical Hebrew is a synthetic language.'[64] Gabriel Josipovici's influential conversation with the biblical text entitled *The Book of God* (1988) is rooted in his sense of the resonance, grammar and rhythm of the biblical Hebrew as essential to our understanding of it, criticizing an authority as established as Gerhard von Rad for his 'neglect of the natural syntax and grammar of the Bible' when it does not fit in with 'certain religious dogmas he accepts independently of the Bible'.[65] But Jospovici, for all of his brilliance, finally dismisses, as we have seen, the 'pious remarks of theologians such as Ulrich Simon'.[66] He responds vigorously to the text of the Hebrew Bible as literature, commenting that, though supremely authoritative for Jews and Christians, the Bible does not seem anything like as authoritative as the *Aeneid* or *Paradise Lost*, but much more 'modern' and 'much quirkier, funnier, quieter than I expected'.[67]

Josipovici's book is much more 'literary' and less historical than a number of text books on the Bible as literature to appear in recent years, including David Norton's comprehensive two-volume *A History of the Bible as Literature* (1993),

---

[63]   Robert Carroll and Stephen Prickett, Introduction to *The Bible: Authorized King James Version with Apocrypha*, p. xi.

[64]   Robert Alter, 'The Glories and Glitches of the King James Bible: Ecclesiastes as a Test-case', in Hannibal Hamlin and Norman W. Jones, *The King James Bible after 400 Years: Literary, Linguistic and Cultural Influences* (Cambridge: Cambridge University Press, 2010), p. 47.

[65]   Gabriel Josipovici, *The Book of God: A Response to the Bible* (New Haven, CT, and London: Yale University Press, 1988), p. 56. Much more recently, and more playfully, the linguistics scholar David Crystal has written on the literary effect of the King James Bible on the English language in *Begat: The King James Bible and the English Language* (Oxford: Oxford University Press, 2010).

[66]   Ibid., p. 125, and see above, p. 112.

[67]   Ibid., p. x.

or the introductory *The Bible as Literature* by John B. Gabel, Charles B. Wheeler and Anthony D. York, originally published in 1986 and now into its fifth edition. Many more textbooks have appeared on the frankly easier subject of the Bible *and* literature, including my own (with Stephen Prickett) *The Bible and Literature: A Reader* (1999), which threads particular passages from Genesis to the Psalms and into the New Testament through a series of literary inter-texts, and the more recent *Blackwell Companion to the Bible in English Literature* (2009), edited by Rebecca Lemon, Emma Mason, Jonathan Roberts and Christopher Rowland, which offers a series of essays on the use of the Bible by specific authors from Old English poetry to modernist writers like T.S. Eliot and Virginia Woolf.[68] Yet the continuing difficulty of critically appropriating the Hebrew Bible *as* literature, even while acknowledging the supreme examples of literary narrative and poetry within its books, lies in the deeply rooted sense, whether we are 'fundamentalists or atheists',[69] that it is essentially and ineradicably different from all other books in both its origins and in its ancient traditions of reading. If the King James Bible remains as a classic of English literature, that was not the purpose of those responsible for it, as T.S. Eliot saw all too well. This difficulty became apparent to myself and my fellow editors, Andrew Hass and Elisabeth Jay, when we were working on the *Oxford Handbook of English Literature and Theology* (2007). For the most problematic part of that book was that entitled 'Literary Ways of Reading the Bible', and the nature of the difficulty was summed up by Peter Hawkins in the opening sentence of his essay, 'The Bible as Literature and Sacred Text':

> Any consideration of the 'Bible as Literature and Sacred Text' must begin by recognizing the problematic nature of that deceptively simple conjunction, 'and'. Although it may imply an easy equivalency – the Bible as both a work of literature *and* the Word of God – these two identities have never rested easily with one another. For centuries, appreciation for Scripture's artistry sprang from the devout conviction that its Divine Author would offer nothing less than perfection.[70]

No less than seven chapters in the *Handbook* deal with specific books of the Old Testament, from the Pentateuch to the Prophets. Tod Linafelt's essay on the Pentateuch expresses well the dilemma for the authors of these chapters. Regarded as a work of literature, Linafelt suggests that the Pentateuch is among

---

68　Both of these books are deeply indebted to the magisterial *Dictionary of Biblical Tradition in English Literature*, ed. David Lyle Jeffrey (Grand Rapids, MI: William B. Eerdmans, 1992).

69　Josipovici, *The Book of God*, p. 3.

70　Peter S. Hawkins, 'The Bible as Literature and Sacred Text', in Andrew W. Hass, David Jasper and Elisabeth Jay (eds), *The Oxford Handbook of English Literature and Theology* (Oxford: Oxford University Press, 2007), p. 197.

the most 'unliterary' of texts. Later poets and writers have responded creatively to the great narratives of creation and fall, of the histories of the patriarchs, the poetic passages. Yet no less important are the cultic and legal texts – to literature far less attractive, but to which Linafelt is 'reluctant to give short shrift'.[71] For the power and complexity of these texts lie precisely in the depths of their religious sensibility, and this can be as profound in their legal ordinances as in the puns, wordplays and alliterations which carry a theology and a religious vision that remains a troubling presence even when they also inspire the imaginations and genius of later generations of poets from Milton to Joyce. We return to the issue of biblical literature as 'poetry with a purpose,' and as Harold Fisch once pointed out, writers and critics from Longinus onwards have acknowledged the Hebrew scriptures as models of literary excellence, and yet 'those writers who have had difficulty in accommodating the Bible to any normal aesthetic have also not been mistaken'.[72] Such writers include St Augustine and Dr Samuel Johnson who was clear, as we have seen, that poetry and the Word of God cannot, finally, mix.[73] The Song of Songs may be the 'most lyrical poetry in the Bible', yet if long ago Origen was clear that it is a wedding song, written in the form of a play, at the same time it is specifically expressing, for our instruction, the heavenly love for a bride for her bridegroom, who is the Word of God.[74]

Thus we are left with the issue expressed by T.S. Eliot almost 80 years ago in his essay on 'Religion and Literature' (1935), that the Bible *as* literature and within the great literature of the world remains powerful and disturbing because it is different from all other books in literature – because it is, in Eliot's phrase, 'considered as the report of the Word of God'.[75]

---

[71]   Tod Linafelt, 'The Pentateuch', in the *Oxford Handbook of English Literature and Theology*, p. 215.

[72]   Harold Fisch, *Poetry with a Purpose*, p. 1.

[73]   In his *Lives of the Poets*, Johnson asserts that the essence of poetry is invention, and from it the reader expects 'the enlargement of his comprehension', while 'whatever is great, desirable, or tremendous, is comprised in the name of the Supreme Being. Omnipotence cannot be exalted; Infinity cannot be amplified; Perfection cannot be improved'. 'The Life of Waller', in the *Lives of the Poets* [1779–81], vol. 1 (Oxford: Oxford University Press, 1952), p. 203. See also my *Study of Literature and Religion: An Introduction,* 2nd edn (London: Macmillan, 1992), pp. 10–12.

[74]   J. Cheryl Exum, 'Song of Songs, in the *Oxford Handbook of English Literature and Theology*, p. 259. Origen, *The Prologue to the Commentary on the Song of Songs*, trans. Rowan A. Greer (The Classics of Western Spirituality) (Mahwah, NJ: The Paulist Press, 1979), p. 217.

[75]   Eliot, *Selected Essays*, p. 390.

Part Two: *Parergon*

And so, after this brief review of the literature and issues concerning the reading of the Bible as literature we return to the specific experience of the study of literature and theology.

It was in 1981 that I first encountered Ulrich Simon's essay 'Samson and the Heroic' in the collection of essays entitled *Ways of Reading the Bible*, edited by Michael Wadsworth.[76] It is a typically dark piece of writing by Simon, immersed in literature from Shakespeare to Proust, and in the heavy tragedy of the twentieth century. The focus is on the 'innocent stupidity' of Samson whose story in the book of Judges has, in Ulrich's terms, an earthiness 'which removes it from mythology'. Regarded by the Jews as a representative of their misfortunes and their capacity to endure, Samson also becomes the model for a kind of 'godly heroism' that emerged, suggests Simon, in Europe in August 1914. It was a year later, after the publication of this essay, in 1982 when Simon delivered his lecture in Durham on Job and Sophocles, reading Job also as a tragic hero. With neither Samson nor with Job is Simon interested in the question of the 'Bible as literature'. Rather it is the Bible as one of the roots of our collective memory, its provocation of theology and its characters – figures of a fallibility that possibly make the world, finally, bearable even despite themselves. In spite of his grimness, Simon, perhaps in the end, does not take the Bible too seriously as either literature or theology – but therefore all the more seriously as an expression of the stuttering admission of our place before God, all the more incomprehensible in the context of the horrors of the twentieth century which we can only face, like Samson, with final weakness and ultimate strength. Simon, for all his darkness and near despair, remains still a theologian even when he is upbraided by Josipovici for sermonizing and for 'removing from the Bible its profound and irresolvable ambiguities'.[77] Actually I think that nothing was further from the truth. In Simon literature steps into the abyss that is theology and shines as a light in its darkness, which yet remains impenetrable though not without hope.

In Job and in Samson, Ulrich clings on to a heroism that is provided by the Hebrew Bible in the face of God and in the mess of this world, but finally we are left with Job in his concluding utterance, made before God relents and returns him to his former prosperity:

> Therefore have I uttered what I did not understand,
> things too wonderful for me, which I did not know ...

---

[76]   See above, Chapter 8, pp. 112–13.
[77]   Gabriel Josipovici, *The Book of God*, p. 125.

therefore I despise myself
and repent in dust and ashes.[78]

But we must not be too hasty. I will return, before this chapter is finished, to Job, but for now I want to go back to another person who has figured more largely in these pages than I had imagined would be the case when I began – the Dutch theorist Mieke Bal. In 1986, Bal wrote an extensive review on the Bible as literature in the journal *Diacritics* (Winter, 1986) entitled 'A Critical Escape'. It dealt with three books that were then attracting considerable attention and to which I have already referred in this chapter, Robert Alter's *The Art of Biblical Poetry* (1985), Meir Sternberg's *The Poetics of Biblical Narrative* (1985), and Phyllis Trible's *Texts of Terror* (1984). By the time I came to read Bal's review I had read all three books and, I admit, had fallen for all of them. Bal came along with a suitable critical reprimand. What she suggests is that such critics, while seeming to offer liberating ways of reading the Bible *as* literature, in fact come to us simply as theologians in disguise, and actually quite old fashioned and conservative ones to boot. Meir Sternberg is the most easily disposed of: writing in the aftermath particularly of Wayne Booth and his already by then standard text *The Rhetoric of Fiction* (1961), Sternberg establishes the biblical narrator as omniscient, thereby duplicating God's divine omniscience. In a perfect hermeneutic circle, the reader creates the narrator who then fulfils the role of ultimate power over the reader.[79] Dismissed as a theologian, even Sternberg's literary credentials are put in question by Bal's crushing opening remark: 'In spite of its appealing title, Sternberg's study is limited rigorously to the least narrative aspects of the biblical narrative: the ideological impact of the later editors who established the canon.'[80] In other words, Sternberg begins ideologically, seems to unpick everything through literature, and then dumps us back in a theology that was always there anyway from the start. It is a supreme example of 'I told you so'.

She is less hard on Alter, though ultimately Alter takes us to a position very similar to that of Sternberg. Playing the game that biblical criticism (with its historical roots in the eighteenth century) suffers from a terminal historical tendency that only the profoundly *a-historical* study of literature can rescue us from, Alter himself is, in fact, rooted in the historical authority of the sacred texts and his 'poetic reconstruction is profoundly historical, in spite of its lack

---

[78]   Job 42:3, 6 NRSV.

[79]   One is reminded of the final sentence of C.G. Jung's *Answer to Job*: 'The religious need longs for wholeness, and therefore lays hold of the images of wholeness offered by the unconscious, which, independently of the conscious mind, rise up from the depths of our psychic nature', trans. R.F.C. Hull (London: Hodder & Stoughton, 1964), p. 178.

[80]   Mieke Bal, 'The Bible as Literature: A Critical Escape'. *Diacritics*, vol. 16 (1986), p. 72. The essay was republished as a chapter in Bal's book *On Story-Telling: Essays in Narratology* (Sonoma, CA: Polebridge Press, 1991), pp. 59–72.

of appeal to historical sources'.[81] In other words, the whole project of the bible 'as literature' gets us precisely nowhere beyond what conservative biblical critics have been saying for well over a hundred years.

Phyllis Trible differs from both Sternberg and Alter in that she works from a position not of literary scholarship, but as a biblical scholar and with an explicitly feminist perspective. Hence, Bal suggests, there is an inherent, and rather similar, contradiction in her argument: that although she would argue from an 'intrinsic reading' of the biblical text, embracing anachronisms in order to expose patriarchy, yet even in her 'texts of terror', 'Yahweh is somehow redeemed from the critique'.[82] In other words, and in spite of Trible's emancipatory aspirations, theology remains intact within the reading of the biblical narratives, and *that*, in all these readings of the Bible as literature, is their limitation. Literature is really just a means to an already established end. In Sternberg's case, the reading is 'actively ideological, and poetics is put to that use'.[83] Alter and Trible go further in their literary concerns, but yet remain limited by theological assumptions that anchor their readings and fail to preserve them, in the first case, from a lack of 'reflection on the link with social concerns' and, in the second, a lack of 'a feminist philosophy that would account for the relations between text and society'.[84]

From Bal's analysis of these key texts in the reading of the Bible as literature, it begins to become clear why our conferences on literature and theology in the 1980s, perhaps instinctively, largely ignored the rush of literary critics to the texts of the Bible and their sense, even in steadfastly 'secular' critics such as Frank Kermode, of the 'centrality of the Bible in the formation of our culture'.[85] For underlying their apparently new claims for reading the Bible was an old fallacy, that somehow, miraculously, our theology, Jewish or Christian, is at once driven by and drives the biblical texts, when, for us, that theology was precisely the problem confronting us. Furthermore, the Bible should be read not as the slave of a very largely later theology but as a cry against its imperialism, even, for us, its impossibility. Far from the trim arguments of Sternberg and Alter, the Bible time and again leaves us like Job who only satisfies God when he is brought to admit his utter self-loathing: 'therefore I despise myself, and repent in dust and ashes' (Job 42:6). Only then is the Lord content: what can one say? '*Sunt lacrimae rerum* ... the world is like that, but heroism and compassion make it bearable.'[86]

---

[81]   Ibid.

[82]   Ibid., p. 73.

[83]   Ibid., p. 78.

[84]   Ibid., p. 79.

[85]   Robert Alter and Frank Kermode, General Introduction to *The Literary Guide to the Bible*, p. 1.

[86]   Ulrich Simon, 'Job and Sophocles', in David Jasper (ed.) *Images of Belief in Literature* (London: Macmillan, 1984), p. 51.

There was one book that slightly predated the 'critical escape' of the studies of the Bible as literature which were exposed by Bal, and that was Herbert N. Schneidau's *Sacred Discontent* (1976), a work which was often quoted in passing but whose radical proposals were ignored by most people, perhaps deliberately. Robert Alter speaks rather haughtily of Schneidau's 'speculative, sometimes questionable, often suggestive study',[87] and takes from it what he wants, leaving the more awkward stuff unchewed and undigested. But no one really rose to the bait of Schneidau's sense of sacred discontent (actually far more interesting than, though as we shall see, not unrelated to, the much better known earlier work of Erich Auerbach) and of what he calls the 'raggedness and incoherence' of the biblical texts.[88] Rather just as Ulrich Simon was to do for us in his reading of Job and Sophocles, Schneidau knocks the biblical texts repeatedly and roughly against other literature and exposes their weird oddity and their refusal to be tied down. Both Alter and Sternberg finally fail to recognize the nature of Schneidau's 'historicized fiction' – that is, not fiction that is finally constricted by history and later theology (as both biblical critics and literary critics finally, in their different ways, insist upon or are forced to admit), but precisely the opposite: a rebellion against all of that as a cry from the human heart. We can take fictions utterly seriously, but 'it is difficult to believe in fictions, that is, to remember that they are fictions'.[89] But that is the point when we are reading the Bible – the real challenge is to forget the safety net of theology and history, and believe in just the fictions in all of their raggedness and incoherence: to believe in them precisely when they *do not* make any sense. Part of the problem is, of course, that, as Schneidau points out, 'fiction, in its literary uses, bears an unsettling resemblance to a historical recounting'.[90] But in the Bible (unlike the Greek tradition) we find a profound resistance to myth, and a sense of history but only in terms, finally of a deep resistance to that as well. And so how do we get at the truth? Everything is fiction, though a great deal of time is spent in both the Old and the New Testaments warning us against the words of false prophets and false Messiahs who tell us lies, though they are extremely difficult to identify. Thus how do we know, since even 'true messages are still fictions in the technical sense, imaginative evocations ... or else beatific visions?'[91] Oddly the 'ring of truth' sounds only in the inconsistency, in the acceptance, finally, of the oxymoron of 'true fiction' as it is found in Scripture.[92]

---

[87]   Alter, *The Art of Biblical Narrative*, p. 24.

[88]   Herbert N. Schneidau, *Sacred Discontent: The Bible and Western Tradition* (Berkeley, CA: University of California Press, 1976), p. 215.

[89]   Ibid., p. 275.

[90]   Ibid., p. 277.

[91]   Ibid., p. 279.

[92]   I take the term 'true fiction' from the title of Douglas A. Templeton's book *The New Testament as True Fiction* (Sheffield: Sheffield Academic Press, 1999), which admits in its

It is found only when we have the courage to move from myth to the mystery of plot and story, which may, or may not, make sense.

Such is the vexed and anxious world that I remember from our early conferences. Although the Bible was present in almost everything that we thought and said, the whole project of 'the Bible as literature' was, and remains in the end, for all of its attractiveness, too smug and too firmly anchored in the past: while, for us, it was the present and what lay behind it that was so unbearable. Theology was only there to be found again, if it was any longer possible at all.

And so I return to Mieke Bal. My first encounter with Mieke was in 1989 when she and Bob Detweiler spoke together on a panel of the Annual Convention of the American Society of Biblical Literature in Annaheim, California. The panel also involved presentations by Alice Bach and Daniel Patte and gave attention to Bal's recent book *Murder and Difference: Gender, Genre, and Scholarship on Sisera's Death* (1988). We later published the papers in an issue of *Literature and Theology*. As a professor of literary theory and a 'narratologist', Bal admits that she came to biblical studies rather rudely 'without even knocking on the door' and to the Bible as a book that attracted her 'because it was going to be difficult'.[93] She writes with panache and took Bob on with spirit – much to his delight:

> I am interested in the detail that is duplicitous, that will not be recuperated, the detail that is troublesome because it keeps confounding us; the detail that resists coherence and points up to its own marginality. With Detweiler we could say that this is so because the detail is supplement and hence, indispensible, and hence, no detail at all. Not marginal at all. Precisely; just like women.[94]

You can see that we had fun in those days, but it was deadly serious at the same time. Mieke was self-confessedly on a mission 'in single combat against the politics of coherence'[95] that lay at the heart of the work of Alter, Sternberg and others. There was the counter-coherence of feminism that drove her readings of the book of Judges in her book *Death and Dissymmetry* (1988), but there was something even more radical in her further work on Judges in *Murder and Difference*, the book upon which the SBL panel was based. There Bal unpicks

---

Preface that the author has been 'unable to convince myself' of what he is saying. It is a book linked to our conferences, as its chapter 2 began life as an essay entitled 'From Myth to Plot' in the volume from the 1992 conference in Glasgow, published in Gregory Salyer and Robert Detweiler (eds), *Literature and Theology at Century's End* (Atlanta, GA: Scholars Press, 1995), pp. 263–76.

[93]   Mieke Bal, 'Murder and Difference: Uncanny Sites in an Uncanny World', *Literature and Theology*, vol. 5, no. 1 (1991) 11.

[94]   Ibid., p. 15.

[95]   Ibid., p. 17.

the various 'codes' and systems that structure our readings of the Bible, these disciplinary codes being the historical, the theological, the anthropological and the literary. To begin with the theological (which is my primary concern here), the problem is stated in the very first sentences of chapter 2 of *Murder and Difference*:

> The theological code interprets the texts as testimonies of specific religious feelings that characterized the Judaic religion at its beginnings. The theme is not unrelated to that of the war of conquest, which is characteristic of the preceding code [the historical]. The motivation underlying the great 'conquest' was constructed as religious.[96]

War and theology seem bound together – and thus theology becomes a problem in its links to violence, its justification *of* violence, as it was a problem for us. And codes have the effect of unifying things, seeming to make sense, but finally dangerously so. What Bal offers in resistance to this are detailed, intricate readings that, far from abandoning the theoretical, deconstruct any possible hegemony of the code by *transdisciplinary* exercises which celebrate what she calls the 'dynamics of cultural life that no power ever manages to eliminate'.[97] It is the imposition of unity on the text that she seeks to avoid, above all the highly dangerous unity of the theologian:

> The theologian who claims at the expense of the obvious pantheism of the text that Yahweh is practically absent from the song of Deborah unifies similarly, but in more subtle fashion. Under the pretext of a historical perspective, differential by definition, he represents the theology of the song as a 'primitive' state of the Yahwist theology that attains its perfection later.[98]

Now, of course, I am well aware of the seeming contradiction in what I am saying here. Theology, in the end, is our business, even if it is not, finally, Mieke Bal's. If I am anything I am a theologian, and so were Ulrich Simon, Peter Walker and all the rest, in their different ways. But they were theologians for whom 'cultural life' in the twentieth century had rendered theology no longer possible in its old forms, and the only recourse was to the energy of the text (with its 'obvious pantheism') – that which Bal's 'theologian' reading the song of Deborah finally ignores. And this must take us back to what Detweiler reminds us of in his

---

96 Bal, 'Murder and Difference', p. 37.
97 Ibid., p. 137.
98 Ibid.

response to Mieke Bal at the SBL meeting:[99] in the proliferation of details in the biblical texts we find ourselves returning to the *parergon*, the Kantian ornamental detail that is picked up by Derrida in his journey in *The Truth in Painting* (1978) beyond the word-image opposition[100] and the capacity of the image to be 'read' beyond (yet through) the verbal text. Derrida carefully describes the *parergon* as the 'supplement outside the work [which] must, if it is to have the status of a philosophical quasi-concept, designate a formal and general predicative structure which one can transport *intact* or deformed and reformed *according to certain rules*, into other fields, to submit new contents to it'.[101] The importance of this for theology should be clear. Derrida reminds us that Kant also uses the term *parergon* in a long Note that is attached to the second edition of *Religion Within the Limits of Reason Alone* (1793) The *parergon* is actually in the concept of the Note itself which is added to the 'General Remark' that closes the second part of the work, in Derrida's words, 'insofar as it defines what comes to be added to *Religion Within the Limits of Reason Alone* without being a part of it and yet without being absolutely extrinsic to it'.

The point is that we are here concerned, as we read the Bible, with that which is 'exterior' and yet that which the interiority of the text lacks, or perhaps, more precisely and more significantly, the details that our coded readings ignore and expel. What we are struggling with here is what Catherine Keller in her lovely book *The Surface of the Deep* (2003), in another close reading of a biblical text, was to call a theology of becoming. Keller goes back beyond the book of Judges to the creation narratives of Genesis and the indeterminacies of chaos struggling into creation, Moses alongside Moby Dick, Augustine, Irigaray (an unlikely and uneasy, though delightful, literary company) in deconstructions of fearful and defensive orthodoxies. Keller begins with a dramatic image: 'The undertow [counter-current, counter-coherence? DJ] has gripped the wave. The salt washes the wound. We begin again or not at all.'[102] Wounded, limping like Jacob from the struggle with the text, we find the mystery of the depths, which can only drown us, on the very surface of the deep where the breath of God moves – theology begun again from the outside in the 'sea of heteroglossia'.

---

[99] Robert Detweiler, 'Parerga: Homely Details, Secret Intentions, Veiled Threats', *Literature and Theology*, vol. 5, no. 1 (1991), 1–10.

[100] The phrase is taken from the subtitle of Mieke Bal's book *Reading Rembrandt: Beyond the Word-Image Opposition* (Cambridge: Cambridge University Press, 1991).

[101] Jacques Derrida, *The Truth in Painting*, trans. Geoff Bennington and Ian McLeod (Chicago, IL: Chicago University Press, 1987), p. 55. See also David Jasper, 'The Return to the Visual in Theological Thinking', *Creativity Studies*, vol. 7, no. 1 (2014) 72–3.

[102] Catherine Keller, *The Surface of the Deep: A Theology of Becoming* (London: Routledge, 2003), p. xv.

Keller starts her journey 'in gratitude for the relations that ebb and flow through every layer of [the book's] sentences'.[103] I am taken back in this ebb and flow of language to the company we enjoyed in our conferences, many now with us only in the echoes of their words, as Detweiler sees Bal 'moving steadily toward more comprehensive expressions of epistemology as a dynamic of relationship'.[104] There is one whom I regret was never part of our company, though his voice sounds with sympathy, and that is Gabriel Josipovici. In his work *The Book of God* (1988), and I have already offered some criticisms of it, Josipovici approaches the Bible, like Bal, as a newcomer, through childhood memories and traditions. He is profoundly suspicious of the impositions of theology upon the text and he is dismissive, as we have seen, of 'such rousing stuff' which might do for a sermon but forgets the Bible in its profound and irresolvable ambiguities.[105] Yet still Simon's grim position remains understandable, after Josipovici has swatted it, though some might see it as a clutching at straws, and we find that finally Josipovici and Simon are not so far apart. For one thing both are habitual readers of Proust and Dante – and share at once, and with all true writers, a profound suspicion of the book and a delight in writing.[106] The theology will look after itself, later arising from our tears and a new found seriousness.

As well as a literary critic, Josipovici is also a distinguished novelist and dramatist. He knows about writing, and is suspicious of the scholars who seek to impose unity on the Bible, to make it 'literature', or drown it in the demands of history. Like all great books, though perhaps uniquely so, it is odd, truculent and impatient of quick comparisons with other texts, not least those which seem to claim some immediate relationship with it. After all, as Simon reminded us, comparisons in literature are usually 'either odious, or boring, or both'.[107] Like the rest of us, the Bible suspects too ready over-familiarity and the unwelcome use of first names as a ploy to gain control over us or sell us something we cannot actually afford – like theology, for instance. As regards the Bible, Josipovici puts it this way in a passage I have already very briefly referred to:

> ... when I turned to it I found myself faced with two very striking things: the first was that this book, though supremely authoritative for Jews and Christians, did not, when one actually read it, appear anything like as authoritarian as the *Aeneid* or *Paradise Lost*. It seemed much quirkier, funnier, quieter than I expected. The second was that it contained narratives which seemed, even in translation, as I first read them, far fresher and more 'modern' than any of the prize-winning

---

[103] Ibid., p. xi.

[104] Detweiler, 'Parerga', p. 9.

[105] Josipovici, *The Book of God*, p. 125. See above note 2.

[106] See further, Gabriel Josipovici, *The World and the Book* (1971), 3rd edn (London: Macmillan, 1994).

[107] Simon, 'Job and Sophocles', p. 42, and see above, p. 17.

> novels rolling off the presses. Far more 'modern', even, than any of the attempts to rewrite those narratives and fill them out, of which the most weighty was no doubt Mann's *Joseph and His Brothers*.[108]

Josipovici is an excellent reader of the Bible (a rare talent indeed), letting it speak and affect us with its rhythms and oddness. His readings run entirely counter to those of the biblical scholar James Barr who, in a lecture entitled 'Reading the Bible as Literature,' insisted that 'the Bible must be read in a theological mode'.[109] I suppose that in the end Barr is saying much the same thing as T.S. Eliot did years ago in his essay 'Religion and Literature' (1935) which insists upon the peculiarity of the Bible as 'the report of the Word of God'.[110] Well, that is fine, and it is where I ended the first part of this chapter, except that it fails to go far enough and in the end it finally stops us reading the Bible at all – reading it, that is, in its compatibility with and yet difference from all other literature. The point is that you don't go to Proust to confirm your theory about memory. You read Proust because you read Proust and you let him speak so that memory becomes something new and strange and living. You might say the same thing about the Bible and theology. The simple truth, whether you are reading Genesis, Proust or Dostoevsky, is that 'the fact of utterance precedes meaning'.[111]

It is easy to forget how disorienting the beginning of Genesis is, even in translation – or the book of Job, many of the Psalms, Daniel, the Gospel of Mark. We forget because most of our reading and certainly our memories of the Bible have been filtered through selection processes in lectionaries or school curricula, so that most of us have simply never read the lists of genealogies or laws – or the last verse of Psalm 137. Only scholars with ulterior motives ever encounter these 'boring' or shocking parts – but they are part of the biblical rhythm, part of its oddity, there on the surface of the deep. In its rhythm the Bible is at once disorganized and ritualized, a sort of organized chaos that often simply confirms our darkest fears about the way things are (if we are honest. Look again at Judges 19, or most of Hosea). But at the same time, the endless repetitions of the Bible, freed from the impositions of typology, work as in all literature. Finally, in spite of all, we begin to know where we are, or at least we think we do, and theology might seem possible again. But the same might equally be said of *Paradise Lost*, or the *Divine Comedy* or even the poetry of William Blake or the writings of

---

108 Josipovici, *The Book of God*, p. x. See above, p. 173.

109 James Barr, 'Reading the Bible as Literature', *Bulletin of the John Rylands Library*, vol. 56 (1973–4), 13; *Holy Scripture, Canon, Authority, Criticism* (Oxford: Oxford University Press, 1983), p. 160.

110 T.S. Eliot, 'Religion and Literature', p. 390.

111 Josipovici, *The Book of God*, p. 61.

James Joyce. In such readings, as David Daiches memorably put it, perhaps we find that 'God is justified, in a way that might perhaps have surprised him'.[112]

This chimes in with our endeavours at the conferences on literature and theology. We trusted the poets and the story-tellers, or at least tried to, because theology had not succeeded in making the world bearable. It was too thin and too formal, and when theologians are faced with Shakespeare or Goethe with their rich rhetoric and literary density, they tend to 'resent this richness of approach'.[113] But the same can be said of the Bible, which for so long has been thinned down – and those who embarked on the project of 'the Bible as literature', as we have seen in the cases of Alter and Sternberg, simply participated in this thinning process. It was all to make the Bible more manageable and comfortable, more digestible, more in keeping with the tradition that for so long had endlessly developed sophisticated strategies to *prevent* the Bible from being read at all.

This might seem a huge claim, but Josipovici's book is just one example of allowing the Bible to slip the noose, and exploring the consequences of that. Simon did the same, in his own way, and perhaps even more seriously because of his anguish for theology. Surprisingly, this does not happen very often. The authorities of Church, biblical 'scholarship', theology itself, are mighty powerful even yet, and it is hard for any of us to read the Bible at all, whatever our position. It takes the intelligence and guts of a Mieke Bal to remind us of what ought to be blindingly obvious to those who have eyes to see. We need to be led back to the 'density' of the Hebrew Bible (let alone the New Testament) and 'the fact that it seems always to escape reduction to a single or simple meaning'.[114]

As a final illustration of this density, Josipovici takes us back to Genesis 37:12–18, and the odd episode of Joseph's encounter with the man in the field in Shechem. The stranger accosts Joseph and asks him who he is looking for. Joseph replies that he is looking for his brethren and asks if the man knows where they are feeding their flocks. The man helpfully replies that he overheard them say that they were going to Dothan – which is exactly where Joseph finds them. But who is this man, and why do we need to know about him? He is not particularly important in the story, which forgets him as quickly as it finds him. To the ancient Jewish midrashic commentators his identity is no problem: he is the angel Gabriel, an agent of Divine Providence.[115] And after all, in David Malouf's novel of the war in Troy, *Ransom* (2009) to which I will allude further in the next chapter, a god appears and we have no alternative but to take it in our stride.

---

[112]   David Daiches, *God and the Poets* (The Gifford Lectures, 1983) (Oxford: The Clarendon Press, 1984), p. 49.

[113]   Ulrich Simon, *Atonement: From Holocaust to Paradise* (Cambridge: James Clarke & Co. 1987), p. 6. See also above, pp. 47–8.

[114]   Josipovici, *The Book of God*, p. 271.

[115]   Ibid., pp. 277–8.

Well, the stranger in the Genesis story might be Gabriel, but the text does not actually say so. It is one way of making sense of the story and ascribing a meaningful place to a stray detail. In his book *The Genesis of Secrecy* (1979), Frank Kermode had similarly highlighted the incident of the boy in the linen cloth in Gethsemane in Mark 14:51–2, who runs off naked and escapes when the soldiers grab his tunic. What are these little details doing within the density of the text? We assume that everything is put there for a purpose in the telling of the story – it must 'mean' *something*.

Well, that is true – but the same dilemma arises from almost every work of literature. Once we have decided what *King Lear* 'means', more or less, we have to decide then what to do with all the bits and pieces that don't quite fit with our sense of meaning. Such critical exercises are is rather like taking a clock to pieces and reassembling it so that it looks exactly the same as it did before and even works reasonably well – but are bothered because there are some bits left over. What were they doing, and what purpose did they serve? Perhaps we are, after all, missing something. I come back, as does Josipovici, to the conclusion of Job. Job's comforters had insisted that there must be meaning and that it could be known, but Job refuses to accept this.[116] There is no meaning. God finally speaks and affirms that indeed there *is* meaning, but we must just accept his word for it as we, being only human, cannot know it. Two things then happen to Job, the first rather alarming and the second reassuring. Job says that he gets the point from God, but as a result now loathes himself.

> I had heard of you by the hearing of the ear,
> but now my eye sees you;
> therefore I despise myself
> and repent in dust and ashes.[117]

And yet as a result of this, God not only restores his fortune he also doubles it, together with seven sons and three beautiful daughters, and a long life. Is this just another assertion of God's awful and, to us, quite arbitrary power? Or is it more what Josipovici notes that the writer Muriel Spark 'intuitively grasps' in her fine novel *The Only Problem* (1984),[118] that the book of Job is not framed by its beginning and end so much as 'it is the assertion of the fact that meaning will never be able to catch up with life'.[119] In the end Job reminds us that there is a story of which we are a part and 'that man must neither simply accept that there

---

[116]   Ibid., pp. 289–99.

[117]   Job 42:6 NRSV.

[118]   It is uncanny how many of the texts, both critical and literary, I find myself coming back to, were published in the early 1980s, within a year or two of our first conference. Something seemed to be happening at that time.

[119]   Josipovici, *The Book of God*, p. 290.

is a story nor refuse to believe that there is one, but that it is his duty constantly to question God (and himself) about it. In Kierkegaard's wonderful phrase, it "keeps the wound of the negative open".[120]

Here might be a good place to begin to draw this long chapter to a conclusion. Josipovici finally takes us back to the work of Herbert Schneidau and his book *Sacred Discontent*. Schneidau had argued that the Bible should be seen in contrast to the epics of the Ancient Near East, in its espousal of the exploratory narratives of fiction and the refusal of myth as a rebellion against the cyclic movement of the pagan world-view. There are no pre-existing truths, and in 'its very raggedness and incoherence [the Bible] forces the beholder into an extra effort of imagination, giving the work a quality of dramatic vividness'.[121] But actually, as Josipovici points out, this is only saying in the end much the same as every other 'Bible as literature' person has said, starting with Eric Auerbach in his endlessly quoted essay 'Odysseus Scar' in *Mimesis* (1946), and going on through Harold Bloom, Meir Sternberg, et al.[122] And furthermore, we find in the Bible 'as literature' exactly what is the case with *all* 'literature' – which seeks to escape from its own literariness into something more profound, even more 'true', but in doing so, inevitably it becomes literature again, with its demands of endless repetition. The hermeneutic circle is nothing new.

And the problem is that in this movement, even as its 'raggedness and incoherence' is welcomed, the Bible as literature becomes just that – *the Bible* as literature. We are back to Mieke Bal's critical review of Alter, Sternberg and Trible with which we began. The method is always, inevitably, circular – heading back to the safety zone of the ideological and the theological, the world of Sacred Scripture, welcoming the framing of the God who is firmly in charge and unprepared to leave the wound of the negative open. But literature always starts again, always anxious even as it looks back and remembers. And we know how difficult it is to read *any* book as it demands to be read. We are often too ready to despise ourselves, like Job, and give the whole thing up, or else impose upon it our own pre-packaged understanding of what it means, like those 'cribs' provided so that students can understand *The Merchant of Venice* 'correctly'. How much more is it so for the Bible? We have been handed it pre-digested, and on the whole we prefer it that way, even when we can see it, to a degree, as literature

---

[120] Ibid. The remark by Kierkegaard is from *Concluding Unscientific Postscript*, trans. David F. Swenson and Walter Lowrie (Princeton, NJ: Princeton University Press, 1941), p. 78. See also above, p. 123.

[121] Schneidau, *Sacred Discontent*, p. 215. See also Josipovici, *The Book of God*, pp. 299–300.

[122] I have not referred here to more recent publications like *Literature and the Bible: A Reader*, ed. Jo Carruthers, Mark Knight and Andrew Tate (London: Routledge, 2014), as they seem to use more or less the same texts I have been referring to. Nothing much seems to have moved on.

(always remembering, deep down, with T.S. Eliot, that, far more importantly, it is mysteriously the report of the Word of God). The proliferation of *parerga* that pile up, in all their uncanniness, when a Mieke Bal gets her hands on the Bible are just too much. They were too much for us at our conferences, and I think that that is why, on the whole, we kept away from the Bible.

The project of the 'Bible as literature' has continued and continues to produce text books and readers. I have even contributed one myself. But I think that it was no accident that when I (with Andrew Hass and Elisabeth Jay) came to edit the *Oxford Handbook of English Literature and Theology* in 2007, by far the most problematic and least successful section was that entitled 'Literary Ways of Reading the Bible'. We simply could not find the proper handle by which to grasp it, and the essays generally fell back into the trap that this chapter has sought to expose. Theology got in the way of reading instead of reading prompting the possibility of theology anew in a place where its impossibility has been admitted.

And so do we just go on in this deconstructive mode, unpicking the coherences and the politics that drive them? I think we probably do. For my part it rests upon the sense of the eschatological in all theological thinking, its anticipatory, poetic and preliminary nature. So we do not abandon it, but we suspect any and all conclusions and comfortings that it might seem to offer. Remember Job's 'friends' and the divine wrath which they brought down upon themselves. As for Bal? Well as a feminist she is quite clear. She will go on in single combat against the male power game (which so often expresses and defends itself theologically). She concludes her response to Bob Detweiler: 'I repeat my offer, as soon as 50% of us are women, 20% black, and 50% of those women again, I will stop reacting to the male power game. I will be delighted.'[123]

In the next two chapters, which bring this section to an end, I will move on from 'themes' and offer some brief reflections on the expansion of the study of literature and theology into a more global perspective. They are drawn from my own experience in Australia and China and how it is in such places, in different ways new worlds to Western scholarship, that creative thinking in theology after literature is taking place. I have avoided saying too much about North America and its study of religion and literature. That is too huge, and perhaps may be the subject of another book.

---

[123] Bal, 'Murder and Difference', p. 19.

Chapter 12
Europe and Australia: New Worlds

> Many roads meet here
> in me, the traveller and the ways I travel.
> Judith Wright

This chapter will be a reflection on the poetry and novels of David Malouf, perhaps the leading writer in Australia in our time. Malouf is not, as far as I am aware, committed to any specific religious belief, yet his work, written on the border between two worlds – the old world of Europe and the new of Australia and more specifically Queensland – does relate closely to the poetics of John Keble and the nineteenth century tradition. Strangely I find here a kind of prolegomenon to theology and a sense of why prayer is so central, and was unselfconsciously practised in our early conferences, to the whole project of literature and theology. But what do I mean by prayer in the context of Malouf's writings?

The pages that follow are perhaps best described as a meditation, or perhaps a conversation, somewhere between literature and theology. One may dare to go even further. It begins and ends in 'a kind of praying', words used to describe Janet's mysterious vision of her childhood in Queensland at the end of David Malouf's novel *Remembering Babylon* (1993). It converses primarily with the writings of Malouf, but there are other voices and at times, perhaps, only one – my own. Its insistence is upon religious presences, most potent and strange when they are least overt and barely articulate; presences as traces or absences, the otherness in our midst. Malouf is not precisely a religious writer, but he is a deeply spiritual one, essentially a poet and a maker even before he is a novelist, and throughout his work there is sounded a tone that can best be described as a kind of praying or a language that effects a grounding in the sacred, even a beginnings of theology, 'as we approach knowledge. As we approach one another.'[1] This is also rooted deeply in the specifics of the landscape, and linking this experience with something that seems particularly Australian, Malouf brings into sharp focus the words of an earlier Australian writer, Patrick White in his novel *Voss*, a work with which Malouf is closely associated through his work on the libretto of the opera:

---

[1]   David Malouf, *Remembering Babylon* (London: Vintage, 1994), pp. 199–200.

Every man has a genius, though it is not always discoverable. Least of all when choked by the trivialities of daily existence. But in this disturbing country ... it is possible more easily to discard the inessential and to attempt the infinite.[2]

But it is not only Malouf's identification with Australia that is important for he writes between many worlds and between many times. It is the liminality of all his writing that must be acknowledged – words caught on boundaries between worlds, Europe, India and Australia, the old and the new, the classical and the contemporary, the finite and the infinite, the immanent and the transcendent. If he looks back to William Blake as a poetic forbear, he looks back also to Samuel Taylor Coleridge and his reflections on the Symbol, caught between the universal and the specific, the general and the particular.[3] In short there is a *sacramental* quality in Malouf's writing that links him through the Romantic sense of symbol and (strange coupling) with the Tractarian poetics and theology of John Keble in his *Lectures on Poetry* of 1832 to 1841 which focus almost entirely on the classical poets and playwrights of Greece and Rome from Homer to Virgil and for whom 'Poetry lends Religion her wealth of symbols and similes: Religion restores these again to Poetry, clothed with so splendid a radiance that they appear to be no longer merely symbols, but to partake ... of the nature of sacraments.'[4] We might compare here the work of another contemporary Australian writer, Les Murray, and his marvelous poem 'Poetry and Religion' which begins with the words, 'Religions are poems', the living substance and energy of words acknowledged in the lines:

Nothing's said till it's dreamed out in words
and nothing's true that figures in words only.[5]

With the poet John Clare (1793–1864), whose apocalyptic verse, along with words of Blake, prefaces *Remembering Babylon*, Malouf shares a 'friendly knowledge' of nature that is at once precise and universal. Arthur Symonds' characterization of Clare, made long ago at the very beginning of the twentieth century, is equally true of Malouf:

---

2   Patrick White, *Voss* (London: Penguin, 1983), p. 35. See also Tony Kelly, *A New Imagining: Towards an Australian Spirituality* (Melbourne: Collins Dove, 1990).

3   S.T. Coleridge, *The Statesman's Manual* (1816), in *Lay Sermons*, ed. R.J. White (Princeton, NJ: Princeton University Press, 1972), p. 30. See also above, p. 15.

4   John Keble, *Lectures on Poetry, 1832–1841*, trans. Edward Kershaw Francis (Oxford: The Clarendon Press, 1912), vol. 2, p. 481.

5   Les Murray, 'Poetry and Religion', available at: http://www.poetrylibrary.edu.au/poets/murray-les/poetry-and-religion-0572031/.

[Of nature] ... the observation begins by being literal; nature a part of his home, rather than his home a part of nature. The things about him are the whole of his material, he does not choose them by preference out of others equally available ... He does not make pictures which would imply aloofness and selection.[6]

Malouf's perception of the natural world has no sense of hierarchy or privilege and every detail (as in Wordsworth or Hopkins) counts with an equal importance, but, seen with a poet's eyes the world appears unexpectedly even in that which seems insignificant or unworthy of our notice. As the character Mr Frazer, the 'odd whitefeller', writes in his field notebook in *Remembering Babylon*, the early European settlers in Australia failed to see the:

> fruit that was all around them and which they could not, with their English eyes, perceive, since the very habit and faculty that makes apprehensible to us what is known and expected dulls our sensitivity to other forms, even the most obvious.[7]

More philosophically Malouf's sense of human indwelling in nature also bears comparison with Heidegger's notion of dwelling poetically, which is to live 'so as to measure oneself against that Nothing – that No-thing – that grants the possibility of the presence of and the Being of the things that there are ... There we struggle against particular ignorances and incapacities to bring forth truth'.[8] But it is also, we must remember, as himself a poet, struggling to bring forth truth, that Malouf dwells, sharing Blake's sense of progression by contraries wherein brightness wars with darkness in the particularities of existence that are never, in fact, trivial. In his poem 'An Ordinary Evening at Hamilton':

> Familiar rooms
> glow, rise through the dark – exotic islands; this house
> a strange anatomy
> of parts, so many neighbours in a thicket:
> hair, eyetooth, thumb.[9]

---

6   Arthur Symonds (ed.), *Poems by John Clare* (London: Henry Frowde, 1908), pp. 18–19. See also Clare Archer-Lean, 'David Malouf's *Remembering Babylon* as a Reconsideration of Pastoral Idealisation', *The Journal of the Association for the Study of Australian Literature*, vol. 14, no. 2 (2014).

7   Malouf, *Remembering Babylon*, pp. 129–30.

8   James C. Edwards, *The Plain Sense of Things: The Fate of Religion in an Age of Normal Nihilism* (University Park, PA: Pennsylvania State University Press, 1997), p. 184. See also above, p. 90.

9   Available at: http://www.poetrylibrary.edu.au/poets/malouf-david/an-ordinary-evening-at-hamilton-0428007/.

Thus Malouf takes his place with his fellow poets – Blake, Clare, Wordsworth, Keble – quietly engaged in his own pastoral recollections in tranquillity with Wallace Stevens and his plain sense of things, but, for me, above all, with the French poet Yves Bonnefoy and the poems of his collection entitled *Ce qui fut sans lumière* (1987) in which place and event are seen so minutely in acts of memory and thus 'language becomes an exercise in chiaroscuro, an interplay of light and dark on which images are carved and explored through a reclusive, submerged narrative which both undercuts and transfigures (translates) our sense of reality'.[10] So it is with Malouf in the beginnings of a rediscovery of the idea of the holy.

The poems of his collection *Typewriter Music* (2007) approach us gently ('I'm not holding my breath for a reply')[11] and move towards silence (*'No need between us/for speech'*),[12] as if the poet was the only speaker of his tongue, yet that tongue is also a universal language and even in silence there is a fullness of speech. I think of the start and the finish of the Fourth Gospel, and the move through the poetry of the narrative from silence and singularity to the overwhelming plenitude of language. 'In the beginning was the Word' ... 'If every one of them were written down, I suppose that the world itself could not contain the books that would be written.'[13] My return to Scripture, and to the beginning and end of the Fourth Gospel is deliberate. For from there we move back but a step further to the poetry of classical Greece and Rome which, for John Keble, prepared the way for theology, alongside the visionary world of the Hebrew Prophets. Perhaps better, for us, there are boundaries, spaces of literature, in which silence begins to speak, enacted (in the words of the theologian Tom Altizer) 'in the dawning of the actuality of silence, an actuality ending all disembodied and unspoken presence'.[14] Nowhere in Malouf's writing are these boundaries more keenly known and felt than in his novel *An Imaginary Life* (1978), his return to the world of the poet Ovid in exile on the edge of the Roman Empire, helplessly caught between civilization and the wilderness of the Russian steppes.

Ovid's account of his exile begins in frozen desolation, his 'life stripped to the simplest terms'.[15] In the desolate village of Tomis he is rendered dumb, a poet

---

[10]   David Jasper, '*"La Même Voix, Toujours"*: Yves Bonnefoy and Translation', in David Jasper (ed.), *Translating Religious Texts* (London: Macmillan, 1993), p. 107.

[11]   David Malouf, 'Revolving Days,' in *Typewriter Music* (Queensland: University of Queensland Press, 2007), p. 1.

[12]   'Afterword', ibid., p. 82.

[13]   John 1:1; 21:4 NRSV.

[14]   Thomas J.J. Altizer, *The Self-Embodiment of God* (New York: Harper & Row, 1977), p. 96.

[15]   David Malouf, *An Imaginary Life* (London: Chatto & Windus, 1978), p. 16.

robbed of language and communicating only 'like a child with grunts and signs'.[16] With the advent of the mysterious Child – Wordsworth might have called it an event of natural piety – worlds combine and boundaries finally are crossed in the merging of all things into something approaching a sense of Total Presence: 'No more dreams. We have passed beyond them into the last reality'.[17] The end becomes a beginning, purpose is forgotten and the approaching conclusion suggests a sense, if only a very slight sense, of resurrection. Ovid finishes with words, speaking of the Child:

> The earth, now that I am about to leave it, seems so close at last ... And yet for all this closeness, he seems more and more to belong to a world that lies utterly beyond me, and beyond my human imagining ...
>
> It is summer. It is spring. I am immeasurably, unbearably happy. I am three years old. I am sixty. I am six.
>
> I am there.[18]

Malouf treasures the life of Ovid precisely because we know so little about him, not only one of ancient Rome's finest writers and poets, but also one of its finest *readers*. Ovid's gestures are always towards the past, which he reworks in poetry and prose with endlessly inventive re-vision. We have never solved the mystery as to why he was so cruelly exiled by Augustus. Ovid remains to us a fiction, though yet rooted in history and speaking to us through his poetry. The central event of the book, Ovid's encounter with the Child, Malouf assures us, 'has no basis in fact'.[19] Even more remote, more tenuous in their hold upon history are events of Malouf's later novel *Ransom* (2009), based upon the narrative of Homer's *Iliad*, and finally filtered only through the stories of the simple Trojan carter Somax, who once took King Priam into the Greek camp as Priam seeks to reclaim the body of his son Hector from Achilles. The story is told and retold, embellished by Somax, the 'old fellow, [who] like most storytellers, is a stealer of other men's tales, of other men's lives'.[20] Like Malouf. But Somax's listeners do not believe him. He suffers the fate of every true storyteller. Across the centuries and the continents, the Russian playwright and storyteller Anton Chekhov sounds the same note at the end of his exquisite story 'The Bishop'. Here, like all parents, the woman tells everyone of her children, and especially 'about her son who had been a bishop. And she spoke hesitantly, afraid they would not

---

16 Ibid., p. 17.
17 Ibid., p. 141.
18 Ibid., pp. 146, 149, 152.
19 Ibid., Afterword: A Note on Sources, p. 153.
20 David Malouf, *Ransom* (London: Chatto & Windus, 2009), p. 218.

believe her. Nor did they all believe her, as it happened.'[21] But these instants of telling are religious moments, crossings of boundaries that challenge assent and belief, rather as King Priam dares, in an act of piety, to step outside the city and his kingship to face, simply, Achilles – the man. These are deeply human moments when we are invited to exercise that willing suspension of disbelief that makes for poetic faith in the truth that is before us. They are moments of remembrance, mixed with the darker dross of the human imagination that is inspired by pride and forgetfulness, yet they are spots of time which draw worlds together across distances of time and space – *sacramental* moments that often lie at the turning points of deep history, and in which (as occurs in *Ransom* with the god Hermes) a divinity may have shown himself, without warning, in the midst of human affairs. Heidegger might have called such barely remembered moments deep history – *Geschichte*, those little noticed things in which 'the rare and simple decisions of history spring from the way the original essence of truth essentially unfolds'.[22] From such moments built into the stuff of life springs also what John Henry Newman knew as the Illative Sense, that cumulative progression of probabilities that proceed 'not from propositions to propositions, but from concrete things to concrete things without conscious recognition of the antecedent or the process of inference'.[23] Newman, too, like Malouf, was a poet and a novelist. In this they are joined.

At key moments the poet speaks – and it is for us to listen. In Malouf's novel *The Great World* (1990), at the wedding of Vic and Ellie, Mr Warrender gets to his feet to deliver the obligatory speech – and instead recites a poem that he has written. At first the noisier members of the wedding party take it as a spoof until finally they are 'shamed into silence'.[24] Others are moved. Some believe – some remain silently sceptical. For Mr Warrender the event is perfectly natural, poetry simply 'a normal manner of address', though he speaks with humour as well. Although *we* read and see the poem on the page, in the text of the novel, within the world of the work itself its words live only in the memory of the character Digger, 'who had a gift in that direction', and in Digger's repetition of it Iris, who had not understood the poem at first, 'got hold of what she had been so moved by'. In Mr Warrender's poem the animal that is within us lowers its head for the sacrifice:

---

[21]   Anton Chekhov, *The Kiss and Other Stories*, trans. Ronald Wilks (London: Penguin, 1982), p. 97.

[22]   Martin Heidegger, *Pathmarks*, trans. Frank A. Capuzzi et al., ed. William McNeill (Cambridge: Cambridge University Press, 1998), p. 146.

[23]   I.T. Ker, Introduction to John Henry Newman, *An Essay in aid of a Grammar of Assent* (Oxford: Oxford University Press, 1985), p. xix.

[24]   David Malouf, *The Great World* (London: Vintage, 1999), p. 235.

being
In love with what is always out of reach:
The all, the ever-immortal and undying
Word beyond word that breathes through mortal speech.[25]

Spoken by Mr Warrender the words are perfectly ordinary, as is the beginning of all that is sacred, until, by repetition (the moment when the poetry that is spoken in remembrance begins to become, in a sense, the liturgical) that which in language, in Wallace Stevens' words, had been laboriously spoken begins to speak the word that is beyond word in mortal speech. This is the moment when, after Heidegger, the word allows the unsayable to be unsaid and the otherness of the mystery to be. At this point, in the language of the theologian Thomas Altizer, that which is wholly 'other' is actualized in a language that realizes a Total Presence. And then:

> actual otherness is without either a centre or a ground. For both its centre and its ground have been spoken, have passed into speech. In being spoken they are self-actualized, and self-actualized in the self-identity of pure voice. Thus pure voice is the self-actualization of all actual otherness, a self-actualization in which all actual otherness is totally and immediately present.[26]

And so, extraordinarily, Mr Warrender offers his 'mixed blessing' at the wedding.

Such poetry that makes way for religion is always a mixed blessing, its hidden life holding its secrets in the stuff of everyday, while the otherness that we seek is deeply hidden in the very stuff itself, yet only known as an absent presence that is also beyond our grasp, though we may be moved by it: 'To you has been given the secret (μυστηριον) of the kingdom of God.' Thus we hear in St Mark's Gospel. But the language holding the secret remains just that – a mystery. Perhaps the best we can hope for is that sense of the holy that *finds us*, it may be, but in those moments, objects and events on the border and the boundary, between worlds, between the old world and the new.[27]

Thus the poet takes us to, and perhaps sometimes, beyond the boundaries of our world, and in Malouf this becomes a kind of analogy with the physical experience of the early British settlers in Australia, a land beyond all known boundaries, and a place where language on the edge becomes 'a kind of praying'. Such a boundary between worlds, and one that initiates the series of encounters

---

[25]   Ibid., p. 236. See also Bill Ashcroft, 'David Malouf and the Poetics of Possibility', *Journal of the Association for the Study of Australian Literature*, vol. 14, no. 2 (2014).

[26]   Altizer, *The Self-Embodiment of God*, p. 82.

[27]   I am deliberately echoing the words of Coleridge writing on how the Bible 'finds him at greater depths of [his] being' than all other books, in *Confessions of an Inquiring Spirit* (London: William Pickering, 1840).

found in *Remembering Babylon*, is experienced in Gemmy's first words to the children: "'Do not shoot,' it shouted. "I am a B-b-british object!'".[28] Like the narrative of Ovid's exile in *An Imaginary Life*, these words have their origin in an actual event, and, Malouf tells us, 'were actually spoken at much the same time and place, but in different circumstances, by Gemmy Morril or Morrell, whose christian name I have also appropriated; otherwise this novel has no origin in fact'.[29] Fiction leaves its trace upon history, invisible cities merge – London, Jerusalem, Babylon, the newly emerging townships of Queensland, Australia. Malouf prefaces his narrative with words from William Blake's epic *The Four Zoas* and apocalyptic lines from the poetry of John Clare. In Blake's radical Christian vision, haunted by history and at once profoundly sacred and deeply profane, the conclusion is finally reached in a radiant vision of peace as Eternal Man beholds 'the depths of wondrous worlds':

> The Sun arises from his dewy bed, & the fresh airs
> Play in his smiling beams giving the seeds of life to grow,
> And the fresh Earth beams forth ten thousand thousand springs of life.
> ...
> the war of swords departed now,
> The dark Religions are departed & sweet Science reigns.[30]

Amidst just such a fresh and radiant Earth Mr Frazer in *Remembering Babylon* is led by Gemmy (as the Child leads Ovid in the countryside around Tomis in *An Imaginary Life*). Mr Frazer's drawings of plants hold a mystical significance for Gemmy, and:

> They are proof that Mr Frazer, this odd whitefeller, has grasped, beyond colour or weight or smell, the *spirit* of what he has been shown. Watching a plant emerge, the swelling bulb or fruit, the perfected leaf, Gemmy is entranced almost to breathlessness, his own spirit suspended as the real, edible object, in its ghostly form, breaks out of itself onto the whiteness of the page.[31]

Object becomes spirit in a new perception of the new world that is Queensland. 'We have been wrong to see this continent as hostile and infelicitous', writes Mr Frazer. The richness that is hidden within Australia is likened by him to that of the milk and honey of the Promised Land of the Bible in his re-imagining

---

[28] Malouf, *Remembering Babylon*, p. 3.

[29] Ibid., p. 201.

[30] William Blake, *The Four Zoas*, in *Complete Writings*, ed. Geoffrey Keynes (Oxford: Oxford University Press, 1966), p. 379. See also Thomas J.J. Altizer, *The New Apocalypse: The Radical Christian Vision of William Blake* (Aurora, CO: The Davies Group, 2000).

[31] Malouf, *Remembering Babylon*, p. 129.

of the land, hitherto unperceived by the other British settlers, 'since the very habit and faculty that makes apprehensible to us what is known and expected dulls our sensitivity to other forms, even the most obvious'. What is experienced by Mr Frazer is nothing short of a spiritual re-awakening, almost, one might say a conversion and a turning around of the mind (μετανοια) so, as he writes, 'We must rub our eyes and look again, clear our minds of what we are looking for *to see what is there.*'[32]

It is this sense of new perception, prompted instinctively by Gemmy who had been cast out by the old world and adopted by the new (which is even older), that returns the poet to the prophetic vision of William Blake, one with the vision of the Hebrew prophets with whom, in his 'Memorable Fancy', he dined as with his fellow poets:

> The prophets Isaiah and Ezekiel dined with me, and I asked them how they dared so roundly to assert that God spake to them; and whether they did not think at the time that they would be misunderstood, and so be the cause of imposition.
>
> Isaiah answered, 'I saw no God, nor heard any, in a finite organical perception; but my senses discovered the infinite in everything, and as I was then persuaded, and remain confirmed, that the voice of honest indignation is the voice of God, I cared not for the consequences but wrote.'[33]

What Gemmy and Mr Frazer recover in their senses is the infinite in everything, truly an apocalyptic moment in a marriage of heaven and hell, a recovery of lost unity that joins together all things, the far distant land with home and the inner with the outer being. *Remembering Babylon* ends with the little girl Janet, now grown up and exploring the religious life within the convent and realizing in her memories 'a kind of praying'. Outer and inner merge so that 'it does not make a house any less vivid out there because she can no longer see its light'.[34] And in the stilled moment of recollection she holds her first image of Gemmy standing on the top rail of the fence, balanced between two worlds, the old and the new, Europe and Australia, but now over-balancing into the excess of love. Thus all becomes one, the vast continent embracing everything in that other life that is found only within, a literal moment of *felix culpa* – a fortunate fall that realizes a redemption. As with Adam and Eve at the end of *Paradise Lost*, at the end of *Remembering Babylon* we fall into a world with which Gemmy has become one, Mr Frazer begins to *see* it in all its radiant detail, and Janet has begun to know it in her new religious vocation. It is perhaps a rediscovery of a sense of the

---

[32] Ibid., p. 130 (emphases added).
[33] William Blake, *The Marriage of Heaven and Hell*, in *Complete Writings*, p. 153.
[34] Malouf, *Remembering Babylon*, p. 199.

holy and even a justifying of God 'in a way that might perhaps have surprised [even] him'.[35]

In the old world, Blake, and Milton before him, know well this moment. For Blake this moment of fall is also the moment of true creation. For Milton, in *Paradise Lost*, we are left with Adam and Eve on unsettled ground, the first night out of Eden, together facing a world that was beautiful in spite of all, not with the mythical perfection of Eden but yet a place of rest and with Providence their guide. The world was all before them ... 'and (in Malouf) in a line of running fire all the outline of the vast continent appears, in touch now with its other life'.[36]

The image of Gemmy on the rail between the ancient wilderness and the newly cultivated land, 'overbalanced but not yet falling', continues to haunt me as a moment of true creation, a borderline or crossing of worlds that is at once a moment in history but also beyond history – like all true religious moments and events that balance and topple over into love. The poetry of this moment links Malouf with that of Yves Bonnefoy, who shares with him a deep theology of the earth, and sense of the creative anxiety of crossroads, where is known both the deep harmony of all things and also its inevitable fracture in human affairs. Of this harmony Bonnefoy writes in *The Arrière-pays* (2012):

> I love the earth, and what I see delights me, and sometimes I even believe that the unbroken line of peaks, the majesty of the trees, the liveliness of water moving through the bottom of a ravine, the graceful façade of a church – because in some places and at certain hours they are so intense – must have been intended for our benefit. This harmony has a meaning, these landscapes, and these objects, while they are still fixed, or possibly enchanted, are almost like a language, as if the absolute would declare itself, if we could only look and listen intently, at the end of our wanderings. And it is here, within this promise, that the place is found.[37]

Yet the anxiety and the fracture remains. On the fence, at the crossroads, in a fallen world, we can, and we have the option to, choose more than one way, away from the profound otherness of the deep interior. It is an anxiety that every poet knows, and knows too its potential for deep tragedy. It is the tragedy that Blanchot perceives in Kafka with his despairing obsession with salvation and his passion for a literature that can provide no final answer. In Australia, Patrick White identifies the tragedy of the moment when identity is formed by a

---

[35] See David Daiches, God and the Poets (Oxford: Clarendon Press, 1984), p. 49. See also David Malouf, 'First Night', in *Typewriter Music*, p. 5. Also Rudolf Otto, *The Idea of the Holy: An Inquiry into the Non-Rational Factor in the Idea of the Divine and its Relation to the Rational* [1917], trans. John W. Harvey (London: Oxford University Press, 1958).

[36] John Milton, *Paradise Lost*, Book 12, line 646; *Remembering Babylon*, p. 200.

[37] Yves Bonnefoy, *The Arrière-pays*, trans. Stephen Romer (London: Seagull Books, 2012), pp. 25–6.

determination in history, a defining of identity, and the fine edge with its visions of eternity (perhaps inevitably) is left behind. It is, wrote White, 'the moment a society wishes to give an official story of itself, [and then] it becomes a lie. This is exactly what happened in the year of the Bicentenary – which is also the year of the great Australian lie.'[38]

In Malouf, the poet, we trace history back to the roots of the lie, where and in which moment is found also the possibility of re-creation, when happiness becomes where nothing is: the nothing and the silence that is a Total Presence. In language it is the beginning again of theology. More brutally than Malouf (though it may apply also to the moment when King Priam meets Achilles in *Ransom*),[39] in his novel *A Fringe of Leaves* (1976), Patrick White concludes Ellen Roxburgh's 'exile' among the aboriginal people after the shipwreck of the *Bristol Maid* off the Australian coast, with a crossing back to 'civilization' which requires for her a literal fall 'among the cowpats', crawling back 'with a lopsided action dictated by the ruts, until halted by the barn and a pair of man's boots, the latter serviceable in the extreme.'[40] Mrs Roxburgh, herself a liminal creature, of humble background but married into English society, her language adaptable to both, has been led to this point by Jack, an escaped convict who finally cannot face a return to European society and the inevitable punishments that he foresees. Ellen is left to cross the line alone, naked, uttering the repeated phrase, 'We must all help one another' as she is 'hoisted over the threshold'. But the return is agonizing:

> Her torn hands were left clawing at the air. 'JACK! Don't leave me! I'd never survive! I'll not cross this field – let alone face the faces.'
> But she did.[41]

The contrast between White's vision and the end of *Remembering Babylon* and with the poetry of Bonnefoy, is stark. In Malouf we stand on the edge between worlds, divided and united by prayer and by love. We are always between worlds – in the autobiographical work *12 Edmonstone Street* (1985) the text moves between Brisbane, Tuscany, India, and even in the 'risky business' and unreality of air travel there are moments of contact with the earth. Stranded between flights in Bombay 'there was still a stretch of real earth to be crossed ... and India imposed itself: light, colour, vegetation, a milling throng of pedestrians, bicycles, animals of every description. I could barely take it in.'[42] It is from this

---

[38] Patrick White, 'A Sense of Integrity', *Arena*, 84 (1988), p. 98.
[39] Malouf, *Ransom*, p. 175.
[40] Patrick White, *A Fringe of Leaves* (London: Penguin, 1977), p. 300.
[41] Ibid., pp. 299, 300.
[42] David Malouf, *12 Edmonstone Street* (London: Vintage, 1999), p. 105.

close attachment to the earth and to the beauty of this world that the spirit of harmony begins to emerge. And for both Malouf and Bonnefoy this earth, in all its particularities and complex beauty, is to be realized in words: in words and the word. Such words open spaces for the transcendent, for the idea of the holy.

In one of Malouf's short stories, though it is hardly a story but rather a fragment of consciousness caught in a brief first person narrative, he is concerned with the end of language, its death and its mystery. 'The Only Speaker of His Tongue' was first published in 1985 in the collection of stories entitled *Antipodes*. It is about the meeting of two worlds in the figures of the narrator who is a lexicographer and a 'famous visitor, a scholarly freak from another continent', and the aborigine, the 'the one surviving speaker of his tongue,' the digger of holes for fencing-posts at the edge of the plain who responds to the call from another continent with the words, 'Yes, boss, you wanna see me?' – words caught between statement and question.[43] To whom does the last speaker of a language speak in words which are thrown out into an uncomprehending world from an alternative universe that 'is still alive in the man's silence'? For words, as the scholar knows, create our world in the names of villages, the pet names given to animals (Little Bean, Pretty Cowslip), in nonsense rhymes, in the blood and breath of things. 'O holiest of all holy things!'[44]

Words, we might say, are sacraments, living powers (as Coleridge once called them) by which the being of all things is realized for us. At the deepest heart of things they are also on the very edge, their silence defeating the curiosity of the scholar and our instinct for preservation. In this last speaker of an almost dead language, words are at an end, but this is also an infinitely mysterious beginning, opening beyond the world that we know through our naming of it, through words. In the second biblical account of the creation of humankind, the man gives names to all cattle and animals of the field (Genesis 2:20). In the first story, God, the only speaker of his tongue, the first and the last, speaks the whole of creation into being. 'The first and the last words of all those generations' are buried in the old aborigine fellow of Malouf's story, 'down there in the earth'.[45] As the keeper of words that fade from this world, the old fellow is both the centre of all things and at the same time on the very remotest edge of a universe, a liminal figure. The scholar, the freak from another continent, in the solitude of his room with washbasin and an engraving of Naomi bidding farewell to Ruth (another story of liminality and creativity), repeats words, almost like the first Adam of the second creation story:

---

[43]   David Malouf, *The Complete Stories* (London: Vintage, 2007), pp. 422–6.
[44]   Ibid., p. 423.
[45]   Ibid., p. 424.

> As if it were only my voice naming them in the dark that kept the loved objects solid and touchable in the light up there, on the top side of the world.[46]

The world, north and south, the old and the new, Europe and Australia, is kept in being by the words that name things: while the words of the old fellow remain silent, deeper than the freaks of modern scholarship.

When God spoke in the beginning, who understood his words – words that we read in Hebrew or in English, in the texts of our bibles? In a famous Jewish midrash on the first verses of Genesis we read that, before anything came into being, the Holy One, blessed be he, was reading: 'He looked into the Torah and created the world.'[47] In the Rabbinic tradition, the Torah is not a physical book but the blueprint of all creation. It is not speculation about the world but of its very essence.

So, in a way, it is in Malouf's story 'The Only Speaker of His Tongue'. Things centre themselves upon the old, silent, aborigine, upon the words and names that are in his mind alone. In him words are no longer simply a means of communication, but that by which a world is kept in being. He is rather like the desert fathers of the late fourth century CE who live, according to the contemporary work known as *Historia Monachorum in Aegypto*, on the edge between heaven and earth, citizens of heaven though here on earth, and it is through them that 'the world is kept in being'.[48] But the story mirrors also the death of God, which is a moment of the radical reversal of consciousness, an annihilation that is also a beginning, a descent into hell, which (in Malouf's writing) becomes identical with an ascension into heaven.[49] The shift to the theological here is made without apology.

Malouf's *Complete Stories* are prefaced by some words from Pascal's *Pensées*, first published in 1670, which look forward to Bonnefoy's reflections in *The Arrière-pays* in their sense of the purpose of all things, could we but know it:

> When I consider the brevity of my life, swallowed up as it is in the eternity that precedes and will follow it, the tiny space I occupy and what is visible to me, cast as I am into a vast infinity of spaces that I know nothing of and which know nothing of me, I take fright, I am stunned to find myself here rather than elsewhere, for there is no reason why it should be here rather than there, and now rather than then.

---

[46]   Ibid., p. 426.

[47]   *Ber. Rab.* 1:1, quoted in Susan A. Handelman, *The Slayers of Moses: The Emergence of Rabbinic Interpretation in Modern Literary Theory* (Albany, NY: State University of New York Press, 1982), p. 38.

[48]   *The Lives of the Desert Fathers*, trans. Norman Russell (Kalamazoo, MI: Cistercian Publication, 1981), p. 50.

[49]   See Thomas J.J. Altizer, *The Descent into Hell: A Study of the Radical Reversal of the Christian Consciousness* (Philadelphia, PA: J.B. Lippincott Company, 1970).

Who set me here? By whose order and under what guiding destiny was this time, this place assigned to me?

The theologian and the philosopher seek for reasons within the mystery of being, for evidence of the hand of God within the interstices of the universal and the particular, of eternity and time. For what reason am I *here* rather than elsewhere, on this edge – like Ovid in Tomis or Priam, a king learning what it is to be an ordinary man in 'the not-unpleasant yielding of the senses' during his journey by cart between Troy and the Greek camp.[50] Ovid, King Priam, and perhaps all of us, are on the journey 'in between'. And while the theologian and the philosopher pray and think, the poet watches and speaks out of the silence. And prayer, perhaps, is a merging of worlds. We have finally returned to Janet's 'kind of praying' at the conclusion of *Remembering Babylon*, with which I began this chapter.

There is a good precedent in poetry. Out of the silence of the nothing God spoke things into being and saw that they were good. The poet is not called to explain. Wilfred Owen knew that as he wrote his poems in blood before his death in the trenches in 1918. 'All a poet can do today is warn. That is why the true Poets must be truthful.'[51] The poet speaks from the particular place where he or she find themselves – here, on this fence, rather than there or somewhere else, and the poet is called to be truthful. At the end of *12 Edmonstone Street*, the place is a train in New South Wales, travelling to Sydney, the author then a young child, watching the world around him: the girls with their smeared lipstick, the business men in their suits, the snotty kids and 'that darker wagon with the Japs',[52] the prisoners of war. The presence of all this imposes silence and at the same time provokes a language that is indiscernible – like the word of God – the otherness that is present in every moment. It is of and from this silence, and its different, unnameable destination, that Malouf speaks and we, the readers, follow his words on the page.

Within the in-between world of pure silence – like the silence of a new, as yet unexplored continent – is the genesis of speech. In the beginning was the word. The true poet falls into language – the Fall, for Blake, being the true moment of creation – and speech becomes the exodus from the ground of speech. And then speech becomes the living chariot that carries us, like Ezekiel's chariot,[53]

---

[50]   Malouf, *Ransom*, p. 149.

[51]   Wilfred Owen, Preface to *War Poems: The Collected Poems of Wilfred Owen*, ed. C. Day Lewis (London: Chatto & Windus, 1963).

[52]   Malouf, *12 Edmonstone Street*, p. 134.

[53]   Ezekiel 1:20. Also, see Coleridge, *The Statesman's Manual*, p. 29. 'These are the Wheels which Ezekiel beheld, when the hand of the Lord was upon him, and he saw visions of God as he sate among the captives by the river of Chebar. *Withersoever the Spirit was to go, the wheels went, and thither was their spirit to go: for the spirit of the living creature was in the wheels also*.' See also above pp. 133, 152.

to the final, necessary encounter when the strangeness and otherness within is found to be the true self which we have been seeking all along. If we have lost our innocence there is yet a moment of salvation, a homecoming and a merging of object and subject in the enactment of speech: 'As we approach prayer. As we approach knowledge. As we approach one another.'

Chapter 13
Europe and China: Old Worlds Meet

Overhanging the earlier chapters of this book is the dark shadow of Auschwitz and the Holocaust with its sense of absolute evil. Here we find ourselves faced with the question of responsibility. In what sense can we be called responsible for such inhuman evil in our world? I concluded Chapter 3 with the account in the Affidavit of SS Grüppenführer Otto Ohlendorf as he described the manner in which he ordered his men to shoot the victims of the concentration camp at the place of execution, and that 'several of the men should shoot at the same time in order *to avoid direct, personal responsibility*'.[1] I now draw towards a close in this book with a return to Auschwitz and the Holocaust but add to it and alongside it another terrible event of the twentieth century, the 10 years of the Cultural Revolution in China between 1966 and 1976. They are the subject of a remarkable essay by the Chinese scholar Yang Huilin, a professor of comparative literature at Renmin University of China in Beijing, who has recently described Auschwitz and the Cultural Revolution as 'two already symbolic tragic events'.[2] Now, as I draw towards the end of my university career, I find myself blest with the privilege of teaching for three months each year in Beijing, in the Communist Renmin University of China where Professor Yang is both a colleague and a friend.[3] As we seek to find ways of mutual understanding between the West and the newly emergent China, fumbling again to establish pathways through the study of 'literature and religion' (a complex and interesting term that now stretches far beyond the limits of the Judaeo-Christian traditions which circumscribed the Durham conference), the familiar issues and problems re-emerge and end, as always perhaps, in both the necessity and the impossibility of theology; its failure and its urgent call heard again at first through the voices of the poet and the philosopher. Yang, who has been at the forefront of establishing humane intellectual conversations between universities in China and the West (in stark contrast to the unseemly scramble of universities in both East and West to form connections based on economic avarice and self-aggrandizement), shares

---

[1]   Simone Gigliotti and Berel Lang (eds), *The Holocaust: A Reader* (Oxford: Blackwell, 2005), p. 182. See above, p. 57 (emphases added).

[2]   Yang Huilin, ch. 5, 'The Contemporary Significance of Theological Ethics: The True Problems Elicited by Auschwitz and the Cultural Revolution', in *China, Christianity and the Question of Culture* (Waco, TX: Baylor University Press, 2014), pp. 61–75, 61.

[3]   Renmin University was founded in 1937 to educate and train the political elite in China. It is now one of the leading universities in the People's Republic.

with Ulrich Simon the direct experience of profound evil in human affairs, for as a young man he lived through the years of the Cultural Revolution. In his writings, Yang returns time and again to the role of theology, knowing (though for very particular reasons in modern and contemporary China) the truth of Gavin D'Costa's remark that 'theology, properly understood, cannot be taught and practiced within the modern university'.[4] Yet, in spirit and in his own way, Yang would also agree, I suspect, with John Henry Newman for whom there cannot possibly be a university where there is no theology. Making this unlikely connection between Newman and Yang (and working as a Western scholar in a Chinese university one quickly learns the need and the necessity to make unlikely connections) through the study of literature as a common academic 'language', will be the task of this chapter.

Most of the chapters of this book so far have been attempts to recover the sense of what we were doing in the early British conferences on theology and literature in the University of Durham and later Oxford and Glasgow in ways that we were not, and could not have been, altogether aware of at the time. The medium of our work, almost always, was literature, but the deep roots lay in the theological and ecclesiological concerns of the nineteenth century, above all in the figure of John Henry Newman, worked out in him at a time when the Christian Church and its theology in Europe were experiencing profound pressures that were at once intellectual, spiritual and social of an unprecedented nature. After Kant and after Romanticism there was a brave new world in which theology had to be thought afresh to survive at all, yet this could only be done by delving deep into the ancient catholic traditions that ultimately form us as Christians. This brave new world reached its terrible climax in the two great world wars of the next century, after which, it might and has been said, there was nothing further to utter but only a terrible silence that was broken at first only by the voice of the poet, the voice of tragedy, poetically creating something out of nothing. It was here that we began with Ulrich Simon, John Coulson, Martin Jarrett-Kerr and Peter Walker and others, who knew deconstructions in their lives, physically, intellectually and spiritually, far more profound in human terms than those articulated later in the cultural theory and criticism of the late twentieth century. Art and literature speak to us through resonances that both invite and defy comparisons. As I teach Western literature in a China that is today fascinated by religion (and perhaps still rather afraid of its power in human affairs), I find resonances in my experience today with what we felt in the early 1980s and with theology in the nineteenth century. The pressures – intellectual, spiritual and social – are immense and daunting at a time in China (as in England in the middle years of the nineteenth century) when China is

---

4   Gavin D'Costa, *Theology in the Public Square: Church, Academy and Nation* (Oxford: Blackwell, 2005), p. 1, 20.

economically expanding at an enormous speed, sometimes at a terrible cost to the natural and social worlds: a time of great wealth and also of great poverty, both experienced on many levels. Strangely, it is only here in Beijing, where it is, in one sense, almost impossible or at least, in Stanley Fish's phrase, so very hard to do, that I am recalling why the study of theology and literature so fundamentally matters – a recollection that is hardly tranquil. For the last few decades in our Western universities it had, I think, simply become too easy, too facile, theology forgotten, and we have forgotten the deadly serious nature of what we were and are doing and why we are doing it. This is not entirely the case, as we have seen, but the return to a genuine theological sense of being human, whether Christian or otherwise, is painfully slow and often barely perceptible. I am aware that many heads will be shaking at this suggestion.

Much of this chapter will be in the form of a kind of conversation with Yang Huilin as he addresses the problems after Auschwitz and the Cultural Revolution and the significance of a return, therefore, not simply to ethics, but, in his term, to theological ethics. It is a conversation that will lift us out of the parochialism of much of this book – which has appeared, it might be said, to take the form of a return to seemingly conservative Christian, Western roots (though often things conservative can also be profoundly radical). For some of us that may be true, but through the universality of literature (a sometimes painful truth learnt again by nineteenth-century European Protestant missionaries in China like James Legge, who acknowledged that what they heard as the voice of God may come as well through the *Tao Te Ching* as through the Bible) we may begin to stretch out across our differences and to 'read religiously' at far more profound levels than those encouraged by Robert Detweiler's sense of the 'erotic space of the text'.[5] Such religious reading should, perhaps, be extended to the more precise term of 'theological reading', from the basis of what Yang, thinking outwards, with the living and creative empathy of a true humanism, from the work of Ernst Bloch in *The Principle of Hope*, describes as the 'inertia of secular theory',[6] that is the deadness of the 'codes' in thinking which contain within themselves 'a set pattern of speech for the other party'.[7] Perhaps a parallel in Western literary and cultural theory might be drawn here with Terry Eagleton's characterization of deconstruction as an exercise in driving a coach and horses through everyone else's position without the inconvenience of having to adopt and be responsible for one of your own.[8] More simply we might call this the habit of putting words

---

[5]   Robert Detweiler, *Breaking the Fall: Religious Readings of Contemporary Fiction* (Louisville, KY: WJK Press, 1995), p. 35, and see above Chapter 6, p. 91.

[6]   Yang Huilin, *China, Christianity and the Question of Culture*, p. 62.

[7]   Maurice Bloch, *Political Language and Oratory in Traditional Society* (London: Academic Press, 1975), p. 9.

[8]   Terry Eagleton, *Literary Theory: An Introduction*, 2nd edn (Oxford: Blackwell, 1996). See above, pp. 45–6.

into other people's mouths. In the West this perhaps goes some way to explain the later 'turn to ethics' after the first outpouring of postmodern enthusiasm, a turn that I endorse here but dare to move beyond, with Yang, if only in anticipation, into theological ethics. There is also the issue of granting freedom to the 'other' and a release from such set patterns of speech.

The experiences of Europe and China and their different cultures and histories in the twentieth century are drawn together in the twentieth century by the two great events of the Holocaust and the Cultural Revolution. Each give us terrible evidence of the frailty of our human existence and that 'collective unconsciousness' in which we are all involved, and the questions of guilt and responsibility that no consoling narratives or systems of religion or politics can finally evade or eradicate.[9] Auschwitz demands absolutely and at once a theological response and refuses any attempt at justification. None of us can stand outside or beyond its dark shadow of suffering or guilt. Poets and writers, survivors of the camps, like Paul Celan and Primo Levi continue to speak, in spite of Adorno, and if Bonhoeffer writes before his death by hanging at Flossenberg in 1945 in *Letters and Papers from Prison* it is the language of poetry which first gives his faith utterance. In China, the 'scar literature' of the 1970s seeks to give a voice to the sufferings of the people of China during the Cultural Revolution in fictions (and later films) now widely read in translation and seen in the West, like Yu Hua's searing novel *To Live* and the work of the Nobel Prize winning writer Mo Yan.[10] Yang also notes the autobiographical novels of women writers who have left China which speak of individual experiences of pain and loss, though these, he says, have tended to foster 'the narcissistic belief that "all persons in the world are drunk and only I am sober"'.[11] But evil wears a darker and more unavoidable face for all of us at the heart of human history.

Yang draws our attention to a moment in Simon Wiesenthal's book *The Sunflower* (1977) in which Wiesenthal quotes the words of a dying Nazi soldier who had been involved in the massacre of Jews: 'I know what I am saying is horrifying. In the long nights, as I am compelled to lie here waiting for death to arrive, I yearn more and more to tell this story to a Jew and seek

---

[9]   See Yang Huilin, *China, Christianity and the Question of Culture*, p. 61.

[10]   So brutal are the depictions of human violence in Yu Hua's novels that Mo Yan, referring to Yu Hua's time as a dentist wrote, 'I've heard that [Yu Hua] was a dentist for five years. I can't imagine what kind of brutal tortures patients endured under his cruel steel pliers.' Mo Yan, 'The Awakened Dream Teller: Random Thoughts on Yu Hua and His Fiction,' in *Yu Hua 2000 Collection: Contemporary China Literature Reader* (Ming Pao: Hong Kong, 1999), p. 1.

[11]   Yang Huilin, *China, Christianity and the Question of Culture*, p. 62. Such works promote the belief that the Cultural Revolution was solely the responsibility of Mao Zedong and the Gang of Four. In the same way Hitler and a few close associates amongst the Nazis might be blamed alone for the Holocaust.

his pardon. However, I do not know if any Jews are still alive.'[12] We return to the impossibility of forgiveness. It is the stories that we hardly dare to utter and yet yearn to tell as we seek forgiveness that alone might offer some comfort if not reconciliation and forgiveness itself; but whom do we write for, and is there anyone left to read or hear them? It is not the death of the author but the death of the reader that is most to be feared for the writer. And if the story is finally read, who will believe me when all belief has been shattered? After the death of God do we still have the strength to summon up the necessary willing suspension of disbelief to read at all, fearing what we might encounter? And yet the poets still continue to write, even in the darkness – lights whom the darkness cannot finally comprehend or subdue. Wiesenthal takes us back to the ancient Christian 'story' of the four daughters of God – Truth, Righteousness, Mercy and Peace – in medieval works like Langland's *Piers Plowman* and the complex bitterness of *The Merchant of Venice* – a play that has fascinated Chinese translators since the nineteenth century, but is, perhaps, finally, untranslatable in the implications of the terrible moment of the 'conversion' of Shylock and in the clash of justice and mercy.[13] After Auschwitz can there be forgiveness (Simon intones, 'May they never rise again!'), is such a move even *ethical* for Wiesel or the Jewish Christian Ulrich Simon? As Emmanuel Levinas, another Jewish teacher, has stated clearly, 'Making forgiveness almighty is creating an inhuman world.'[14] Everything changes after Auschwitz and all ethics are held in question before such absolute evil.

Drawing upon the work of Dideir Pollefeyt and his essay 'Ethics, Forgiveness and the Unforgiveable after Auschwitz'[15] Yang offers three models or 'views of evil'. (As I sat in my study in Beijing in 2014 where this chapter was first drafted, an outsider to the Cultural Revolution, I realize that only now and through this re-encounter with evil in human history, am I reliving in China the deep, impossible narratives and imperatives of our conference in Durham in 1982.) The first model of evil is called 'diabolicization'; that is identifying the perpetrator of evil as satanic (Hitler, Mao Zedong, Stalin) and perceiving him (or her) as simply an inhuman monster, outside the realm of common humanity.[16] Such a model falls inevitably into a form of dualism, dividing the good from the evil, the world

---

[12] Simon Wiesenthal, *The Sunflower* (New York: Schocken Books, 1977), p. xx.

[13] See above, p. 43. More recently, of course, the Four Daughters of God are re-born in the poetry of William Blake, in his *Songs of Innocence and Experience* (1789, 1794), 'The Divine Image'.

[14] Emmanuel Levinas, *Het menselijk gelaat: Essays*, ed. Ad Paperzak (Baarn: Ambo, 1984), p. 46. Quoted in Yang Huilin, *China, Christianity and the Question of Culture*, p. 63.

[15] Didier Pollefeyt (ed.), *Incredible Forgiveness: Christian Ethics between Fanaticism and Reconciliation* (Leuven: Peeters, 2004), pp. 121–59.

[16] As, for example in Harry Mulisch's novel *Siegfried* (2001), in which Hitler is portrayed as a grey, inhuman quality of absolute evil, the 'totally other' and 'the absolutely

of light from the world of darkness in a manner finally eschewed by Christian theology and its ancient, endless theodical reflections. Under this model, Auschwitz or the Cultural Revolution can be regarded as tragic dislocations in the great flow of human history, discontinuities rather than the profound continuities which Richard L. Rubenstein so agonizingly described and in which it 'became morally acceptable for normal men and women to participate in the project of mass extermination *with a good conscience*'.[17] We, you and I, dear reader, surely cannot be held responsible for the actions of those inhuman monsters, wholly other, who perpetrate such evils in our midst, distanced always from us as the 'other' which can take on manifold forms – from the diabolical to the inhuman in Jews, homosexuals – or anyone not like 'us'. It is, of course, perfectly possible to find support for something like such a position even in the Bible literature itself, which can offer us the image of the God of vengeance. But in a secular age, and as we have seen in Hannah Arendt's *The Human Condition*,[18] revenge is transferred back and purely so to the human sphere – it becomes ours alone either to forgive or else to exact vengeful punishment – each, in itself, perhaps, following Levinas, merely the pathway to an inhuman world. At the end of the age of 'revenge tragedies' in Elizabethan England it was Shakespeare's *Hamlet* – the most profoundly theological of all of his plays – which explored in the agony of Hamlet the impossibility and the 'cursed spite' of thus being called and seeking to repair a world that is out of joint and that God has abandoned. For the evil is also within him, his conscience, too, 'caught' by the play.

The second model of evil Pollefeyt describes as 'banalization', taking the term, again, from the writings of Hannah Arendt. This is closer to the painfulness felt at the 1982 Durham conference that at least acknowledged the continuities rather than the discontinuities in the history in which we also played, and still play, our part. Society is not finally good but partakes of the evil in a kind of ghastly structure of line-management (so beloved of the modern university) that minimizes the freedom of the individual who becomes a mere cog in the machinery of evil that somehow is the very realization of Kafka's Joseph K in *The Trial* and his 'melancholy conclusion' at the end of the Parable of the Door Keeper, that lying has been turned into a universal principle. In both of these models I can console myself that it is not, finally, my fault. I take no responsibility within the inevitable and all-powerful machinery of state.

Pollefeyt's third model he calls the 'apology of evil'. This is essentially the redefinition of ethics on the principle that certain situations sometimes require

---

foreign, the denial of everything that exists and can be thought '. *Siegfried*, trans. Paul Vincent (London: Penguin, 2004), p. 136.

[17] Richard L. Rubenstein, *After Auschwitz: History, Theology, and Contemporary Judaism*, 2nd edn (Baltimore, MD: Johns Hopkins University Press, 1992), p. 183. See further above, p. 46.

[18] See above Chapter 8, p. 114.

us to act radically in a particular kind of way to restore a society that has fallen out of joint. As Yang puts it, 'even Hitler believed that Germany's decline was the outcome of moral depravity and that Germany's salvation lay in "revitalizing morality"'.[19] In literature, we might say, this is the model that gives rise to the modern and postmodern fictions of dystopia – from Aldous Huxley's *Brave New World* to Margaret Atwood's *The Handmaid's Tale*, portraying a culture of discontinuity under the dissimulation of continuity with the biblical tradition, and therefore, to a degree, reminiscent of Bakhtin's portrayal of Russia under Stalin in *Rabelais and His World* (1965).

Through the 'apology of evil' model history itself makes the Holocaust not only morally acceptable but even morally necessary, a 'necessary price' to pay. But we have seen that it was the genius of Newman which recognized in the tradition of Christian theology the great and absolute necessity of continuity in the development of Christian doctrine based not so much on the principle of *consistency* but rather as *connectedness* and the 'gradual influence of truth over error'.[20] Even though the formal expression of a truth or position may not have been actually spoken and articulated, as Newman puts it in his last University Sermon entitled 'The Theory of Developments in Religious Doctrine', it has been 'all along the secret life of millions of faithful souls'.[21] And it is finally in his *Essay on the Development of Christian Doctrine* that Newman, appealing to his doctrine of revelation, states the principles of development in Christianity that utterly contradict the 'apology of evil' model and its argument for the necessary revision of ethical principles – that is, that radically new definitions of the ideas of good and evil may sometimes be necessary under certain circumstances. Newman puts it starkly, and with a startlingly contemporary tone:

> [We] must determine whether on the one hand Christianity is still to represent to us a definite teaching from above, or whether on the other its utterances have been from time to time so strangely at variance that *we are necessarily thrown back on our own judgement* individually to determine what the revelation of God is, or rather if in fact there is, or has been, any revelation at all.[22]

---

[19] Yang Huilin, *China, Christianity and the Question of Culture*, p. 66. We might even recall that the saintly Archbishop William Temple, recognizing the evil of war in 1939, nevertheless remarked that sometimes we are called to commit a lesser evil that a greater evil may be prevented.

[20] J.H. Newman, *The Arians of the Fourth Century*, quoted in Gerard H. McCarren, 'Development of Doctrine', in *The Cambridge Companion to John Henry Newman*, eds Ian Ker and Terrence Merrigan (Cambridge: Cambridge University Press, 2009), p. 119.

[21] J.H. Newman, *University Sermons* 3rd edn [1871] (London: SPCK, 1970), p. 323.

[22] J.H. Newman, *Essay on the Development of Christian Doctrine*, ed. J.M. Cameron (London: Penguin, 1974), p. 74 (emphases added).

What is most interesting for our discussion here, as we turn now from Auschwitz to Yang's reflections on the Cultural Revolution in China, is the specific terms in which Newman writes; those of Christianity and the ultimate dependence on divine revelation. The issue with regard to the 'apology of evil' model is clear – that ultimately the redefinition of ethics is not dependent upon our own judgement (although the principle of development does not negate in any way the process of change within human history and culture). The question as regards divine revelation may finally be crucial or even debatable, but the principle is clear – that it cannot be for us to undertake to change the course of human history by redefining nothing less than what it means to be human. We cannot change our humanity except at the cost of losing it: hence, in the end it might be said, *all* ethics must be *theological* ethics, and perhaps it is the tragic in literature that points to this – points, but no more. Thus, as we have seen, it was the power of Ulrich Simon's book *Pity and Terror* that it sought a synthesis between Christian existence and tragic involvement, but finally *failed* to bring this about.[23] And so the utterly serious study of literature and theology is in the end based upon a necessary impossibility in its requirement of theology.

A brief illustration of what has just been argued may be found in a startling passage in Pat Barker's novel of the First World War, *Regeneration* (1991). The novel (which is based on a real encounter with Siegfried Sassoon) concerns the work of an army psychologist, W.H.R. Rivers, in Craiglockhart, Edinburgh who is treating young men sent back from the Front and the trenches in Europe suffering from various forms of shell shock, what we might now call post-traumatic stress syndrome.[24] One young soldier, David Burns, who has witnessed scenes of unbelievable horror in battle, eventually suffers a total breakdown and, while walking with the doctor by the sea at Thorpeness, becomes dangerously violent. The doctor is not a young man and although Burns is 'terribly emaciated' he is 30 years younger and still dangerous. As Rivers witnesses the utter psychological disintegration of a human being, almost, we might say, his loss of a sense of his humanity as a result of human evil and violence in war, the doctor concludes that *nothing* in human reason can possibly justify this: 'He looked up at the tower that loomed squat and menacing above them, and thought. *Nothing justifies this. Nothing, nothing, nothing.* Burns's body remained rigid in his arms.'[25] The scene is a kind of ghastly pastiche of the *Pietà*. There can be no argument for war or even its inevitability in history that can justify or make tolerable such an effect upon even one person and rob him of all that is human. The implication in the passage is clear. It puts a human question mark beside even the image of the cross

---

23   See above, p. 54.

24   Another example of this in literature is found, of course, in Virginia Woolf's *Mrs Dalloway* (1925).

25   Pat Barker, *Regeneration* (London: Penguin, 1992), p. 180.

of Christ itself. Does even the salvation of the world justify the indescribable, inhuman sufferings of one young Jewish man, inflicted by human decision, perhaps on the excuse of the greater good of society as a whole – or have we, in those particular sufferings, lost our own humanity as well?

This passage in fiction, it seems to me, throws down the gauntlet to Christian theology and Christology. Have *we* the right, as human beings, to offer any justification of the cross as somehow a means to our final well-being and the salvation of our souls? Have *we*, even though commanded to seek reconciliation with our brethren before we seek God, the right, therefore, to forgive or to condemn? Are the monsters of evil in the end *our* creations? The poet – and Wilfred Owen, facing almost inevitable death in France, knew so well that it is not the poet's task to offer resolutions – the poet offers no answer. Yet through the poet we merely know profoundly of the pity of war, and here pity is indeed a hard, inadequate term. And true Poets must be truthful.

And so we return to Yang Huilin's essay, to the problem of forgiveness and to the Cultural Revolution in China. Yang, who as a young man experienced the 10 years of the Revolution, describes it in this way.

> Like Auschwitz, the Cultural Revolution typically manifested a kind of combined historical force of collective unconsciousness, and also typically exposed the one-sidedness and limitations of values and ideals in the earthly world. 'Evil' could be wrought and 'monsters' could have their way precisely because each of us was a participant from one angle or another. In the ultimate sense, there could be virtually no pure 'victims' amid this sustained and enormous evil.[26]

Of course Auschwitz and the Cultural Revolution cannot simply be equated. They were not the same, and they had a profoundly different effect upon the German and the Chinese peoples respectively. As Yang himself admits, it is not altogether possible entirely to 'negate' the Cultural Revolution as it did eventually bring about forms of independent thinking and even, arguably, the economic reforms that have brought China into the forefront of the global economy, to the point that there is now even a kind of nostalgia, or more, felt for Mao himself amidst the current corruption scandals. Furthermore, it cannot be placed (any more than Yang himself) directly within the European religious and theological traditions of Christian and Jewish literature and theology and its narratives. It is therefore only within our literary traditions that deep similarities are to be felt and perceived and new, yet recognizable, versions of Pollefeyt's three models or views of evil are to be found. The model of diabolization, Yang suggests, is most clearly seen in the Chinese 'scar literature' of the late 1970s, which Yang, by and large, dismisses, without further elaboration, as something approaching

---

[26] Yang Huilin, *China, Christianity and the Question of Culture*, p. 70.

fantasy literature. The second model is that of banalization, which in China Yang locates amongst the intellectuals and within theoretical circles of thought, the determinism of which he sums up in a telling phrase, that it is unable to 'make choices that transcend the present environment'.[27] Here we are trapped by our own horizons, temporally, culturally and perhaps even geographically. The third model, that of the 'apology of evil', is different as regards the Cultural Revolution from the Holocaust inasmuch as the passing of the years has changed and even softened the effects of some 40 years ago so that, says Yang, 'there is no way to pursue the reasons and responsibilities for the catastrophe'.[28]

For different reasons forgiveness cannot be the simple response or solution to the evils of either the Holocaust or the Cultural Revolution. In China, as participant in an event that involved the whole population (as opposed to an act of genocide) there remains, as Yang has noted, no one to take responsibility for the evil, and so who is there to forgive? Even Chairman Mao, in the present new age of economic dislocation and acknowledged corruption, has been the subject of new myths which place him back on his 'sacred altar' and portraits of Mao used to 'ward off evil' are commonplace today.[29] And so we come back to where we began with the word 'responsibility'. It lies at the very heart of our humanity, as Milton realized in *Paradise Lost*.

In both the Western and the Eastern traditions there is, in different ways, the problem of the delicate balance between intention and action. Yang Huilin notes that in the Daoist tradition in China one finds the proposal to 'judge by the intention and not the deed with regard to filial piety, otherwise there is no filial son in poor families', and to 'judge by the deed and not the intention with regard to pruriency, otherwise there is no moral man since the Creation'. He continues:

> [In China] evil behaviour has always been argued from two aspects, the *xin* (conception or motive) and the *ji* (the action or the result), and may thus be exculpated. This has never had the effect of preventing new evil, however; the Cultural Revolution is only one example of this.[30]

But at the end of Chapter 3 I made a reference to the fateful scene in Goethe's *Faust, Part One* in which Faust alters the opening of St John's Gospel, retranslating it as 'In the beginning was the Deed'.[31] The deed stands, and though we, perhaps, temper somewhat the rule of law with loving intentions, or seek the roots of

---

27   Ibid., p. 71.
28   Ibid., p. 72.
29   Ibid.
30   Ibid., p. 73.
31   See above, pp. 56–7.

justice as opposed to law, like Derrida, in a mystical imperative,[32] yet the logic of the tradition takes us inevitably to the place of execution and to the foot of the cross, as it always has done: *God is dead, and we have killed him.*[33] In Christianity the cycle is broken only by the divine act of kenosis, though for some there is no salvation: the chant yet goes forth, 'May they never rise again.' The evils of neither Auschwitz nor the Cultural Revolution can be finally absolved or obliterated by forgiveness.

If the Chinese tradition has always tended towards the integration of the sacred and the secular, such that Confucianism moves towards the idea of a 'Confucian religion', in the West the processes of secularization and de-sacralization since the sixteenth century, accelerating in the nineteenth and twentieth centuries, have perhaps reached a point of no return. Before the horrors of Auschwitz, coming at the end of millennia of anti-Semitism and perhaps necessary but ultimately futile just-war arguments in the Christian Church, theology is finally silenced, and there is no synthesis, as Ulrich Simon would wish or hope to argue, between Christian existence and tragic involvement.[34] I was once persuaded that he might be right in his hope, but this can no longer be the case. The poet, who is of the Devil's party, and therefore a true poet (as Blake once said of Milton with an irony that transcends irony)[35] can only be true to his or her vocation and show us what we prefer not to contemplate, and show us its pity.

Yang, with whom most of this chapter has been in dialogue, ends his essay on Auschwitz and the Cultural Revolution on a note of grim realism. 'Most theories of ethics and morality since modern times insist, to a certain extent, on "contracts," the balancing of interests, and operability.'[36] In other words, such theories are simply pragmatic and practical, seeking balance if not resolution. This is like a reading of Romans 13 which stops half way through, ends at verse 7, and believes that that is all there is to be said. For the Pauline ethics of love, which know neither limit nor balance, are simply inaccessible in the 'pursuit of responsibility', but it can only be in such a pursuit that the possibility of a theological ethics is shadowed forth if never actually present.

---

[32] See Jacques Derrida, 'Force of Law: The "Mystical Foundation of Authority" "Mystical Foundation of Authority"', in Drucilla Cornell, Michel Rosenfeld and David Gray Carlson (eds), *Deconstruction and the Possibility of Justice* (London: Routledge, 1992), pp. 3–67.

[33] See Friedrich Nietzsche, *The Gay Science* [1882], trans. Josefine Nauckhoff (Cambridge: Cambridge University Press, 2001), pp. 119–20.

[34] Ulrich Simon, *Pity and Terror: Christianity and Tragedy* (London: Macmillan, 1989), see above, p. 54.

[35] William Blake, *The Marriage of Heaven and Hell* (1790–93), in *Complete Writings*, ed. Geoffrey Keynes (Oxford: Oxford University Press, 19723), p. 150.

[36] Yang Huilin, *China, Christianity and the Question of Culture*, p. 74.

Yang explains this in the Christian tradition through the work of Johan Verstraeten for whom 'the significance of the Bible is metaethical or transethical'.[37] I have to admit that I am not persuaded by the postmodern slippages of Verstraeten's essay and its argument which ultimately appears to absolve the Bible itself from ethical responsibility in the name of some higher calling that finally transcends ethics. (I suppose this might be some kind of understanding of the idea of grace.) But is this a legitimate reading of the gospels? In the Daoist tradition in China Yang suggest this possibility in terms of an abandonment of *li* (behaviour and manners) for the sake of *Dao* (the Way), again a possible transcending of the ethical, perhaps? But there are overtones here of Derrida's resort to the mystical foundations of justice, and I am deeply conscious that such mystical tendencies are not entirely absent from the dark arguments of this book, though I am myself suspicious of them.

However, before returning to that theme of the mystical in the final chapter, I would like briefly to offer a rather different idea and possibility of a theological ethics in the light of the irresolutions of the present chapter and its heavy sense of responsibility under the shadow of Auschwitz and the Cultural Revolution. When we met in Durham in 1982 to discuss theology and literature I do not think we were aware of that issue of responsibility, though if Ulrich Simon could end his lecture reminding us that the best we could hope for (by heroism and compassion) was to make the world a bearable place, then surely something more than that was needed and called for. It is not enough, by human qualities, to make life simply bearable. Yet there were, and are, no trite theological solutions, no possible actions of a *deus ex machina*, the 'wholly other' or Barthian transcendence, but only, for us, the words of the poets, like Sylvia Plath in *Ariel*, words that were not in any sense 'good for us'. And still in all of our discussions there was a theological seriousness that was inescapable and yet somehow always beyond us. Since that time much has been said and written about theological aesthetics and the forms of beauty, particularly in the magnum opus of Hans Urs von Balthasar, though I am profoundly wary of his theological position in both its deep patriarchalism and its religious use of literature, and have written so elsewhere at more length.[38] Nevertheless, it is perhaps the vision and form of beauty that calls us beyond (and perhaps, mysteriously, even *in*) our acts of heroism and compassion in the face of evil towards an unaccountable moment of transformation and transfiguration, in spite of all. How can we know this?

---

[37]   Johan Vertraeten, 'The "World" of the Bible as Meta-Ethical Framework of Meaning for Ethics', in Hendick M. Vroom and Jerald D. Gort (eds), *Holy Scripture in Judaism, Christianity and Islam: Hermeneutics, Values and Society* (Amasterdam: Rodopi, 1997), p. 140.

[38]   See David Jasper, 'God's Better Beauty: Language and the Poetry of Gerard Manley Hopkins,' *Christianity and Literature*, vol. 34, no. 3 (1985), 9–22.

Is it because in the poet we might glimpse the form of beauty as in a sacrament, a form which is indissoluble and beyond the merely intellectual? For:

> Our meddling intellect
> Mis-shapes the beauteous forms of things: -
> We murder to dissect.[39]

And so our assent to the beautiful has to be through an act of the imagination but therefore no less intelligent as, in Newman's words in the *Grammar of Assent*, a 'complex act both of inference and assent' elicited 'by arguments too various for direct enumeration, too personal and deep for words, too powerful and concurrent for refutation'.[40] Yet words return, inevitably and necessarily, to this risky business of mere beauty that remains, even if only as a forgotten dream, in our scarred world.[41] Has the dream abandoned us or we the dream? As St Augustine wrote, so long ago:

> I have learnt to love you late, Beauty at once so ancient and so new! I have learnt
> to love you late! You were within me, and I was in the world outside myself.[42]

The poet begins *within*, in the human heart and mind, with remembrance and recollection of those spots of time, of the 'unhistoric acts' upon which the growing good of the world is partly dependent, or those 'moments of reprieve'[43] that, relived in the poem realize, if only at first as a trace imprinted on the face of things, the form of beauty, the beauty even of Auschwitz, to which praise is given. Yet such a word, as John Coulson has noted, seems 'too large for our actions; and we can only use [it] ironically and with qualification'.[44] We are back to the theme and trope of irony, its tragedy and its distance, its flexibility with

---

[39] William Wordsworth, 'The Tables Turned', *Poetical Works*, ed. Thomas Hutchinson, revised, Ernest de Selincourt (Oxford: Oxford University Press, 1969), p. 377.

[40] J.H. Newman, *A Grammar of Assent*, quoted in John Coulson, *Newman and the Common Tradition: A Study in the Language of Church and Society* (Oxford: Clarendon Press, 1970), p. 29.

[41] See Peter Baelze, *The Forgotten Dream: Experience, Hope and God* (The Bampton Lectures for 1974) (London: Mowbrays, 1975).

[42] St Augustine, *The Confessions*, trans. R.S. Pine-Coffin (London: Penguin, 1961), Book X, 27, p. 231.

[43] George Eliot, *Middlemarch* (1871–2); Primo Levi, *Moments of Reprieve* (1981).

[44] John Coulson, 'Faith and Imagination', *The Furrow* Series on 'Belief and Unbelief', no. 7 (1983), p. 542.

sense and meaning that can, perhaps, alone 'liberate the stale religious positions of our time'.[45]

Beauty has had its place throughout the Christian tradition in the poetic beauty of the hymn to love in I Corinthians 13, to St Augustine, the icon, Thomas Aquinas and John Henry Newman. It is credible to the imagination, its form indissoluble – as if it were possible to explain or reduce by analysis the *meaning* of Bach's *B Minor Mass*, the Isenheim Altarpiece, or Wordsworth's *Prelude*. And so religion and theology begin with granting priority to the imagination in the language of ultimate concern, that language understood only as *fiduciary* rather than analytic, presupposing a prior unity and requiring us to take on trust the metaphorical, the analogical, and the ironic as the only possible conditions in words of that prior vision. And beauty itself, perceived and heard even, and most deeply, in the scars of human history, or known only as trace, calls forth again religion and theology; as von Balthasar suggests in his great work theological aesthetics, *The Glory of the Lord*, beauty must be loved and fostered by religion. For without this, it departs, as a mask lifted from the face of humankind, and that face then becomes incomprehensible and indecipherable to us. It becomes the inhuman. With this responsibility we were called, and continue to be called, to our task in seeking theology through the voice and beauty of the poet and literature and in the midst of suffering.

---

[45]   Ulrich Simon, 'Job and Sophocles', in David Jasper (ed.) *Images of Belief in Literature* (London: Macmillan, 1984). See above, p. 51.

PART IV
Conclusions

Chapter 14

Becoming Innocent Again: Looking Back on Theory in Literature and Theology

This is the first section of a conclusion in two parts. It will tell half the story, in a final retrospective glance backwards, and the rest will have to wait until the second section. If, in the last few pages we have been reviewing new life in literature and theology in current activity in Australia and China, giving signs of new hope, most of this book has been solidly Eurocentric. It has looked back to the nineteenth century, things taught then and now largely, sadly, forgotten, and the loss has been terrible. Werner Jeanrond, you will recall, reminded us of Schleiermacher's teaching of the risk in interpretation, every act of reading being new and preliminary as the mystery of the text is approached again and again.[1] It was Schleiermacher too, according to Rudolf Otto, who rediscovered the *sensus numinis*,[2] most fully articulated in his lectures *On Religion: Speeches to its Cultured Despisers* (1799). Otto's essay on Schleiermacher holds curious echoes of Newman's *Grammar of Assent* as it reflects on Schleiermacher's injunction to 'learn devout contemplation, that you may experience in your own beings the mysterious stirrings of the universe, the divine manifestation of nature, history, and life.'[3]

In some ways this whole book has been about recovering this capacity for devout contemplation through literature in the face of evil and the impossibility of theology. Strictly speaking this brief chapter does neither of the things suggested in its title: it would be impossible for us now to become innocent again – and, furthermore, I am not really looking back on theory. Irony is present everywhere.[4] I am also very aware that what I am saying now to a certain degree contradicts certain things that I have said in my published writings in

---

[1] See above, p. 74.

[2] Rudolf Otto, 'How Schleiermacher Rediscovered the *Sensus Numinis*', in *Religious Essays*, trans. Brian Lunn (Oxford: Oxford University Press, 1931), pp. 68–77.

[3] Schleiermacher, *On Religion*, quoted in Otto, 'How Schleiermacher Rediscovered the *Sensus Numinis*', p. 76.

[4] Looking back it now seems no surprise that in 1993 I wrote a whole book in the ironic mode, with a nod thereby to the doctrine of reserve so beloved of Keble and the Tractarians. It remains one of my favourite books, described in a letter to me by Tom Altizer (who did not like it very much!), as 'a series of exercises intended as a burning away of your own deeper temptations.' Indeed – literature as purgation and salvation. David Jasper, *Rhetoric, Power and Community: An Exercise in Reserve* (London: Macmillan, 1993).

the past. Such is progress, and a certain consistency requires the ability to change even to the point of contradiction. Over the past few months and years I have spent a great deal of time reading through my early papers and publications in the field of literature and theology beginning with the run up to the conference in Durham in 1982 and up to the time of the conference in Leuven in 2014. It proved to be quite a formidable task given the sheer volume of paper involved, and in the process I began to think that a more appropriate title for this exercise might have been 'Notes Towards a Supreme Fiction', though Wallace Stevens thought of it as a title first. But I will return to this theme later.

In 2009 I received an invitation to publish an article in a book edited by R.S. Sugirtharajah.[5] The book consisted of essays by a group of senior academics and they were all asked to return to a significant moment in an early stage of their academic thinking. It was called *Caught Reading Again*, and each essay was supposed to be a reflection on a book 'that inspired [you] most at the outset of [your] career'. My choice was Nathan A. Scott's *The Wild Prayer of Longing* (1971), which I had picked up second hand by accident in Blackwell's Bookshop in Oxford in 1975. It was the initial sentence of Nathan's book that first caught my attention: 'The new theologians of the present time, whatever their affiliation ... have of late been nervously remarking a profound erosion of the theological terrain as the chief religious fact of our period.'[6] As I was a theology student and ordinand at the time this clearly struck me as of some significance. Was there any future in what I was studying? Nathan's book goes on to suggest that in this context, literature and poetry have accordingly grown in importance 'independent of the supernaturalist projections of traditional piety'.[7] Well, over the years I have become more and more attached, in an odd way, perhaps, to 'traditional piety', (perhaps it is just getting older that does it), but not, I hope uncritically and certainly with no delusions about its present context in the Church, of which I sometimes despair. Actually, my continuing obsession with literature has developed more and more questions about ecclesiology – and to that also I will return later on.

I was certainly not alone in my struggles with theology in the university in the 1970s. In an article in *Literature and Theology* published in 1992, and taken from a paper read at a conference on literature and theology in Pannonhalma, Hungary, organized by my old friend Tibor Fabiny – and at which I was present – Werner Jeanrond remarked that 'early in the 1970s when I began my theological studies in Germany, my fellow students and I were very unhappy about the rigid

---

5   R.S. Sugirtharajah (ed.), *Caught Reading Again: Scholars and Their Books* (London: SCM, 2009), pp. 41–53.

6   Nathan A. Scott Jr., *The Wild Prayer of Longing: Poetry and the Sacred* (New Haven, CT: Yale University Press, 1971), p. xi.

7   Ibid., p. xiii.

division of labour in our theological faculties'.[8] Above all it was the isolation of biblical studies from theology that was problematical – and Werner, as we have seen in Chapter 5, turned to what he called the 'hermeneutical imperative', while I (though concerned for hermeneutics in a different, less philosophical way, having been trained in the first instance as a literary critic in the rather vaguely Marxist atmosphere of the Cambridge of the late 1960s), read poems and novels and went to the theatre to keep myself sane. True, in Oxford in those days there were fine theological thinkers like Maurice Wiles, John Macquarrie and Peter Baelz, but in different ways they were under fire and the theological world was fragile, not least within the Church. Wallace Stevens (to whom reference has already been made in this chapter) puts my case nicely in a tribute he wrote to T.S. Eliot, with an image that appeals to me in spite of all its unhappy connotations: 'Reading Eliot out of the pew, so to speak, goes on keeping one young. He remains an upright ascetic in a world that has grown exceedingly floppy and is growing floppier.'[9]

Whatever you might think about Eliot now, that image of the upright ascetic, tough and a bit old-fashioned and out of key with the present, read 'out of the pew', is important. It reminds me a bit, and I do not feel inclined to apologize for it, of that 'old, Anglican, patristic, literary, Oxford tone' of our first conferences.[10] One of the enduring obsessions in the writings I have been revisiting is their profound sense of the suffering endured by the twentieth century, and of the dislocation with the theology that had gone before, to be drowned first in the blood-bath of the First World War. In the very first cyclostyled *Newsletter of the National Conference on Literature and Religion* that we produced in January 1983, the humble precursor of the journal *Literature and Theology*, I wrote in the Editorial: 'The point is that the old order has passed away. Some would say that the new chaos has taken its place.'[11] We felt that we were caught in a continuous stream of evil and suffering above all symbolized by Auschwitz, and this utterly dislocated us from a past in theology that could no longer articulate for us any true vision. Theology, at least in the Church, it seemed, had ceased to work. Heather Walton expressed this feelingly in her Introduction to the published papers from the 1996 Conference held in Oxford which was entitled 'The Trace of the Other': 'Emphasis shifts away from what is communicated in the text towards the unutterable loss it amplifies, and literature assumes the mystical task

---

[8]   Werner G. Jeanrond, 'Biblical Criticism and Theology: Towards a New Biblical Theology', *Literature and Theology*, vol. 6, no. 3 (1992), 219.

[9]   Wallace Stevens, *Opus Posthumous: Poems, Plays, Prose*, revised edn, ed. Milton J. Bates (New York: Vintage Books, 1990), p. 240.

[10]   See above, p. 13. The words are Cardinal Manning's of Newman.

[11]   David Jasper and T.R. Wright, Editorial, *National Conference on Literature and Religion*, Newsletter I, January, 1983, 1.

of making readable a silence.'[12] Theologically there was a profound silence, and yet somehow theology remained at the very heart of our concerns. The question was, how to recover it. For many if not most people it suggested a turn to critical theory, dominated by Derrida and poststructuralist thinking in those days, and a placing of theology within the traditions of European Enlightenment and post-Enlightenment thinking from Kant onwards, that is within what we now know as continental philosophy and theory. Accordingly, and in this context, what I want to do is revisit another book that was important to me then, but with which I now profoundly disagree – Walter Lowe's *Theology and Difference: The Wound of Reason* (1993), one of a number of books mentioned by Heather in her Introduction, including also works by Carl Rashke and Charles Winquist, in which 'theology is being challenged to revisit the catacombs and begin again from the place of the dead'.[13]

But before doing that I need to take one further step back to our 1992 conference in Glasgow and the volume of papers from that entitled *Literature and Theology at Century's End* (1995) edited by Robert Detweiler and Gregory Salyer. As the millennium approached, Bob, by then, in a way, our elder statesman at the conferences,[14] in his Preface also took us back to the theme of suffering and dislocation, to the radical hiatus in theology, adding a further theme to which we were then just beginning to be open – that is how very *Western* we were in our thinking, and largely unaware of how complicit we were (most of us perhaps still *are*) in a hegemony that permeates our religious thinking and literature. (I think that this is still true, by and large, 20 years later, though as we have seen in our last chapters perhaps things are slowly beginning to change.) Bob reminded us of Edward Said's book *Culture and Imperialism* (1993) as 'required reading for persons concerned with the future of literature and theology',[15] in which Said expands the chauvinist readings of the Christian Gospel as heritage of Western Imperialism, now further enlarged in secular variations that render most of us complicit in perpetuating that hegemony, only now, even only now, struggling to hear other voices from elsewhere in the global economy. But the overwhelming theme of this particular collection of papers, once again, is the absolute necessity of theology (Christian or otherwise) and its utter impossibility at century's end. An essay by Jim Champion explores what he calls 'sacramentality', that is 'an orientation to what's given with the world, and in its depth' in thinkers like Jung, Heidegger and Gadamer – but in

---

[12]   Heather Walton, 'Re-visioning the Subject in Literature and Theology', Introduction, in Heather Walton and Andrew W. Hass (eds), *Self/Same/Other: Re-visioning the Subject in Literature and Theology* (Sheffield: Sheffield Academic Press, 2000), p. 11.

[13]   Ibid., pp. 11–12.

[14]   See above, Chapter 6.

[15]   Robert Detweiler, Preface, in Gregory Salyer and Robert Detweiler (eds), *Literature and Theology at Century's End* (Atlanta, GA: Scholar's Press, 1995), p. x.

the end, it is clear to me, this cannot be enough, cannot even be 'theoretically' enough. Something is missing, and it is perhaps what Champion calls that lost and '*hidden theological dimension* underlying the attitudes of interpretive suspicion and interpretive trust'.[16] It is with this in mind I find myself returning (with a degree of embarrassment at the language) to a work of literature quoted by Said at the very outset of *Culture and Imperialism* – Joseph Conrad's *Heart of Darkness* (1899), a work caught in the abyss between the old world of the nineteenth century and the brave new world of our own times.

> The conquest of the earth, which mostly means the taking it away from those who have a different complexion or slightly flatter noses than ourselves, is not a pretty thing when you look into it too much. What redeems is the idea only. An idea at the back of it; not a sentimental pretence but an idea ...[17]

I will come back to the crucial question of the *idea* and its life in theology and Christian doctrine in due course. For now I would go behind the idea to what it means to *think* about the idea – something tough and enduring and not merely a sentimental pretence. It is where, perhaps, theology may begin again.

Here what I want to reflect on is the notion of 'theological thinking' as suggested by Carl Rashke in his 1988 book of the same name. Such thinking, it may be always emerges from the place of the dead, and in that sense is a thinking in hope, a thinking to which assent must be properly and, in Newman's term, 'grammatically' given. Raschke clearly states that 'it is our task here not to be concerned simply with thinking, but with *theological thinking*. The inquiry that amounts to thinking theologically may be regarded as a kind of "inquest" into the mysterious contention that "God is dead" for which the corollary is that theology has "ended"'.[18] In other words, theological thinking begins precisely when theology is impossible. It is thinking across the abyss. I suppose that this is exactly what we were trying to do in the early conferences on literature and theology, and my contention has been that it started to go wrong when we encountered the so-called 'turn to theory' – though we had our own methods, rooted in something much older than post-structuralism and postmodernism. We looked back to the nineteenth century.

Here I turn at last to Walter Lowe's book *Theology and Difference*. I agree heartily with its spirit and purpose. Lowe begins with the statement that 'this book is an effort to do two things: acknowledge the chasm which separates us

---

[16] James Champion, 'Sacramental and Prophetic Interpretation', in *Literature and Theology at Century's End*, pp. 15–42; 28, 17 (emphases added).

[17] Frontispiece to Edward W. Said, *Culture and Imperialism* (London: Vintage, 1994).

[18] Carl Raschke, *Theological Thinking: An Inquiry* (Atlanta, GA: Scholars Press, 1988), p. vii.

from the nineteenth century and *think* across it'.[19] That is exactly right – but *how* we think (and perhaps where we think from) is the issue. Lowe sets out to try and solve what he calls 'the problem of finding a *conceptual framework* within which to place the various theological options of the twentieth century'.[20] He, like some others, seems to be hooked on linking together the twentieth century (at least after 1918) and the nineteenth century by yoking the dialectical theology of Karl Barth with the postmodernism of Jacques Derrida – a largely fruitless enterprise it seems to me even if it seems to make sense at one level – although that is a debate for another time. My primary point here is that by seeking for a conceptual framework for theology in the form of critical and cultural theory that has actually already abandoned, in the main, theological thinking is doomed from the start, for theology can only be formed within the terms of theological thinking, and not a discussion reconstituted, as Giles Gunn once put it, you will recall, 'on the plane of the hermeneutical rather than the apologetic, the anthropological rather than the theological, the broadly humanistic rather than the narrowly doctrinal'.[21] But the study of literature and theology, whether we like it or not, must finally be constituted in some way within the realms of the apologetic, the theological and the doctrinal. Thus, we might all, in our different ways, acknowledge the centrality of Heidegger in religious reflection in the culture and thought of the later twentieth century, but we cannot run away with the idea that Heidegger is himself a religious thinker or a theologian. He is neither, nor would he have acknowledged so. George Pattison has put clearly my position in his book *The Later Heidegger* when he refers to what he calls Heidegger's 'religious sources'. And religious thinkers, too, have their limitations, and that is important to confess, as Pattison expresses it:

> He acknowledges that they provide the material, the ontic evidence upon which the ontological analysis will build. However, such analysis is alien to the religious thinker, and a Luther or a Kierkegaard, no matter how acute their psychological observations on the human condition, remain at the level of the ontic or *existentiell*. Their question was never the question of Being but such individual, personal questions as 'How can I find a gracious God?' or 'How can I become a Christian?' *How* they addressed such questions shows us, their readers, what *resolute confrontation with finitude, guilt and death might mean*, but they themselves never understood the ontological meaning of their works.[22]

---

[19] Walter Lowe, *Theology and Difference: The Wound of Reason* (Bloomington, IN: Indiana University Press, 1993), p. ix.

[20] Ibid.

[21] Giles Gunn, *The Interpretation of Otherness: Literature, Religion, and the American Imagination* (New York: Oxford University Press, 1979). See also above, p. 70.

[22] George Pattison, *The Later Heidegger* (London: Routledge, 2000), pp. 196–7 (emphases added).

This description better describes our questions in literature and theology (finally at one with both Luther and Kierkegaard in religion), and those questions were pursued, after the death of theology, through a theological thinking that found its first home in the living works of the poets and writers who did not address the questions, in the first instance at least, in the terms of philosophy or even theory but, with John Bunyan's Pilgrim who continually 'brake out with a lamentable cry, saying, "What shall I do?"'[23]

At this point I turn to a more recent essay of mine entitled 'Interdisciplinarity in Impossible Times' published in Heather Walton's book *Literature and Theology* (2011). The book was reviewed at some length by Mark S. Burrows in the journal *Worship* (2013),[24] and my comments here, to some degree, play off against that review. The description in my essay of the times as 'impossible' (impossible both for ourselves and for theology) was adjusted by Burrows (after Hölderlin) to the notion of 'destitute'. That may indeed be a better description. My central concern was to remind us that we can only return to theology (via theological thinking) by looking, if I may be allowed to quote from myself, 'not outward to systems but inwards to the founding power of the creative imagination and its capacity to transform and illuminate our sense of the "sacred" and its effects'.[25] In other words the task was contemplative and even, though I hesitate to use that very vexed word, spiritual – though not the less rigorous and intelligent for that. Things began to go wrong in our enterprise when, with the turn to theory, and in Pattison's terms, we became too philosophical and started asking the wrong questions. I suppose that, in a sense, we stopped being 'religious'. Rather, I suggested, somewhat boldly, that 'literature, perhaps, naturally sustains the practice, which was so important in the early Christian Church, of the *disciplina arcani* – the discipline of silence and secrecy whereby the things of greatest sanctity and importance are not spoken of lightly or loudly, but preserved in their mystery as an act of acknowledgement'.[26] As Edward Yarnold once put it in his book on baptismal homilies of the fourth century, *The Awe-Inspiring Rites of Initiation* (1971):

> It is a natural instinct to be reticent about something one holds precious. Publicity cheapens; *omne ignotum pro magnifico*. In the publication of everything we hold sacred, there has been a loss, not only for ourselves, but perhaps also for

---

23   John Bunyan, *The Pilgrim's Progress* [1678], (London: Everyman's Library, 1954), p. 11.

24   Mark. S. Burrows, review in *Worship*, vol. 87 (2013), 180–82.

25   David Jasper, 'Interdisciplinarity in Impossible Times: Studying Religion through Literature and the Arts', in Heather Walton (ed.), *Literature and Theology: New Interdisciplinary Spaces* (Farnham: Ashgate, 2011), p. 10.

26   Ibid., p. 11.

non-Christians, but the loss is irreparable. There is no way in which secrecy can be re-established.[27]

But that secrecy is exactly what we were concerned with, well expressed in literature by Frank Kermode's book *The Genesis of Secrecy* (1979) which took literary criticism back to its roots in biblical interpretation and St Mark's Gospel. Yet Kermode famously ended his book on an utterly negative note with an oblique reference to Kafka's great parable of the doorkeeper in *The Trial*, concluding with the utter despondency of the final closure of the door. 'Our sole hope and pleasure is in the perception of a momentary radiance, before the door of disappointment is finally shut on us'.[28] Kermode's pessimism looks back to Roland Barthes' view that literature is, as Susan Sontag puts it, already a posthumous affair. In *Writing Degree Zero* (1953), Barthes also famously asserts that 'literature is like phosphorous. It shines with its maximum brilliance at the moment when it attempts to die'.[29]

We were, I think, perhaps more naively or even more innocently, acknowledging something in literature different from Kermode or Barthes, something finally less miserably 'unfollowable' if no less aware of the suffering and passion of the world, though, in Mark S. Burrows' telling words in his review, it was 'a largely obsolete gesture in the critical discourse of the academy we inhabit'. Perhaps that is why, in the end, the enterprise of literature and theology has been – indeed, *had* to have been – a failure in the academy, always liable to be taken over by more contemporary, more easily defensible modes of discourse through which theology finally tends to disintegrate into the less serious enterprise of religious studies, whether through the route of philosophy, social theory, anthropology, or a variety of other possibilities. I suggested, unfashionably, in my essay in Heather's book, that literature and art still have the capacity to invite us into those 'spaces for the revisiting of things of deepest importance' through 'the faith and wisdom of the past – that is 'those enduring theological "traditions" that constituted the central horizon in which the arts once lived but have long since been displaced or chastened in late-modern cultures'.[30]

Chastened by the dialectic of Enlightenment, rendered dumb by the holocausts of the twentieth century, or dazzled by the allurements of postmodernity and its cleverness, few people heeded this call to theology, and the loss has been incalculable. The project known as theological humanism,

---

[27]   Edward Yarnold SJ, *The Awe-Inspiring Rites of Initiation: Baptismal Homilies of the Fourth Century* (Slough: St. Paul Publications, 1971), p. 54.

[28]   Frank Kermode, *The Genesis of Secrecy: On the Interpretation of Narrative* (Cambridge, MA: Harvard University Press, 1979), p. 145.

[29]   Roland Barthes, *Selected Writings*, ed. Susan Sontag (London: Fontana/Collins, 1983), p. viii.

[30]   Jasper, 'Interdisciplinarity in Impossible Times', p. 15.

spearheaded by David Klemm and Bill Schweiker in the USA, with its roots in the culture of Renaissance Europe and its gaze upon the future, went some way to remind us of our responsibility for the integrity of life upheld between theology and humanism, and the dangers of the extremes of what Klemm and Schweiker call '*hypertheism*' and '*overhumanization*' – but it has largely fallen on deaf ears in spite of its considerable intelligence.[31] What theology and literature set out to explore was precisely what theology (admittedly almost exclusively Christian theology, at least in its early stages) was most deeply concerned to explore and express, recognizing that theology only comes alive within religious praxis when its methods are thought *through – back* to – theological thinking – precisely as literature only flourishes as 'a search for some supremely acceptable fiction'. The point is, of course, that the fiction has to work hard to sustain our willing suspension of disbelief and our faith in it. We have to be able to fall in love with Elizabeth Bennet – or perhaps, in the end, even Mr Darcy. Wallace Stevens beautifully summarizes the whole matter, both personally and universally, in his poem to Henry Church, 'Notes Towards a Supreme Fiction':

> And for what, except for you, do I feel love?
> Do I press the extremest book of the wisest man
> Close to me, hidden in me day and night?
> In the uncertain light of single, certain truth,
> Equal in living changingness to the light
> In which I meet you, in which we sit at rest,
> For a moment in the central of our being,
> The vivid transparence that you bring is peace.[32]

And so we have started a conversation, between literature and theology, among ourselves and in the space of the text, unshielded by the comforts of abstractions and theory, and now we must ask how such a conversation might be what St Benedict, in his monastic rule, calls a *conversatio morum* – a way of living that includes the art of *lectio divina* and is more just than a method of talking.[33]

Our vocation has a kind of monastic discipline at its root: as did that of John Henry Newman, to whom I finally return, as I have so often in this book, a voice expressing the language of Church in society, a hidden ecclesiology that was grounded in an *idea* and a secrecy that Kermode perhaps knew more of than he was willing to admit (in his championing of Austin Farrer, for example) and

---

[31] See further, David E. Klemm and William Schweiker, *Religion and the Human Future: An Essay on Theological Humanism* (Oxford: Blackwell, 2008).

[32] Wallace Stevens, *Selected Poems* (London: Faber and Faber, 1963), p. 99.

[33] See *The Rule of St Benedict*, trans. Carolinne White (London: Penguin, 2008), ch. 58, pp. 85–6. Also, Michael Casey, *Sacred Reading: The Ancient Art of Lectio Divina* (Liguori, MO: Liguori Publications, 1996).

the Romanticism of Coleridge within the traditions of a fiduciary, rather than an analytic, understanding of language. Recalling John Coulson's reminder that our access to both religion and poetry shares complex acts of inference and assent, and that 'understanding religious language is a function of understanding poetic language',[34] I turn again to what I believe is one of the key texts for understanding the nature and processes of our project in literature and theology, that is Newman's *Essay on the Development of Christian Doctrine* in the edition of 1845 – the work that finally carried Newman into the Roman Catholic Church.

I will be quite brief. Newman's constant theme in the 30 years from *The Tamworth Reading Room* (1841) to his greatest work the *Grammar of Assent* is that 'man is *not* a reasoning animal; he is a seeing, feeling, contemplating, acting animal'.[35] Newman carries us back to Pascal's reasons of the heart and forward to John S. Dunne's sadly forgotten book entitled *The Reasons of the Heart* (1978) – another 'must' for the student of literature and theology if only for its searing readings of Camus, Kafka and Rilke[36] – which roots intelligent faith in suffering and solitude before the community can be again entertained. In the *Grammar of Assent* Newman observes that:

> the heart is commonly reached, not through the reason, but through the imagination, by means of direct impressions, by the testimony of facts and events, by history, by description. Persons influence us, voices melt us, looks subdue us, deeds inflame us. Many a man will live and die upon a dogma: no man will be a martyr for a conclusion.[37]

Writing as a poet and novelist, Newman then turns to theology and the development and coherence of doctrine within the two millennia of the Christian Church. He begins with an 'idea' within which the whole of what develops is implied. As everyone who has watched a great production of *King Lear*, or read *The Brothers Karamazov* knows, the idea of the work in itself can, perhaps should, never be precisely grasped, and yet it must be spoken of, explored, developed – and the key is how to do this with fidelity and without corruption to the essential idea itself. In a key passage from the last of his *University Sermons*, Newman, recognizing that the inexhaustible riches of a real idea defy full expression in words, notes how:

---

[34] John Coulson, *Newman and the Common Tradition* (Oxford: Clarendon Press, 1970), p. 4, and see above, Chapter 2.

[35] Quoted in J.M. Cameron, Introduction, in John Henry Newman, *An Essay on the Development of Christian Doctrine* [1845] (London: Penguin, 1974), p. 37.

[36] See also above, p. 32.

[37] Newman, *Essay on the Development of Christian Doctrine* , p. 37.

One proposition necessarily leads to another, and a second to a third; then some limitation is required; and the combination of these opposites occasions some fresh evolutions from the original idea, which indeed can never be said to be exhausted. This process is its development, and results in a series, or rather body, of dogmatic statements, *till what was an impression on the Imagination has become a system or creed in the reason.*[38]

The evolutionary language used here, moving from the imagination to creed, is, indeed, remarkable in a sermon preached in 1843.

As we move into Newman's analysis of the process of the development of an idea (or perhaps a supreme fiction, where the credentials of truth and fiction are blurred to the point of near mergence) we become ever more aware of the correlation between the demands of theology and the discipline of reading demanded by literature, each holding a *conversatio* with the other in which the mutual resonances are familiar. Early in his *Essay on the Development of Doctrine*, Newman refers to the *disciplina arcani* of the early Church, not as an exercise in exclusion so much as a recognition of the nature of the secrecy that shrouds the truth whereby to those who are outside everything comes in parables.[39] And as we slowly introduce our students to those great literary texts from Aeschylus to Proust with which we have long lived ourselves and have something to say of them, though the mystery always remains finally hidden, we know that, as Newman puts it:

the highest and most wonderful truths, though communicated to the world once for all by inspired teachers could not be comprehended all at once by the recipients, but, as received and transmitted by minds not inspired and through media which were human, have required only the longer time and deeper thought for their full elucidation. This may be called the *Theory of Developments*.[40]

It is very clear that the seven tests which Newman proposes for the true development of an idea – that is the coherence of doctrine consistent with the revealed truth of the original idea – are perfectly familiar to students of the canon of literature, and also, for example, to readers of David Tracy's discussion of the nature of the Classic work in his book on theology and cultural pluralism *The Analogical Imagination* (1981) where he begins by introducing systematic theology as hermeneutical.[41] Such tests recognize the synchronicity and the universality of literature (as of doctrine) which finally must submit to

---

[38]   John Henry Newman, *University Sermons*, 3rd edn [1871] (London: SPCK, 1970), p. 329 (emphases added).

[39]   Mark 4:11.

[40]   Newman, *Essay on the Development of Christian Doctrine*, p. 90.

[41]   David Tracy, *The Analogical Imagination: Christian Theology and the Culture of Pluralism* (London: SCM, 1981), pp. 99–107.

the Vincentian Canon – '*quod ubique, quod semper, quod ab omnibus creditum est*' ('what has been believed everywhere always, and by all'). And if Newman acknowledges that his theory of development, like the art of grammar, is merely an expedient, then it is so 'to enable us to solve what has now become a necessary and an anxious problem'.[42] What we are doing profoundly matters, and it is not simply an academic game or pastime.

Continually through the *Essay* one is struck by how Newman anticipates what would much later become the professional tools and insights of literary study and criticism in the twentieth century. For example, at the beginning of Chapter 2 he outlines in half a page a clear description of the essentials of reception theory or 'reader-response criticism'. For, he says, Holy Scriptures were 'intended to create an idea, and that idea is not in the sacred text, but in the mind of the reader'.[43] Yet, acknowledging the genius of inspiration in the text, Newman recognizes also the place and demands on the later reader who, though lacking the poetic and creative genius of what Coleridge would have called the Primary Imagination, yet nevertheless 'on these recipients the revealed truths would fall ... at first vaguely and generally, and would afterwards be completed by developments'.[44] Reading, like religion, grows on you and, indeed, in you. Later, in a remarkable anticipation of Wolfgang Iser and his notion of the implied reader, Newman admits the creative necessity of the 'gaps' in Holy Scripture, stimulating the reader in the proper exercise of the imagination. It is an insight more fully developed for biblical studies in a book edited by Robert Detweiler and William G. Doty entitled *The Daemonic Imagination: Biblical Text and Secular Story* (1990), to which I contributed an essay, though I note that this book does not once mention Newman.[45]

In his analysis of the development of Christian doctrine in the early centuries of the Church, Newman continually returns to the theme of the book and its 'mystical',[46] rather than its literal interpretation. Indeed, he finally seems almost to conflate the idea of the Church itself with the nature of the text, with its narrative of secrecy, its arcane discipline, its mystery and its demand for interpretation. Writing of the officials of the Roman state, Newman notes that they, like all 'public men', 'care[d] very little for books; fine sentiments, the most luminous philosophy, the deepest theology, inspiration itself, moves them but little; they look at facts, and care only for facts'.[47] In this reading, what the

---

[42]   Newman, *Essay on the Development of Christian Doctrine*, p. 91.
[43]   Ibid., p. 149.
[44]   Ibid.
[45]   See Wolfgang Iser, *The Implied Reader: Patterns of Communication in Prose Fiction from Bunyan to Beckett* (Baltimore, MD: Johns Hopkins University Press, 1974).
[46]   On the mystical, see above, Chapter 4, p. 60.
[47]   Newman, *Essay on the Development of Christian Doctrine*, p. 259.

ancient Gradgrinds, M'Choakumchilds and Bounderbys of the Roman Empire utterly failed to interpret was the mysterious, even perverse truth of the Christian Church.[48] It was all a question of interpretation, of hermeneutics and of seeing below the surface and reading between the lines in the supreme fiction that was only possibly accessible, in the first instance, through the willing suspension of disbelief for the moment, which constitutes poetic faith.

In conclusion, it has become perfectly clear to me that the enterprise of theology and literature upon which we embarked in the early 1980s very largely lost its way about 10 years later, though we are perhaps slowly recovering something of its original sense and purpose. It is not that a great deal of valuable things have not been said and done since then in its name, but we have been too eager to be seen to be a junior partner in larger and separate contemporary conversations in both literature and theology when we should have been content to be less fashionable and continue to describe what Mark Burrows called 'a largely obsolete gesture in the critical discourse of the academy we inhabit.' (That, of course, is as much a criticism of the academy as anything else.) Ten years after the first publication of the journal *Literature and Theology* the editors, which then included myself and Graham Ward, among others, produced a Joint Editorial Statement in which we linked ourselves in a critical pluriformity with the 'adventurous projects' of critical theorists, semioticians, anthropologists, philosophers, psychologists and so on, in the fields of film, painting, music, social and political practice – the list went on with vaunting ambition.[49] It was hopeless, and we were too stupid to see it at the time, wanting, perhaps, the manage of unruly jades. Within all of this cacophony, too, were intelligent voices like that of Walt Lowe. Some younger voices today have gone largely unheard (partly because they have been schooled in a way of writing that is more or less incomprehensible even to the average intelligent reader) – I mean Daniel Whistler in his excellent, perverse book on Schelling's theory of symbolic language.[50] Daniel is there looking for the tools which will help us back to the ideas that can rescue us from our destitute times, bridging the gap that is an abyss, as was Newman in his day – as is Heidegger too in is *Elucidations of Hölderlin's Poetry* (1981) which, he says in the Preface to the Fourth Edition, 'spring from a necessity of thought'.

---

[48]   I deliberately allude here to Slavoj Žižek's book *The Puppet and the Dwarf: The Perverse Core of Christianity* (Cambridge, MA: The MIT Press, 2003).

[49]   The Joint Editorial Statement was published as a separate flyer with *Literature and Theology*, vol. 6, no. 3 (1992), and signed by Kirsten Anderson, Colin Crowder, Mark Ledbetter, Graham Ward, Terry Wright and myself.

[50]   Daniel Whistler, *Schelling's Theory of Symbolic Language: Forming the System of Identity* (Oxford: Oxford University Press, 2013).

Indeed – but then, led by the poet, we move to think beyond thinking, not in search of any hidden meaning but 'letting the unsayable be unsaid'[51] in the theological moment whose possibility remains, if only in an act of faith.

51   See Timothy Clark, *Martin Heidegger* (London: Routledge, 2002), p. 118. One is reminded here of Heather Walton's phrase about making silence readable.

Chapter 15

Conclusion: Prospero's Books

I've a terrible errible lot todue todie todue tooterribleday
Finnegans Wake

My conclusion begins with the oldest, darkest and most brilliant passage in Joyce's *Finnegans Wake*; the dream mass, a Eucharistic feast that is celebrated in the coinherence of the cosmic sacrament with Irish mythology and Dublin pub. It is an end which is at the same time a beginning, centred upon a death in a cosmic and historical Holy Week that is re-enacted again and again throughout the *Wake*. It is the dark heart, for me, of a deeply sacramental theology and literature reflected in the history of Western consciousness.

The writing of this book has been a mixture of personal reflection and a review of a local history in which many people have played their part. Not all of them, perhaps very few of them, would agree with my sense and assessment of the study of literature and theology through the perspectives of the series of conferences which began in Durham in 1982 and end for me, and for the present at least, with my own lecture given at our most recent conference in the University of Leuven in 2014.[1] As I write further international conferences are planned, and so the story is not yet at an end: or should I say stories? It has not been my purpose to argue with those who disagree with me or seek to impose my own sense of theology and its future on other participants in that history, both past, present and perhaps future. The theology, known most deeply in the sacramental tradition of the liturgy and worship, has remained largely implicit and what, for me, lies at the heart of the enterprise is more precisely *a sense of theology*. I will spend some time later in this final chapter comparing that sense, which is necessarily both catholic and liturgical, with another enterprise in Christian theology, in its way, perhaps, both far more theologically coherent and intellectually more consistent in its critique of modernity, that project known as Radical Orthodoxy. Of course, the study of literature and theology has never professed to be a theological movement such as that developed largely in the mind of John Milbank, for it is far less systematic, perhaps even less strictly academic[2] in its attention to the voices of literature: it is more of a sense of theology. But it

---

[1]   The lecture provides the origins of Chapter 8 in this book.

[2]   I struggled here with the alternative word 'intellectual', but finally decided that 'academic' was more appropriate, being harder and a little more brittle. If the life of the

is no accident that not a few of the people most closely associated with Radical Orthodoxy – Milbank himself, Graham Ward – have also been participants in the conferences and the journal *Literature and Theology*, which Ward edited with great distinction for a number of years after my own editorship came to an end. And there are clear commonalities; the centrality of sustaining the tradition, the importance of ecclesiology, a suspicion of modernity. But having said that our roots and methods are very different.

For a long time it has been clear to me that theology is not simply communicated in *what* is said but in *how* it is said and written. The study of literature and theology has never been a systematic enterprise, but has partaken of the life of literature and poetics upon which it has been nourished. At its best it has been self-consciously creative and therefore has been risky in daring to offend both the theologian and the literary critic, sometimes at the same time, and this has something to do with the inescapable life of prayer at its heart. It has never taken off with any success within the formal walls of the academy and university, and although that has saddened me it should not have surprised me. Although scholars in the UK and North America have worked closely together it is clear that both the roots and the fundamental nature of their concerns are different. Perhaps the formative figure in the USA was Amos Wilder, who took part in the First World War and was Nathan Scott's mentor, while in the UK, as has been clear from this book, it was the Second World War which impressed itself most deeply, for us, on the serious study of literature and theology. Furthermore, this latter term, theology, has never held in America the place it maintains in the British tradition even, though it is fading, to a degree, today.

Yet for myself it is an American theologian, though one largely marginalized, whose work haunts me and returns to me time and again. Twentieth-century British theology, in its self-preoccupations, has never experienced the death of God. Perhaps finally it is too parochial, too closely linked with the establishment of the Church. But no engagement with Christian theology through literature can finally avoid an event that is known most deeply, after Hegel, through the literary imagination of Nietzsche, and therefore the consequences of which can only be faced in the subtleties of the literary imagination. For Thomas J.J. Altizer theology begins in the death of God and becomes articulate only in the European poetic tradition of Dante, Milton, Blake and Joyce. For Altizer, therefore, 'the truth is that it is only radical secular thinkers and scholars who have rescued or renewed the most revolutionary expressions of Christianity, Christian spokesmen have either buried or disguised these expressions, thereby

---

academy has, by and large, come to bore me, the life of the intellect certainly has not. They are, for me, increasingly separate.

giving Christianity itself a sterile or reactionary mask'.[3] Our early conferences were, I think, addressing, beyond their own knowing, a horrified realization of the death of God. Where theology is rendered silent only then does its voice becomes absolutely insistent. Where the Church becomes the tomb of Christ, ecclesiology and liturgy remain as urgent imperatives.[4] Furthermore, it is Altizer who insists upon a depth of freedom, known both theologically and imaginatively most deeply in the *Inferno* of Dante and in the Eucharistic celebration of Joyce's *Finnegans Wake*, a freedom that theology calls prevenient grace – a freedom of the will that alone allows the possibility of forgiveness. Thus the drama of Holy Week is grounded in the literary imagination, and into this drama the energies of all our endeavours have finally flowed.

If Altizer suggests a long poetic history that is, in the end and always has been, marginal to the mainstream of Christian theology, then the tradition that we have traced is even older and more diverse, though it finally achieves a degree of focus and clarity within the intellectual, literary and spiritual insistencies of the nineteenth century in England, at a time when the fortress of Christianity was, for many beginning to crumble and the sea of faith beginning its retreat with 'its melancholy, long, withdrawing roar'.[5] Its consequences in the twenty-first century have spread much further afield and its future remains unclear. If the death of God has borne itself upon us but lately, then the vehicle, both intellectual and spiritual, that will enable theology to continue to speak has revealed more ancient and, more recently, surprising roots. It was no accident that two of the earliest voices to be heard in a lecture at our conferences were those of Job and Sophocles from the biblical and classical traditions. Job remains unsatisfied with all glib answers in the face of unmerited suffering, insistent upon his freedom to be himself before God. From the depths of such suffering we move, in our partiality and our sense of evil, to Boethius' *Consolation of Philosophy*, written in exile, and from thence to Pascal and his profound sense of predestination and freedom within prevenient grace, and his deep sense of the reasons of the heart. And from Pascal we are drawn, inevitably, to the theology of John Henry Newman.

In every sense the deep well springs of our concern for the absolute importance of theology and literature flow from the fathers of the Oxford Movement, and

---

3   Thomas J.J. Altizer, 'The Ultimate Ground of Catholicism', unpublished essay, 2014, p. 25.

4   See above, Chapter 3, pp. 48–9, for the image of the Church and the tomb of Jesus, in Thomas J.J. Altizer, 'William Blake and the Role of Myth in the Radical Christian Vision', in Thomas J.J. Altizer and William Hamilton, *Radical Theology and the Death of God* (London: Penguin, 1966), p. 182.

5   Matthew Arnold, 'Dover Beach'. I have deliberately avoided any discussion of the bleak theology of Don Cupitt. See Don Cupitt, *The Sea of Faith: Christianity in Change* (London: British Broadcasting Corporation, 1984).

above all John Henry Newman and John Keble. They provide the context and the energies from which the theological and literary roots grow in often strange and diverse ways. Both men were poets before they were theologians, and Keble, as Oxford Professor of Poetry dedicated his *Lectures on Poetry* (1832–41), to William Wordsworth. Delivered in Latin, unlike those of Matthew Arnold which, in 1857, were the first to be delivered in English, Keble's lectures deserve more attention than they have received. Newman described the *Lectures* as Keble's 'greatest literary work',[6] while Dean Church in his posthumous masterpiece, *The Oxford Movement: Twelve Years, 1833–1845* (1891), describes them as 'the most original and memorable course ever delivered from the Chair of Poetry in Oxford'. George Saintsbury, in his *History of Criticism* (1900–1904) compares Keble on poetry with the 'undogmatized and secularized' lectures of his successor at Oxford, Matthew Arnold. Criticism since has been silent on Keble's *Lectures*, which were published in English only in 1912,[7] failing to trace the crucial link between them and their intellectual origins in Romanticism.

Keble devotes almost all of his stately lectures, to which I have returned so often in this book, to a consideration of classical poetry from Homer to Virgil. There are passing references to Dante, Spenser, Shakespeare and Dryden, and even fewer to contemporary poets. Byron, in particular, is criticized and dismissed for his want of reserve,[8] a constant theme in Tractarian theology. In short, Keble anchors his sense of the close relationship between poetry and religion in close readings of Greek and Latin poets, above all Homer, and the tragic dramas of Aeschylus, and Virgil. The profound theology of the lectures is allowed to speak through the poetry, and from the outset Keble does not underestimate the significance of his theme at a time when his theological energies are in demand for the defence of the Church;

> I did not foresee that in these last few years it would be perils threatening the Church more than perils threatening the State which would withdraw the minds of us all from the delights of quiet literary study. Yet so it has been, and had I not been encouraged by the opinion of those to whose judgement I chiefly defer on such a point that there is a real possibility that discussions on poetry may not be without profit even in the sphere of religion, I should neither at the outset have undertaken the task of delivering these lectures, nor have decided now to publish them.[9]

6　　J.H. Newman, Preface to John Keble, *Occasional Papers and Reviews* (Oxford: James Parker and Co., 1877), p. xii.

7　　Edward Kershaw Francis, trans. *Keble's Lectures on Poetry, 1832–1841*, 2 vols (Oxford: The Clarendon Press, 1912). The references to Church and Saintsbury are drawn from the Translator's Note by Francis, vol. 1, p. 3.

8　　Ibid., vol. 1, pp. 258–9.

9　　Ibid., To the Reader, vol. 1.

Keble allows the poetry to speak for itself in a rediscovery of the theology that is always at the heart of his concerns. He writes in the tradition of his predecessor in Oxford as Professor of Poetry, Bishop Robert Lowth and his lectures on the *Sacred Poetry of the Hebrews* (1753),[10] also given in Latin and, and first translated into German, only published in English in 1787. It was within such a broad tradition that we embarked on our work in the early 1980s, the link with Lowth and subsequent Romanticism being most overtly evident in the early lectures in the conferences of Stephen Prickett.[11]

Intellectually, and most explicit in the early programmes on theology and literature taught in the University of Bristol by John Coulson, the key to our sense of interdisciplinarity was John Henry Newman, and above all in his late work on faith and reason, and the epistemology of belief, the *Essay in Aid of a Grammar of Assent* (1870) with its 'logic loose at both ends'. But here, before returning finally to Newman's understanding in that book of the Illative Sense, I focus on his earlier *University Sermons*, delivered in Oxford between 1826 and 1843 as illustrating in a more preliminary way what Donald MacKinnon has called 'the pedigree, the subtlety, the complexity, and the profoundly interrogative character of Newman's explorations in these sermons'.[12] Rather more poetically and long before MacKinnon, Henri Bremond had described the reserve of Newman as 'effacing the boundaries between the reasonings of the intelligence and the exercises of living piety'.[13] That also describes, in a sense, the spirit of our study of literature and theology, though for some of us the term 'piety' must necessarily have been elastic, rooted in the literature, intuitions and anxieties of European Romanticism, the visions of Blake and the tortured intelligence of Coleridge. Yet theology was taken seriously by us, as for Newman, as he sought to express the grounds of belief and faith within that 'subtle empiricist temper which he found so congenial'.[14]

For if the Joseph Butler of the *Sermons in the Rolls Chapel*, with his concern for the primacy of conscience, is everywhere evident in Newman's *University Sermons*, ever in the background is the empiricist tradition of Locke and Hume, 'whose depth and subtlety all must acknowledge', despite his fallacies,

---

[10] Keble refers to Lowth's work more than once in his lectures. See for example, footnote 1 in vol. 1, p. 59, on Genesis 4:23, and referring to Lowth, *Sacred Poetry of the Hebrews*, Lecture IV, p. 56 (1763). It relates to the scholarly conclusion that Lamech's address to his wives is 'the most ancient of all songs that remain to us'.

[11] Prickett had published his book *Romanticism and Religion: The Tradition of Coleridge and Wordsworth in the Victorian Church* in 1976.

[12] D.M. MacKinnon, Introduction to *Newman's University Sermons*, 3rd edn [1871] (London: SPCK, 1970), p. 9.

[13] Henri Bremond, *The Mystery of Newman*, trans. H.C. Corrance (London: Williams and Norgate, 1907).

[14] MacKinnon, *Newman's University Sermons*, p. 14.

says Newman in Sermon X, 'Faith and Reason, Contrasted as Habits of Mind'.[15] Throughout the untidinesses of his *Sermons* Newman balances the necessary, a priori demands of revelation with the equally necessary exercise of reason within the habits of the imagination, while in the intellectual background (via the unseen presence of the Coleridge of the *Biographia Literaria*) ever looms the figure of Kant.[16] For Newman, the self-confessed rhetorician, as for us, such exploration can never be merely abstract, but rooted in the relations of things and the living power of words, even 'the Inspired Word [of the Bible] being but a dead letter (ordinarily considered), except as transmitted from one mind to another'.[17] In the language of the *Sermons* there are haunting echoes which sound for us through strange corridors: to the words of T.S. Eliot in his 1935 essay on 'Religion and Literature' which acknowledge that the Bible only survives as literature at all as long as it is recognized, in some sense, as the Word of God;[18] to the processes of reason in faith which are powerful only because they are 'weak'.[19] The glimpse here is caught of the 'weak' (post)Catholic thought and theologies of our own time, of Gianni Vattimo and John Caputo.

Our enterprise, any more than that of Newman, was never systematic, being founded upon a faith that Coleridge in the *Biographia* would call 'poetic', promoted only by the 'willing suspension of disbelief', and the faith of Newman which he describes in the *Grammar of Assent* as a 'principle of action'. Yet the influences upon him, both unrecognized and acknowledged, were never less than serious. Behind the *University Sermons* there are also the *Nichomachean Ethics* and that form of ethical process that 'emphasizes that in any inquiry we can only achieve that degree of *akribeia* (accuracy) that its subject matter permits'.[20] Literature, even more than theology as understood in its doctrinal and systematic forms, provides the grounds for such enquiry. Or, to put this another way, it is in what Maurice Blanchot has named the space of literature that is recovered the possibility, in Newman's words – 'a presumption, yet not a mere chance conjecture'[21] – of faith by a reason that is thereby nourished as it is 'the true office of a writer, to excite and direct trains of thought':[22]

---

[15] MacKinnon, *Newman's University Sermons*, p. 195.

[16] Newman, of course, did not read German. The standard work on Kant's influence in England remains René Wellek, *Immanuel Kant in England, 1793–1838* (1931).

[17] MacKinnon, *Newman's University Sermons*, p. 94.

[18] T.S. Eliot, 'Religion and Literature', in *Selected Essays*, 3rd edn (London: Faber and Faber, 1951), p. 390.

[19] Ibid., p. 208.

[20] MacKinnon, *Newman's University Sermons*, p. 13.

[21] Ibid., p. 249.

[22] Ibid., p. 275.

> A moving forward in the twilight, yet not without clue or direction; – a movement
> from something known to something unknown ...[23]

This epistemology is given clearer, more precise and more accurate expression in
the *Grammar*, as we have seen:

> Nor need reason come first and faith second (though this is the logical order), but
> one and the same teaching is in different aspects both object and proof, and elicits
> one complex act both of inference and assent. It speaks to us one by one, as the
> counterpart, so to say, of ourselves, and is real as we are real.[24]

Although at the end of his life Newman forgetfully denied that he had ever read
any of Coleridge's works, in the 1830s, after reading Coleridge's *Church and
State* and *Aids to Reflection*, he admitted that he found there 'much I thought
to be mine'.[25] In the *Apologia*, as we have seen, he acknowledges his intellectual
debt to Coleridge and Romanticism, though hardly his theology of the Church.
In the second of the *University Sermons*, entitled 'The Influence of Natural and
Revealed Religion Respectively' (preached on Easter Tuesday, 13 April 1830),
Newman admits that, although he had not read Coleridge at this point, there is
'a remarkable passage in his *Biographia Literaria*, in which several portions of
this Sermon are anticipated'.[26] Above all it is in Coleridge's sense of a fiduciary
language and the power of the living word, that both Newman's epistemology
of faith and the energy of the study of literature and theology find their origins.
Newman begins, as did we in our way, with the problems of and facing theology,
and he was, throughout his life, a controversialist, frequently making more
enemies than friends. By the later part of the twentieth century, the Church was,
institutionally, a very much frailer vessel than in Newman's time, abandoned by
many even of those most closely committed to our enterprise, yet we too were
searching for ways of thinking and being through which theology could yet speak
in a manner recognizable within the traditions that were seeking legitimacy in
a world that was becoming at once irreligious (at least in the West) and inter-
religious. Newman's was never more than a problem for Christianity, yet its

---

[23]   Ibid., p. 249.

[24]   J.H. Newman, *Grammar of Assent* (1906), pp. 391–2. Quoted in J.D. Holmes,
Introduction to *Newman's University Sermons*, p. 40. See also above, p. 134.

[25]   See A.J. Boekraad and H. Tristram, *The Argument from Conscience to the Existence
of God* (Louvain, 1961), p. 29. See also John Coulson, *Newman and the Common Tradition:
A Study in the Language of Church and Society* (Oxford: Clarendon Press, 1970), Appendix,
'How Much of Coleridge had Newman Read?', pp. 254–5. David Newsome, *Two Classes
of Men: Platonism and English Romantic Thought* (London: John Murray, 1972), ch. 4,
'Coleridge and Newman', pp. 57–72.

[26]   MacKinnon, *Newman's University Sermons*, footnote on p. 23.

challenges remain issues for faith and belief in our contemporary much broader world of suffering and uncertainty, a world of many faiths and none. As Owen Chadwick expressed it long ago in his own work on doctrinal development, Newman was facing 'the ultimate theological problem of the nineteenth-century Church, Catholic or Protestant – the problem of the relation between Christian certainty and the inevitable failure of historical inquiry ever to produce results which are more than probable results'.[27]

Not just the failure of historical enquiry, but the failure of history itself now looms darkly in our world, and therefore the ultimate failure of that enquiry and all theological reflection on it to provide any clear answers to our deepest problems. At the heart of our investigations into the relationship between literature and theology lay what Newman would have known as the Illative Sense. In the second part of the *Grammar of Assent* he addresses this as the intellectual counterpart of Aristotle's understanding of *phronesis* in the *Nichomachean Ethics*, that sense of wisdom which is rooted in concrete situations which later Heidegger was to build into his ontology of human existence.[28] The sense of converging probabilities allows us to shift from the abstract to the particular and to engage with the variety of human experience, its divergences held in check by an act of faith made moral by the demands of conscience, obedience and a sense of the holy that remains as a light that shines in the darkness even when that darkness is total – a darkness visible in a final *coincidentia oppositorum* that theology, in its deepest intimacies, knows, but barely acknowledges, as the death of God. Our enterprise could never commend itself fully to the academic world, for it still demands that we say our prayers, though in a manner and with what Newman would have named 'certitude' that the Church has more often than not failed to comprehend, an 'underground Catholicism', of which the implicit knowledge is 'not the explicit confession of the Divine Objects of Faith revealed by the Gospels and Catholic Dogmas [known as] only symbols of divine fact which could not be adequately understood or exhausted by a thousand propositions'.[29]

And so our recourse was to literature and the living power of words found in particular situations that bring us to the limits of human suffering and experience. In such situations utterance stutters towards silence and narratives collapse into the stillness of Holy Saturday, a moment of waiting that is at the very heart of our humanity lived before the absent presence that we know simply as God. In the words of George Steiner:

---

[27]   Owen Chadwick, *From Bossuet to Newman: The Idea of Doctrinal Development* (The Birkbeck Lectures, 1955–56) (Cambridge: Cambridge University Press, 1957), p. 71.

[28]   See also Alasdair MacIntyre, *After Virtue: A Study in Moral Theory* (London: Duckworth, 1981).

[29]   J.D. Holmes, Introduction to *Newman's University Sermons*, pp. 34–5.

But ours is the long day's journey of the Saturday. Between suffering, aloneness, unutterable waste on the one hand and the dream of liberation, of rebirth on the other. In the face of the torture of a child, of the death of love which is Friday, even the greatest art and poetry are *almost* helpless.[30]

But the 'almost' is crucial: almost, but not quite. For here only the voice of the poet dares to speak, and so we turn, inevitably and necessarily, to the poets. Edmond Jabès, in 1975 in *The Book of Margins*, writes of the memory of a meeting with Paul Celan, the poet and survivor of the Holocaust:

> That day. The last. Paul Celan at my house. Sitting in this chair that I have right now been staring at for a long time.
>
> Exchange of words, closeness. His voice? Soft, most of the time.
>
> And yet it is not his voice I hear today, but his silence. It is not him I see, but emptiness, perhaps, because on that day, each of us had unawares and cruelly revolved around himself.[31]

The moment, in memory, is sacramental – a real presence that is known only as an absence, yet utterly real, a survival. Mark Rudman, writing in the *New York Times Book Review*, situates Jabès 'in the spiritual company of Kafka and Beckett. The three inhabit the same no-place, which is everywhere, creating works that miraculously cleave to the essential while avoiding the generic'.[32] Here alone, as in all of Kafka, though in him it is hopeless, is salvation sought – a Eucharistic moment of Here Comes Everybody that is finally celebrated, holding its secrets, in *The Divine Comedy* or in Book II, chapter 3 of *Finnegans Wake*, re-enacted for theology in the words of Joyce and Thomas Altizer:

> *I've a terrible errible lot todue todie todue tooterribleday* – a death that is the centre not only of a cosmic Holy Week, but which is reenacted again and again throughout the course of the epic. If the universal humanity of the *Wake* is both legendary Ireland and a contemporary Dublin pub, and H.C.E. is both a local innkeeper and the most glorious and divine king of our archaic past, then the action and the speech of the *Wake* are divine and human simultaneously, a simultaneity which is present in a mystery play or drama that is the universal history of humanity.[33]

---

[30]   George Steiner, *Real Presences* (London: Faber and Faber, 1989), p. 232 (emphasis added).

[31]   Edmond Jabès, 'Memory of Paul Celan', *The Book of Margins* (Chicago, IL: Chicago University Press, 1993), excerpted in Robert Detweiler and David Jasper (eds), *Religion and Literature: A Reader* (Louisville, KY: Westminster John Knox Press, 2000), p. 172.

[32]   Mark Rudman, quoted in Detweiler and Jasper, *Religion and Literature*, p. 172.

[33]   Thomas J.J. Altizer, 'The Ultimate Ground of Catholicism', pp. 9–10.

You see how impossible was the task we had embarked upon, and how far we have travelled in such a short space in this concluding chapter from the measured, archaic, Latin language of John Keble's lectures, through John Henry Newman to the Jewish mystic Edmond Jabès and the Dublin of Joyce. But as was once said of Joyce's *Ulysses*, 'we're all in the bloody book'. And Keble writes at length of Virgil, Homer and the sacred tragedies of Aeschylus. We are back with Job and Sophocles – it all coheres in a living language of literature that speaks finally of silence.

Ours was, undeniably, a deeply Catholic and at times mystical enterprise, taking us back to the liturgical language of the Christian Eucharist, and yet, at the same time profoundly hospitable in its halting entertainment, at least in our later days, of wider traditions. Hence, there is the chapter in this book which converses with contemporary China and its spiritual emergence from its ancient religions and modern, secular roots. To that I will return shortly. But for now, and in a brief comparison, how do we differ from another theological project, that known as Radical Orthodoxy? We, too, I think, are largely post-liberal in our thinking, following Alasdair MacIntyre in his argument, as formulated by Steven Shakespeare, that 'rationality and ethics needs to be shaped by narratives, by traditions of enquiry and virtue'. We, too, were rooted in tradition, in the idea of the Church and in an opposition to the 'myths' of secularism. Sadly Hans Blumenberg's *The Legitimacy of the Modern Age* was only translated into English in 1983, too late for us to cut our teeth on in Durham in 1982. But, paradoxically, we have never for one moment dared to offer a master discourse against the threat of nihilism, even one that asserts its *non*-mastery. John Milbank, on the other hand, has written that:

> Only Christian theology now offers a discourse able to position and overcome nihilism itself. This is why it is so important to reassert theology as a master discourse; theology, alone, remains the discourse of non-mastery.[34]

The heart of our difference from Radical Orthodoxy lies, it may be, in its rejection of the theology of Duns Scotus and the difference of that theology from the 'analogical' world-view of Thomas Aquinas (*c.*1225–1274). Duns Scotus (upon whom the poetry of Gerard Manley Hopkins is so reliant) sees language as 'univocal' – that the words we employ when applied to God are used in the same way as when applied to any- and everything else. For Aquinas, on the other hand, language is 'equivocal', inasmuch as the language used of God is entirely different from ordinary language. Analogy thus becomes the means whereby we are not rendered utterly speechless before God. We may say that

---

[34]   John Milbank, *Theology and Social Theory: Beyond Secular Reason*, 2nd edn (Oxford: Blackwell, 2006), p. 6.

'God is truth' inasmuch as God is the source of all truth, yet our words remain equivocal, lost in a mystery that is finally beyond our telling.

For Radical Orthodoxy, the univocal language of Duns Scotus fails to preserve this unique otherness of God, rendering God finally as 'being' just in the same way as everything else 'is'. Thus, in the end, so the argument might go, we are left in such univocity with a godless world in which 'God' seems to be replaced with something simply like pure power. Now as Steven Shakespeare has noted, let it be said, Radical Orthodoxy's reading of Duns Scotus (as with many of the thinkers that it addresses both positively and critically) is extremely controversial, indeed, questionable.[35] For us, so deeply rooted in Coleridgean and Romantic thought, the picture was very different – and, it has to be admitted, not without its theological dangers also. Deeply univocal, the thinking that underlies the conferences on literature and theology celebrates the essential interconnectedness of all things, sometimes even moving towards the pantheistic tendencies of a poem like Wordsworth's *Lines Written a Few Miles Above Tintern Abbey*. A systematic defence, or even definition, of such a broad position would be difficult to mount, and we have never done so. Like Newman and Keble, we can acknowledge our profound debt to Coleridge and Wordsworth (to whom, as I have noted, Keble even dedicated his *Lectures on Poetry*) while recognizing their spiritual and theological distance from us in many ways. Our position, like Newman's with regard to the British empiricist tradition of Locke and Hume, is untidy and with a necessary and admitted inconsistency that allows us to draw from Coleridge's language of the symbol, especially in *The Statesman's Manual*, a sense of the sacramental, and in the end to admit in faith that within all change, variety and paradox there may be an underlying consistency that, like Job before God, we can only acknowledge and no more. Beyond that is silence.

This shift back to the univocality of Duns Scotus (who, as far as I can remember, has never been mentioned in any of our conferences), both preserves us from the exclusive Christian rhetoric of Radical Orthodoxy, and grants an entirely different *tone* to our theological discourse, one less systematic, more inclusive and more 'poetic'. Such a tone develops from that sense in language that *how* you say something is as important, or even more important, as *what* you say: manner (and manners) thus becomes crucial in a deeply humanistic approach to theological thinking. I would agree entirely with Milbank that 'neither a reiteration of Christian orthodoxy in identically repeated handed-down formulas, nor a liberal adaptation to postmodern assumptions will serve as well'.[36] But I would see this assertion firmly in the context of Newman's *Essay*

---

[35]   Steven Shakespeare, *Radical Orthodoxy: A Critical Introduction* (London: SPCK, 2007), p. 11.

[36]   John Milbank, *Being Reconciled: Ontology and Pardon* (London: Routledge, 2003), p. 196.

on Development in Christian Doctrine. As we have seen in the previous chapter, in this *Essay*, with its organic sense of continuity within change, we find some of Newman's most perceptive 'literary criticism', not least in his development of the idea that the Bible remains dead upon the page until enlivened in the processes of reading and reception.[37]

Where, I think, we parted company most profoundly with Radical Orthodoxy was in its ultimate failure to take wholly seriously the materiality of the created world and our place within it. In the pages of all literature the body suffers and feels, the 'meadows and the woods' are living presences that evoke the 'still, sad music of humanity', and the world is a place of tears and joy in physical creation. It is from such actual, inescapable participations that we return, haltingly, to the mysteries of the incarnation and the Passion. Marcella Althaus-Reid, however, has suggested, on the other hand, that while 'liberation theology takes account of the fragility of God in history ... radical orthodoxy seems to have a God-ideal outside failures and platitudes of destitution.'[38] It was just such a sense that was borne in upon me years ago when I was asked to review the volume *Radical Orthodoxy: A New Theology* (1999), edited by John Milbank, Catherine Pickstock and Graham Ward: a sense I then felt that there were essays on the body, yet as if this body had never felt pain or ecstasy; on music, though no note had ever been heard or wept over; on art, yet no image presented itself to the eye or to the soul. As Katie Terezakis has suggested in an essay on Milbank's reading of his 'hero' Johann Georg Hamann (1730–1788) that exposes a profound contradiction;

> But if we are assured, as Milbank would assure us, that bodies are not really bodies and nature not really nature, nor the limitations of our experience as they appear to be, then that which Hamann considers the site of our embrace of divinity would be emptied of the features which, for Hamann, characterize it.[39]

But I should not press the point too far, for my purpose here is not to provoke controversy or argument. What is at stake, rather, is the future of theology within a global cultural economy, and yet one which holds within its voice and practice the deep memory of the past in which it necessarily participates. The liturgical has ever been present in the study of literature and theology, not least inasmuch as it must be enacted, something 'done in remembrance' as a testimony and as

---

[37]   See above, pp. 232.

[38]   Marcella Althaus-Reid, in Rosemary Radford Ruether and Marion Grau (eds), *Interpreting the Postmodern: Responses to 'Radical Orthodoxy'* (New York and London: T&T Clark, 2006), p. 111.

[39]   Katie Terezakis, 'J.G. Hamann and the Self-Refutation of Radical Orthodoxy ', in Lisa Isherwood and Marko Zlomislić (eds), *The Poverty of Radical Orthodoxy* (Eugene, OR: Pickwick Publications, 2012), p. 51.

a hope for the future. In my own writing this sense of the centrality of liturgy reached a culmination in my volume *The Sacred Community* (2012) and is heard most clearly there in the voices of Martin Heidegger and Yves Lacoste. And it remains most deeply in the practice of the liturgy that cannot simply look back to the 'middle voice'[40] of earlier liturgies but demands constant rediscovery and re-authentication in the language and forms of literature. Whether this has actually been the case in much twentieth-century liturgical reform in the Christian churches is another matter. One thing is quite clear. Liturgical utterance, while rooted in history and tradition, can only be truly alive within the words of a living language that is honed and spoken from within the darkest actualities of human experience and the world. But, as Marko Zlomislić has suggested:

> Within the universe proposed by Radical Orthodoxy the individual is reduced to a predictable machine, God becomes an abstraction and society becomes a panopticon driven by disciplines of control. The critics of nominalism stifle individualism in order to maintain a spiritual aristocracy along with a theological elitism.[41]

And so what of the future? I have admitted more than once to my overall sense of failure to achieve what we set out to do in the early 1980s in the field of literature and theology. There are many reasons for this. It is very difficult for genuine interdisciplinarity to flourish in the over-specialized and increasingly philistine world of contemporary Western universities. Although the rhetoric of comparative studies (not least in religion, literature, and literary studies) sounds in all the academic prospectuses, the crossing of boundaries between our strictly defined scholarly colonies is, by and large, professionally suicidal, especially for younger scholars. Second, it was not long before we abandoned the deep intellectual and spiritual roots in Romanticism and the nineteenth century that were sown in the early conferences. And we forgot the fundamental importance of theology. As we moved into the brave new world of postmodernism – which we never really embraced – we began to seem old fashioned and even rather embarrassingly pious as well as a little forgetful, which was the opposite of that cynical cleverness that was increasingly in vogue. We also lost our way between theological liberalism and post-liberalism – which I think was partly a loss of nerve, though not unmixed with a degree of intellectual confusion. 'Literature and theology' increasingly became its much tamer partner 'literature and religion', and started simply to repeat itself in endless textbooks on the Bible

---

[40]   The term used by Catherine Pickstock.

[41]   Marko Zlomislić, 'Paper Cut-Outs of Christ in Plato's Cave', in Isherwood and Zlomislić, *The Poverty of Radical Orthodoxy*, p. 208.

and literature, essays, starting with Auerbach, endlessly recycled. The primary imperatives and the vision began to fade. Christian theology was moving in different directions, all of them with varying degrees of conservatism even within the language of postmodernity, and the explosion upon the imaginative spirit of the death of God began to be treated with, at best, a failure of understanding and mild disdain.

But the event of the death of God, first anticipated and known in modernity in Hegel and Nietzsche, was again actually enacted in the trenches of the First World War, and then the genocide and nuclear horror of the Second World War (both of the latter moments which our history, to a degree, has sought to obliterate), and from them theology in the West has never truly recovered, for Western theologies have failed to 'embody the radically new understandings of the Bible that were born in this period, nor could they embody the radically new expressions of the imagination that are now fully born'.[42] No study of the Bible in the later part of the twentieth century has fully acknowledged its necessary rebirth into a post-theological age that demands forms of attention and articulation that we have barely begun to even to dare to consider. Or is it that we simply lack the imagination? In his stately Latin prose Keble knew something of this as he patiently read the poetry and the tragedies of Homer, Aeschylus, Sophocles, and Virgil against the Bible, and vice versa, acknowledging also the later tradition of Dante and the Renaissance tragedies of Shakespeare. But Keble's theological insights as Oxford Professor of Poetry were quickly swallowed up in the shallower and safer waters of Matthew Arnold. Newman, too, in his way and in his anticipations of what Heidegger would imaginatively call *Geschichte* – 'deep history' – knows his deep unspoken fears of that nihilism that it was to take all of Heidegger's philosophical purpose to overcome. The connections I am drawing here are long and fragile, and I think that, in the end, we lacked the courage or the intelligence, or the imagination – or all three – to sustain them in those spaces of literature that alone might dare to frame new expressions of a genuinely apocalyptic and universal Christianity.

Such a Christianity will need to be absorbed into a universal and global cultural context that was virtually unknown to us 30 years ago, and is still barely emerging in any authentic manner within either universities or the Church. Its most radical expression is to be found in small endeavours in China, and conversations between thinkers in China and the West. I will keep specifically to these examples in China not because there are no other conversations, but because, as Zhang Longxi has put it in his crucial book on literary hermeneutics in the West and East, *The Tao and the Logos* (1992), 'such an arbitrarily synecdochic use of the word *East* is not meant to deny the distinctions among the various cultures of the East, but arbitrariness of the word serves to call in

---

[42]   Altizer, 'The Ultimate Ground of Catholicism', p. 26.

question the very name of the East as opposed to the West'.[43] This admission is indicative of the still preliminary and unclear nature of our task. Theology in its traditional expressions, like the churches, in the West is dying. Since the heady days of Max Müller in Oxford at the end of the nineteenth century and his stupendous 50-volume project on *The Sacred Books of the East*, the serious study of comparative religion has faltered, and it is now in literary hermeneutics and the study of texts and translation that Christian theology is slowly rediscovering itself anew, not in churches but in the academies and between intellectuals, and the arbitrary distinctions between 'East' and 'West' are slowly, very slowly, dissolving. It is here that we are gradually regaining our vision, born, as chapter 13 on the work of Yang Huilin has sought to indicate, from the imperatives of recent history and in sufferings which are China's equivalent to the sufferings of Europe in the middle years of the last century. As Zhang Longxi's book indicates, the terms of this new interpretative pluralism must be the finally untranslatable words of religion – *tao* and *logos* – words from cultures far apart, and words on the edge of life and death whose creative power is first addressed by the philosopher, and then the mystic and poet.

Such dialogues in literature and theology, therefore, must now move on from the exclusively Christian discourses of our early days. They must be engaged in *between* religions and cultures (as the only creative readings of the Bible have always been), in a sense illicit, but sensitive to those points of convergence that shun mastery and privilege, and recognize compatibilities beyond cultural enclosures yet without denying difference. Only by this will new spaces appear, a rebirth of images in which the imagination can extend into new visionary expressions. As I embark upon a new adventure in literature in China (alas, in translation only), a literature which is far less concerned to define the differences between poetry, philosophy, religion and ethics than the Western tradition, I end with some words that I myself wrote 15 years ago with my old friend Bob Detweiler, shortly before his death, at the end of our Reader in religion and literature, and after a consideration of Wallace Stevens' poem 'Sunday Morning':

> The vocabulary of kenosis is deep within the Christian tradition and the imagery of the passion narratives, but in the words of the poet is far more radical than any conclusion dared by most theologians. Perhaps Christ himself, though not the articulate tradition that appropriated his memory, ventured this utterly post-modern moment that the poet knows. Perhaps the greatest literature has always been within this moment of transition, speaking to us yet beyond us in fictions that we know to be fictions yet, imaginatively, know also to be true. Such literature

---

43   Zhang Longxi, *The Tao and the Logos: Literary Hermeneutics, East and West* (Durham, NC: Duke University Press, 1992), p. xii.

can, in spite of all, realize the "divinization" of our world in an apocalypse that we have barely begun to appreciate.[44]

Such is the vision, such the transformation, the old books must be buried – and so we move on.

---

[44]   Detweiler and Jasper (eds), *Religion and Literature*, p. 177.

Brief Bibliography

It was while editing the *Oxford Handbook of English Literature and Theology* (Oxford University Press, 2007) with Andrew W. Hass and Elisabeth Jay that the early ideas for the present volume started to develop.

Proceedings of the Conferences on Literature and Theology

1982: David Jasper (ed.), *Images of Belief in Literature* (London: Macmillan, 1984).

1984: David Jasper (ed.), *The Interpretation of Belief: Coleridge, Schleiermacher and Romanticism* (London: Macmillan, 1986).

1986: David Jasper and T.R. Wright (eds), *The Critical Spirit and the Will to Believe* (London: Macmillan, 1989).

1988: David Jasper and Colin Crowder (eds), *European Literature and Theology in the Twentieth Century* (London: Macmillan, 1990).

1992: Gregory Salyer and Robert Detweiler (eds), *Literature and Theology at Century's End* (Atlanta, GA: Scholars Press, 1995).

1996: Heather Walton and Andrew W. Hass (eds), *Self.Same/Other: Re-visioning the Subject in Literature and Theology* (Sheffield: Sheffield Academic Press, 2000).

2000: Erik Borgman, Bart Philipsen and Lea Verstricht (eds), *Literary Canons and Religious Identity* (London: Ashgate, 2004).

Chapter 2

John Coulson (ed.), *Theology and the University: An Ecumenical Investigation* (London: Darton, Longman & Todd, 1964).

John Coulson, *Newman and the Common Tradition* (Oxford: Clarendon Press, 1970).

John Coulson, *Religion and Imagination: 'In aid of a grammar of assent'* (Oxford: Clarendon Press, 1981).

Chapter 3

Ulrich Simon, *A Theology of Auschwitz* (London: Victor Gollancz, 1967).
Ulrich Simon, *Sitting in Judgement, 1913–1963* (London: SPCK, 1978).
Ulrich Simon, *Atonement: From Holocaust to Paradise* (Cambridge: James Clarke & Co, 1987).
Ulrich Simon, *Pity and Terror: Christianity and Tragedy* (London: Macmillan, 1989).

Chapter 4

Martin Jarrett-Kerr, *Studies in Literature and Belief* (London: Rockliff, 1954).
Martin Jarrett-Kerr, *D.H. Lawrence and Human Existence*, 2nd edn (London: SCM, 1961).

Chapter 5

Werner G. Jeanrond, *Theological Hermeneutics: Development and Significance* (London: Macmillan, 1991).

Chapter 6

Robert Detweiler, *Breaking the Fall: Religious Readings of Contemporary Fiction* (San Francisco, CA: Harper & Row, 1989).

Chapter 7

Mieke Bal, *On Story-Telling: Essays in Narratology* (Sonoma, CA: Polebridge Press, 1991).

Chapter 9

John Keble, *Lectures on Poetry, 1832–1841*, trans. Edward Kershaw Francis, 2 vols (Oxford: Clarendon Press, 1912).
John Henry Newman, *An Essay on the Development of Christian Doctrine* (1845), ed. J.M. Cameron (London: Penguin, 1974).

John Henry Newman, *An Essay in Aid of a Grammar of Assent* (1889), 8th edn, ed. I.T. Ker (Oxford: Clarendon Press, 1985).

John Henry Newman, *Apologia Pro Vita Sua* [1864], ed. Ian Ker (London: Penguin, 1994).

Chapter 10

David Jasper, *The Sacred Community: Art, Sacrament, and the People of God* (Waco, TX: Baylor University Press, 2012).

Chapter 11

Robert Alter and Frank Kermode (eds), *The Literary Guide to the Bible* (London: Collins, 1987).

David Jasper and Stephen Prickett (eds), *The Bible and Literature: A Reader* (Oxford: Blackwell, 1999).

Chapter 12

David Malouf, *Remembering Babylon* (London: Vintage, 1994).

David Malouf, *12, Edmonstone Street* (London: Vintage, 1999).

Tony Kelly, *A New Imagining: Towards an Australian Spirituality* (Melbourne: Collins Dove, 1990).

Chapter 13

Yang Huilin, *China, Christianity and the Question of Culture* (Waco, TX: Baylor University Press, 2014).

Index

Note: Page numbers in **bold** denote main entries.

12, Edmonstone Street (Malouf) 199, 202

Abrams, M.H. 20, 17
Absolute tragedy 113
Adams, A.K.M 170
Adorno, Theodor 87
Africa Answers Back (Nyabongo) 169
African Pulse (Jarrett-Kerr) 68
After Auschwitz (Rubenstein) 47
Aids to Reflection (Coleridge) 16, 33
Alberoni, Albert 96
Alter, Robert 126, 164, 166, 173, 177
Altizer, T.J.J. 48–9, 51, 81, 92, 120, 122, 195, 236–7, 243–4
Analogical Imagination, The (Tracy) 231
Analogy of Religion (Butler) 34, **131**, 138–40
Anatomy Lesson of Dr. Nicholas Tulip (Rembrandt) 156
Anderson, Pamela Sue 99
Angelus Novus (Klee) 83
Anglican Revival, The (Brilioth) 108
Anna Karenin (Tolstoy) 54
Anti-semitism 115
Apocalyptic Trinity, The (Altizer) 122
Apologia Pro Vita Sua (Newman) 31, 33, 107, 129, 131, 241
Apostolic Tradition (Hippolytus) 144, 148
Arendt, Hannah 112, 113–14, 121, 210
Ariel (Plath) 216
Aristotle 34, 115, 120
Arnold of Bonneval 149
Arnold, Matthew 14, 65, 127, 238
Arrière-Pays, The (Bonnefoy) 198, 201
Art of Biblical Narrative, The (Alter) 164

Art of Biblical Poetry, The (Alter) 166, 177
Atonement (McEwan) 117
Atonement: From Holocaust to Paradise (Simon) 47, 118–19
Atwood, Margaret 95
Auden, W. H 18, 39–40
Auerbach, Erich 160, 187
Augustine of Hippo, St. 60, 217
Aurora (Boehme) 136
Auschwitz **44–57**, 76–7, 87, 115, 122, 207, 209, 213–15
Austen, Jane 53

Baez, Joan 28
Baker-Smith, Dominic 25–6
Bakhtin, Mikhail 97
Bal, Mieke **101–8**, 126, 165, 168, 177–8, 180–83, 185, 188
Balthasar, Hans Urs von 216, 218
Barr, James 184
Barrett, C.K. 144–5
Barth, Karl 15, 44, 49–50, 51, 100, 104, 226
Bataille, Georges 101
Bathsheba (Lindgren) 162
Baudrillard, J 95, 155
Bauman, Zygmunt 155
Beaumont, Sir George 132
Believing in the Church (Church of England Doctrine Commission) 163–4
Bell, Bishop George 94
Benjamin, Walter 83, 104
Bible and Literature, The (Jasper and Prickett) 174
Bible as Literature, The (Gabel, Wheeler and York) 174

Bible: Authorized King James Version
(Carroll and Prickett) 172–3
Biographia Literaria (Coleridge) 29, 36,
130, 141, 240, 241
Black Prince, The (Murdoch) 119
Black Sun (Kristeva) 75
*Blackwell Companion to the Bible in English
Literature* 174
Blake, William 24, 48, 49, 50, 190, 191,
196, 197, 215
Blanchot, Maurice 76, 79, 91, 100–101,
118, 122, 198, 240
Blind Side of the Heart (Franck) 112–13
Bloom, Harold 171–2
Blumenberg, Hans 244
Body of the Dead Christ in the Tomb
(Holbein) 74–5, 78, 121
Boehme, Jacob 136
Böll, Heinrich 47, 116
Bonhoeffer, Dietrich 17, 40, 48, 94, 208
Bonnefoy, Yves 192, 198
Book of God, The (Josipovici) 173, 183
Book of J (Rosenberg and Bloom) 171–2
Book of Margins, The (Jabès) 243
Borgman, Eric 99
Bouyer, Louis 152
Brave New World (Huxley) 211
Breaking the Fall (Detweiler) 88, **90–98**
Bremond, Henri 239
Brink, André 116–17
Bunyan, John 227
Burrell, David B. 28, 32, 39
Burrows, Mark S. 227, 228, 233
Butler, Bishop Joseph 34, 90, 138–40, 239
Bynum, Caroline Walker 149–50
Byron, Lord 132, 238

Caputo, John 240
Caroline Divines 23, 38, 128
Catharsis 127
Caught Reading Again (Sugirtharajah) 222
Celan, Paul 45, 50–51, 81, 243
Chadwick, Owen 134–5, 140
Champion, Jim 224–5
Chekhov, Anton 193

Chicago, University of 14
Christian Year, The (Keble) 127, 131, 135,
138, 140–41
Christianity and Symbolism (Dillistone) 20
Church and the Bomb, The 20
Church Dogmatics (Barth) 49
Church, R.W. 238
Clare, John 190, 196
Colenso, Bishop John William 65–7
Coleridge, S.T. 4, 6, 13, 15, 16, 22, 23, 24,
25, 29, 30–34, 36, 96, 107, 108,
127, 129–30, 131–4, 136, 141, 143,
152, 190, 230, 231, 240, 241
Concluding Unscientific Postscript
(Kierkegaard) 123
Congregation (Rosenberg) 163
Conrad, Joseph 225
Consolation of Philosophy (Boethius) 237
Coulson, John 5, 6, 13, 16, 21–3, **27–41**,
64, 117, 127–8, 129, 141, 217, 230,
239
Coverdale, Miles 172
Craig, David 46
Crime and Punishment (Dostoevsky) 76
Critical Spirit and the Will to Believe, The
(Jasper and Wright) 3, 59
Cross on the Mountains, The (Friedrich) 73,
83, 109
Crowder, Colin 93
Cultural Revolution 205–15
Culture and Imperialism (Said) 224–5
Cunningham, Valentine 104
Cupitt, Don 106, 149

Daemonic Imagination, The (Detweiler and
Doty) 232
Daiches, David 185
Dark Gaze, The (Hart) 100–101
Dawkins, Richard 33, 81
Death and Dissymmetry (Bal) 168, 180
Death of Tragedy, The (Steiner) 51
Derrida, Jacques 32, 39, 76, 80, 95, 96, 102,
161, 172, 182, 215, 226
Descartes, René 121
Descent of the Dove, The (Williams) 145

Detweiler, Robert 8, 24, 69, **87–98**, 102, 123, 180–83, 207, 224
Development of Christian Doctrine, Essay on (Newman) 31, 35, 130, 134–5, 136, 138, 211, 230–32, 246
D.H. Lawrence and Human Existence (Jarrett-Kerr) 68–9
Diacritics 177
Dialogue with Trypho (Justin Martyr) 143
Dickinson, Emily 35
Didion, Joan 28
Dido and Aeneas (Purcell) 105. 108
Diefrenbach, Lorenz 115
Dillistone, F.W. 13, 20–21
Dinesen, Isak 111–12
Disciplina Arcani 131, 227–8
Discourses on the Scope and Nature of University Education (Newman) 7, 36
Dix, Dom Gregory 145, 157
Don Quixote (Cervantes) 120–21
Donne, John 39, 138
Dostoevsky, F. 6, 49, 74–5, 76, 121
Dr. Faustus (Marlowe) 57
Dream of Gerontius, The (Newman) 40, 89–90, 108, 136
Drury, M. O'C 56
Dry White Season, A (Brink) 116–17
Dunne, John S. 230
Duns Scotus 39, 244–5
Durham, University of 1, 2, 3, 7, 13, 44, 73, 104, 206

Eagleton, Terry 17, 45, 207
Eckhart, Meister 88, 101, 106, 123, 148
Eclipse of Biblical Narrative, The (Frei) 163
Edwards, Michael 93
Eliot, T.S. 6, 40, 46, 68–9, 93–4, 160, 161, 175, 184, 223, 240
Enright, D.J. 52
Erasmus, Desiderius 75, 78
Erotic Phenomenon, The (Marion) 146
Eucharist (Bouyer) 152
Eucharist and sacrament **143–57**
Euripides 115

European Literature and Theology in the Twentieth Century (Jasper and Crowder) 7
Ezekiel 133, 152, 202

Fabiny, Tibor 222
Fackenheim, Emil 46, 48
Farrer, Austin 62, 164–5
Fateless (Kertész) 76–7, 80
Faust, Part I (Goethe) 56–7, 214
Feng, Yü-Hsiang, General 70–71
Fiduciary language 15, 32, 128, 218, 230
Finnegans Wake (Joyce) 235, 237, 243–4
First Apology (Justin Martyr) 143
Fisch, Harold 166, 175
Fish, Stanley 33, 90, 207
Forgiveness 44, 99–100, 112–13, 114, 119, 209, 214
Foucault, Michel 155
Four Quartets, The (Eliot) 93–4
Four Zoas, The (Blake) 196
Frank, Manfred 82
Frankenstein (Shelley) 156
Frazer, Sir James George 160
Friedrich, Caspar-David 73, 109
Fringe of Leaves, A (White) 199
Frost, Robert 91

Gadamer, H-G 32, 74
Galileo 121
Gay Science, The (Nietzsche) 48, 89
Geertz, Clifford 91–2
Gelassenheit 88, 90, 98, 123
Genesis of Secrecy, The (Kermode) 186, 228
Geselligkeit 90, 123
Glasgow, University of 2, 8
Glory of the Lord, The (Balthasar) 218
God and the Rhetoric of Sexuality (Trible) 167
Golden Legend, The (Voragine) 147
Grammar of Assent, A (Newman) 5, 6, 13, 15, 16, 32, 33, 34, 35, 60, 108, 128, 134, 217, 230, 239, 241, 242
Great World, The (Malouf) 194–5
Greene, Graham 19
Greene, Sharon 96

Gruppenbild mit Dame (Böll) 47, 116
Guéranger, Dom Prosper 153
Gunn, Giles 69–70, 226

Hamann, Johann Georg 246
Hamilton, William 48
Hamlet (Shakespeare) 210
Hampson, Daphne 168
Handelman, Susan A. 77, 161
Handmaid's Tale, The (Atwood) 95, 211
Hardy, Thomas 105
Hart, Kevin 100–101
Hartmann, Geoffrey 162
Hass, Andrew 2
Hawkins, Peter 174
Heart of Darkness, The (Conrad) 225
Hegel, G.W.F. 89
Heidegger, Martin 32, 88, 90, 98, 123, 191,
     194, 195, 226, 233, 242, 248
Henchard, Michael 54–5
Henn, T.R. 160
Henry V (Shakespeare) 16
Herbert, George 138
Heyendaal Institute for Theology, Science
     and Culture 99
Hill, Geoffrey 18
Himmler, Heinrich 115–16, 122
Hippolytus, St. 144
Historia Monachorum in Aegypto 201
Hitler, Adolf 115
Hoban, Russell 95
Holbein, Hans, the Younger 74–5, 77, 78,
     82, 121
Holloway, Richard 30–31
Honest to God (Robinson) 17, 35
Hopkins, G.M. 6, 39, 90
Horae Canonicae (Auden) 18, 39, 93
Hosea 47
Houlden, Leslie 30
Huddleston, Bishop Trevor 62
Hügel, Baron von 59–62, 70
Human Age, The (Lewis) 67–8
Human Condition, The (Arendt) 115, 210

Idea of a University, The (Newman) 108, 141

Idea of Biblical Poetry, The (Kugel) 160, 166
Idiot, The (Dostoevsky) 74–5, 82, 121
Illative Sense 5, 16, 34, 92, 194, 239
Images of Belief in Literature (Jasper) 3, 25
Imaginary Life, An (Malouf) 192–3, 196
Imagination 29, 36, 39, 130, 133, 152, 231
In Good Company (Jasper and Ledbetter) 96
In Memoriam (Tennyson) 131
In Praise of Folly (Erasmus) 78–9
Inferno (Dante) 236
Inge, Ralph 16
Institute for Theology, Imagination and the
     Arts, St. Andrew's University 8
International Society for Religion,
     Literature and Culture (ISRLC) 1
Interpretation of Belief, The (Jasper) 3, 73,
     82, 109
Interpretation of Otherness, The (Gunn) 69–70
Irony 41, 51, 52, 89
Iser, Wolfgang 231

Jabès, Edmond 170, 172, 243
Jacobson, Howard 168–9
James of Vitry 150
James, William 60
Jarrett-Kerr, Martin CR. 8, 19–20, **59–71**, 117
Jasper, David 104
Jay, Elisabeth 2, 104–5, 108, 109
Jeanrond, Werner **73–83**, 222–3
Job 16, 51, 52–3, 123, 178, 186, 188, 237
'Job and Sophocles' (Simon) 52–3
John of the Cross, St. 148, 149
Joseph and His Brothers (Mann) 102, 162
Josipovici, Gabriel 112, 119, 173, 183–4,
     185, 186, 187
Joyce, James 49, 235
Judas Iscariot 50
Julian of Norwich 148
Justin Martyr 143, 144, 156

Kafka, Franz 79, 100, 117, 122, 198, 210, 228
Kant, I 38, 182
Keble, John 9, 64, 126, 127, 130, 131–2,
     135, 138–41, 189, 190, 192, 238–9,
     245, 248

Kermode, Frank 22, 129, 164, 228, 229
Kertész, Imre 76–7, 78, 122
Kierkegaard, S. 49, 123, 227
King James Bible after 400 Years, The
    (Hamlin and Jones) 173
King Lear (Shakespeare) 48, 55
King's College, London 43
Kirwan, Michael 25
Klee, Paul 83
Klemm, David E. 100, 123, 229
Knights, Ben 6
Knights, L.C. 22, 36, 63, 129
Knox, Alexander 130
Kristeva, Julia 75, 78

Lacoste, Jean-Yves 143
Lady Chatterley's Lover (Lawrence) 19, 62
Last of the Just, The (Schwarz-Bart) 79, 80,
    81, 122
Later Heidegger, The (Pattison) 226
Lausiac History, The (Palladios) 151–2
Lawrence, D.H. 19, 21, 68–9
Leavis, F.R. 20, 22, 63, 129
Lectio Divina 229
Lectures on Justification (Newman) 130
Lectures on Poetry (*de poeticae vi medici*)
    (Keble) 9, 127, 131–2, 190, 238–9
Lectures on the Sacred Poetry of the Hebrews
    (Lowth) 159, 166, 239
Ledbetter, Mark 96
Legge, James 207
Letters and Papers from Prison (Bonhoeffer)
    208
Leuven, University of 1, 111, 235
Levi, Primo 77–8
Levinas, Emmanuel 209
Lewis, C.S. 161
Lewis, Wyndham 67–8
Linafelt, Tod 174–5
Literary Guide to the Bible, The (Alter and
    Kermode) 160–61, 170–71
Literature and Theology 1, 2, 4, 13, 24–5, 26,
    104, 113, 119, 180, 222, 223, 233
Literature and Theology at Century's End
    (Detweiler and Salyer) 9, 224

Liturgical Movement 153
Liturgy 93, 246–7
Living the Death of God (Altizer) 49
Loades, Ann 55–6, 151
Lot's Wife 109
Loughlin, Gerard 35
Lowe, Walter 224–6, 233
Lowth, Robert 239
Lumen Fidei (Pope Francis) 74–6
Luther, Martin 21, 227
Lux Mundi (Gore) 142
Lyotard, J-F 169, 170
Lyra Apostolica 135–8
Lyrical Ballads, The (Wordsworth and
    Coleridge) 132, 135, 139

'Memorable Fancy, A' (Blake) 197
Machiavelli 114–15
Mackinnon, Donald 239
Malouf, David 9, 126, 185, **189–203**
Mann, Thomas 16, 102, 103
Manning, Cardinal 13
Manzoni, Alessandro 19
Mao Zedong 214
Marion, J-L. 143, 146
Martin, David L. 156
Mary of Egypt, St. 146–7
Mauriac, François 19
Maurice, F.D. 66
Maximus the Confessor, St. 145, 153
Mayor of Casterbridge, The (Hardy) 54–5, 120
McHale, Brian 95
Measure for Measure (Shakespeare) 47–8
Meditations on the Passion (Rolle) 151
Memoirs of the Life of Sir. Walter Scott
    (Lockhart) 127
Merchant of Venice, The (Shakespeare) 43, 209
Midrash and Literature (Hartmann and
    Budick) 162
Milbank, John 24, 106, 235–35, 244–7
Milton, John 50, 162, 197–8, 215
Mimesis (Auerbach) 160
Mo Yan 208
Moore, Stephen D. 170
Morgan, D.N. 64

Moulton, Richard Green 159
Mozley, Thomas 23
Murder and Difference (Bal) 180–81
Murdoch, Iris 119
Murray, Les 190
Mystical Element of Religion, The (Hügel)
    61–2
Mystical Experience 148–9

National Socialism 46
Natural Supernaturalism (Abrams) 20
Newman and the Common Tradition
    (Coulson) 22, 32
Newman, Cardinal J.H. 5–6, 7, 13, 15–16,
    21, 22, 23–4, **27–41**, 60, 61, 89,
    90, 105, 106, 107–8, 126, 128–31,
    132–8, 140–42, 153, 194, 206,
    211, 229–33, 237, 239–42
Newsletter of the National Conference on
    Literature and Religion 223
Ngidi, William 66
Ngugi Wa Thiong'o 21
Nichomachean Ethics (Aristotle) 34, 240,
    242
Niebuhr, Reinhold 21, 62–3
Nijmegen, University of 1, 9, 99–109
Norton, David 159, 173
'Notes Towards a Supreme Fiction'
    (Stevens) 229
Novelist and the Passion Story, The
    (Dillistone) 21

Odyssey (Homer) 160
Ohlendorf, Otto 57, 205
On Consulting the Faithful in Matters of
    Doctrine (Newman) 5, 91
On Religion (Schleiermacher) 221
Only Problem, The (Spark) 123, 186
'Only Speaker of His Tongue, The'
    (Malouf) 200–201
Origen 147, 175
Ostriker, Alicia 167
Otto, Rudolf 221
Ovid 192–3
Owen, Wilfred 45, 202, 213

Oxford Handbook of English Literature and
    Theology, The (Hass, Jasper, Jay) 4,
    174–5, 188
Oxford Movement 33, 106, 107, 126,
    127–42, 143, 153, 238

Paradise Lost (Milton) 162, 197–8
Parergon 182, 188
Pascal, Blaise 201–202, 237
Patterns of Christian Acceptance (Jarrett-
    Kerr) 70
Pattison, George 93
Pattison, Mark 24
Perfume (Süskind) 47
Phillips, D.Z. 14, 22, 27, 28, 55, 129
Philoctetes (Sophocles) 17, 52–3
Philosopher and His Poor, The (Rancière) 115
Philosophical Investigations (Wittgenstein) 32
Phronesis 34, 92, 242
Pity and Terror (Simon) 44, 54–5, 113, 212
Pius XII 46
Plath, Sylvia 216
Plotted, Painted and Shot (Exum) 167–8
Poetics of Belief, The (Scott) 107
Poetics of Biblical Narrative, The (Sternberg)
    165–6, 177
Poetry and the Religious Imagination (Knox
    and Lonsdale) 2
Poetry with a Purpose (Fisch) 166
Pollefeyt, Dideir 209–10, 213
Postmodern Bible Reader, The (Jobling,
    Pippin, Schleifer) 171
Postmodern Bible, The 170
Postmodern Condition, The (Lyotard) 169, 170
Postmodern Use of the Bible (McKnight)
    169–70
Pound, Ezra 63
Power of Symbols, The (Dillistone) 20
Prelude, The (Wordsworth) 22, 32, 132
Prickett, Stephen 2, 133
Principal of Hope, The (Bloch) 207
Protestant Era, The (Tillich) 8, 87
Proust, Marcel 102, 111, 184

Quincuplex Psalterium (d'Etaples) 26

Rabelais and His World (Bakhtin) 211

Radical Orthodoxy 4, 101, 105–6, 235–36, 244–7

Radical Orthodoxy: A New Theology (Milbank, Pickens, Ward) 246

Radical Theology and the Death of God (Altizer and Hamilton) 48

Ramsey, Bishop Ian 35

Rancière, J. 115, 120–21

Ransom (Malouf) 193–4, 199

Rashke, Carl 225

Ratcliff, E.C. 148

Ratushinskaya, Irina 103

Reader-response criticism 133

Reading religiously 91

Reading Rembrandt (Bal) 103

Real Presences (Steiner) 76

Reason and Commitment (Trigg) 63–4

Reasons of the Heart, The (Dunne) 230

Regeneration (Barker) 212

Religion and Imagination (Coulson) 15, 23

Religion Within the Limits of Reason Alone (Kant) 182

Religious Experience and Christian Faith (Dillistone) 21

Remembering Babylon (Malouf) 189, 190–91, 196–8, 199, 202

Remembrance of Things Past (Proust) 102

Renan, Ernest 115

Renmin University of China 126, 205

Rhetoric of Fiction, The (Booth) 177

Richter, Hans Werner 87

Ricoeur, Paul 97

Riddley Walker (Hoban) 95

Robinson, Bishop John 14, 15, 17

Rolle, Richard 151

Romans, Epistle to 215

Römerbrief, Der (Barth) 44, 49, 120

Roszak, Theodor 87

Rubenstein, Richard L. 45, 46, 47, 48–9, 50, 51, 113, 210

Rudman, Mark 243

'Samson and the Heroic' (Simon) 112, 176

'Shibboleth' (Derrida) 162

Sacred Body, The (Jasper) 143

Sacred Books of the East (Müller) 249

Sacred Community, The (Jasper) 143, 247

Sacred Desert, The (Jasper) 70

Sacred Discontent (Schneidau) 179, 187

Sagovsky, Nicholas 59–61

Saintsbury, George 238

Samson and Delilah (de Mille) 168

Schleiermacher, Friedrich 5, 31, 74, 75, 78, 80, 82, 221

Schneidau, Herbert N. 179, 187

Schwartz, Regina 168–9

Schwarz-Barth, André 79, 122

Schweiker, William 123, 229

Scott, Nathan A. Jr. 14, 25, 62, 69, 107, 222

Scott, Sir Walter 129, 131–2

Scrutiny 63, 129

Secular Promise, The (Jarrett-Kerr) 69

Sermons in the Rolls Chapel (Butler) 239

Shakespeare, Steven 245

Shakespeare, William 45, 47–8, 131

Shape of the Liturgy, The (Dix) 145

Shelley, P.B. 132, 136

Sikes, Thomas 130

Simon, Ulrich 4, 9, 16–18, 29, 35, **43–57**, 99, 104, 112, 113, 118–19, 119–20, 176, 183, 212, 215

Singer, Isaac Bashevis 163

Sitting in Judgement (Simon) 54

Solzhenitsyn, Alexander 55

Song of Songs 147, 175

Sophocles 16, 45, 52–3

Sophronius, St. 146, 147

Southey, Robert 33, 130

Spark, Muriel 123, 186

Spiegelman, Art 115

Statesman's Manual, The (Coleridge) 15, 25, 133, 152, 245

Steinberg, Leo 150

Steiner, George 18, 25, 51, 55, 76, 81, 113, 120, 242–3

Steinschneider, Moritz 115

Sternberg, Meir 126, 165, 177

Stevens, Wallace 195, 222, 223, 229, 249

Strugnell, John 9
Sugirtharajah, R.S. 169
Sunflower, The (Wiesenthal) 208
Surface of the Deep, The (Keller) 182–3
Sutherland, Stewart R. 119
Sykes, Stephen 73

Tamworth Reading Room, The (Newman) 134
Tao Te Ching 207
Temple, William 62–3
Teresa of Avila, St. 148
Terezakis, Katie 246
Tertullian 136, 144, 156
Testament, The (Wiesel) 116
Texts of Terror (Trible) 177, 178
Theological Humanism 123, 229
Theology and Difference (Lowe) 224, 225–6
Theology and the University (Coulson) 23,
        36, 129, 142
Theology of Auschwitz, A (Simon) 44, 47,
        49, 51–2, 112, 120
Thomas Aquinas 244
Thomas of Cantimpré 150
Tillich, Paul 8, 15, 21, 48, 87
Time and Narrative (Ricoeur) 97
Time and Western Man (Lewis) 67
Timon of Athens (Shakespeare) 120
Tinsley, Bishop John 35
To Live (Yu Hua) 208
To the Lighthouse (Woolf) 17
Todorov, T. 164
Torah 77, 201
Total presence 81, 193, 195
Trace 80, 95
Tracy, David 73, 231
Treatise on Method (Coleridge) 36
Trial, The (Kafka) 53, 210, 228
Trible, Phyllis 167, 177, 178
Trollope, Anthony 99
Tutu, Bishop Desmond 62
Tyndale, William 161, 172
Typewriter Music (Malouf) 192

Unamuno, Miguel de 55
Uncivil Rites (Detweiler) 69

University Sermons (Newman) 134,
        230–31, 239–40, 241

Vatican, Second Council 6, 30, 31, 109, 153–4
Vattimo, Gianni 240
Very Model of a Man, The (Jacobson) 169
Vincentian Canon 231
Voragine, Jacobus de 147

Waiting for Godot (Beckett) 95, 111
Walker, Bishop Peter 8, 18–19, 39–40,
        93–4, 117, 145
Walton, Heather 223–4, 227, 228
Ward, Graham 25, 50, 105, 233
Ward, Wilfrid 16, 34, 61
Waugh, Patricia 95
Weil, Simone 24, 55–6, 150–51
Whistler, Daniel 233
White, Patrick 189, 198–9
Whitehead, Alfred North 19
Wiesel, Elie 116, 163
Wiesenthal, Simon 208–9
Wild Prayer of Longing, The (Scott) 222
Wilder, Amos 236
Wilkinson, Alan 70
Will to Believe, The (James) 60
Williams, Charles 18–19, 39, 145
Williams, Rowan 4, 123, 145
Wittgenstein, L. 22, 28, 29, 32, 39
Woolf, Virginia 17
Wordsworth, Mary 132
Wordsworth, William 20, 22, 27, 32, 33,
        127, 130, 132, 138, 139, 141, 245
Work of Mourning, The (Derrida) 102
Wright, T.R. 3, 59, 113
Writing Degree Zero (Barthes) 228

Yang Huilin 10, 126, **205–16**, 249
Yarnold, Edward 227
Yeats, W.B. 30

Zhang, Longxi 248, 249
Zim zum 114
Zlomislić, Marko 247
Zulu Wars 65–7